Orkney
& Shetland

Orkney
& Shetland

THE
SCOTTISH ISLANDS

NEW EDITION REVISED AND UPDATED

Orkney
& Shetland

James &
Deborah Penrith

This edition published in Great Britain in 2007 by
Crimson Publishing
Westminster House
Kew Road
Richmond
Surrey
TW9 2ND

First published 2002
Third edition 2007

A catalogue record for this book is available from the British library.

ISBN 978 1 85458 371 0

Printed and bound in Singapore

Contents

SHETLAND

Background Information

Practical Information

EXPLORING SHETLAND

Preface

As the VisitScotland Orkney brochure says, 'experience the magical ebb and flow of the tides and seasons'. Apply this to both Orkney and Shetland and you will begin a life-long love affair with the Northern Isles of Scotland that stretch like a generous handful of coins flung across the Pentland Firth from John o' Groats, scattering north-eastwards for nearly 186 miles (300 km) to lie between the Atlantic Ocean and the North Sea. They form two vividly distinct archipelagos that are Britain's remotest northern stepping stones. Orkney and Shetland together offer you more than 170 islands and islets – fewer than 35 inhabited – and for island lovers these are destinations whose unique history and culture means that they literally have no equal.

Although the northern tip of Orkney on North Ronaldsay is a scant 50 miles (80 km) from the southern tip of Shetland at Sumburgh Head there are noticeable differences between the two island groups. One major difference lies in their geological complexion. Orkney's sandstone has eroded over millennia to produce not only some stunning coastal cliffs, but also and more importantly for the islanders it has weathered to lay down larger areas of fertile soil than are found on Shetland. This is why Orkney was the first island group to be extensively settled, with the result that they have a greater mass of antiquities than can be found anywhere else in Europe. Scratch the earth, you'll be told, and Orkney bleeds archaeology.

Another major difference, also a result of Nature's caprice in doling out arable land, is that Shetlanders look to the sea for sustenance and a livelihood where Orcadians rely more on their island granary. Having said that, the stretch of water between them is a belt holding them together, rather than a barrier keeping them apart. Shetlanders and Orcadians alike have a reserve natural to islanders the world over, but scratch that and, like the land, there's hidden wealth - courtesy, friendliness and a helpfulness that can at time be positively embarrassing. There's also a fair amount of whimsy. A visitor to Shetland recalls finding an old man flat on his back by the footpath. Somewhat alarmed, she asked him what he as doing. 'Tinkin' he replied.

Don't go to Orkney and Shetland if all you want to do is lie on a beach and tan. There are some exquisite beaches, but breezy days and less than Mediterranean temperatures don't exactly encourage sun-worshipping. Those who believe there's more to life than toasting in the sun will find plenty of other attractions. Twitchers will be thrilled by the vast numbers and species of seabirds, migrants and rarities that literally flock to Orkney and Shetland, making them wonders of the ornithological world; ancient stone circles, standing stones, burial chambers, Viking remains and treasures and, more recently, monuments and relics of two World Wars, offer fascinating windows into the islands' history; the wonderful luminous light draws artists and photographers alike; the wildflowers, some found nowhere else on earth, the land and marine wildlife – whales, dolphins, and otters – make the islands hotspots for nature lovers; the lochs and voes yield magnificent fighting trout and salmon, while the surrounding waters offer sea angling on an epic scale; divers are attracted by unpolluted waters and the prospect of diving for treasure in Shetland and in the largest graveyard of battleships and cruisers in the world in Orkney's Scapa Flow; walkers and cyclists will find miles of beckoning tracks and pathways, some of which have criss-crossed the islands since prehistoric times; yachtsmen, canoeists and kayakers can face testing waves and currents for the reward of close-ups of spectacular sea stacks, geos and caves – views only to be guessed at from the land; even geology takes on a new shine in islands formed hundreds of millions of years ago in an equatorial lake.

There's more, of course: the arts and crafts of island folk, the food and drink, the guided tours, the riveting living museums, the wonderful music, the festivals, the people and, finally, just being there.

Deborah Penrith
May 2007

Acknowledgements

We should acknowledge and thank all the people of Orkney and Shetland, but we just don't have the space. The following, however, helped in many ways to ensure that what you find between these covers is comprehensively informative, up-to-date, entertaining and, hopefully, at times amusing.

Colin Keldie, Marketing Assistant, VisitOrkney; Misa Hay, Marketing Executive, VisitShetland; Erik Meek, RSPB Orkney; Leslie Fettes, Orkney Islands Sea Angling Association; Helen Hadley, Northcroft Partnership, Orkney; Susan Blacklaw, Sales & Marketing Manager, Loganair; Sita Hughson, PR Coordinator, Shetland Museum and Archives; Karen Fraser, Customer Services Librarian, Shetland Library; David Polson, Ferry Services, Shetland Islands Council; and Deryk Shaw, Warden, Fair Isle Bird Observatory.

Sources of Information
We cannot praise too highly the combined services of VisitScotland, VisitOrkney, and VisitShetland, their helpful staff, and their publications. Other mines of information were *The Orcadian* weekly newspaper and its annual freebie *The Islander*, the *Orkney Economic Review*, Orkney Museum Services, Stromness Museum, Shetland Museum, National Trust for Scotland, Royal Society for the Protection of Birds, WWF Scotland, Scottish Wildlife Trust, Scottish Natural Heritage, Historic Scotland, *Scottish Islands Explorer* magazine, *The Shetland Times* weekly newspaper, and *Shetland Visitor*, its free annual magazine, *Shetland Life, The New Shetlander*, and the *Orkneyinga Saga*.

Photography
Front cover photograph of Kirkwall harbour and rear cover photograph of the Ring of Brodgar, both courtesy of VisitScotland (www.visitscotland.com).

Photographs of Orkney are by Deborah Penrith, and courtesy of Helen Hadley, Northcroft Partnership.

Photographs of Shetland are by Deborah Penrith, and courtesy of Shetland Island Tourism, taken by Charles Tait, except the photo of Lerwick harbour on page 139 which is courtesy of VisitScotland and Scottish Viewpoint.

THE NORTHERN ISLES

Practical Information

THE NORTHERN ISLES
Practical Information

Island-bound travellers have a choice of reaching Scotland by air, sea, rail, or road, depending on which country they are coming from. Trains and coaches are the prime carriers of passengers. On the main London- to- Glasgow and Edinburgh routes there are frequent rail and coach departures every day. There are also regular services from London to Aberdeen, Dundee and Inverness. There are good bus and train links with all the ferry ports around Scotland's coast.

BY AIR

Glasgow is the hub for onward air travel to the islands, along with Edinburgh, Aberdeen and Inverness. *British Airways* (✆0870-850 9850; www.britishairways.com) operated by *Loganair* (✆0141-848 7594) flies from these airports to Kirkwall Airport on Orkney and Sumburgh Airport on Shetland. There are direct flights all year round from European cities to Edinburgh, Glasgow, Aberdeen, and Inverness and from North America to Glasgow and Edinburgh. Daily flights operate from Dublin and Belfast to Aberdeen, Edinburgh, and Glasgow.

Glasgow Airport is particularly well served by transatlantic flights. *Continental Airlines* (www.continental.com) operates a year-round non-stop service to Glasgow via Newark from 96 airports across North America. From May to October, *American Airlines* (www.aa.com) operates a daily direct service to Glasgow from Chicago's O'Hare, offering connections from 66 other points across the US. *Icelandair* (www.icelandair.com) also has convenient connections to Glasgow via Reykjavik from Boston, New York, Baltimore/Washington, Minneapolis/St Paul, and Orlando, while *Air Canada* (www.aircanada.ca) can fly you from 32 US cities to Glasgow via Toronto, and *Air Transat* (www.airtransat.com) from Toronto between April and October. Scotland's major airports can also be reached via London Heathrow/Gatwick on United Airlines and Delta from the USA, and via Europe on Air France and KLM.

Flights from London
British Airways: (✆0870-850 9850; www.britishairways.com) to Glasgow, Edinburgh, Aberdeen, and Inverness.
Flybe: (✆0871-522 6100; fax 01392-366151; www.flybe.com) to Edinburgh, Dundee, and Glasgow from Birmingham.
Flybmi: (✆0870-607 0555; fax 01709-314993; www.flybmi.com) to Glasgow, Edinburgh, Aberdeen and Inverness.
Easy Jet: (✆0870-600 0000; fax 01582-443355; www.easyjet.com) to Glasgow, Edinburgh, Aberdeen, and Inverness.
Ryanair: (✆0871-246 0000; fax 01279-666201; www.ryanair.com) to Glasgow, Edinburgh, Aberdeen and Inverness.
ScotAirways: (✆0870-606 0707; fax 01223-292160; www.scotairways.co.uk) to Edinburgh, and Dundee.

If you are going to Scotland via London check the fares offered by no-frills airlines such as Ryanair, EasyJet, and Flybe. Several air fares offered by British Airways and Flybmi include airpasses.

The Highland Rover special gives you five separate flights within Scotland on routes operated by British Airways and Loganair for less than a normal one-way fare. You can add extra flights at bargain rates. There is also the option to add a connection to and from Belfast or Londonderry from Glasgow. Tickets can be issued only outside Scotland. For enquiries, reservations, and full details contact British Airways Reservations (✆0870-850 9850; www.britishairways.com).

Bikes

If you are planning a cycling holiday and want to take your own bike with you many airlines consider bikes to be part of the normal baggage allowance provided they are carefully packed, but you might be obliged to sign off their liabilities for compensation – Limited Release is the official term. Budget flights usually charge extra to carry a bike and inter-island flights on small aircraft have limited luggage space, so check beforehand.

TOUR OPERATORS

Scotia Travel: Mercantile House, 53 Bothwell Street, Glasgow G2 6RF (&0141-305 5050; fax 0141-305 5001; email bill@scotiatravel.com; www.scotiatravel.com).

Scotland Touring (Orkney & Shetland Touring Company): 14 Harbour Street, Kirkwall KW15 1LE (✆0845-094 0405; fax 0845-094 0499; email sales@orkneyshetland.com; www.scotlandtouring.com). Holidays and tours, self-drive and fly/drive to Orkney and Shetland. Group package tours, ferry passage and island tours for coach groups, shore excursions for cruise ships. Multilingual local guides.

McGrory Short Breaks: 13 Stirling Drive, Burnside, Glasgow G73 4JH (✆/fax 0141-634-4876; email dan@mcgrory.fsbusiness.co.uk; www.mcgrory.fsbusiness.co.uk). Self-drive packaged breaks from Aberdeen to Orkney and Shetland.

BY SEA

Numerous regular ferry services link Europe with ports along the southern and east coasts of England. The closest to the Scottish border are Newcastle-upon-Tyne and Hull in northern England. There is also a ferry service from Belgium to Rosyth, in Edinburgh.

Ferry Operators

DFDS Seaways: (Göteborg, ✆+46 042-266000; fax +45 33-423011; email info@dfdsseaways.se; www.dfdsseaways.se) Esbjerg to Harwich, Amsterdam to Newcastle, Bergen, Haugesund and Stavanger to Newcastle.

Fjord Line: (Royal Quays, North Shields, Tyne & Wear NE29 6EG; ✆0191-296 1313; fax 0191-296 1540; email fjordline.uk@fjordline.com; www.fjordline.com) Bergen, Haugesund and Stavanger to Newcastle.

Norfolkline: (Norfolk House, Eastern Docks, Dover, Kent CT16 1JA; ✆0870-870 1020; fax 0130-421 8420; email doverpax@norfolkline.com; www.norfolkline-ferries.com) fast car ferry, up to 12 daily departures Calais to Dover and Dieppe to Newhaven twice a day in season.

P&O Ferries: (King George Dock, Hedon Road, Hull HU9 5QA; ✆0870-520 2020; email reservations.admin@poferries.com; www.poferries.com) from Zeebrugge and Rotterdam to Hull. Offices in Holland, Belgium, Germany, France and Spain.

P&O Ferries: (Channel House, Channel View Road, Dover, Kent CT17 9TJ; ✆0870-520 2020; email customer.services@poferries.com; www.poferries.com) up to 35 trips a day, Calais to Dover.

SeaFrance: (Eastern Docks, Dover, Kent CT16 1JA; ✆0870-443 1653; www.seafrance.net) from Calais to Dover.

Smyril Line: (J Broncksgota 37, PO Box 370, FO-110 Torshavn, Faroe Islands, ✆+298 34-59 00; fax +298 34-59 50; email office@smyril-line.fo; www.smyril-line.com) Bergen, Denmark, Faroes and Iceland to Lerwick and Scrabster.

Stena Line: (Charter House, Park Street, Ashford, Kent TN2 48EX; ✆0870-570 7070; Göteborg, ✆+46 31-704 00 00; fax +46 31-85 85 95; email info@stenaline.com; www.stenaline.com) from Hook of Holland to Harwich; Dublin to Holyhead, and Rosslare to Fishguard. Offices in Belgium, Denmark, Germany, Holland, Norway, Sweden and Ireland.

Superfast Ferries: (The Terminal Building, Port of Zeebrugge, Doverlaan 7, Box 14, 8380 Zeebrugge; ✆+32 50 252252; fax +32 50 252259; email info.belgium@superfast.com; www.superfast.com) from Zeebrugge to Rosyth.

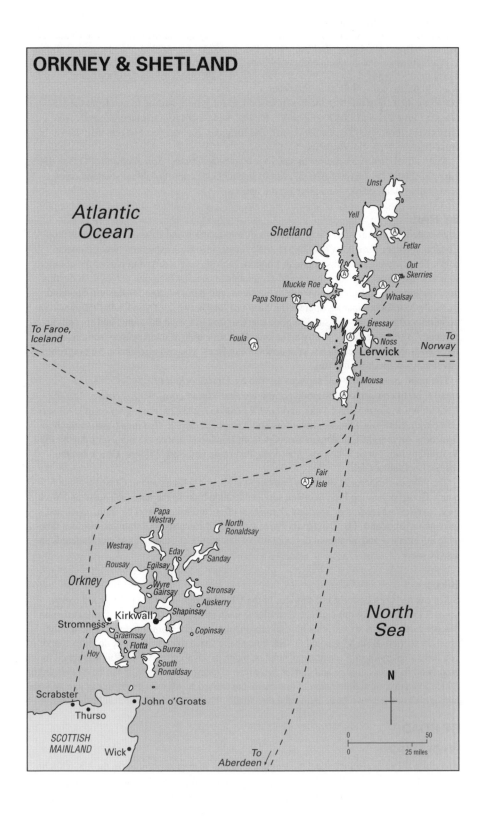

ORKNEY & SHETLAND

Atlantic
Ocean

Shetland

Unst

Yell

Fetlar

Out
Skerries

Muckle Roe

Papa Stour

Whalsay

Bressay

To Faroe,
Iceland

Foula

Noss

Lerwick

To
Norway

Mousa

Fair
Isle

Papa
Westray

North
Ronaldsay

Westray

Eday

Rousay

Egilsay

Sanday

Orkney

Wyre
Gairsay

Stronsay

Auskerry

Shapinsay

Kirkwall

Stromness

Copinsay

North
Sea

Graemsay

Flotta

Burray

Hoy

South
Ronaldsay

Scrabster

John o'Groats

N

Thurso

SCOTTISH
MAINLAND

Wick

0   50

To
Aberdeen

0   25 miles

Getting to Scotland from Ireland

P&O Irish Sea: (✆0870-242 4777; fax 01574-872147; www.poirishsea.com) Larne to Cairnryan. *Seacat:* (Donegall Quay, Belfast; ✆0870-552 3523; fax 02860-331344; email belfast. reservations@seacontainers.com; www.seacat.co.uk) high-speed crossings, Belfast to Troon. *Stena Line:* (✆+353 1-20 47700; fax +353 1-20 47620; email info@stenaline.com; www.stenaline.com) Belfast to Stranraer.

For a one-stop shop offering the best prices on all ferry lines sailing to and from the UK contact *Ferry Savers* (✆0870-066 9612; fax 0870-444 1484; email customerservices@ ferrysavers.com; www.ferrysavers.com); and for cross-channel ferry tickets visit www. cross-channel-ferry-tickets.co.uk.

Alternatively, you can charter or sail your own boat. Contact *Sail Scotland* (PO Box 8363, Largs KA30 8YD; ✆01309-676757; fax 01309-673331; email info@sailscotland.co.uk; www.sailscotland.co.uk) for advice on the options.

BY RAIL

High-speed trains run from Paris–Calais–Ashford–London and Brussels–Lille–Ashford– London. Contact *Eurostar* (✆0870-518 6186; email info@eurostar.com; www.eurostar. com). There are eight main stations in London, each serving a different part of the country, so if you are travelling from the capital remember to check which one serves your destination. Euston is the terminus for Western Scotland, and King's Cross for Eastern Scotland. Britain's 26 train companies operate the *National Rail* network (✆08457-484950; www.na-tionalrail.co.uk) and its website is a good place to find out what discounts and specials each company is offering. You can buy a National Rail timetable at main railway stations and some bookshops. As well as tracking down cheap fares, you can also check the best times to travel at www.thetrainline.com.

The main cross-border rail services are run by *First ScotRail* (✆0845-755 0033; email scotrail.enquiries@firstgroup.com; www.firstscotrail.com), *Virgin Trains* (✆08457-222333; www.virgintrains.co.uk), and *GNER* (✆08457-225225; www.gner.co.uk). All serve Edinburgh, Glasgow, Dundee, Inverness and Aberdeen; GNER also runs trains through to Inverness. Overnight Caledonian Sleepers from London (Euston) are run every day by First ScotRail to Edinburgh, Glasgow, Aberdeen, Inverness and Fort William. Check out the special book-ahead deal.

The journey time from London to Edinburgh is about 4½ hours and to Glasgow about 5 hours. Good connecting First ScotRail services include links to the north at Thurso and Wick. First ScotRail's *Freedom of Scotland Travelpass* offers unlimited travel by train, coach and ferry across Scotland. The *Travelpass Pack*, available at First Scotrail stations, includes time-table information and additional discount offers. International Student Discount Railcards can also be used.

Bikes

Bikes can be taken on most rail services in the UK, although there are no standard regulations. A leaflet on bike rail carriage is available from most railway stations. The Caledonian Sleeper carries up to six bicycles in reservable spaces, except from Inverness, where only three are carried. Both Virgin and GNER trains have space to carry bikes at no extra charge if you have a reservation. Reservations must be made in advance. First ScotRail has space for at least two bikes per carriage and carries them free of charge. Bikes which can be dismantled or folded to a maximum dimension of one metre are treated by all rail companies as part of your luggage allowance (two large items and one small). This may be enforced on busy trains.

BY ROAD
From Europe

An option for motorists crossing the English Channel is the Eurotunnel (in the UK ✆0870-535 3535; in France ✆03 2100 6100; www.eurotunnel.com) which operates its drive-on service 24 hours a day every day of the year with four departures an hour during summer

peak periods and a crossing time from Calais to Folkestone of 35 minutes platform to platform (45 minutes at night). Fares are fluid and depend on demand and when you are travelling. National Express division Eurolines (✆0870-580 8080) operates a European express coach service to and from more than 500 destinations.

Within the UK

Long-distance coaches run cross-border services and serve all major towns and are a relatively inexpensive way to travel. Two of the major companies which operate a nationwide network are *National Express* (✆0870-580 8080; www.nationalexpress.com) and *Scottish Citylink* (✆0870-550 5050; email info@citylink.co.uk; www.citylink.co.uk). Many National Express services – known as 'Rapide' – have toilet facilities, movies and light refreshments. Scottish Citylink coaches have toilet facilities. There are good value discount passes when travelling by bus to most areas of Scotland. There are a number of options depending on where you visit and how long you want to travel. The Discount Coachcard, for instance, offers a discount of up to 30% off adult fares on all National Express and Scottish Citylink services. It is available to passengers that are between the ages of 16 and 25 inclusive, full-time students, or the over 50s. If you are over 60 you can get 50% off travel with the national concessionary fare scheme. Check discounts and special offers for Eurolines at www.nationalexpress.com.

Postbuses

Scottish Royal Mail Postbuses run in many remote areas of Scotland, carrying mail and fare-paying passengers where there is no other form of public transport they can use. If you are using Postbus it pays to study the timetable and route carefully as Postbuses follow postal delivery and collection schedules and do not always travel the same routes on their return journeys. You can flag down a Postbus at any point and it will stop to pick you up. Some Postbuses are adapted for wheelchair users. Space is limited so don't make travel plans that rely totally on the Postbus service. Details and timetables from Royal Mail Customer Service Centre (Drake House, Breakwater Road, Plymouth PL9 7HJ; ✆08457-740740; www.royalmail.com/postbus).

Bikes

In general, bus companies will carry dismantled and wrapped bikes, provided there's space and you do not exceed your passenger luggage allowance. Scottish Citylink does not carry conventional bikes, but will carry folded bikes in appropriate bags.

RED TAPE

VISAS

If you are coming from a country that requires you to have a visa to visit the UK the British government has introduced a new type of visa to make entry easier. Previously, a visa was issued at a British mission abroad, but the decision to let you enter the UK was taken by an immigration officer at the port of entry. That has now changed. The entry clearance officer issuing a visa abroad now also grants leave to enter, and the immigration officer's job is now simply to verify that the visa is valid and in a genuine passport. The new standard visa costs the same as the previous single-entry visa, but it allows unlimited travel in and out of the UK for its validity period. A new visa is usually valid for six months from the date of issue, but you can now ask for it to come into effect up to three months after its date of issue. For more information on visa requirements contact UKvisas, Foreign and Commonwealth Office, King Charles Street, London SW1A 2AH; ✆0845-010 5555; www.ukvisas.gov.uk.

VAT REFUNDS

Value Added Tax (VAT) of 17.5% is levied on most purchases in the UK. In some circumstances tourists and business travellers can claim a refund of this when they leave.

Procedures for applying for a refund are detailed in *A Traveller's Guide to the Retail Export Scheme*. This booklet is available free at all customs points, as well as at www.hmce.gov.uk/forms/notices/704-2.htm. Non-EU visitors to Scotland can claim VAT refunds through the *Foreign Exchange Tax-Free Shopping* scheme. A tax-free shopping form must be obtained and completed at the shop where you make your purchases (take your passport with you), although this service is not available in every shop. This form is presented to HM Revenue & Customs as you leave the country. Further details on the conditions and procedures for refunds can be obtained from HM Revenue & Customs (National Advice Service, Alexander House, Victoria Avenue, Southend, Essex SS99 1BD; ℂ0845-010 9000; www.hmrc.gov.uk).

FIREARMS

You can tranship or import firearms into the UK for sport or hobby-shooting only if you comply with strict regulations. For guidelines check the Metropolitan Police Service Firearms Enquiry Team at www.met.police.uk/firearms-enquiries/index.htm. You should also ask the airline at the time you book your ticket about their rules and regulations on carrying firearms.

MONEY

PLASTIC CASH

Major credit cards are accepted in many establishments but it is still advisable to carry cash in UK sterling or Scottish banknotes in the event a smaller business or merchant does not have the facility to accept plastic. You can use your credit card to withdraw cash from a network of more than 2,000 cash dispensers – auto teller machines – throughout Scotland. Between them the ATMs of the Bank of Scotland, the Royal Bank of Scotland, Clydesdale Bank and Lloyds TSB Scotland accept most credit cards, among them Eurocard, American Express, Mastercard, Visa Card, Multibanco and Mistercash.

BANKS AND BANKING

Three of Scotland's traditional banks issue their own banknotes. The Royal Bank of Scotland, the Bank of Scotland and Clydesdale Bank. Banknotes come in £5, £10, £20, £50 and £100 denominations. The £1 coin is in general circulation throughout Scotland, although the Royal Bank of Scotland still produces a £1 banknote. Bank of England and Bank of Northern Ireland notes are welcome in Scotland, although you might have difficulty using them the further south of the border you go in England. Change your Scottish money before leaving if you can. Exchange rates are the same for Scottish and English notes.

All Scottish banks use the same basic colours to distinguish the different banknote values – blue for £5, brown for £10, purple for £20, green for £50, and red for £100 (the Bank of England also used the same colours for Sterling). In the main, the notes differ in their designs. The portrait on all Bank of Scotland notes is that of Scottish author Sir Walter Scott; Royal Bank of Scotland notes feature Lord Ilay (1682–1761), who was the bank's first governor; and Clydesdale Bank marks its different denominations with portraits of poet Robert Burns (£5); missionary Mary Slessor (£10); Scottish warrior king Robert the Bruce (£20); economist Adam Smith (£50); and the researcher and inventor Lord Kelvin (£100). There's some interesting information on Scotland's currency on www.scotbanks.org.uk and www.saor-alba.fsnet.co.uk. Information on British currency is available at the Bank of England website at www.bankofengland.co.uk, and the Royal Mint's site at www.royalmint.com. If you live outside the sterling area and need a currency converter try www.oanda.com/converter/classic.

HEALTH

Good medical services are widely available, but free care under the National Health Service applies only to UK and European Union residents, and nationals or residents of a country with a reciprocal healthcare agreement with the UK. All others are expected to pay. This means adequate travel insurance is a good policy. If you become ill while in Britain you are eligible for free emergency treatment provided under the National Health Service (NHS). For details read the *Overseas Visitors' Eligibility to Receive Free Primary Care* and *Are You Visiting the United Kingdom? Did you know you may have to pay for hospital treatment whilst here?* which are available to download from the Department of Health at www.dh.gov.uk and to order as hard copies from the Department of Health (PO Box 777, London SE1 6XH; ℂ08701-555 455; fax 01623-724524; email dh@prolog.uk.com). For more information contact the Department of Health (Richmond House, 79 Whitehall, London SW1A 2NL; ℂ020-7210 4850; fax 020-7210 5454; email dhmail@dh.gsi.gov.uk; www.dh.gov.uk).

SMOKE-FREE SCOTLAND

Smoking in enclosed public spaces, such as restaurants, cafés, pubs, hotels, B&Bs, most public places and on most forms of public transport in Scotland is (like the rest of the UK) against the law. Some accommodation establishments have designated dedicated bedrooms where smoking is allowed. Contact them beforehand to check.

HAZARDS

There are no natural hazards to speak of. The dense blitzes by the ferocious Highland midge (*Culicoides impunctatus*) that raise irritation levels on many West Coast islands in summer are virtually non-existent in Shetland and in Orkney are in evidence mainly in July, depending on the weather. Recommended are repellents based on either dimethyl phthalate (DMP or Dimp) or di-ethyl toluamide (DEET). *Shoo!* is a popular DMP version. Old fishing manuals recommend pipe smoking; all authorities suggest you should wear light-coloured clothing at dusk, when *Culicoides impunctatus* likes to dine. A midge forecast sent direct to your mobile phone may help you plan your trip. The information supplied will let you know whether to expect neglible, low, moderate, high or nuisance midge levels. More information at www.midgeforecast.co.uk.

CLOTHING

Pack lightweight clothing, but be flexible enough to allow for the variable weather. May to September is often warm, but an umbrella or light (waterproof) jacket is still advisable to cope with rain or cool evenings. A heavier waterproof jacket and a decent sweater – buy one in Orkney or Shetland – is a good idea from October and on through the winter months. Pack waterproof trousers if you plan to do a lot of walking, and take stout and comfortable shoes or boots.

ACCOMMODATION

VisitScotland produces four accommodation guides, revised annually, which cover *Hotels & Guest Houses*, *Bed & Breakfast*, *Self-Catering*, and *Caravan & Camping*. Accommodation in these categories is graded on a one-to five-star system. The more stars, the better the quality, and these are the determining factors – the quality of the welcome and service, the food, the hospitality, ambience, and the comfort and condition of the establishment – not the size of accommodation or its range of facilities. This easy-to-understand system tells you at a glance the quality standard of all types and sizes of accommodation from the smallest B&B or self-catering cottage to the largest countryside or city centre hotel: Five-star-Exceptional, World-class; Four-star-Excellent; Three-star-Very Good; Two-star-Good; and One-star-Fair and Acceptable.

For caravan holiday accommodation meeting the required high standards VisitScotland gives its colourful *Thistle Award* symbol. Other signs to look out for are the square 'Walkers Welcome' and 'Cyclists Welcome' ones which mean the establishments have met a rigorous string of requirements aimed at making your walking or cycling holiday even more enjoyable. VisitScotland also operates a national accessibility scheme, identifying and promoting accommodation that caters for people with mobility problems. It awards symbols in three different categories: Unassisted wheelchair access; assisted wheelchair access; and access for people with mobility difficulties. For more information contact Quality Assurance Department, VisitScotland (Thistle House, Beechwood Park North, Inverness IV2 3ED; ✆01463-723040; fax 01463-717244; email quinfo@visitscotland.com). Accommodation listings can be obtained from VisitScotland (Ocean Point One, 94 Ocean Drive, Leith, Edinburgh EH6 6JH; ✆0131-472 2222; www.visitscotland.com). Local tourist information centres operate the national Book-a-Bed-Ahead Service, reserving your accommodation for a nominal fee. To find a quality assured eating establishment visit www.eatscotland.com.

HOSTELS

A Scottish Youth Hostels Association (SYHA) membership offers a good way to avoid expensive hotel bills. SYHA is a member of the Hostelling International network, offering self-catering or meals, common rooms, hot showers, dormitories, family rooms and private rooms at some hostels. *SYHA* (7 Glebe Crescent, Stirling FK8 2JA; ✆0870-155 3255; fax 01786-891333; email reservations@syha.org.uk; www.syha.org.uk. Open Monday to Friday 9am to 5pm).

Scottish Independent Hostels (Secretary, PO Box 7124, Fort William PH33 6YX) has an online search facility at www.hostel-scotland.co.uk for hostels in Orkney and Shetland. You can then book direct with the individual hostel. They cater for all ages, do not require membership and have fully equipped kitchens and hot showers.

Scottish Farmhouse Holidays (2 Barefoots Avenue, Eyemouth TD14 5JH; ✆01890-751830; fax 01890-751831; email info@scotfarmhols.co.uk; www.scotfarmhols.co.uk) is a central reservation service for working farms and crofts. Prices for B&B start from £15 per person per night up to an average of £24 for a double room with private facilities; *Scottish Country Cottages* (Stoney Bank, Earby, Barnoldswick BB94 0AA; ✆0870-078 1100; www.scottish-country-cottages.co.uk) are worth a browse.

CAMPING

There are not a lot of official camping areas in the islands, but hill and coastal camping is normally easy to find. Get advice and permission from farmers, crofters, or estates where these exist.

HELP AND INFORMATION

TOURIST INFORMATION CENTRES

VisitScotland has a network of tourist information centres which can give detailed information and advice on most things concerning their area. Contact them for information on things to see and do, places to visit, events, transport within their area and full accommodation listings. The central office of *VisitScotland* is at Ocean Point One, 94 Ocean Drive, Leith, Edinburgh EH6 6JH (✆0131-472 2222; fax 0131-343 1513). Otherwise you can contact the booking and information centre at Fairways Business Park, Deer Park Avenue, Livingston EH54 8AF (✆0845-225 5121; fax 01506-832 222; email info@visitscotland.com; www.visitscotland.com) which is open Monday to Friday 8am to 8pm, and Saturday 9am to 5.30pm.

WOMEN TRAVELLERS

If you are nervous about travelling alone one solution is offered by *Women Welcome Women World Wide* (5W), a non-profit trust which fosters international friendship by enabling women of different countries to visit one another. There are more than 2,500 members in nearly 70 countries, including in the Scottish Isles. Visit, call or write to Women Welcome Women World Wide (88 Easton Street,

High Wycombe, Bucks HP11 1LT; ✆/fax 01494-465441; www.womenwelcomewomen.org.uk). Their office is open from 9.30am to 1.30pm from Monday to Friday, excluding public holidays.

DISABLED TRAVELLERS

VisitScotland produces *Accessible Scotland*, a useful booklet on accommodation with disabled facilities. *Capability Scotland* is the country's leading disability organisation and provides a national advice and information service. For more information on their services contact *Advice Service Capability Scotland (ASCS)* (11 Ellersly Road, Edinburgh EH12 6HY; ✆0131-313 5510; fax 0131-346 1681; email ascs@capability-scotland.org.uk; www.capability-scotland.org.uk).

You can also get practical advice and information from *Tourism for All UK*, formerly *Holiday Care* (c/o Vitalise, Shap Road Industrial Estate, Kendal, Cumbria LA9 6NZ; ✆0845-124 9971; fax 01539-735567; email info@tourismforall.org.uk; www.tourismforall. org.uk). In particular, it can help with information on accessible accommodation, visitor attractions, transport and activity holidays for people with disabilities, as well as holidays for children with disabilities and sources of holiday funding.

A referral service that can put you in touch with local disability advice centres is *Update* (27 Beaverhall Road, Edinburgh EH7 4JE; ✆0131-558 5200; email info@update.org.uk; www.update.org.uk).

GAY TRAVELLERS

Organisations and establishments catering for the needs and interests of gay travellers continue to blossom in the major mainland cities and towns of Scotland and the islanders have a relaxed attitude towards gay visitors. One starting point is the *Gay and Lesbian Switchboard* (PO Box 169, Edinburgh EH3 6SG; ✆0131-556 4049). Another is the *Glasgow Gay & Lesbian Centre* (11 Dixon Street, St Enoch, Glasgow G1 4AL; ✆/fax 0141-221 7203; www.glgbt.org.uk), open Monday to Sunday 11am to midnight.

DRUGS AND THE LAW

If you violate British law, even unknowingly, you can be expelled, arrested or imprisoned. Penalties for possession, use or trafficking of illegal drugs are strict, and if you are convicted you can expect a jail sentence, a heavy fine, or both. If you are on medication and using prescribed medicinal products containing drugs controlled under the Misuse of Drugs Act 1971 you are permitted to import these in limited quantities. You must be able to prove that your drugs have been prescribed and that you require such medication during your visit. The Home Office (Drugs Licensing, DSU, 6th Floor, Peel, London SW1P 4DF; www.drugs. gov.uk) is responsible for controlled drug licensing. Information and advice is also available from the Department of Health (Richmond House, 79 Whitehall, London SW1A 2NL; ✆020-7210 4850; fax 020-7210 5454; email dhmail@dh.gsi.gov.uk; www.dh.gov.uk). If you want to avoid problems at your point of entry carry a letter from your doctor and make sure that your medicines, pills etc are in their original prescription bottles or packets. If you need a prescription from a British doctor it is advisable to know the generic rather than brand names of all your prescribed drugs.

POST OFFICES

In many rural areas post office services are available as part of a shop. Post offices vary in size and in rural areas may have only one postal collection a day. Local staff are usually quite knowledgeable about their area and helpful with any queries. Post offices are generally open Monday to Friday 9am to 5.30pm, Saturdays 9am to 12.30pm or 1pm. Smaller branches (sub-post offices) often close for lunch.

TELEPHONES

Telephone boxes/pay-phones operated by British Telecom can be found in all towns and most villages. These accept coins or BT phonecards. Coin-operated pay-phones will not give you any change, so start with lower-value coins and add larger value coins for as long as you want to speak. Many organisations provide directory enquiry services at a cost. To get local or national directory, try BT at 118500 (23p a minute plus 40p a call); or other services at 118119 (30p a minute, plus 25p a call); and 118118 (14p a minute, plus 49p a call). For international directory there is BT's at 118505 (£1.50 a minute, minimum charge £1.50), or 118190 (£1 a call, plus 60p a minute).

Check mobile phone coverage with your service provider before you go as signals in many islands are weak to non-existent, especially in mountainous areas.

WEATHER

Lots of websites offer weather forecasts, but if you want the most authoritative information, check out the Met Office's home page for detailed five-day regional forecast at www.met-office.gov.uk or www.weathercall.co.uk. Other useful weather websites for the Northern Isles are www.zetnet.co.uk/sigs/weather and www.northisles-weather.co.uk.

USEFUL ADDRESSES AND TELEPHONE NUMBERS

The Automobile Association (AA) of the UK (Contact Centre, Lambert House, Stockport Road, Cheadle SK8 2DY; ✆09003-401100; www.theaa.com) provides information and updates on traffic-related issues.

British Sub-Aqua Club branches in Scotland are supported by two regional coaches, each with a team of area coaches, covering northern and southern Scotland. Coaches can be contacted at email scotland.north.coach@bsac.com. Branches can be contacted at www.bsac. com. ScotFed is the Scottish Federation of BSAC branches and the current website is www. arcl.ed.ac.uk/scotfed.

Historic Scotland (Longmore House, Salisbury Place, Edinburgh EH9 1SH; ✆0131-668 8600; fax 0131-668 8669; email hs.friends@scotland.gsi.gov.uk; www.historic-scotland.gov. uk; for information about opening times, ✆0131-668 8800) has more than 300 historic sites in its direct care. These are conserved and presented for the enjoyment of visitors and the proceeds from admissions and purchases at the sites support Historic Scotland in its conservation and presentation work. Wherever possible merchandise in the shops is sourced from Scotland, with an emphasis on supporting local craft industries.

National Cycle Network: Sustrans (2 Cathedral Square, College Green, Bristol BS1 5DD; ✆0117-915 0101; email info@sustrans.org.uk; www.sustrans.org.uk).

National Museums of Scotland (Chambers Street, Edinburgh EH1 1JF; ✆0131-225 7534; fax 0131-220 4819; email info@nms.ac.uk; www.nms.ac.uk) includes the Royal Museum, where many of the more striking and important archaeological finds made in the islands are now on display. Entry is free.

The National Trust for Scotland (NTS) (Wemyss House, 28 Charlotte Square, Edinburgh EH2 4ET; ✆0131-243 9300; fax 0131-243 9301; email information@nts.org.uk; www.nts. org.uk) is a conservation charity which aims to protect and promote Scotland's natural and cultural heritage for present and future generations. Membership of the trust literally opens some of the most famous doors in the country.

The Royal Society for the Protection of Birds (RSPB) (Scotland Headquarters, Dunedin House, 25 Ravelston Terrace, Edinburgh EH4 3TP; ✆0131-311 6500; fax 0131-311 6569; email rspb.scotland@rspb.org.uk; www.rspb.org.uk/scotland) is a registered charity working throughout the UK. RSPB Scotland works to secure a healthy environment for birds and wildlife and to conserve and enhance Scotland's natural heritage. It manages more than 70 reserves in Scotland, covering 153,205 acres (62,000ha) and ranging from mountains to moorland, ancient Caledonian pine forests, wetlands and thousands of miles of coastline.

Scottish Canoe Association: Caledonia House, South Gyle, Edinburgh EH12 9DQ (✆0131-317 7314; fax 0131-317 7319; email enquiry@scot-canoe.org; www.scot-canoe.org).

Scottish Natural Heritage (SNH) (12 Hope Terrace, Edinburgh EH9 2AS; ✆0131-447 4784; fax 0131-446 2277; email enquiries@snh.org.uk; www.snh.org.uk) works to assure the long-term health of the country's natural high level of biodiversity, and to maintain and improve a rich variety of plants and animals, their habitats and the natural processes which support them. Much of SNH's work is about caring for special sites and areas which have been designated because of the importance of their plants, animals, habitats, rocks, land-forms and scenery. SNH also works with landowners and managers to maintain and, where appropriate, enhance Sites of Special Scientific Interest, National Nature Reserves and the National Scenic Areas which have been designated to protect landscapes.

The Scottish Wildlife Trust (SWT) (Cramond House, Cramond Glebe Road, Edinburgh EH4 6NS; ℂ0131-312 7765; fax 0131-312 8705; email enquiries@swt.org.uk; www.swt. org.uk) is a voluntary body working for all wildlife of Scotland, representing more than 28,000 members who care for wildlife and the environment. SWT seeks to raise public awareness of threatened habitats and species and manages more than 120 reserves through-out Scotland, including its most northerly reserve at Linga Holm, Stronsay, which is home to a wealth of wildlife and hundreds of grey seals.

NATIONAL ANTHEM, FLAG AND SYMBOL

Anthem. *Post-devolution Scotland is looking for a new Scottish national anthem to replace the current British national anthem,* God Save the Queen. *A number of polls have show that the leading contender is* Flower of Scotland, *followed by* Scotland the Brave. *The former is already Scotland's unofficial anthem and is sung at international rugby and football matches. Apart from any nationalist sentiments the Scots haven't forgotten that when first written the British national anthem contained the following verse:*

> *God grant that Marshall Wade,*
> *May by thy mighty aid,*
> *Victory bring,*
> *May he sedition hush,*
> *And like a torrent rush,*
> *Rebellious Scots to crush.*
> *God save the King*

Flag. *The flag you will see flying throughout the islands is the cross of St Andrew, also known as the Saltire, a white cross shaped like the letter X on a blue background. This is said to be one of the oldest national flags of any country, dating back at least to the 12th century. Legend says that St Andrew, an apostle of Jesus in the Christian religion and Scotland's patron saint, was crucified by the Romans in Greece in AD60 on a cross of this shape. St Andrew's Day is celebrated on 30 November every year.*

Symbol. *The thistle as a Scottish symbol recalls an incident in an early clash with Viking raiders. The Norse invaders were advancing barefoot under cover of darkness when one of them trod on a thistle. His yell roused the Scots in time to repel the attack.*

FURTHER READING

The saga of the Earls of Orkney written around AD1200 by an unknown Icelandic chronicler is the only medieval work to use Orkney as the pivotal point for its action and presents the islands' history as a lively fusion of myth and legend, anecdote and poetry. The *Orkneyinga Saga* (Penguin Books, London 1981) is the classic translation by Hermann Pálsson and Paul Edwards and is not only an excellent source book, but a rollicking good read.

The Alban Quest: by Farley Mowat (Weidenfeld & Nicolson, London 1999).
The Scottish Nation 1700–2000: by TM Devine (Allen Lane, The Penguin Press, London 1999).

The Isles: by Norman Davies (Macmillan, London 2000).

Scotland – History of a Nation: by David Ross (Lomond Books, 1999).

Invaders of Scotland: by Anna Ritchie and David J Breeze (Historic Scotland, Edinburgh, 1991).

Scotland: an archaeological guide to more than 200 sites from earliest times to AD1200, by Anna and Graham Ritchie (Oxford University Press, Oxford and New York 1998). For an introduction to the life of the Picts, we recommend Anna Ritchie's *Picts* (Historic Scotland 1999).

Prehistoric Scotland: by Ann MacSween and Mick Sharp (BT Batsford, London 1989).

Hoy, the Dark Enchanted Isle: by John Bremner (Bellavista Publications, Kirkwall 1997).

Shipwrecks of Orkney, Shetland and Pentland Firth: by David Ferguson (David & Charles 1988).

The Wrecks of Scapa Flow: compiled by David M Ferguson (The Orkney Press, Stromness 1985).

John Gow the Orkney Pirate: by George Watson (Caithness Field Club, Wick 1978).

The Lighthouse Stevensons: by Bella Bathurst (Flamingo, London 2000).

Shetland Shipwrecks: compiled and published by the Shetland Sub-Aqua Club (Lerwick 1989).

Walks on Shetland: by Mary Welsh (Westmorland Gazette, Kendal, Cumbria 1995).

The Birds and Mammals of Shetland: by LSV and UM Venables (Oliver & Boyd, Edinburgh, 1955).

Birds of Britain & Europe: translated and adapted by Ian Dawson (HarperCollins, London 1994).

Wild Flowers of Britain & Europe: translated and adapted by Martin Walters (HarperCollins, London 1994).

Reflections on Scotland: by Ian Wallace (Jarrold Colour Publications, Norwich, UK, 1988).

The Scottish Islands: by Hamish Haswell-Smith (Canongate Books Ltd, Edinburgh 1999).

An Island Odyssey: by Hamish Haswell-Smith (Canongate Books Ltd, Edinburgh 2000).

ORKNEY

Background Information

Practical Information

ORKNEY
Background Information

GEOGRAPHY

Orkney's 70 or so islands and islets lie at the turbulent crossroads where the Atlantic Ocean and the North Sea meet and, like those of Shetland, are nearer to the Arctic Circle than they are to London. Orkney is about 6 miles (9km) off Duncansby Head, on the north coast of Scotland, and the archipelago stretches about 53 miles (85km) from top to bottom. Its northernmost island, North Ronaldsay, is about 50 miles (80km) from the southern tip of Shetland, roughly double the distance across Orkney at its widest point. There is no land due west of Orkney until you reach Labrador, in Canada. The confluence of the Atlantic and the North Sea produces some extremely wild and dangerous tidal rips in the Pentland Firth.

The archipelago can roughly be divided into three areas – the North Isles, the South Isles and in between, the largest, central island known as the Mainland, which is divided into East Mainland and West Mainland. These are connected by an isthmus less than 2 miles (3km) wide between the capital, Kirkwall, and Scapa Flow. The small islands of Burray and South Ronaldsay, to the south of the East Mainland, are joined to it by concrete causeways built during World War II by Italian prisoners of war to prevent enemy submarines entering the naval base there. After Mainland, Hoy is the largest island and on it is Ward Hill, at 1,571ft (479m) the highest point on Orkney. Only 18 of the islands are now inhabited, with a total population of around 20,000. The islands are still gradually moving northwards at the rate of nearly an inch (2.5 cm) a year.

Geology

Like Shetland, Orkney rocks are formed mainly from mud and sand deposited in freshwater Lake Orcadie during the Devonian (Old Red Sandstone) Age, some 400–360 million years ago. Evaporation and the variable rainfall associated with its then sub-tropical climate led to successive deposits of sand, silt and mud, which were eventually compressed into finely laminated sandstone layers. In them, ancient colonies of dead algae form distinctive bun-shaped masses of banded rock known as stromatolites. Fossil fish are also abundant in the sandstone layers. Lake Orcadie eventually dried up and at Yesnaby on Mainland the sands of the long gone resultant desert are preserved in the spectacular sea cliffs and the Castle of Yesnaby sea stack. On the exposed westerly coasts the sandstone has been remorselessly scoured by the Atlantic, producing at St John's Head, on Hoy, perpendicular cliffs towering 1,135ft (346m) above the sea, and the famous Old Man of Hoy sea stack, whose vertical rock pillar rears 450ft (137m).

Topography

During the last Ice Age sea levels were more than 330ft (100m) lower than they are today. Orkney was then a range of hills and valleys surrounded by low-lying land stretching to the Scottish mainland. Around 10,000 years ago global warming caused sea levels to rise again and gradually the lower valleys were submerged. The sea level stabilised about 6,000 years ago, by which time the islands looked roughly as you see them today. Variation in rock hardness causes erosion at different rates; headlands have formed where the rock is harder, bays where it is softer. The glacial erosion that fashioned Orkney's low hills was followed by flooding that left a gently undulating Orkney with broad open bays, generally sheltered by sand dunes, and a coastline whose indentations give it a total length of 500 miles (805km).

Orkney manages to give the impression of a somehow more orderly and tidy place than Shetland. This is possibly because it has been shaped by a longer agricultural partnership between land and man, whose intensive cultivation of the more fertile parts of its 247,105 acres (100,000ha) has tamed and smoothed most of its rougher corners. The bits that are still rough are really wild, presenting huge cliffs, caves, carved rock arches, and dizzying sea stacks, usually on the side bearing the full brunt of the Atlantic breakers. In calm weather, stretches of sea virtually hemmed in by land, such as Scapa Flow, look like vast, clear lakes with barely a ripple disturbing their surface.

Virtually the only remaining wild trees left in Orkney today are the gnarled and stunted stands in the sheltered Berriedale valley on Hoy, but in other places so-called tall herb vegetation and scrub hint at a different vanished landscape. Orkney was undoubtedly more wooded when the first primitive agriculturalists stepped ashore from their skin-covered boats. A scrub woodland of hazel, aspen, birch, willow and rowan covered much of the lower lying parts of the islands, but once the new settlers began chopping down trees for firewood and building material and clearing land for farming and for their grazing animals the indigenous woods had little chance of regeneration. Wind and changes in climate also contributed to the problem. These factors and the depletion of the soils by early farming methods also contributed to the expansion of the peatlands. Upland areas of the larger islands are dominated by heather moorland, although this is slowly being reduced through agricultural improvements. Trees can be successfully grown if protected from grazing animals, as can be seen in stands at Binscarth, near Finstown, and at Balfour Castle, on Shapinsay.

All parts of Orkney are too close to the sea for true rivers to form, but sparkling burns, lochs and lochans (small lochs) are pleasant common features of the landscape.

CLIMATE

You can sometimes experience all four seasons in one day in Orkney – that's how changeable the weather can be. The good thing is that the climate is much milder than you'd expect at this latitude (59°N), with little variation between winter and summer and hardly any snow or frost. The tail effects of the warm Gulf Stream temper the islands' northerly location. Summers are mild and fairly dry, although the coasts and higher land may experience cool onshore winds. Winter temperatures compare well with those of southern English seaside resorts.

Weatherwise the best time to visit Orkney is during the sunniest and driest months of May and June. It is warmest in June–September, the wettest months are October–January, and the windiest November–March. On average, there is a gale every 13th day, with the relatively flat, open terrain seemingly magnifying the power of the wind. Rain totals anything up to 39 inches (1,000 mm) a year, but rainfall doesn't usually last long.

The islands bask in an average of 1,100 hours of sunshine a year, with highest number of hours in May (160) and August (185), although July and August are the hottest months, with average maximum day temperatures of 59°–65°F(15°–18°C). These are also the months when it is warmest at night. Days and nights seem to blend into one in mid-summer as the sun barely dips below the horizon. In June, the sun rises about 3am at Kirkwall and does not sink until nearly 9.30pm and, as in Shetland, golf matches can be played at midnight and you can read all night long. Minimum sea temperature is 42°F (6°C) in February; maximum is around 55°F (13°C) in July.

HISTORY

While Shetland was undoubtedly the first archipelago to face the Viking sword, Orkney was the place that attracted substantial numbers of Norse settlers once they realised that its fertility could easily support them, their families and their livestock. The fact that it was even closer to mainland Scotland and the Western Isles was an added bonus for the rovers who regularly sailed there to pillage the wealthier religious communities and villages. As in Shetland, the Norsemen had to subdue the population before they could settle, although the archaeological record seems to suggest that to a great extent they absorbed rather than exterminated the resident Picts. The distinctive bone pins and combs of the Picts have been unearthed in a number of Viking settlements and there is also evidence that their administration and land tenure systems were respected and even adopted by the invaders.

When the Vikings arrived Orkney had already been home to farmers and fishermen for more than 5,000 years, unknown people who constructed elaborate tombs and erected religious

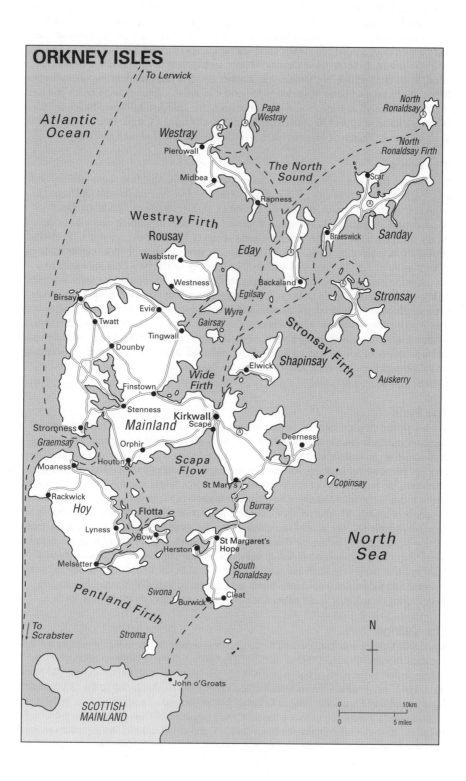

ORKNEY ISLES

To Lerwick

Atlantic
Ocean

North
Ronaldsay

Papa
Westray

Westray

Pierowall

The North
Sound

Midbea

Scar

Rapness

North
Ronaldsay Firth

Westray Firth

Braeswick

Sanday

Rousay

Eday

Wasbister

Stronsay

Westness

Egilsay

Backaland

Birsay

Evie

Wyre

Stronsay Firth

Twatt

Gairsay

Tingwall

Dounby

Elwick

Shapinsay

Auskerry

Finstown

Wide
Firth

Stenness

Kirkwall

Mainland

Scapa

Deerness

Stromness

Graemsay

Orphir

Moaness

Houton

Scapa
Flow

Copinsay

Rackwick

Hoy

St Mary's

Lyness

Burray

Bow

Flotta

St Margaret's
Hope

Herston

North
Sea

Melsetter

South
Ronaldsay

Swona

Cleat

Pentland Firth

Burwick

N

To
Scrabster

Stroma

John o'Groats

SCOTTISH
MAINLAND

0   10km

0   5 miles

monuments long before the Great Pyramids at Giza in Egypt, England's Stonehenge or the Great Wall of China were built. One of the things that makes Orkney unique is its concentration of accessible archaeological remains in such a small area. There are hundreds of sites and the past is all around you. While there are far too many to see in the space of a single visit you should try not to leave Orkney without seeing Neolithic Maes Howe chambered tomb, Skara Brae village, the Bronze Age Ring of Brodgar and Stones of Stenness, Gurness Broch, the Norse and Later Medieval St Magnus Cathedral, Orphir Round Church and Earl's Bu, and the Brough of Birsay (all on the Mainland); the Iron Age Midhowe Broch and tomb (Rousay); Knap of Howar Neolithic farmstead (Papa Westray); Cubbie Roo's Castle and St Mary's Church (Wyre); St Magnus Church (Egilsay); and the Dwarfie Stane (Hoy).

The Iron Age

It is obvious from archaeological excavation that by the Iron Age there was a wealthy and well-organised society in Orkney. By about 500BC the Iron Age inhabitants had begun to build strong circular houses as the main dwellings of their steadings. Gradually these became more sophisticated in design and formed the centres of small agricultural settlements, often enclosed by outer defences in the shape of ditches, banks or walls. By around 100BC the defensive stone towers known as brochs were standing or under construction in more than 50 places. Technologies such as iron working had arrived from the south. Iron was easier to obtain and work with than bronze. Copper ore was scarce, but there was plenty of low-grade bog iron ore in Orkney. While large amounts of this were needed to produce even small amounts of metal, the remains of furnaces and smithing hearths surrounded by iron-working slag show that it was a thriving industry. Metal and stone imports and, later, Roman jewellery, glassware and pottery, suggest extensive sea-trading links with the east and west coasts of Scotland and with Shetland, although actual contact with Roman Britain was slight and there is dispute about whether the Romans ever actually set foot on the islands.

The Picts

Orkney played an important part in the common culture which existed throughout northern Scotland and these links brought the Picts of Orkney into the broader northern Pictish kingdom sometime around the sixth century. It is recorded in Irish chronicles that Columba, then abbot of the powerful Irish religious community on the island of Iona, visited Brudei mac Maelchon, the pagan 'King of the Northern Picts,' in 565. While visiting the Pictish king, Columba met a 'king' from Orkney, who offered safe passage to missionaries travelling among the northern islands. The motive for Columba's journey into the heartland of the Picts, an area decidedly hostile to Celts, is not clear although it is believed he was keen to spread the Irish version of Christianity before the British version then spreading northward from Northumbria could sway them. His mission failed, as Orkney's gradual conversion to Christianity took place at a time during the sixth and seventh centuries when the whole of Pictland was being accepted into the fold of the Roman church through the influence of Northumbria and the proselytising priests of Ninian and his Candida Casa community on the Solway Firth.

The Vikings

By AD800 Orkney was firmly established as a Norse colony and in AD875 it became a Norse Earldom. It was not until AD995 as that Olaf Tryggvason, King of Norway, persuaded the Viking settlers at the point of his sword to accept the 'White Christ' and forsake the old Norse gods. The King, a recent convert himself, didn't mince words. According to the *Orkneyinga Saga* he told Earl Sigurd the Stout of Orkney: 'I want you and all your subjects to be baptised. If you refuse, I'll have you killed on the spot, and I swear that I'll ravage every island with fire and steel.' It was an offer Sigurd the Stout couldn't, and didn't, refuse. The mass conversion to Christianity brought many changes. The pagan burial rites of the Vikings had been abandoned by the end of the 10th century. A church was built at Birsay in the 11th century and by the 12th century the estate of every Norse family of any consequence had its own church.

Until their conversion the Vikings used lettering known as runes, which had a 16-character alphabet developed in Scandinavia around AD200. Its straight, uncomplicated strokes made it perfect for cutting into wood and stone. In Orkney, it was mainly used for writing colloquial messages on the walls of buildings and handy rock faces. Well-known runic graffiti include the inscriptions carved into the rock at Maes Howe chambered tomb. 'Thorny was bedded here' and 'Ingigerd is the best of them all' stand out among the 24 inscriptions. When the Viking's simple runic lettering was replaced by the Latin alphabet they acquired the new skill of writing on animal skin parchment with quill pens and ink made from vegetable dyes. In those days the people of Orkney and Iceland spoke the same Old Norse language. In Iceland, a whole new literary tradition was founded, based on the culture and memories of the Viking past and preserving its oral legends and poetry. At a time when most writing in Europe was in Latin and concerned mainly with religious matters the Norse sagas were written for entertainment, to be read aloud to members of a household gathered around the fire. Today these are among the classics of world literature. It is through the pages of the *Orkneyinga Saga*, written around AD1200, that so much of Orkney's history is known. The saga tells the story of successive *Jarls*, or Earls, of Orkney, many of whom were as powerful as kings. The saga has been of particular help to local archaeologists through its detailing of prominent people, places, events and sites in the period AD900–1200. Nowadays, Scandinavians visit Orkney in increasing numbers each year, as the islands display aspects of the way their Viking ancestors lived more readily than anything they can see in their own countries.

The historical roll call of the early Norse who ruled Orkney – and Shetland – is full of wonderfully eponymous names, but while they all made their mark in one way or another Thorfinn lingers on as a beer named 'Skull Splitter' in his honour, and Magnus, martyred on Egilsay in 1115 and later canonised, is commemorated in stone in the shape of Kirkwall's magnificent red sandstone cathedral, St Magnus. As is the usual fate of invaders, the Norsemen were assimilated rather than driven out.

The Scots

The last truly Norse earl was murdered sometime around 1231 in a debauched evening and within a few years the rulers of the islands were Scots paying homage to the King of Norway. One of these was Earl Henry Sinclair, a colourful Scot of Norman ancestry who is remembered chiefly for the voyage he made in 1391 from Orkney to Greenland and is credited with the discovery of America for Europeans in 1398, nearly a century before the Genoese seaman, Christopher Columbus. Credence is given to this story by the fact that when the Sinclairs built a chapel on their estate in 1446 it bore carvings of corn-cob and aloe cactus – plants not officially discovered until the voyage of Columbus to the New World 56 years later. Norse power waned in the islands and in the Scottish mainland territories under its rule after the disastrous battle of Largs in October 1263, which saw King Haakon's armada of 120 galleys scattered and destroyed by storm and the forces of Scots king Alexander III, who disputed Norway's claim to the Western Isles. The defeated Haakon fell ill on the voyage home to Norway and died in the Bishop's Palace in Kirkwall.

Three years later a treaty of friendship was signed by Scotland and Norway and in return for an annual payment the Norse relinquished the Hebridean islands they had ruled for centuries. They held on to Orkney and Shetland. This deal led to the financial wrangles of the late 15th century when unpaid Scottish compensation had grown into huge arrears and was now due to Denmark, which had ruled Norway since the union of 1397. The arrears and annual payment were abolished with the marriage in 1469 of King James III of Scotland and Princess Margaret of Denmark. Her father, King Christian I, could not raise the money promised for her dowry, so he pledged Orkney and Shetland. To this day Shetlanders are still somewhat miffed by the fact that Orkney was pledged for 60,000 gold florins while Shetland was pawned for only 8,000. When Christian didn't redeem his pledge all the islands were incorporated into the Scottish kingdom and were rapidly colonised afresh by Scots who often proved more rapacious than the Vikings.

In the 1500s earls and landlords of the stripe of Robert Stewart and his son Patrick put their stamp on Orkney and Shetland with their palaces and castles, bleeding the islanders to pay for them and forcing their tenants to build them. The 17th and 18th centuries were times of boom and bust as fortunes ebbed and flowed with the kelp industry, which saw islanders collecting, drying and burning hundreds of thousands of tons of kelp, a seaweed that was used to make potash and soda for the glass and soap industries and helped to make the landlords even wealthier. After this business collapsed came the time of the herring fisheries boom. This in turn petered out towards the end of the 19th century and men turned either to the Greenland whaling fleets or the Royal Navy for berths. During the 19th century the Hudson Bay Company used Orkney as its main recruitment centre and 80% of the men it employed in its exploration and trading activities in Canada were Orcadians.

World Wars

The precarious existence eked out by most islanders was momentously relieved by two World Wars which brought thousands of free-spending servicemen to the islands to man the forward defences and support the Royal Navy's Grand Fleet based in the sheltered anchorage of Scapa Flow. One never to be forgotten chapter in the saga of the Scapa Flow took place shortly after the end of World War I when 74 ships of the German High Seas Fleet, interned there after their surrender, were scuttled by their crews on the orders of their commander, Rear-Admiral Ludwig von Reuter. Many were subsequently salvaged but three battleships, four light mine-laying cruisers and four destroyers still lie on the bottom with other German and British warships and draw marvelling scuba divers from all over the world.

World War II also saw tragedy in the Flow. Despite the entrances being obstructed by sunken blockships a German U-boat slipped into the anchorage on the night of 14 October 1939 and sank the 29,150-ton battleship *HMS Royal Oak*. The ship went down in 13 minutes with the loss of 833 men out of a crew of 1,200 and is now an officially designated war grave (see *Diving* in *Sport and Recreation*). As a result of this audacious attack, which he admitted was a 'magnificent feat of arms', Winston Churchill ordered the construction of the barriers which block off the four channels leading into Scapa Flow from the east and are now causeways linking the main southern islands to the East Mainland. Between 1942 and 1944 more than 500 Italian prisoners of war helped to build the 1½ miles (2.4km) of concrete barriers. As well as this feat of construction the Italians left behind a unique memorial, the beautiful little chapel they built from corrugated iron Nissen huts on Lamb Holm. Scattered around Scapa Flow, particularly on Hoy, are modern man's monuments – wartime coastal defence installations, shore batteries, crumbling piers, blockships, signal stations, storage tanks and buildings, and rows of dilapidated huts.

Oil

Prosperity arrived in Orkney, as in Shetland, in the mid-1970s and the symbol of it was, and is, the tall gas flare which can be seen from afar burning night and day on the little island of Flotta, between Hoy and South Ronaldsay. Flotta is Orkney's counterpoint to Shetland's Sullom Voe, a terminal for the North Sea oilfields. This has plugged Orkney into new sources of revenue, helped to halt depopulation, and created hundreds of jobs to the point where unemployment in Orkney is now virtually unknown.

CLAIMS TO FAME
For such a small area of the world Orkney can claim links with an impressive array of historically famous names and events. Women's suspenders have become a design classic, influencing both female fashion and modern sexual imagery. The patent for them was lodged in 1896 by two young Orkney apprentice tailors, **Andrew Thomson** *and* **James Drever,** *who invented them to hold up crofters' trousers. On emigrating to California they registered their patent for 'a clasp serving to secure the stocking.' Thomson later returned to his native Hoy, where the patent was recently found. American hero* **General George Custer,** *the youngest general in the Union army in 1863 and killed by Sioux Indians at the Little Bighorn, was of Orkney stock, descended from the islands' Cusiter family.*

US writer Washington Irving, *author of* Rip van Winkle, *was the son of a Shapinsay man, whose home can still be seen on the island. The grandfather of* Herman Melville, *author of* Moby Dick, *came from the Northern Isles. The British Army greatcoat was designed by* Peter Shearer, *a Kirkwall tailor. Some authorities believe that the family of* Brigham Young, *leader of the Mormons, came from Graemsay. Ancestors of American film star* Greer Garson *came from Sandwick. During an Indian uprising in 1885 Orcadian* James Mowatt *rode nearly 200 miles (322km) in 36 hours from Edmonton to Calgary, Canada, to raise the alarm. This puts American Paul Revere's famous 20-mile (32km) ride from Charlestown to Lexington in 1775 in the shade.*

Novelist Eric Linklater, *known for* White Maa's Saga *and* Poet's Pub, *was born in 1899, the son of Captain Robert Linklater of Dounby, on Orkney's West Mainland. Poet* Edwin Muir *was born in 1887 in Deerness and spent his childhood on the island of Wyre.* Dr John Rae, *who was brought up at the Hall of Clestrain, Orphir, made four Arctic searches before he solved the mystery of the missing North-West Passage expedition led by Sir John Franklin. He shocked Britain in 1854 by reporting that Sir John Franklin's crews had turned to cannibalism in a desperate attempt to survive.* Jo Grimond, *the man once described as the 'greatest politician never to become prime minister,' was MP for the Northern Isles from 1950 to 1983. He died in 1993 and was buried near his Orkney home. The island of Sanday is the home of acclaimed composer* Sir Peter Maxwell Davies, *who helped to inaugurate the annual St Magnus Festival, an event regarded as one of the highlights of the national arts calendar.*

ECONOMY

Farming and stock raising have always been the basis of life in Orkney, with fishing a secondary source of food and income – so much so that Orcadians are known as crofters with boats, unlike the Shetlanders, who have always been regarded as fishermen with crofts. Farming is a prosperous sector of the economy and the predominant form of agriculture. Modern mechanical methods result in high productivity. The neat, cultivated landscape reflects the hard work of countless generations of farmers as much as the fertility of the land. Crofts average 148 acres (60ha) in size, many of the smaller old crofts having been amalgamated with others to make more viable farms. The climate does not favour arable farming, so most farmers breed and rear beef cattle. Dairy cows and sheep are also kept. Naturally reared Orkney beef and lamb is renowned for tenderness and flavour and is widely marketed throughout Britain. In addition to fodder crops such as turnips, swedes and beet, oats and an ancient form of barley called bere are also grown. Beremeal is still popular in island baking.

It is estimated that 15,396 of the resident population of around 19,245 live on the Mainland. In all there are about 8,250 households. Orkney households spend more than twice as much on fuel and power as families on mainland Scotland. Their travel costs are also noticeably higher. In remote and island areas prices of most goods tend to be anything from 5% to 25% higher than on the Scottish mainland, depending on the commodity or service. The pump price of petrol, for instance, is usually about 10–13% higher.

Other major contributors to island income are tourism, fishing, oil terminal activities and jewellery manufacture. Recent figures show that over 12 months about 125,000 tourists visit Orkney. This might not seem a large number but the majority of them are A-B income group spenders and what they lack in quantity they make up for in quality, injecting into the economy more than twice the amount brought in by fish and shellfish, and nearly as much as agriculture. Around 128,000 passengers and 38,000 accompanied cars cross to and from Orkney on the main Stromness to Scrabster route every year, along with 7,800 commercial vehicles. On the Stromness–Aberdeen route more than 28,000 passengers and 2,800 vehicles are carried annually. Kirkwall Airport handles more than 89,700 passengers and around 11,600 flights a year.

The Orkney fishing fleet is made up of around 177 vessels, 130 of them shellfish vessels of 33ft (10m) and under. Marine food exports, particularly lobster, scallops and crabs, are growing and production of farmed salmon topped 8,400 metric tons in the year 2000. The craft industries are dominated by the two highly successful jewellery firms, Ortak and Ola Gorie, but also include a large number of smaller firms, which together account for about 22.5% of value-added in the manufacturing sector. Orkney jewellery has a well-established name for image and quality.

Work to transform part of the island of Flotta into a major oil terminal began in 1973, and four years later the terminal opened for business. Construction of the terminal saved Orkney from the depressing unemployment experienced in other remote areas of Scotland at the time. Today, terminal staff work in what is virtually a self-sufficient community. Since its inauguration in January 1977, more than two billion barrels of crude oil and liquid petroleum gas have been processed through Flotta – the equivalent of around 15% of Britain's total North Sea oil output – and carried by nearly 4,000 crude oil tankers. North Sea oil passing through the Flotta system in 2001 totalled 6,825 metric tons. The economic contribution of the oil age to Orkney cannot be overstated and it is gratifying that any adverse impact on the ecology it might have had has been minimised by corralling operations on one tiny island. Plans are now in hand to create a major container port in Scapa Flow to serve the Atlantic route from America to north-west Europe. This could create up to 2,000 new jobs and is expected to cost at least £135 million to build. If everything goes to plan the first superships could be docking in Scapa Flow within the next few years.

LANGUAGE

English is the common language, but Orkney shares with Shetland a dialect and vocabulary owing much to the old Norse settlers. Words that the Vikings would have used when talking to each other about farming, fishing or weather conditions still find echoes in the everyday speech of the islanders and in local place-names. There are slight regional differences, such as *peedie*, which means small in Orkney, whereas Shetlanders use *peerie*. Other words you might come across are:

breck – slope	*grind* – gate	*noup* – peak
bring – breast	*hest/russ* – horse	*quoy* – enclosure
brim – surf	*holm* – isle	*skip/scap* – ship
brinian – burnt clearing	*hope* – shallow bay	*sourin* – swampy place
bu – farm (chief)	*hund* – dog	*stack* – rock pillar
croo – sheepfold	*kirk* – church	*stove* – house *t*
ey – island	*knap* – hill-top	*swart* – black
furse – waterfall	*ling* – heather	*ward* – beacon
graenn – green	*myre* – wet	*wick* – bay

Orcadian names for some common birds include:

aak – guillemot	*mallimack* – fulmar
caloo – long-tailed duck	*moosiehaak* – kestrel
chucket – blackbird	*pickieterno* – Arctic tern
cooter-neb – razorbill	*sawbill* – red-breasted merganser
corbie – raven	*scootie allan* – Arctic skua
dunter – eider	*scootie* – starling
gauk – cuckoo	*smyril* – merlin
kattabelly – hen harrier	*sula, solan goose* – gannet
laverock – skylark	*tammie-norie* – puffin
loon, rain goose – red-throated diver	*whaup* – curlew and
lyre or lyrie – Manx shearwater	*whitemaa* – common gull

Practical Information

GETTING THERE

BY AIR

British Airways (℗0870-850 9850; www.britishairways.com), operated by Loganair
(St Andrew's Drive, Glasgow Airport, Paisley, Renfrewshire PA3 2TG; ℗0141-848 7594;
fax 0141-887 6020; www.loganair.co.uk), flies to Kirkwall on the Orkney Mainland from:

Aberdeen, three every day, 45-minute flight.
Edinburgh, two a day Monday to Friday, two on Saturday, and one on Sunday, 90-minute flight.
Glasgow, one every day, 90-minute flight.
Inverness, two a day Monday to Friday, one on Saturday and Sunday, 30-minute flight.
Shetland, two a day Monday to Friday, one on Saturday and Sunday, 35-minute flight.
Flights during the peak season are busy so it is advisable to book well in advance. For departure times and further details contact the airline.

There are also good connections from Europe to Glasgow, Edinburgh and Aberdeen. If you are flying from the USA or Ireland you can fly direct to Glasgow.

Distances to Orkney from Major European cities

London: 580 miles (933km)
Berlin: 830 miles (1,336km)
Madrid: 1,350 miles (2,173km)

Oslo: 500 miles (805km)
Paris: 800 miles (1,288km)
Rome: 1,450 miles (2,334km)

As well as scheduled services from the Scottish mainland and Shetland, Kirkwall Airport is the base for the original inter-island services introduced and continuously operated by Loganair. Services to island airstrips include the Westray to Papa Westray route which, with a flying time of less than two minutes, is the shortest scheduled air service in the world. The small island airstrips are maintained by Orkney Islands Council.

For fare and timetable information: scheduled flights to/from Orkney: *British Airways* (℗0870-850 9850; www.britishairways.com).
Local island schedules: *Loganair* (℗01856-872494/873457; fax 01856-872420; www.loganair.co.uk).

Kirkwall Airport: Kirkwall KW15 1TH; ℗℗01856-872421; fax 01856-871882. Open Monday to Friday 6.15am to 7.45pm, Saturday 6.15am to 6.45pm, and Sunday 9am to 7.45pm. A bus service operates from the airport to Kirkwall, single fare £2, return £3. Service times are available at the Airport Information Desk (℗01856-886210). Car hire and taxis are available.

Charter aircraft: Loganair (℗01856-872420) and Tayflite Executive Air Charter (℗01738-550088; www.tayflite.co.uk.

Airport: The airport is about 4 miles (6km) from Kirkwall. Ramp and wheelchairs are available and ambulift equipment is available to assist with embarkation/disembarkation. Facilities at Kirkwall Airport have been improved significantly, including a new airport terminal, and the installation of an Instrument Landing System. There is a café, bar, shop and broadband facilities. A free-of-charge car park is available.

BY SEA

You have a choice of four ferry routes. From Aberdeen there's a *NorthLink* passenger and vehicle 6-hour ferry trip to Kirkwall; from Scrabster (Caithness), a passenger and vehicle ferry sailing daily all year round and taking about 90 minutes; from John o' Groats a passenger-only ferry sails daily from May to the end of September and takes 40 minutes to reach Burwick; and from Gill's Bay, near John o' Groats, *Pentland Ferries* runs a car and passenger service to and from St Margaret's Hope, South Ronaldsay. The crossing takes about an hour.

If you are piloting your own vessel contact *Orkney Harbours* to advise on your schedule. You can contact them at *Orkney Islands Council* (Department of Harbours, Harbour Authority Building, Scapa KW15 1SD; ℂ01856-873636; fax 01856-873012; email harbours@ orkney.gov.uk), or visit www.orkneymarinas.co.uk.

NorthLink Ferries Ltd (Kiln Corner, Ayre Road, Kirkwall KW15 1QX; reservations ℂ0845-600 0449; fax 01856-879588; email info@northlinkferries.co.uk; www.northlinkferries.co.uk; also at New Ferry Terminal, Ferry Road, Stromness KW16 3BH and Jamieson Quay, Aberdeen AB11 5NP) operate the Aberdeen to Kirkwall and Scrabster to Stromness ferry routes to Orkney. The Kirkwall office is open for walk-up bookings from 9am to 5pm Monday to Friday. Closed at weekends. The check-in and reservations desk in Stromness is open from 5.30am to 4.45pm Mon-Fri and 7.30am to 4.45am Sat/Sun (5.30am to 4.45pm on Sats 9 June to 18 August).

The *MV Hjaltland* and *MV Hrossey* passenger and car ferries from Aberdeen to Kirkwall carry 600 passengers and 153 cars and the crossing takes 6 hours. The 410ft (125m) ferry leaves Aberdeen at 5pm on Tuesday, Thursday, Saturday and Sunday. The adult single fare is £24.30 in peak season (July and August), £20 mid-season (April, May, June, September and October, 19 Dec–8Jan), £15.90 in low season (January, February, March, November and December). The additional charges are added for the following; single car fare is £86.30, £82, £62.80 respectively and motorcycle is £19.50, £16.80, and £14.10. The single fare for an outer two-berth cabin is £86.30, £77.70 and £56.10. An inner cabin (up to four-berth) will cost you £84.10, £75.50, and £53.90 respectively. All cabins are en suite. There are specially equipped cabins for disabled passengers. The 361ft (110m) *MV Hamnavoe* sails from Scrabster to Stromness carrying 600 passengers, 95 cars and takes 90 minutes. It leaves Scrabster at 8.45am, 1.15pm and 7pm Monday to Friday, and at 12 noon and 7pm on Saturday and Sunday. Peak season summer schedule includes an 8.45am departure from Scrabster from Saturday 9 June–Saturday 18 August. The adult passenger single fare is £15.10 in peak season, £14.10 mid-season, £13 low season. Car £45.30, £42.10, £41, and motorcycle £15.70, £14.10, and £12.40. This route gives you a good view of the famous sea stack, the Old Man of Hoy, and the towering red sandstone cliffs of St John's Head.

There is a 10% discount available on standard passenger and vehicle fares to senior citizens, those in full-time education and the disabled. Self-service restaurants offer a wide range of menus featuring local produce, and on the longer routes there is the choice of the la carte restaurant. Each ferry has lounge areas, bars, a well-stocked shop, and children's play areas. On the longer routes a modern cinema shows the latest releases.

John o' Groats Ferries: (Ferry Office, John o' Groats, Caithness KW1 4YR; ℂ01955-611353; fax 01955-611301; email info@jogferry.co.uk; www.jogferry.co.uk) operates a daily passenger-only (and bicycles) ferry service, with sailings at 9am and 6pm (4.30pm in September) from John o' Groats to Burwick from 1 May to 30 September. The trip on *MV Pentland Venture* takes 40 minutes. There are additional sailings from 1 June to 2 September at 10.30am and 4pm. No booking is required. The ferry ticket of £28 return includes the connecting coach fare to Kirkwall, 17 miles (27km) from the Burwick landing. Fares to Burwick (on the southern tip of the island) cost £26 return. The ferry takes the short route – just 40 minutes. It's quite scenic, passing the deserted isles of Stroma and Swona along the way. These islands provide sheltered breeding grounds for a wealth of marine wildlife to view on the trip. In recent years there have been numerous sightings of killer whales. Generally the sea is calm during the summer months, but look out for the occasional forecast of bad weather, which can be testing for queasy passengers.

Pentland Ferries Ltd (Pier Road, St Margaret's Hope, South Ronaldsay KW17 2SW; ℂ01856-831226; fax 01856-831614; email sales@pentlandferries.co.uk; www.pentlandferries.co.uk) with the *Pentalina*, an ex-Caledonian MacBrayne ferry boat of 1,900 tons which can carry 50 cars and 250 passengers, sails from Gill's Bay, about 3 miles (5km) from John o' Groats, through Scapa Flow to a terminal at St Margaret's Hope, South Ronaldsay. Crossing takes about an hour; buy your tickets on board. The single adult fare is £10, children 5–16 £5, car, caravans and motorhomes (up to 6m) £25 (motorhomes over 6m, £40), motorcycle £7, and bicycle £2. Operates 3–4 times a day in summer, seven days a week. Owner Andrew Banks Jnr (Coel na Mar, St Margaret's Hope; ℂ01856-831538).

BY ROAD

Head north using the motorway system for the A9 to Inverness. From here the bridges over the Moray, Cromarty and Dornoch firths have taken hours off the old journey time. Roads to Wick (for John o' Groats) and Thurso (for Scrabster) are well signposted. From Perth to Inverness is 114 miles (184km) and takes about 2¾ hours by car, from Inverness to Scrabster is 111 miles (179km).

By Coach

Coach services are operated by *Scottish Citylink* (Buchanan Bus Station, Killermont Street, Glasgow G2 3NP; ℂ0870-550 5050; fax 0141-332 4488; email info@citylink.co.uk; www.citylink.co.uk) from all major UK cities via the National Express network. If you are travelling from southern England, you may have to overnight in Glasgow, Edinburgh or Inverness.

The Orkney Bus (John o' Groats Ferries, John o' Groats, Caithness KW1 4YR; ℂ01955-611353; fax 01955-611301; email info@jogferry.co.uk; www.jogferry.co.uk) is a direct express coach leaving Inverness Bus Station (Platform 1) every day during May at 2.20pm, and June to September at 7.30am and 2.20pm, to meet the ferry from John o' Groats to Kirkwall. A bus waits at the pier in Burwick to drive arriving ferry passengers to Kirkwall, which takes about 45 minutes. The return Inverness to Kirkwall fare is £42. You can buy your ticket on the bus. Bicycles cannot be carried.

Distance to Scrabster from major UK cities:

Aberdeen: 216 miles (348km)	**Inverness:** 110 miles (177km)
Carlisle: 368 miles (592km)	**Newcastle:** 378 miles (608km)
Edinburgh: 268 miles (431km)	**Perth:** 224 miles (361km)
Glasgow: 268 miles (431km)	**Stanraer:** 376 miles (605km)

BY RAIL

For Scrabster you can travel by train to Thurso, leaving Inverness at about 7.14am. On arrival at Thurso Railway Station a free bus to John o' Groats connects with the Orkney ferry at Scrabster at about midday. Contact *First ScotRail* (Atrium Court, 50 Waterloo Street, Glasgow G2 6HQ; ℂ0845-755 0033; email scotrail.enquiries@firstgroup.com; www.firstscotrail.com) for more information and timetable.

TOUR OPERATORS

Discover Orkney Tours: John Grieve, 44 Clay Loan, Kirkwall KW15 1QG (ℂ/fax 01856-872865; email john@discoverorkney.com; www.discoverorkney.com). Guided tours and walks throughout Orkney with an accredited guide. Tours suitable for individuals or groups and collection from your accommodation, the ferry, or airport. From an hour to all day tours.

Scotsell for Scottish Island Holidays: 20 Hydepark Business Centre, 60 Mollinsburn Street, Springburn, Glasgow G21 4SF (ℂ0141-558 0100; fax 0141-558 4040; email holidays@scotsell.com; www.scotsell.com). Scottish island specialists with imaginative car touring holidays, by ferry to Orkney and Shetland.

Puffin Express and Go-Orkney: 30 Culduthel Road, Inverness IV2 4AP (✆01463-717181; email sdunnett@btconnect.com; www.puffinexpress.co.uk). For packages, including road and ferry travel between Inverness and Orkney, and guided tours.

Wildabout Orkney Tours: Michael and Christie Hartley, 5 Clouston Corner, Stenness KW16 3LB (✆/fax 01856-851011; email info@wildaboutorkney.com; www.wildaboutorkney. com). Year-round tours for groups and individual travellers. Focus on Orkney history, archaeology, wildlife, folklore, spirituality and culture.

John o' Groats Ferries: Ferry Office, John o' Groats, Caithness KW1 4YR;✆01955-611353; fax 01955-611301; email info@jogferry.co.uk; www.jogferry.co.uk. In addition to the service to Orkney they also operate a number of tours. The Inverness to Orkney day tour leaves from Inverness Bus Station at 7.30am from 1 June to 2 September, return 9pm. It costs £47 per person return, and includes a six-hour tour of the islands. Bookings are essential. The Maxi Day Tour leaves at 9am (1 May to 30 September), return 7.45pm. It costs £38 for adults, £104 for a family ticket (two adults, two children). The shorter Highlights Day Tour leaves at 10.30am 1 June to 2 September, returns 6pm. It costs £35 return, children £10. The 90-minute Wildlife Cruise from John o' Groats costs £15 per person. This leaves every day at 2.30pm from 20 June to 31 August to view marine wildlife in the Pentland Firth. No booking is required.

COMMUNICATIONS

MAIL

The main post office in Kirkwall is in Junction Road (✆01856-874249), open Monday, Tuesday, Thursday and Friday from 9am to 5pm, Wednesday 9am to 4pm, and Saturday 9.30am to 12.30pm. The Stromness post office is at 37 Victoria Street, Stromness (✆01856-850201), open Monday to Friday 9am to 1pm, 2pm to 5.15pm, and Saturday 9am to 12.30pm. You will find other post offices throughout the islands (see *Help and Information* in each section).

NEWSPAPERS AND MAGAZINES

The Orcadian (Hell's Half Acre, Hatston, Kirkwall KW15 1DW; ✆01856-879000; fax 01856-879001; www.orcadian.co.uk) newspaper is published every Thursday. It also publishes *The Islander*, an annual tabloid paper aimed at visitors and available throughout the islands free of charge. *Orkney Today* (Unit 1, Kiln Corner, Ayre Road, Kirkwall KW15 1QX; ✆01856-888810; fax 01856-888811; email info@orkneytoday.ltd.uk; www.orkneytoday.ltd. uk), every Friday. British national newspapers are usually flown in early each day. Even the more remote islands get their newspapers delivered later the same day. *The Press & Journal* (www.pressandjournal.newsstand.com), published on the Scottish mainland in Aberdeen, carries news reports on Orkney and Shetland.

RADIO

BBC Radio Orkney (Castle Street, Kirkwall KW15 1DF; ✆01856-873939; fax 01856-872908; email radio.orkney@bbc.co.uk) might be one of the smallest outposts of the BBC but it claims the widest reach of any BBC station, with research showing that 7 out of 10 adults in Orkney tune in at least once a week. It broadcasts on 93.7MHz FM each weekday. News, weather and'what's on' diary are aired between 7.30am and 8am; music and topical programmes are broadcast from 6.15pm to 7pm during October–May. There is music from 7pm to 8pm every Friday.

BBC Radio Shetland can also be heard on the same waveband between 5.30pm and 6pm, as can *BBC Radio Scotland* which broadcasts news and traffic reports on flights and ferries.

MAPS

Ordnance Survey maps in the Landranger series are recommended for all the islands. These are covered by Sheet 5 (North Isles), Sheet 6 (Mainland), and Sheet 7 (South Isles). All are 1:50000 scale, which means 1¼ inches to 1 mile (2 cm to 1km). The official tourist map obtainable from VisitOrkney in Kirkwall is useful for motorists and general planning with a scale of 1:28,000, or about 2½ miles to the inch (4 km to 2.5 cm). The OTB has a good range of books, maps and material on the islands, and further along Broad Street the Orkney Museum in Tankerness House has a selection of Orkney books and other material not seen in many other places and worth browsing when you visit.

GUIDES

Booklets on various aspects of Orkney are produced by Historic Scotland. They are written by specialists in their fields and are recommended for good all round reading. Particularly interesting and useful are *Invaders of Scotland*, by Anna Ritchie and David J Breeze, and Anna Ritchie's *Picts*. The locally produced *Orkney Guide Book*, by Charles Tait (Charles Tait Photographic, Kirkwall 1999) is fairly expensive (£17.95) but meticulously comprehensive 276-page introduction to the islands.

Before hitting the water divers should hunt for a copy of *The Wrecks of the Scapa Flow*, compiled by David M Ferguson (The Orkney Press, Stromness 1985), which is dry but thorough.

The liveliest guide to the islands through the centuries remains a book written more than 800 years ago, the Orkneyinga Saga (translated by Hermann Pálsson and Paul Edwards, Penguin Books, London 1981).

BY AIR

Loganair (✆01856-872494/873457), flies from Kirkwall to six of the islands: Eday (twice a day on Wednesday), Sanday (twice a day Monday to Saturday), Stronsay (once a day Monday and Wednesday), Westray (twice a day Monday to Saturday), Papa Westray (twice a day Monday to Saturday, and once a day on Sunday) and North Ronaldsay (twice every day). Special tickets are available on Orkney's inter-island air service.

An **Excursion** return fare is available on all flights to North Ronaldsay and Papa Westray with a minimum stay of one night. Discounts of up to 50% are available to passengers over the age of 60 on many of the full economy fares, but not on services to North Ronaldsay and Papa Westray, or in conjunction with already rebated fares.

BY SEA

Orkney Ferries (Shore Street, Kirkwall KW15 1LG; ✆01856-872044; fax 01856-872921; email info@orkneyferries.co.uk; www.orkneyferries.co.uk) operate the inter-island passenger and car ferry services to the north and south islands – nine ferries between Orkney Mainland and 13 of the smaller islands, with daily sailings to most. Adult fares range from £6.60 to £13.10 return. Children under five travel free. Children aged 5–16, senior citizens and registered disabled passengers travel half price. A 25% discount is available on a 10-journey ticket, or 30% on a 20-journey ticket. They also have special Sunday excursions, in addition to scheduled sailings, to the Outer Isles (Eday, Sanday, North Ronaldsay, Stronsay, Westray, and Papa Westray) from May to August. Timetables for Orkney Ferries are published for summer (1 April–30 September) and winter (1 October–31 March) services.

BY ROAD
Bus

Orkney Coaches (Scotts Road, Hatston Industrial Estate, Kirkwall KW15 1GR; ✆01856-870555; fax 01856-877501; email orkneycoaches@rapsons.co.uk; www.rapsons.com) operates a comprehensive network throughout the Orkney Mainland, linking the main towns of

Kirkwall and Stromness with most of the other communities. In addition, buses connect with ferries to Hoy, Rousay, Egilsay and Wyre all year.

There are also summer connections at Burwick for the John o' Groats ferry. During the summer months a service links Stromness and Kirkwall with Skara Brae, the Ring of Brodgar, Standing Stones of Stenness, and Maes Howe. One-day *Orkney Rover* tickets are available for £7 and three-day £18. For the best value ask the driver for a Day Return. For more details and a free timetable contact the customer helpline (✆01856-870555).

Causeway Coaches (Alec Rosie, Church Road, St Margaret's Hope KW17 2TR; ✆01856-831444; fax 01856-831476) operates a taxi, minibus and coach business on service, contract and private hire basis. Main coach route is Kirkwall-Wilderness-Holm-Burray-St Margaret's Hope.

Taxis
Cabs are readily available in both Kirkwall and Stromness.

Driving
Orkney has about 150 miles (241km) of good motoring roads, though sinuous enough to call for extra careful driving and slower than normal speeds. This seems always to have been the case. A well-known official notice says: 'Driving at a speed of over four miles an hour within the limits of the narrow streets will be considered furious driving. Penalty of 40 shillings. By Order of the Magistrates 1833-37.'

Car Hire. Main vehicle hire companies are based in Kirkwall and Stromness and serve the ferry terminals. *WR Tullock* is the only official car hire company operating at Kirkwall Airport. British drivers must produce a current licence which must have been held for at least a year. Drivers must be 21-75. Overseas visitors should have a current licence valid in their own country or an international licence. Vehicle mileage is usually unlimited and vehicles come with a full fuel tank and should be returned full. Most credit cards, Maestro (debit card), cheques with bank card and cash are accepted. Vehicles can be collected from, or delivered to, the airport. Ferries are met by arrangement.

EATING AND DRINKING

EATING
Crofters of old needed around 4,300 calories a day to keep going and while meals relying on such staples as oats, bere, kale, and fish might seem boringly repetitive, modern nutritionists have given their plain fare the thumbs-up for healthy eating. On the other hand, Orkney's beef, lamb, fish, lobster, crab, shellfish, cream, butter, cheese and other dairy products definitely have the edge when it comes to taste. The choice of turf versus surf is a personal matter, but whichever you opt for you can be sure of meals ranging from excellent to superb. When you have had a surfeit of trout, salmon or scallops try the local black pudding or marinated herring with a plate of Orkney 'tatties' (potatoes) that are more heavenly than ordinary, oatcakes, or bannocks made from Orkney's oldest grain, bere. This used to be ground to meal in stone querns, which were always turned with the sun, left to right. The other way was considered unlucky. If you are an adventurous eater look out for *spoots*. These are difficult-to-catch shellfish better known as razor shells, because their long shiny outer looks like an old cut-throat razor.

Increasingly hedged about by European Union dairy restrictions, cheese-making in the islands has been shrinking in recent years, although the flag is still admirably waved for traditional Orkney farmhouse cheese by award-winning *Grimbister Farm Cheese*, and the hand-made ice cream of *Orkney Creamery*. Standards are kept high in the islands by the annual Orkney Food Awards, presented by VisitOrkney in collaboration with Orkney Quality Food and Drink Ltd, a group of companies committed to the promotion of excellence in local produce and manufacture.

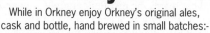
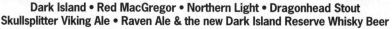

DRINKING

The great *Orkneyinga Saga* recounts that Svein Asleifarson of Gairsay was a guest of Earl Paul Hakonarson in the great drinking hall of Bu, near the round church at Orphir, when Svein Breast-Rope accused him of quaffing less ale than anyone else by using a smaller drinking horn and having it refilled before it was completely empty. Asleifarson was so enraged by this insult that he split his accuser's skull with an axe and also killed Breast-Rope's nephew for good measure. The Vikings made their ale from malted beer barley, and the stuff they brewed for Christmas was much stronger than that downed in everyday carousing. Earls went to a lot of trouble to ensure that their Yule ale would be strong. In about 1046, Earl Rognvald Brusason sailed his longboat from Kirkwall to Papa Stronsay just to get the especially good malt he wanted for his Christmas brew. The trip cost him his life. He was surprised and killed on the orders of his uncle, Thorfinn the Mighty. The Vikings were men who took their drinking seriously. Orcadians still do and residents of Stromness must have hailed the repeal in 1947 of the temperance ordinance which had left Orkney's second largest town 'dry' for more than 27 years. They certainly cheered the news that the Orkney beer 'Skull Splitter' was the Supreme Champion Winter Beer of Britain 2001. The strong ale, weighing in at 8.5% alcohol by volume, clinched the prize in the National Winter Ales Festival organised by the *Campaign for Real Ale* (CAMRA) in Manchester. It beat off competition from beers across the length and breadth of Britain to take the title. Described as a fruity barley wine, 'Skull Splitter' snatched the award from a final selection of more than 20 ales, strong milds, stouts and porters. *Orkney Brewery*, set up in an old school in 1988, is Britain's second most northerly. Its 'Skull Splitter' is named after Thorfinn, seventh Viking Earl of Orkney, and is said to be 'dangerously drinkable' with fish, curries and chocolate. The prestigious award follows the success of 'Dark Island' – also from the Orkney Brewery in Quoyloo (Sandwick, KW17 3LT; ℂ01856-841802; fax 01856-841754; www.orkneybrewery.co.uk) – which was voted champion Scottish beer in November 2000. Other Orkney Brewery tipples are Raven Ale, Dragonhead Stout, Red MacGregor, and Northern Light.

Established in 1798, *Highland Park* (see *Exploring: Kirkwall*) is the northernmost whisky distillery in the world, its distinctive pagodas a prominent landmark overlooking Kirkwall. Still adhering to traditional methods of distilling, Highland Park uses local peat to fire the kilns below the pagodas to dry the all-important maltings. The result is an internationally lauded product described by one leading expert as 'The greatest all-rounder in the world of malt whisky.' Highland Park 12-year-old (40% alcohol by volume) has a nose that is said to be 'smoky, like a garden bonfire, with a finish that is teasing, heathery, delicious'. The finish of the 14-year-old (55.2%) is said to be 'matty, like chewing on heather,' and its 24-year-old (43%) has a finish that is 'smooth, honeyish with light fruitiness, soothing'.

Distilling began in the islands in the 18th century. Their very remoteness made them ideal hideaways for what at the time was an illegal activity. One of the moonshiners of old was Magnus Eunson, an outwardly respectable preacher by day and an illicit whisky distiller by night. Legend has it that Eunson kept his full casks under the kirk pulpit, away from prying Excisemen. Eunson pursued his twin careers until his arrest in 1813. It is rumoured that his ghost roams the distillery at night – an understandable haunting, since Orkney's first legal distillery was opened on the site by James Robertson, one of the officers who arrested him. Another reason for the preacher's ghostly visitations could be the constant evaporation of the stored whisky which fills the air with the so-called 'Angel's Dram'.

Soft drinks. For those who eschew alcohol the best-selling brand of soft drink is a sweet, orangey concoction called *Irn Bru* (pronounced 'iron brew'), which is said to 'knock down' a meal of black pudding wonderfully well. It is also a best-seller in Russia where, oddly enough, it is regarded by trendies as a sophisticated drink.

ENTERTAINMENT

There is a cinema on the Mainland, the *Phoenix Cinema* (✆01856-879900) in the Pickaquoy Centre, Kirkwall, but entertainment in Orkney usually means music, music, and more music. It's played and practised in the home, in clubs, pubs, bars, community centres and at festivals – especially festivals (see *Calendar of Events*), which draw people from far and wide throughout the summer season. There are festivals for folk, traditional, jazz, blues, country and Irish, with the May folk festival one of the major events in both the Orkney and Scottish music calendar. For details contact Johnny Mowat, Folk Festival Office (PO Box 4, Stromness KW16 3AA; ✆01856-851331; fax 01856-851636; email orkneyfolkfestival@btinternet.com; www.orkneyfolkfestival.com). In between, from April to September, there are music 'sessions' everywhere in Stromness and Kirkwall and *ceilidhs* in the more rural areas. You'll find the *Orkney Accordion and Fiddle Club* playing Orcadian and Scottish traditional music in the Ayre Hotel, Kirkwall (✆01856-873001), at 8.30pm on the last Wednesday of each month from April to October at open evenings where everyone is welcome, and the *Orkney Strathspey and Reel Society* getting up steam every Thursday night. Visiting players and listeners are welcome. For venues enquire at VisitOrkney. From July to September it's 'Rolling in the Isles' with traditional music sessions in most hosteleries, including Sands Hotel, Burray; Pier Restaurant, Rousay; and Stronsay Hotel, Stronsay. The Stromness Hotel is a focal point for sessions all year round and hosts the April jazz and the September blues festivals, attracting groups from as far afield as Australia and America.

June, when the sun barely dips below the horizon at night, is also the time for the **St Magnus Festival** (60 Victoria Street, Kirkwall KW15 1NV; ✆01856-876214; fax 01856-876284; email science@orkney.com) the brainchild of Orkney's resident composer, Sir Peter Maxwell Davies. This has grown since its inception in 1977 to become one of Scotland's most prestigious classical festivals, attracting leading orchestras and world-class performing artists. Ask VisitOrkney for more details or check *The Orcadian* newspaper, published every Thursday (see *Communications*).

THE GREAT OUTDOORS

WILDLIFE ON ORKNEY

Orkney has more than 30 sites of Special Scientific Interest, areas specially protected for wildlife, with many of national importance. It also has a National Scenic Area. Charged with the responsibility for such protection is *Scottish Natural Heritage* (SNH), a government agency created by the Natural Heritage (Scotland) Act 1991. SNH works closely with the *Royal Society for the Protection of Birds* (RSPB) and the Orkney Islands Council (OIC) and has an office in Kirkwall where local staff are involved in giving conservation advice, grant work, research and survey, and projects to promote public access and enjoyment of the islands. SNH is funding an assessment of moorland management and conservation measures and finances farm conservation projects that help farmers and others managing land to factor into their plans the needs of local wildlife. 54–56 Junction Road, Kirkwall KW15 1AW; ©01856-875302; fax 01856-876372.

FLORA

Much of the land is either pasture for cattle and sheep or used to grow hay and silage, grassland areas that are intensively farmed and of little botanical interest. The edges of fields, ditches and wet uncultivated patches are often much richer in plant life such as the **yellow flag iris**, **meadowsweet** and **marsh marigold**, as well as **pink ragged robin**, **purple northern marsh orchid** and **lilac cuckoo flowers**. On moorland you'll find **tormentil** and **heather** and berry-bearing plants such as **crowberry**, **cloudberry** and **blueberry**. Plants commonly found on the shore include **sea-mayweed**, several types of **orache**, **Scots lovage**, **sea-sandwort** and large concentrations of **oysterplant**. Many upland plants are found at much lower altitudes than usual and salt-tolerant plants grow on maritime coastal heaths constantly exposed to sea spray. Places such as Yesnaby, Papa Westray, the coasts of Westray and Rousay are full of **sea pink** or thrift, **wild thyme**, **white grass of Parnassus** and **scurvy grass**.

The **Scottish primrose** (*Primula scotica*), a beautiful flowering plant confined to Orkney and the north coast of Scotland, is a rare find. This tough little primrose survived the Ice Age and is found only in maritime heath at about 15 sites in Orkney. Best places to find it are on clifftops between Stromness and Yesnaby, the west coast of Rousay, Westray, and the North Hill in Papa Westray, which is a wildlife reserve managed by the Royal Society for the Protection of Birds under an agreement between Scottish Natural Heritage and the owners. The tiny amethyst flowers of Scottish primrose open up in May and again from July to late September. Some plants may not flower until they are 10 years old.

In the East Mainland the Bay of Buckquoy has an area of saltmarsh which is not a common habitat in Orkney. Plants found here include **glasswort** and long-bracted **sedge**. Graemeshall Loch with its thick bed of reeds and **grey club rush** is possibly the best site for wetland plants. The West Mainland has probably the widest range of habitats for wild flowers in Orkney, from salt marsh, at the Bridge of Waithe, to alpine species on the Rendall Hills. The dales of the West Mainland support a unique fern and rush flora. This is normally associated with woodland and is thought to be a relic of the birch and hazel scrub which was widespread before the arrival of the Stone Age settlers. Botany buffs should make a beeline for the **Stromness Museum**, where there is a comprehensive herbarium which belonged to Magnus Spence, author of the first complete *Flora Orcadensis*.

FAUNA

The *Nuckelavee* is a sea monster of Orkney folklore. When crops failed or disease struck, the breath of this mythical monster was held to blame. Memories of the *Nuckelavee* survived on Hoy and Sanday until as recently as the 20th century. Seals, or *selkies*, are also part of island folklore, although these are mammals you can actually see. The confluence of the North Sea and Atlantic results in some fearsome tidal races, but the waters are rich in fish and shellfish, which means lots of **Atlantic grey seals** and, to a lesser degree, populations of **common seal**. At least 7,100 common seals frequent Orkney waters, roughly a quarter of the British and 1% of the world populations. There are also about 25,000 grey seals, 35% of the British and about 17.5% of the world populations.

Eighteen different species of whale have been recorded off Orkney, but the ones you are most likely to see are **minke whales**, **killer whales** (orca) and long-finned **pilot whales**. Scapa Flow and the waters around Deerness are good for **harbour porpoises**. The **white-beaked dolphin** is the most common of Orkney's dolphins, which you are more likely to see from a boat than from the shore. **White-sided** and **Risso's dolphins** are also regularly spotted. Late summer is the best time to see whales and dolphins. There is no guaranteed best spot, but generally the west side of the island is a good bet and places such as Cantick Head (Hoy), Noup Head (Westray), and North Hill (Papa Westray) are also good.

Most terrestrial mammals have been introduced, among them the **hedgehog**, **rabbit**, **brown hare**, **mountain hare**, **brown rat**, and **vole**. The mountain hare, which is found only on the relatively high land of Hoy, could have reached Orkney under its own steam. It is thought the hare arrived there at the end of the last Ice Age, when Orkney was still connected to mainland Scotland. **Otters** can also be regarded as indigenous. Island coastlines provide excellent habitat for these engaging creatures, but sightings are rarer in Orkney than on Shetland.

In 1904, the naturalist JG Millais, son of Pre-Raphaelite painter JE Millais, noted that the **vole** of Orkney was different from the common vole of mainland Britain and similar to the continental vole, of which it is now regarded as a sub-species. This distinction had already been noticed by the minister on the island of Shapinsay in 1805. There are slight variations in size and colour on different islands. Bergman's Rule says that animals generally get bigger and darker the further north they live, in order to absorb and retain heat. The voles of Westray, which are the smallest and darkest, are the most distinct. There are also voles on the Mainland, Sanday, Rousay, Burray and South Ronaldsay. The vole is the main prey of **kestrels**, **short-eared owls** and, for at least part of the year, **hen harriers**.

Caterpillars of the **winter moth** turn some areas of heather quite red in summer by eating away the leaves to expose the woody stems. Flocks of **gulls** feast on these caterpillars, which have been recorded at a density of 1,500 per sq metre. The small natural wood at Berriedale on Hoy and the area around it is the most important place for **butterflies** and **moths** in Orkney, with more than 30 species found nowhere else in the islands.

BIRD-WATCHING

More than 20 species of seabirds are found in Orkney and the human population is probably outnumbered 100 to one by the feathered residents. Although there have been marked declines in recent years as a result of food shortages, there have been up to 200,000 **guillemots**, 20,000 **Arctic terns**, 70,000 pairs of **kittiwakes**, 10,000 **razorbills** and, everybody's favourites, some 50,000 pairs of **puffins**. The majority of puffins are found on the very remote island of Sule Skerry. Puffins have to beat their paddle-like wings 300–400 times a minute to fly, but can average 50 mph (80 km/h) in flight. Nearly a fifth of the entire British population of **curlews** – more than 5,000 pairs – breeds in moorland areas.

The 70 pairs of **short-eared owls** – known locally as *cattie-faced owls* – represent one of the strongest populations in Britain, while one of the country's rarest birds of prey, the **hen harrier**, still survives on Orkney's moorlands along with the **merlin**. The best time for bird-watching depends on the species that interest you. Mid-May to mid-July is excellent for breeding birds; late April to late May covers the spring migration of most species; autumn migration is at its height in September and October.

Corncrakes were once widespread in Britain, but are now confined to Orkney, the Western Isles and a handful in northern Scotland. The reasons for their decline are complicated, but changes in agricultural practices are high on the list. A joint initiative funded by the RSPB and SNH, and supported by the Scottish Crofters Union, has helped to substantially increase numbers in both the Outer and Inner Hebrides but the future of these birds in Orkney is still uncertain due to the intensity of grassland management in the islands. If you've heard this bird calling on your outings report it to the RSPB (℡01856-850176).

The RSPB owns, leases or manages by agreement almost 21,000 acres (8,400ha) of land in the islands with the specific aim of protecting birds and other wildlife within its 11 wildlife nature reserves on Orkney Mainland (4), Copinsay, Shapinsay, Egilsay, Hoy, Rousay, Westray and Papa Westray. Interpretation facilities and bird-watching hides are provided at several sites. Vast numbers of birds nest in these reserves, with the largest concentrations on sea cliffs, and important populations on moorlands and marshes. Mid-April to mid-July is the **best time** for seeing breeding birds. Outside this period, many reserves can be virtually deserted. Orkney is also internationally important for its wintering seafowl. **Great northern divers** from Iceland and Greenland, and **Slavonian grebes, velvet scoters** and hundreds of **long-tailed ducks** from northern Europe arrive to join resident **eider ducks, red-breasted mergansers** and **black guillemots**. They tend to concentrate in and around sheltered Scapa Flow. More than 50,000 waders feed on the shoreline in winter. For more information contact *RSPB Scotlandy* at its Orkney office (12/14 North End Road, Stromness KW16 3AG; ✆01856-850176; fax 01856-851311; email orkney@rspb.org.uk).

WALKING

The Orkney Islands Council, VisitOrkney, and bodies such as Scottish Natural Heritage and the Royal Society for the Protection of Birds encourage visitors to bring their boots to Orkney as walking is by far the best way to adjust to the slower pace of island life and take advantage of the network of country roads and tracks to enjoy the natural splendour of the islands, the myriad prehistoric brochs, stone circles, chambered tombs, and other ancient sites. Walking also gives you the chance to experience something of the more recent history of Orkney, its crofting, fishing, milling, herring and kelp industries, and evidence of its long seafaring heritage. On walks around Scapa Flow, for instance, you can see remains of coastal installations and gun batteries placed to defend the British naval fleet in two World Wars.

A *Walks in Orkney* leaflet is available free from the VisitOrkney in Kirkwall which offers a choice of 19 walks across the Mainland and the other islands. Walks recommended are around 1.8 miles (3km) and are suitable for all ages and abilities provided you follow the advice contained in the map key and give yourself ample time to cover the distance. Each listed walk is identified by Ordnance Survey map references. Maps make walks more interesting and help you to decipher the surrounding landscape much more easily. Walks criss-cross working rural areas so all the usual cautions of the countryside code apply. Don't forget your camera and binoculars and be sure to pack food and drink.

CYCLING

Orkney's fairly flat terrain means that two-wheel touring is easier on the legs than in hillier Shetland. Check with the tourist office in Kirkwall or Stromness for recommended routes. The Orkney leg of the **North Sea Cycle Route** starts at Stromness and takes in the coastline of the West Mainland, passing through Kirkwall and continuing southwards over the World War II Churchill Barriers, which join the main South Isles to the East Mainland. The route ends at the Burwick ferry pier at the southernmost tip of South Ronaldsay. A short sea ferry ride to John o' Groats from here links up with the cycle route on the Scottish mainland. The Orkney stretch winds through areas of great natural beauty, as well as taking in a wide range of attractions, particularly a number of fascinating archaeological sites. Check out the national cycling website www.cycling.visitscotland.com.

FISHING

Fly-fishing

Island lochs hold some of the finest wild **brown trout** to be found anywhere. The Mainland Loch of Harray is the biggest draw. Its 1,500 acres (607ha) of water usually produces fish averaging around ¾lb (340g) from the first day of the season to the last, with June and July providing the best sport. Larger fish of 1–2lb (453 g-lkg) are fairly common, and every season sees a few of 2lb (1kg) or more landed. Wading is rewarding early and late in the season, with boat fishing a better bet during summer.

The neighbouring Loch of Stenness is one of the most challenging on the Mainland. Stenness is an arm of the sea and, to an extent, is tidal. This adds migratory **sea trout** to the native brown trout. Each season fish of 3lb (1.4kg) and more are recorded. The Loch of Skaill, in Sandwick, is trophy fish water and the angling here is reserved for *Orkney Trout Fishing Association* (OTFA) members only. Trout average more than 2lb (1kg) and anything under this weight is put back. In Evie, Peerie Water is stocked with the most beautiful vermilion-spotted trout, averaging 1¼lb (794g). Kirbuster in Orphir is an ideal beginner's loch, with bags averaging three to the pound. Many of the smaller lochs and lochans also offer excellent sport.

A trip to the North Isles is a must for the fly-fisherman – Westray, Stronsay and one of the most fished islands, Sanday, where trout of up to 6lb (2.7kg) have been caught. For more information on angling contact OTFA (c/o Malcolm Russell, Caolila, Heddle Road, Finstown KW17 2EG; ©01856-761586; www.orkneytroutfishing.co.uk), which is a non-profit-making, voluntary body, dedicated to the preservation and enhancement of game fishing throughout Orkney. The work of the association includes provision of access and boat-launching facilities on six of Orkney Mainland's prime trout fishing lochs. Most of these OTFA sites also provide shelter, piers, car parking and toilet amenities. For a small subscription visiting anglers can use all its sites and facilities. You can join at *WS Sinclair* (25–27 John Street, Stromness; ©01856-850469). Stan Headley's excellent book *A Trout Fishing Guide to Orkney* is available from most newsagents and booksellers in Orkney.

Sea Angling

Sea trout are generally caught in the shallow bays on the east coast of the Mainland, Hoy and Scapa Flow. Most are taken in spring and autumn and average around 1lb (453g), although fish of up to 5lb (2.2kg) are landed every year. Cold, clean waters and sheltered shores around the many islands make for memorable sea angling from boats for **cod**, **ling**, **pollack**, **coalfish**, **skate**, and **halibut**, as well as wreck fishing from the shore around Scapa Flow and rock fishing from the Churchill Barriers. For more information contact the *Orkney Islands Sea Angling Association* (c/o Leslie Fettes, 2 Buttquoy Place, Kirkwall; ©01856-874089; email info@anglingorkney.co.uk; www.anglingorkney.co.uk). Sea angling charters can be organised throughout the year from Stromness on the *MV Welcome Home*, with a OISAA qualified skipper. Charter trips cost £110 for 4 hours and £220 for 8 hours, for a minimum of 5 and a maximum of 12 people. Rod and reel hire can be included, with tackle available for purchase.

DIVING

Scuba divers come primarily to dive on the wrecks of British and German warships sunk during two World Wars and now lying at the bottom of Scapa Flow, where you can expect average visibility of 20–33ft (6–10m) in summer and 39–66ft (12–20m) in winter, when vis of up to 150ft (45m) is not uncommon. Thousands of divers enjoy exploring these wrecks each year.

GRAVEYARD OF THE GERMAN FLEET

Entombed in the depths of Scapa Flow are the World War I wrecks of the German High Seas Fleet warships, scuttled on 21 June 1919 towards the end of the Versailles armistice negotiations. On the order of the German Fleet Commander, Rear-Admiral Ludwig von Reuter, 74 ships were scuttled by their crews. Fifty-two sank completely; the rest were either beached or saved by boarding parties of the Royal Navy. Early salvage reduced the number of wrecks on the bottom and today only seven of note are regularly visited by divers – four light mine-laying cruisers, Brummer, Dresden, Cologne, and Karlsruhe; and three great battleships each up to 568ft (173m) long and each displacing more than 25,000 tons, SMS König, SMS Markgraf, and Kronprinz Wilhelm. These wrecks lie in depths varying from 79–148ft (24–45m), along with two torpedo-boat destroyers, V83 and S54; one submarine, UB116, and the four 600-ton main armament gun turrets of the Bayern.

This huge fleet was sunk as the result of a misunderstanding. After surrendering the German Imperial Fleet in November 1918 and sailing it into captivity in Scapa Flow, Rear-Admiral von Reuter waited for the outcome of the Versailles peace talks, due to end on 21 June 1919. They were not concluded by this date and negotiations were extended for a further two days. The German commander was not informed and assumed on 21 June that hostilities were due to be resumed. He did not want his fleet used by the Allies against his homeland so he decided to sink the entire fleet. One after another the ships of the great German battle fleet capsized and sank. As a result, the 120 sq mile (311 sqkm) bay of Scapa Flow now offers the best wreck-diving sites in Britain and undoubtedly ranks as one of the five top wreck-diving areas in the world, with more shipwrecks than any other place on earth – some 430,000 tons of shipping. Dives to these ancient warships are eerily spectacular. Unfortunately, many of the wrecks are in deep water – up to 151ft (46m) – and require decompression scuba dives or technical mixed gas descents. The 19,560-ton battleship HMS Vanguard *went down off Flotta in 112ft (34m) of water on 9 July 1917 after an accidental explosion in her magazine.*

World War II has also contributed its share of wrecks to the Flow, with a further 20 blockships sunk to seal off enemy access to the bay, and 16 known British wrecks, as well as a further 54 unidentified wrecks. This, too, is the grave of the 29,150-ton battleship HMS Royal Oak. *The sinking of* Royal Oak *on 14 October 1939 by a lone German U-boat was a catastrophic blow, both to the Royal Navy and to the belief that Scapa Flow was impregnable to enemy attack. Under cover of darkness and on a fast incoming tide German Commander Gunther Prien manoeuvred his* U47 *past blockships and anti-submarine netting in one of the most daring attacks of the war.* U47 *fired two salvos of torpedoes at the battleship. The first salvo inflicted only minor damage and the confused crew thought the muffled bow explosion was a minor problem in the ship's paint store. This gave Prien another 20 minutes to reload and fire a second salvo which scored three direct hits and sent* Royal Oak *to the bottom in less than 15 minutes, with the loss of 833 men. This is how Gunther Prien's logbook records the attack:*

'There are massive groans, steel plates buckling and further detonations. We look through the periscope as columns of water shoot into the air, flames and bellowing fire erupt into the night sky... One battleship has been hit, another damaged and the other ship received three hits. It's time to leave quickly.'

In March 1941, HMS Wolverine *caught up with U47 and sank her off Iceland.* HMS Royal Oak *now lies upside down in 89ft (27m) of water, camouflaged by growths of kelp, soft coral and anemones. In October 2000 the ashes of a widow whose husband went down with the battleship were placed inside the wreck in a unique ceremony, which coincided with the annual remembrance service held at the site of the wreck by the Royal Navy.*

The wreck is now a designated war grave and diving on her is forbidden. As a direct result of the sinking the eastern approach channels to Scapa Flow were completely blocked by the now-famous Churchill Barriers.

For those who have planned and adequately prepared themselves according to their experience and ability, it is a challenging but safe experience, but on average one diver dies in Scapa Flow every year and 15–20 get decompression illness (DCI) requiring treatment. Two common factors are relatively inexperienced divers attempting long, deep dives, often before acclimatising, and divers failing to take account of the nitrogen load taken on by repetitive deep-diving over the period of their holiday. Many of the wrecks in Scapa Flow are at depths in excess of 100ft (30m) so if you're doing multiple dives, your nitrogen load will build up. As your nitrogen load increases, the possibility of inadvertently straying from recommended decompression stops will increase. Diving with oxygen-enriched nitrox may add a safety factor but does not guarantee immunity from DCI and the mix can produce other serious problems for the inexperienced. Danger is minimised if you follow the basic rules of safe diving.

If you think you might have DCI, or if you've missed a decompression stop, tell your divemaster and tell the skipper of the boat. The commonest signs of DCI are skin tingling, rashes, joint pains, numbness in hands, feet or a limb, headaches, and limb weakness. The immediate treatment is with oxygen and rehydration, both of which can be done on the boat. The skipper will contact the coastguard, who will inform the Stromness recompression chamber operator and the doctor on call. If necessary, an ambulance will meet the boat. It is important to get treatment as soon as possible, before your condition gets worse, and the system can be triggered while you are still on your way back to port. Heriot Watt University's dive unit operates its own recompression facility in Stromness (℡01856-850605) and in conjunction with Orkney Health Board and the Hyperbaric Medicine Unit in Aberdeen, this is used to treat divers with DCI. Evacuation to Aberdeen for specialist care is also available.

It's surprising how many divers still mix drinking and diving. Alcohol dehydrates and it vasodilates. Even small amounts make you more liable to nitrogen narcosis. If you are planning to dive you should not spend the evening in the bar the night before. Basic dive safety and common sense: *Don't drink and dive*. If you are flying home, remember it's best not to dive the day before you leave.

You can, of course, explore some of the wrecks without even getting your feet wet. A three-hour cruise on the *MV Guide* from Houton Pier takes you to one of the scuttled German warships and includes a visit to Hoy. A remote operated vehicle (ROV) is manoeuvred around the wreck while you watch the video pictures it transmits. Booking is essential and can be made at Kirkwall and Stromness tourist offices. For schedules and rates contact *Roving Eye Enterprises* (Westrow Lodge, Orphir KW17 2RD; ℡01856-811309; fax 01856-811737; email k2bichan@aol.com; www.rovingeye.co.uk).

SAILING

Summer cruising yachts flock to the sheltered waters and anchorages of the archipelago and regattas are held throughout the islands. Main host and principal club in the islands is the *Orkney Sailing Club* in the port of Kirkwall. The club welcomes all visitors, whether yachties or tourists. Kirkwall is an ideal base for touring or a stop-off en route to Shetland and Norway. There are showers and bar facilities for visiting boat crews. The club runs Royal Yacht Association (RYA) approved sailing courses and has several RYA instructors and senior instructors. Club-owned Wayfarers and Picos are used for instruction. On racing nights members are usually willing to introduce you to the sport by taking you as crew. The club also takes part in other local club regattas and hosts an inter-county against Shetland every second year. Contact Orkney Sailing Club at The Girnel, Harbour Street, Kirkwall KW15 1LE (℡01856-872331; www.orkneysailingclub.org.uk). The Girnel takes its name from the building's original purpose. It was built in the 1600s for storing the Earl of Orkney's rent corn from the northern islands and is one of Kirkwall's oldest buildings. If you need help and advice on cruising the islands or to charter a bareboat yacht contact *Sail Orkney* (Mike Cooper, 20 George Street, Kirkwall KW15 1PW; ℡01856-871100; email mike@sailorkney.co.uk; www.sailorkney.co.uk).

GOLF

There are three courses on the Orkney mainland. The Kirkwall course is on a hill above the town and harbour; Stomness is a shore-side course with the cliffs of The Kame of Hoy as background; and there is a new nine-hole course at St Margaret's Hope.

CLIMBING

If you want to try some virgin sandstone stack and cliff rock **climbing** check out the Orkney Climbing Club at www.orkneyclimbingclub.co.uk or www.orkney-seastacks.co.uk. There is also a climbing wall at the Kirkwall Grammar School.

CRAFTS

Like neighbour Shetland, Orkney is noted for its **knitted** woollen garments and more than 50,000 are produced every year. Traditional Orkney **chairs**, with their curved woven straw backs to keep out draughts and canopy designed to ward off drips from leaky roofs are unusual buys. Silverwork, jewellery, pottery, artwork and handcrafts are usually best bought direct from the craft workers. Several organisations promote and sell the work of their members:

Orkney Craft Industries Association: Andi Ross, Outerdykes, Stenness KW16 3HA (℡01856-850207; fax 01856-850819; email ocia@e-scotland.co.uk; www.orkneydesignercrafts.co.uk).
Orkney Craftsmen's Guild: Jean Tulloch, Dalcomera, Holm Road, Kirkwall (℡01856-873754; email jeanick321@hotmail.com).
The Workshop: Front Road, St Margaret's Hope, South Ronaldsay (℡/fax 01856-831587; www.orkneydesignercrafts.com). A craft producers' co-operative specialising in crafts and knitwear using wool from the rare North Ronaldsay sheep, soft Icelandic Lopi, and authentic Shetland. Open April to December: Monday to Saturday from 10am to 5pm; and February to March: 10am to 1pm.

FOODSTUFFS

Orkney is famed for the quality of its foodstuffs: fish and shellfish from its cold, pollution-free waters, its tender beef and flavoursome lamb, and its baking. Its Highland Park malt whisky is also justly acclaimed. For local goodies with a taste of the islands try:

Grimbister Farm Cheese (Grimbister Farm, Kirkwall KW15 1TT; ℡/fax 01856-761318), family-run business producing traditional unpasteurised Orkney farmhouse cheese.
The Original Orkney Hamper Co (36 Victoria Street, Stromness KW15 3AA; ℡/fax 01856-850551; email info@orkneyhampers.co.uk; www.orkneyhampers.co.uk), which makes up food and drink hampers from cheese to malt whisky. Select from flavoured oatcakes, fresh mussels, oysters and scallops, salmon, marinated herring, Orkney beers, baking from Westray, jams and marmalades from Shapinsay, pure and natural clover honey from the Orkney Honey Farm, and Stenness whisky truffles. There's also a mail order service with UK next-day delivery promised.
The Orkney Salmon Company (Crowness Point, Kirkwall KW15 1RG; ℡01856-876101; fax 01856-873846; email enquiries@orkneysalmon.co.uk; www.orkneysalmon.co.uk), is a consortium of island salmon farmers who grow salmon using low-intensity methods to produce a firmly textured and subtly flavoured fish. They also raise organically grown salmon produced to the organic aquaculture standard set by the UK Soil Association, as well as shellfish.
The Orkney Creamery (Crantit Dairy, St Ola KW15 1RZ; ℡/fax 01856-872542; info@orkneyicecream.com; www.orkneyicecream.com), is a family-run company established in 1949 and still provides Orkney's liquid milk requirements. It also produces the popular hand-made ice cream and a selection of fudge. In 1998 the farm received added attention when a 5,000-year-old Neolithic tomb containing four skeletons was discovered on one of the fields and this has now been excavated.
William Jolly (Scott's Road, Hatston, Kirkwall KW15 1GR; ℡01856-872417/873317; fax 01856-874960) has a wide range of Orkney fare and take-home vacuum-packed salmon and other cured and smoked specialities. They'll also mail anything from a packet to a hamper for you.
Tods of Orkney (The Granary, 25 North End Road, Stromness KW16 3AG; ℡01856-850873; email info@stockan-and-gardens.co.uk; www.stockan-and-gardens.co.uk) makes Stockan and Gardens oatcakes, shortbread and biscuits. Oatcakes come in various shapes and flavours and, along with shortbread, are available in gift boxes. Tods also operates a mail order service.

WINE

Wines made in the traditional way using berries, flowers and vegetables rather than grapes is made locally at Britain's most northerly winery the *Orkney Wine Company* (Operahalla, Holm Road, St Ola, Kirkwall KW15 1SX; ℂ01856-878700; fax 01856-878701; email info@orkneywine.co.uk; www.orkneywine.co.uk). All wines are sulphur-free and suitable for vegetarians. You can visit the winery and its shop and taste a range of wines, including *Strubarb*, made with locally-grown rhubarb and strawberries; *Blaeberry Hairst*, blueberry wine; or *18 Carat*, more like a liqueur, made from Orkney carrots and fortified with eight-year-old Orkney single malt whisky.

MUSIC

Music lovers should enjoy the sounds Orcadians produce on their fiddles, accordions, pipes, guitars, mandolins, banjos and other, stranger, instruments such as the *bodhrán*, a goatskin drum, and the *clarsach*, a small Celtic harp. VisitOrkney in Broad Street, Kirkwall, stocks Orkney music CDs and cassettes. They are also available in local stores and at *Grooves Records* (40 Albert Street, Kirkwall; ℂ01856-872239; fax 01856-875585; email info@groovesrecords.co.uk; www.orkneymusic.co.uk). Good introductory buys are Hullion's *Leave the Land Behind*, sisters Jennifer and Hazel Wrigley's *The Watch Stone*, (both Attic Records), and Fiona Driver's *The Orkney Fiddler* (Newton Hill Records).

CRIME AND SAFETY

Crime is rare in Orkney. One case reported in *The Orcadian* newspaper concerned a bicycle that had 'gone missing and could the person who took it by mistake please return it'. There are cases of drunkenness and petty theft but nothing major. Locals say there is no point in stealing cars as there is nowhere to hide them. They recall some London tourists who did steal a car only to have the local police follow them until they ran out of petrol. Hard drugs are unknown, although some cannabis is smoked, especially during the summer music festivals.

HELP AND INFORMATION

TOURIST INFORMATION CENTRES

VisitOrkney: 6 Broad Street, Kirkwall KW15 1NX (ℂ01856-872856; fax 01856-875056; email info@visitorkney.com; www.visitorkney.com). The *Kirkwall Tourist Information Centre* is also housed here. It is open in May, Monday to Sunday 9am to 6pm; June to October, Monday to Saturday from 8.30am to 8pm; and October to April, Monday to Friday from 9am to 5pm, Saturday 10am to 1pm and 2pm to 4pm.

USEFUL ADDRESSES AND TELEPHONE NUMBERS

British Airways: (ℂ0870-850 9850); or at Kirkwall Airport; (ℂ01856-873611; fax 01856-876321).
John o'Groats Ferries: (ℂ01955-611353).
Kirkwall Airport (Highlands and Islands Airport): ℂ01856-872421; fax 01856-871882. Information desk ℂ01856-886210.
Loganair at Kirkwall Airport (ℂ01856-872494/873457; fax 01856-872420).
NorthLink Ferries: Kirkwall (reservations ℂ0845-600 0449).
Orkney Islands Council: Council Offices, School Place, Kirkwall KW15 1NY (ℂ01856-873535, fax 01856-875846).
Police Station: Watergate, Kirkwall (ℂ01856-872241).
Police Station: North End Road, Stromness (ℂ01856-850222).
RSPB: 12/14 North End Road, Stromness KW16 3AG (ℂ01856-850176; fax 01856-851311).

Scottish Natural Heritage: 54-56 Junction Road, Kirkwall KW15 1AW (✆01856-875302; fax 01856-876372).

Orkney Wildlife Emergency Response Group. First contact points for you if you come across a wildlife casualty are:

Dead birds (unusual kills) – *RSPB* (✆01856-850176);
Dead and injured seals – *Orkney Seal Rescue* (✆01856-831463);
Dead stranded whales, dolphins and turtles – *Scottish Natural Heritage* (✆01856-875302, fax 01856-876372);
Heath fires – *Fire Brigade* (✆999) or *RSPB* (✆01856-850176);
Injured birds, oiled birds and animals, dead and injured animals, trapped whales and dolphins, stranded live whales, dolphins and turtles – *Scottish SPCA* (✆01856-761267);
Oil spill – *OIC Oil Pollution Officer* (✆01856-873636).

CALENDAR OF EVENTS

Music festivals cater for jazz, folk, traditional fiddle, country and Irish, and other musical tastes. The internationally acclaimed **St Magnus Festival** held every June. VisitOrkney organises **sea angling** competitions every month from May to August. One of the biggest events in Orkney is the annual **County Show** held in Kirkwall in August. The show is organised by the Orkney Agricultural Society at Bignold Park. Other **agricultural shows** are held in August at Sanday, East Mainland, Shapinsay, South Ronaldsay and Dounby. The Stromness Hotel holds an annual **beer festival** for lovers of fine ales. Food and drink is celebrated in September with the 'Taste of Orkney' festival weekend bringing together producers, processors, cooks and customers to sample the best of Orcadian fare. The seven-day **Orkney Science Festival** is also held in September.

THE BA'

On Christmas Day and New Year's Day hundreds of people pack the streets of Kirkwall for a sporting free-for-all that revives a tradition going back to 1650. This is the game of mass street football known as the Ba'. The game is played with no written rules and with no limit on the number of players. Orcadians return from all over the world to watch or take part. A Boys' Ba' game starts at 10.30am with the main event Men's Ba' starting at 1pm. The game starts when the leather ball, the ba', is thrown from the Market Cross in front of St Magnus Cathedral to the waiting teams, the Uppies and the Doonies – Up-the-Gates and Down-the-Gates, the name coming from the old Norse word Gata, meaning a road or path. Whether you play for the Uppies or the Doonies depends on which side of the Market Cross you were born, or where you first entered Kirkwall. The aim of the Doonies is to get the ba' to Kirkwall harbour, where it must touch the water for a win, while the Uppies have to reach a goal at the opposite end of town. The result is a wild scrum of players with games lasting up to six hours and usually ending in darkness. Tradition says a win for the Doonies brings luck with the fishing, while an Uppies win means good crops. There have been other ba' games in the past. A Youths Ba' played from 1892 to 1910 was intended to stop the men from joining in the boys' game. A Women's Ba' played on Christmas Day 1945 and New Year's Day 1946 was not continued because it was considered too violent.

Another tradition lives on in South Ronaldsay where the **Festival of the Horse** is held every August. Youngsters dress up in colourful costumes, some handed down through several generations, and compete in a ploughing match at the Sands o' Right with miniature ploughs.

Annual Events

January	*The Ba'* - Traditional street football/rugby match on New Year's Day (www.bagame.com).
February	*Sea trout season opens (25th)*
March	*Brown trout season opens (15th)* (www.orkneytroutfishing.co.uk)
	Scarecrow Festival
April	*Orkney Ceilidh Weekend*
	Orkney Jazz Festival
	Rugby Sevens (www.orkneyrfc.co.uk)
	Flotta Fun Weekend
May	*Norwegian Constitution Day Celebrations*
	Orkney Homecoming (www.orkneyhomecoming.com)
	Orkney Folk Festival (www.orkneyfolkfestival.com)
June	*Hoy Half Marathon*
	Harray Community Association Ceilidh
	St Magnus Festival (www.stmagnusfestival.com)
	Midnight Golf
	Rousay, Stronsay and Longhope Sailing Regattas
July	*Stromness and Westray Sailing Reggatas*
	Stromness Shopping Week
August	*Annual Agricultural Shows*
	Kirkwall Regatta
	Vintage Rally Show
	Festival of the Horse and Boys' Ploughing Match
	Riding of the Marches
	Orkney Beer Festival
September	*Orkney Middle Distance Triathlon*
	Orkney Science Festival
	Taste of Orkney Food Festival
October	*Close of brown trout season (6th)*
	Close of sea trout season
November	*Maes Howe Winter Solstice*
December	*Christmas Tree Lighting*
	Christmas Day Ba' Game
	Hogmanay – The clock of St Magnus Cathedral and ships' whistles announce the New Year.

EXPLORING ORKNEY

Kirkwall & the East Mainland

Stromness & the West Mainland

South Isles

North Isles

Kirkwall & the East Mainland

Mainland Orkney is not only the biggest island in the archipelago, it contains more land than all the other islands put together. It is known simply as 'the Mainland'. It falls roughly into East and West sections at the narrow waist of land between Kirkwall and Scapa Flow. Included in the East Mainland area are the parishes of St Ola, which surrounds Kirkwall, Holm (pronounced 'Ham'), which includes the small island of Lamb Holm, Deerness, and St Andrews, which itself splits into the districts of Tankerness and Toab. The islands of Burray and South Ronaldsay are connected to the East Mainland by the concrete Churchill Barriers. Excluding the linked southern islands the East Mainland stretches 12 miles (19km) east from Kirkwall to Skaill in Deerness and 10 miles (16km) south from Rerwick Head in Tankerness to Rose Ness in Holm. The area is relatively low lying farmland where many of Orkney's beef herds are raised. You can tour the area by a circular route covering some 37 miles (60km), including several interesting shore walks. There are superb views of Orkney's North Isles from Tankerness and Deerness, and from Holm you can easily see the Scottish Mainland on a clear day. In the days of the Vikings Thorfinn Sigurdarson, the powerful Earl of Orkney, fought and routed Karl Hundason, King of the Scots, in a fierce sea battle off the coast of Deerness.

KIRKWALL

Capital and port Kirkwall is an ancient city dating back to the years when the Orkney islands were ruled as a Norwegian dominion. With its roots deep in the Norse past, Kirkwall immediately strikes the eye as being Scandinavian. Kirkwall is the most northerly cathedral city in Britain and still retains many signs of its former political and ecclesiastical importance. The old town clusters round the cathedral and is notable for its picturesque streets and buildings.

Kirkwall's name comes from the Old Norse *Kirkjuvagar*, meaning 'church-bay,' and refers to the 11th century church of St Olaf. All that's left of this church is a carved arch which has been incorporated into St Olaf's Wynd at the north end of the old town. The magnificent red sandstone minster which stands at the heart of the town is St Magnus Cathedral.

St Magnus Cathedral
This was founded in 1137 by Norse Earl Rognvald Kolsson in memory of his uncle, the martyred Magnus, and built by the master masons of Durham under the initial supervision of the Earl's father, Kol Kalason. The cathedral took 300 years to complete and is one of two surviving cathedrals in Scotland which remain intact and have never ceased to be places of worship. The other is Glasgow Cathedral. The old statues, ornaments, and other signs of its Catholic past are long gone and St Magnus Cathedral is now part of the Protestant Church of Scotland. It was built as a result of what was in effect a pagan vow. Earl Rognvald pledged to build a noble minster in memory of his murdered uncle, Earl Magnus, at a time when the Norse were still being converted to Christianity.

THE MARTYRDOM OF MAGNUS
According to the Orkneyinga Saga, the sons of the great Earl Thorfinn bore joint rule over the earldom after their father's death. Their names were Erlend and Paul. In 1098, when Magnus Erlendsson was a young man, Magnus Bare Legs, King of Norway came to Orkney with a fleet of ships. The king asserted his power as overlord by sending the two earls to Norway. He took the young Magnus with others to accompany him on an expedition. After raiding in the Hebrides they sailed as far as Anglesey. There the Norwegian force attacked two Welsh earls whose ships were in the Menai Strait.

When the order was given to prepare for battle, young Magnus did not arm himself, but remained seated on the deck of the king's ship. He said that he had no quarrel with any man there and would not fight. Magnus took a psalter and sang while men fought around him. He managed to escape from the ship during darkness. Some years passed before he appeared again in Orkney.

After the death of King Magnus of Norway the way became clear for Magnus to return to Orkney. By this time Earls Erlend and Paul were dead. Paul's son Haakon was established as earl. Magnus, finding that a number of influential people were prepared to support him, put forward a claim to his father's share of the earldom. In this he was successful. After some years there came to be ill-feeling between the followers of the two earls. Some of the wiser men on either side sought to bring about a reconciliation. It was proposed that the two earls should meet on the island of Egilsay. It was agreed that each earl should come to the meeting with only two ships and a limited number of men. The date of this meeting is uncertain, but it was probably in 1115. Magnus came to the island after Easter. His cousin Haakon broke the agreement and came with eight ships and a large force of men.

While Magnus awaited the arrival of Haakon, he spent much time in prayer. It soon became plain that there was to be no conference. Magnus asked that his life be spared and declared that he was willing to submit to torture: 'And God knows that I am looking more to your souls than to my life.' He said to Haakon: 'Maim my body as thou likest, or pluck out my eyes and put me in a darksome dungeon.' Haakon was willing to stop short of murder, so long as Magnus was deprived of power, but certain powerful chiefs insisted that Magnus must die. Haakon commanded his standard-bearer to kill him, but he indignantly refused. Then Haakon laid the unwelcome duty on Lífólf, his cook. Lífólf began to sob, and Magnus said: 'Stand thou before me, and hew on my head a great wound, for it is not seemly to behead chiefs like thieves. Take good heart, poor fellow, for I have prayed that God grant you his mercy.' So Lífólf took up the axe, and Magnus received his death-wound on the head. He was buried in the church his grandfather had built at Birsay. When the new cathedral was ready for use, the saint's relics were transferred from Birsay to Kirkwall.

The Earl fulfilled his vow, became Christian, and was buried in the cathedral along with Magnus, who was shortly afterwards canonised. The remains of St Magnus were accidentally discovered during repairs to the cathedral in 1919 when some of the ashlar stones on the large rectangular pier of the south arcade of the choir were found to be loose. In a cavity behind these stones a box was found containing most of a human skeleton. The gash in the skull confirmed the story in the *Orkneyinga Saga* about the death wound inflicted on St Magnus on Egilsay in 1115. The bones were returned to their resting place. A century before this a similar find had been made in the corresponding pier on the north side of the choir. A re-examination of the remains established that they were the bones of St Rognvald and metal plaques bearing their names are now attached to the two pillars which contain the remains of both the cathedral's founder and its patron saint.

One of Norway's greatest warrior kings died in Kirkwall in 1263. In October that year King Haakon anchored his fleet in Orkney after his defeat at the Battle of Largs, on the west coast of Scotland. He decided to winter in Orkney, but fell ill and died in December in the Bishop's Palace. He was buried in the cathedral but the following year his body was returned for burial in Norway. In 1963, the Norwegian Government sent a marble **memorial slab** bearing a short inscription in Latin, which can now be seen in the floor of the choir.

The spectacular new **west window** of the cathedral, unveiled by the Queen on 9 August 1987 was commissioned by the Society of the Friends of St Magnus Cathedral to mark the 850th anniversary of its founding and is regarded as a fine example of contemporary stained glass art. In the interior are interesting **tombstones** of Kirkwall's eminent men from the 16th century down to the present day. Among the tombs in the nave aisles are those of two 19th-

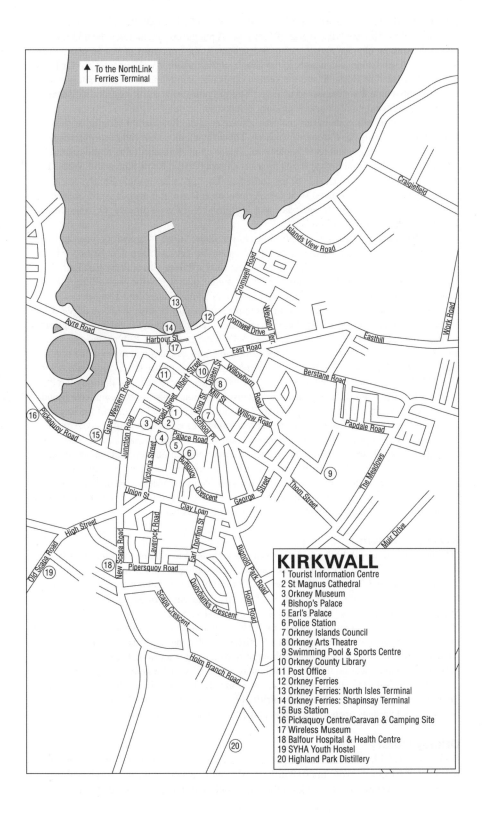

To the NorthLink
Ferries Terminal

Craiglefield

Islands View Road

Cromwell Road

Wevland Terr.

Cromwell Drive

Avre Road

Harbour St

East Road

Easthill

Work Road

13

12

14

17

Berstane Road

Albert Street

Willowburn Road

11

10

Queen St.

Papdale Road

Great Western Road

Broad Street

King St.

Mill St.

8

Pickaquoy Road

16

Junction Road

3

1

7

Willow Road

School Pl.

2

15

4

Palace Road

5

6

The Meadows

9

Victoria Street

Burnquoy

Crescent

George Street

Thom Street

Union St

Muir Drive

Clay Loan

High Street

Laverock Road

Old Scapa Road

New Scapa Road

Earl Thorfinn St.

Bignold Park Road

19

18

Pipersquoy Road

Quoybanks Crescent

Holm Road

Scapa Crescent

Holm Branch Road

20

KIRKWALL

1 Tourist Information Centre
2 St Magnus Cathedral
3 Orkney Museum
4 Bishop's Palace
5 Earl's Palace
6 Police Station
7 Orkney Islands Council
8 Orkney Arts Theatre
9 Swimming Pool & Sports Centre
10 Orkney County Library
11 Post Office
12 Orkney Ferries
13 Orkney Ferries: North Isles Terminal
14 Orkney Ferries: Shapinsay Terminal
15 Bus Station
16 Pickaquoy Centre/Caravan & Camping Site
17 Wireless Museum
18 Balfour Hospital & Health Centre
19 SYHA Youth Hostel
20 Highland Park Distillery

century Orcadians, African explorer WB Baikie (1824–65) and John Rae (1813–93), Arctic traveller and the 'intrepid discoverer of Franklin.' A plaque commemorates the 833 men lost in the sinking of *HMS Royal Oak* in Scapa Flow at the beginning of World War II. The beautiful red sandstone which adds to the charm of the cathedral was quarried not far from Kirkwall, at Head of Holland, and the yellow sandstone, sometimes used alternately with red, probably came from the island of Eday. This polychrome work is regarded as Britain's best medieval example of two such colours in a pattern.

For more information about this majestic edifice read the Rev Harald Mooney's illustrated booklet *St Magnus Cathedral, Orkney*. This is available at the cathedral entrance, from the Tourist Office, and local bookshops. The story of the cathedral is also depicted in a 15-minute multilingual film at the *St Magnus Centre* (Palace Road, Kirkwall KW15 1PA; ©01856-878326) on the east side of the cathedral. The centre has a study library, coffee lounge and toilets with disabled facilities. Admission is free and it is open April–September 9.30am to 5.30pm Monday to Saturday, and 1.30pm to 5.30pm on Sunday; October–March 12.30pm to 2pm, closed on Sunday.

From the top of the cathedral's 125ft (38m) tower, added in the 14th century, you can look down on two other antiquities, the Bishop's Palace and the Earl's Palace. The **Bishop's Palace** was built about the same time as the cathedral; the **Earl's Palace** was built by Earl Patrick Stewart, who was executed before he could carry out his plan to join the two buildings. Few more interesting ancient domestic buildings survive in Scotland than these two palaces. The Earl's Palace is now roofless, but it is still an imposing building bearing the scars of two 17th-century sieges. Cannon balls from these assaults are still unearthed in the gardens from time to time. The earliest visible parts of the Bishop's Palace date from the 12th century. As you approach the building up Palace Street, the formidable bulk of the round tower at the north-west corner of the episcopal hall is an impressive sight. In this palace the hapless little seven-year-old 'Maid of Norway' died in September 1290 on her way to Scotland to marry the Prince of Wales (later Edward II). The palace was extensively reconstructed and the massive round tower added around 1550 by Bishop Robert Reid, one of the last and greatest of the medieval Orkney prelates and the man regarded as the real founder of Edinburgh University. Around 1600, the episcopal palace was once again reconstructed, this time by Earl Patrick Stewart who had a grandiose scheme to link the two palaces to make himself one fortified and garrisoned residence. In 1607, Earl Patrick, 'drowned in debt', and his plan fell apart. Not until 1671 did it again become a bishop's residence. The last bishop, Murdoch Mackenzie, died there on 17 February 1688. During the 18th century the palace was allowed to fall into ruin. Both palaces are open in summer, closed in winter. There is an admission charge.

Orkney Museum

'The houses, white with harl, present crowstepped gables and picturesque chimneys to the street... through an arched gateway, one catches a cool glimpse of a paven entrance court.' This is how in 1868 Robert Louis Stevenson saw the buildings that now house the Orkney Museum (©01856-873191; fax 01856-871560; email museum@orkney.gov.uk) in Broad Street, opposite St Magnus Cathedral. One of Scotland's finest town houses, Tankerness House, contains a vivid introduction to Orkney's rich archaeology from 4000BC to AD1800, including some beautiful and mysterious Pictish symbol stones and a spectacular Viking whalebone plaque with dragon heads, thought to be a linen smoothing board from a boat grave excavated at Scar on the island of Sanday. Open all year Monday to Saturday and Sunday afternoon from May to September. Admission is free, although donations are welcome. There is a toilet for the disabled, and stairlifts give access to all floors. There are also extensive sheltered gardens open to the public at the back of the museum.

Orkney Library

Founded in 1683 by William Baikie, the Orkney Library & Archive (44 Junction Road, Kirkwall; ©01856-873166; fax 01856-875260; email general.enquiries@orkneylibrary. org.uk; www.orkneylibrary.org.uk) is the oldest public library in Scotland. Temporary membership is available for visitors. The Orkney Room and Archive is a reference treasure trove for history buffs. Open Monday to Saturday.

At the **Ortak Visitor Centre**, at Hatston (✆01856-872224; fax 01856-875165; email ortak@ortak.co.uk; www.ortak.co.uk), you can watch a video presentation of how Ortak's renowned jewellery is made. There is a permanent display and an opportunity to see jewellery-making demonstrations. Admission is free and the centre is open all year round.

Orkney Wireless Museum

You don't have to be a radio nut to enjoy the Orkney Wireless Museum (Kiln Corner, Kirkwall KW15 1LB; ✆01856-871400; www.owm.org.uk). This small museum near the harbour is a fascinating treasure house of memorabilia from the early 20th century. Early wireless sets of wood and Bakelite jostle with phonographs and gramophones, magazines, catalogues, advertisements and domestic ephemera of the period. Featured are wartime communications, and you can see transmitters used for short-range contact with fighters and for long-range morse to bombers, replica radar equipment, original gun operations maps, army signal equipment, and the original Scapa Flow boom defence chart. There's also a spy's radio transmitter, trinkets made by Italian prisoners-of-war, and albums of photographs of the wartime service personnel who created 'Fortress Orkney' for the defence of Scapa Flow. Open April to September, Monday to Saturday 10am to 4.30pm, Sunday 2.30pm to 4.30pm. Admission charge. Wheelchairs welcome.

Highland Park Distillery

Highland Park Distillery (Holm Road, Kirkwall KW15 1SU; ✆01856-874619; fax 01856-876091; email pretson@edrington.co.uk; www.highlandpark.co.uk) was founded more than 200 years ago and is the northernmost whisky distillery in the world. Highland Park's distilling process has remained almost entirely unchanged since 1798. The malt is dried in kilns fired with peat and heather cut from the distillery's own land at Hobbister, a blend of fuel that gives the malt its distinctive aroma. Highland Park is owned by Highland Distillers and its single malts are exported worldwide. Around 45,000 casks are locked behind the doors of the distillery warehouses – that's more than 1.8 million gallons, or 8 million litres' of whisky. The tour of the distillery culminates with a complimentary taste of the famous malt and a short audio visual presentation.

The Highland Park shop at the visitor centre sells gifts and souvenirs. Open all year April–October, Monday to Friday 10am to 5pm, guided tours every half-hour; May–August, Monday to Saturday 10am to 5pm, and Sunday midday to 5pm; November–March, Monday to Friday tour at 2pm. Shop open 1pm to 5pm. Group bookings by appointment.

Kirkwall Airport

About 4 miles (6km) from Kirkwall, Kirkwall Airport is the legacy of an enterprising young pilot, Lieutenant Fresson, who on 8 May 1933 inaugurated the first regular domestic air service between Orkney and Inverness in a Dragon Rapide. The *Orkney Herald* reporter who saw Fresson at Wideford sniffed that in his plus-fours he looked more like 'an ordinary golfer' than a pilot. One of Fresson's later passengers recalled how the pilot would often zoom along the cliffs at 50ft (15m) to count fulmars' nests.

FURTHER AFIELD

Tankerness

North-east of Kirkwall Airport, on the west side of the Tankerness peninsula, are the twin **Lochs of Weethick**, both brackish and both impounded by a double ayre, or shingle bar, which is the only example of its kind in Orkney. *Nousts*, where boats were hauled out when not in use, can be seen along the northern bank of the outer lagoon and are evidence of its use as a harbour, perhaps as far back as Viking times. Most of the farms in the vicinity of the **Loch of Tankerness** were established in the days when the sea was the main means of transport. The enormous loch lies in the centre of the Tankerness peninsula and is the focal point for feeding and breeding curlews, lapwings and oystercatchers.

There's a pleasant walk around **Rerwick Head**, where remains of the World War II coastal defence installations which once guarded the sound between Tankerness and Shapinsay are evident on the headland. There are a number of sandy beaches on both sides of the peninsula, notably at Hall of Tankerness, Heatherhouse and Redbanks, as well as broad **Mill Sands** which is a good place to watch birds and seals and to collect cockles and the razor shells known locally as *spoots*. During spring and autumn the shore around the bay of Deer Sound is frequented by redshank, turnstone and sometimes bar-tailed godwit. Shelduck spend the summer here, breeding in old rabbit holes.

Mine Howe

An ancient enigma was uncovered in Tankerness in 1946 when a massive earthen mound known as Mine Howe was excavated for the first time on Veltigar Farm (Tankerness KW17 2QU; ©01856-861234; email minehowe@ukonline.co.uk; www.minehowe.com). The dig uncovered a mysterious structure sunk in the earth. After an examination produced polished stones, hundreds of bones, teeth, cockleshells and other detritus, the mound was covered up again and remained so until 1999 when local farmer Douglas Paterson reopened it. Within the mound he found a three-chambered structure, like a tower sunk into the ground. Access to this sunken chamber is by a steep, ladder-like staircase made of 12 stone steps that take you down to a narrow landing from which two long, low chambers branch out at almost right angles. From here more steps lead down into the darkness and a drop of about 5ft (1.5m) into the lower chamber, some 20ft (6m) below the surface.

Archaeologists are still puzzling over the purpose of the structure and its age, uncertain whether it dates from the Neolithic period 4,500 to 6,000 years ago, or the Iron Age, a mere 2,000 years ago. It is thought possible that Mine Howe was associated with ritual or religion, especially as a stone hammer was found lying next to a dog's skull in one of the chambers. Mine Howe is privately run by the Paterson family. An exhibition of photographs illustrates the archaeological dig. Open May: 11am to 3pm (Wednesday and Sunday only); June, July and August: Daily from 11am to 5pm; 1–10 September: Daily from 11am to 4pm; 12–30 September 11am to 2pm (Wednesday and Sunday only). Admission charge.

Deerness

The road connecting Deerness to the Mainland runs over a sandy isthmus where an old defensive broch mound, **Dingieshowe**, is strategically sited among the dunes to the south of the road. It takes its name from the Old Norse for 'parliament mount.' The **Deerness War Memorial** can be found in the churchyard of St Ninians along with an unusual hogback gravestone of a type dating back to the 10th–12th centuries.

The Gloup on the east coast of Deerness gets its name from the Old Norse *gluppa* (a chasm), and the local name for a blowhole. It is a dramatic collapsed sea cave separated from the sea by a land bridge about 80 yards (73m) wide. The blowhole is about 40 yards (37m) long and 80ft (24m) deep. Great care should be taken here, especially at the seaward end of the underground passage. In the right weather, it is possible to sail a small boat into the Gloup. For details of boat hire contact the Tourist Office.

On the Deerness shore within sight of the rocks of Scarvataing, stands a 40ft-high (12m) square stone tower, a **memorial** to a tragic sea disaster that happened in the late 17th century. A simple inset granite slab tells the story: 'To the memory of 200 Covenanters who were taken prisoner at Bothwell Bridge and sentenced to transportation for life, but who perished by shipwreck near this point on 10 December 1679.' The Covenanters who died had been taken prisoner after Charles II had defeated their army five months earlier. The Covenanters had resisted the introduction by Charles I of the English Common Book of Prayer. The ship *Crown* taking them into slavery in the new American colonies foundered on the nearby rocks in a violent storm after its captain ignored local advice to seek shelter. He and his crew survived, but most of the religious dissenters battened in the hold perished. An obelisk in Broad Street, Kirkwall, commemorates the same tragedy.

North from the Gloup is the **Brough of Deerness**, accessible only by a narrow and dangerous cliff track and almost cut off by the sea at high tide. This is the site of an early Christian monastery of the Celtic Church where hermit monks lived contemplative lives. The remains of their chapel can still be seen.

Before you leave the Mainland to cross the first barrier to Lamb Holm you pass through the picturesque village of **St Mary's** which grew up on the Bay of Ayre during the herring fishing days. St Mary's is the venue for a variety of water-based sports and hosts a regatta every July. Near St Mary's is Graemeshall House, a 19th-century laird's mansion containing a private collection of antiques gathered over more than half a century. Spread over five rooms, **Norwood Museum** exhibits some fine lustreware, furniture, clocks, watches and musical boxes. There is an admission charge, but the tour includes a peek inside the private chapel dedicated to St Margaret of Scotland, consecrated in 1898. The house was owned by the Graeme family of Sutherland. Limited opening on certain weekdays May to September.

The Churchill Barriers

These carry the road linking the islands of Lamb Holm, Glimps Holm, Burray and South Ronaldsay with the Mainland and were built between mid-1941 and 1945, largely by Italian prisoners of war whose uniforms had a bright red disc on the back for marksmen to aim at if they tried to escape. One who did make a break was recaptured in a Kirkwall bookshop, where he was trying to find an atlas. The barriers were constructed to seal off the eastern approaches to Scapa Flow after a German U-boat crept through one of the channels in 1939 to torpedo the British battleship *HMS Royal Oak*. The channels were sealed by dumping more than 250,000 tons of stone and concrete on the seabed between the southern islands. On top of this foundation the barriers were built from 66,000 massive concrete blocks of up to 10 tons. After the war, a road was built along the top of the causeways enabling the south isles to become part of the main Orkney road system.

Lamb Holm

Lamb Holm is connected to the Mainland by the first of the four Churchill Barriers. On the tiny island is a unique memorial to the Italian prisoners of war who helped to build them. This is the remarkable **Italian Chapel** (Lamb Holm, Holm KW17 2RT; ✆01856-781268) which, apart from a concrete statue of St George slaying the dragon, is the only relic of Camp 60, which housed the Italian prisoners. The prisoners built the little chapel using two Nissen huts and an assortment of scrap metal and wood. An impressive façade was erected to hide the ugliness of the huts. The work was supervised by POW Domenico Chiocchetti, whose artistic talents were responsible for the arresting frescoes that decorate the interior. Chiocchetti returned to Orkney in 1960 to restore the chapel's paintwork and touch up the interior. A wayside shrine erected near the chapel in 1961 is a token of the friendship which has grown up between Orkney and Chiocchetti's home town of Moena, in the Italian Alps. The carved figure of Christ crucified was a gift from Moena and the cross and canopy were made in Kirkwall following instructions sent by Chiocchetti. The Italian Chapel has weathered many storms and is one of Orkney's most visited tourist attractions. Open 1 April–30 September 9am to 10pm; 1 October–31 March 9am to 4.30pm.

Burray

At the **Fossil and Heritage Centre** (Viewforth, Burray KW17 2SX; ✆01856-731255; email orkneyfossils@btconnect.com) is an unlikely marriage of an exhibition recounting the story of Orkney over millions of years, and displays by the Orkney Vintage Club. Fossil fish 300 million years old, vintage exhibits not so old. There's a café and gift shop, and all in all this is a pleasant place to stop for coffee on a trip over the Churchill Barriers. Open daily April to September from 10am to 6pm. Admission charge for exhibition rooms.

South Ronaldsay

St Margaret's Hope is a picturesque village around a sheltered bay where houses dating from the 17th and 18th centuries congregate along the shoreline. In the 19th century the village was a busy fishing station. It's now the terminal of a new ferry service, has a top gourmet restaurant (see *Eating and Drinking*), and is a favourite hang-out for divers, artists and lovers of peace and quiet. St Margaret's Hope is traditionally but wrongly connected with Margaret, 'Maid of Norway,' the young daughter of King Erik of Norway, who died in Orkney in 1290. The village is more probably named after Margaret, saint and Queen of Scotland. The restored smithy is now the **William Hourston Smiddy Museum** and recalls the days when the village blacksmith was a person of importance in a rural community. There's an admission charge to view the collection of horse-drawn implements and smithy-forged articles. Large and small hand-woven tapestries inspired by the rhythm of life and landscape of Orkney are the forte of the **Hoxa Tapestry Gallery** (Leila Thomson, Neviholm, Hoxa, St Margaret's Hope KW17 2TW; ✆/fax 01856-831395; email neviholm@gmail.com; www.hoxatapestrygallery.co.uk). Tapestries, samplers, cards and prints for sale. Open April to September Monday to Friday 10am to 5.30pm, Saturday and Sunday 2 to 6pm.

An enterprising farmer excavated a prehistoric chambered tomb on the farm Isbister, South Ronaldsay, to unearth remains of more than 300 people, along with fine pottery and the talons of at least 10 white-tailed sea eagles, which is the reason for the dramatic name **Tomb of the Eagles** (Liddle, South Ronaldsay KW17 2RW; ✆01856-831339; email info@tomboftheeagles.co.uk; www.tomboftheeagles.co.uk). This has given rise to a family-run visitor centre with guided 'hands on' interpretation of the original Neolithic artefacts. A 1.2-mile (2km) guided walk along the cliff-top takes you to the 5,000-year-old stalled chamber tomb. The farm is a 30-minute drive from Kirkwall. Seasonal bus service Kirkwall/Burwick. Partial access for disabled to sites. Open March 10am to midday, April to October 9.30am to 5.30pm, November to February visitors welcome by arrangement). Admission charge. Near the Liddle farmhouse is a Bronze Age burnt mound, one of the few to have been excavated, although more than 400 have been recorded in Orkney and Shetland.

From fossil fish to present day, marine life has played an important part in Orkney island life and *The Orkney Marine-Life Aquarium* (Pool Farmhouse, Grimness; ✆01856-831700; fax 01856-831711; email orkneymarinelife@btopenworld.com; www.orkneymarinelife. co.uk) is worth a look-in. Admission charge.

NATURE RESERVES

The only nature sanctuaries of note in East Mainland are on the tiny offshore island of Copinsay, and at Mull Head on the northern headland of Deerness, where a reserve has been established by the *Orkney Islands Council* (OIC) in collaboration with *Scottish Natural Heritage* (SNH).

Copinsay

The 180-acre (73ha) nature reserve on Copinsay, about 1½ miles (2.4km) off the East Mainland, comprises the main island and its four surrounding islets, to the west Ward Holm, Black Holm, Corn Holm, and to the north the small, steep Horse of Copinsay, which is said to have 'enough grass to fatten one sheep, feed two or starve three'. The whole group is now the **James Fisher Memorial Reserve**, owned by the Royal Society for the Protection of Birds (RSPB). Island vegetation is dominated by various grasses, except on Black Holm where there is a dense covering of **scentless mayweed**. The major botanical attractions of the island are, however, the fine spreads of **oyster plants** and luxuriant **sea asters**. Nearly 2,000 pairs of **fulmars** nest on Copinsay, which has almost a mile (1.6km) of vertical cliffs rising up to 249ft (76m) and topped by a lighthouse. These hold another vast seabird colony of around 19,545 **guillemots**, 671 **razorbills** and some 3,750 pairs of **kittiwakes**. **Puffins**, **black guillemots** and **shags** also nest here, and there is a large **great black-backed gull** colony. Small numbers of **arctic** and **common terns**, **eider ducks**, **ringed plovers**, **twites**, rock doves and ravens are among the other attractions during the breeding season. There is also a growing colony of more than 1,000 seals.

During migration, almost anything can turn up in Orkney. In April or May, and again from late August to October, easterly winds and rain can cause large numbers of small migrant birds to seek shelter here. Scores of chats, warblers and flycatchers may make a landfall on the island while waiting for the weather to clear before continuing their flight. Bluethroats, barred warblers and red-backed shrikes occur annually, while rarities have included Richard's pipit, Bonelli's warbler and rustic bunting.

The reserve is always open, weather permitting. There is no admission charge. There is no ferry service, but there are day trips by boat from Skaill, about 3½ miles (5.5km) from Copinsay (contact S Foubister; ✆01856-741252). The old farmhouse on Copinsay may be available for basic overnight accommodation. Details from the Senior Site Manager (✆01856-850176).

Mull Head

Mull Head Nature Reserve covers an area of around 300 acres (121ha) of coastal grassland, heath and sea cliff providing opportunities for walking, bird-watching and nature study. The reserve was established by OIC in 1992 and is managed with the needs of both visitors and wildlife in mind. A comprehensive network of paths stretches from the Covenanters' Memorial on the north coast to the Gloup on the west coast; circular walks of 2½–5 miles (4–8km) are signposted from the Gloup Car Park.

Features of interest on the reserve include sea cliffs that provide nesting sites for guillemots, terns, shags, fulmars, kittiwakes, razorbills, puffins, and their predators, great black-backed gulls and both great and Arctic skuas. On the Brough of Deerness are the remains of a Norse settlement and church; caves and sea stacks around which seals play and a wealth of wild flowers on the maritime heath and grassland. Otters are frequently seen rummaging in the seaweed along the shoreline. You can go anywhere you like in the reserve, so long as you don't disturb the wildlife. The Gloup car park is north from Skaill Farm. The Covenanters' Memorial car park is signposted on the left from Deerness shop.

GETTING AROUND

Buses

Causeway Coaches: Alec Rosie, Church Road, St Margaret's Hope KW17 2TR (✆01856-831444; fax 01856-831476). Operate a Kirkwall–Wilderness–Holm–Burray–St Margaret's Hope service.

Orkney Coaches: Scotts Road, Hatston Industrial Estate, Kirkwall KW15 1GR (✆01856-870555; fax 01856-877501; email orkneycoaches@rapsons.co.uk; www.rapsons.co.uk). Operate a Kirkwall town service, and a Kirkwall Airport service, as well as services from Kirkwall to Finstown-Stromness; East Holm (Monday only); Tankerness–Deerness; Finstown–Tingwall–Evie–Newton–Birsay; Scapa–Orphir–Houton Ferry; Ring of Brodgar–Skara Brae–Stromness; Holm–Burray–St Margaret's Hope–Burwick Ferry; and Wilderness–Holm–Burray–St Margaret's Hope. They also service the ferry terminals at Houton, Tingwall, and Burwick. All vehicles are non-smoking. Free timetable from the tourist office.

Taxis

There are plenty of taxis in Kirkwall. There is a taxi rank outside the tourist office, at the harbour and at the airport.

Bob's Taxi: 58 Junction Road, Kirkwall (✆01856-876543; email ivanleslie@aol.com; www.bobstaxis.com).
CD Taxis: The Workshop, Dakota Road, Kirkwall (✆01856-875000; email info.cdtaxis@btconnect.com; www.cdtaxis.com).
Craigies Taxis: West Tankerness Lane, Kirkwall (✆01856-878787).
Finstown Taxis: (✆01856-761368).
George's Taxi: (✆01856-873000).

Kirkwall 5000 Taxis: Westbank Cottage, St Ola, KW15 1TR (✆01856-875000; fax 01856-875005).

Rainbow Taxis: Kirkwall (✆01856-872063).

Vehicle Rental

Orkney Car Hire: James D Peace & Co, Junction Road, Kirkwall KW15 1JY (✆01856-872866; fax 01856-875300; email info@orkneycarhire.co.uk; www.orkneycarhire.co.uk). Self-drive cars and minibus hire. No mileage charge, from £28 a day for a small car.

John G Shearer & Sons: Ayre Service Station, Burnmouth Road, Kirkwall KW15 1QY (✆01856-872950; fax 01856-875460; email jgshearerandsons@talk21.com). Free airport collection and delivery. Ferries met by arrangement. No mileage charge. From £175 a week.

WR Tullock Car Rental: Castle Street, Kirkwall KW15 1HD (✆01856-876262; fax 01856-874458; email airportcarrental@btconnect.com; www.orkneycarrental.co.uk). Orkney's only franchised airport car hire company. Town centre and airport offices (Terminal Building, Kirkwall Airport, Grimsetter; ✆01856-875500). Competitive rates, no mileage charges. Ferries met by arrangement. Group A (Ka and Fiesta) costs £32 for one day to £165 for a week; Group D (Mondeo) costs £45 for one day to £220 for a week. Check full tariff on www.orkneycarrental.co.uk. Interesting company: founded in 1901 and the oldest family Ford dealership in the UK; great grandfather knew Marconi and Henry Ford.

Drive Orkney: Hatston Industrial Estate, Kirkwall KW15 1RE (✆01856-870000; fax 01856-870001; email info@driveorkney.com; www.driveorkney.com). Self-drive cars and vans, unlimited mileage. Free delivery/collection in Kirkwall and free airport transfer.

Alternatively, you can hire a motorhome at *Orkney Motorhome Hire* (Eastmount, East Road, Kirkwall KW15 1LX; ✆01856-874391; email info@orkney-motorhome-hire.co.uk; www.orkney-motorhome-hire.co.uk). Unlimited mileage. Courtesy airport/ferry transfer.

Cycle Hire

Cycle Orkney: Tankerness Lane, Kirkwall, KW15 1AQ (✆/fax 01856-875777; email cycleorkney@btconnect.com). Mountain bikes available from £10 a day; one week £60; £6 a day for children; £15 a day for a tandem. Trailers can also be hired for £5 and baby seats for £5. All bikes are hybrids. Open in summer Monday to Saturday from 9am to 5.30pm; winter Monday to Saturday 10am to 5pm.

Tours

Explorer Fast Sea Charters: Office 5, Harbour Terminal, Kirkwall Pier, Kirkwall KW15 1HU (✆01856-871225; fax 01856-871228; email expcharters@aol.com; www.explorercharters.co.uk). Wildlife, coastal, birdwatching tours. Private charters.

Orcadian Wildlife: Gerraquoy, Grimness, South Ronaldsay (01856-831240; email enquiries orcadianwildlife.co.uk; www.orcadianwildlife.co.uk). Tailor-made wildlife and history tours.

Orkney Archaeology Tours: Bayview, Birsay KW17 2LR (✆01856-721450; email info orkneyarchaeologytours.co.uk; www.orkneyarchaeologytours.co.uk). Holidays and day tours led by professional archaeologists who are qualified Orkney guides.

ACCOMMODATION

Hotels

Albert Hotel: Mounthoolie Lane, Kirkwall KW15 1JZ (✆01856-876000; fax 01856-875397; email enquiries@alberthotel.co.uk; www.alberthotel.co.uk). Newly-refurbished, in the town centre, 19 en suite rooms. From £50 to £75 a room a night. The *Stables Restaurant* serves lunches from midday to 2pm and dinner from 6pm to 9.30pm. Bar meals are available at *The Bothy* between midday to 2pm and 5pm to 9.30pm, and *Matchmakers* lounge bar has lunch, dinner and high teas in summer Sundays from 4pm to 6pm.

Ayre Hotel: Ayre Road, Kirkwall KW15 1QX (✆01856-873001; fax 01856-876289; email ayrehotel@btconnect.com; www.ayrehotel.co.uk). Three-star hotel overlooking the harbour, five-minute walk from town centre. From £45 to £55 a night.

Foveran Hotel: St Ola, Kirkwall KW15 1SF (℡01856-872389; fax 01856-876430; email foveranhotel@aol.com; www.foveranhotel.co.uk). Three miles from town on A964 Orphir road. Three-star small hotel, B&B from £49.50. Vegetarians welcome.

Kirkwall Hotel: Harbour Street, Kirkwall KW15 1LF (℡01856-872232; fax 01856-872812; email enquiries@kirkwallhotel.com; www.kirkwallhotel.com). Three-star, Victorian building opposite the North Isles ferry terminal. Restaurant, lounge, 36 en suite rooms. £46 to £70 a night.

Lynnfield Hotel: Holm Road, St Ola, Kirkwall KW15 1SU (℡01856-872505; fax 01856-870038; email office@lynnfield.co.uk; www.lynnfieldhotel.com). Three-star, overlooking Kirkwall, Scapa Flow and Kirkwall Bay, once a manse of St Magnus Cathedral. Open all year, four twin rooms, four double/family rooms, two honeymoon suites, and one single. From £60 to £75 a night. Three bars.

Merkister Hotel: Harray KW17 2LF (℡01856-771366; fax 01856-771515; email merkister-hotel@ecosse.net). Three-star, on the shore of Harray Loch, with panoramic views of the loch and hills of Hoy. Halfway between Stromness and Kirkwall, 16 bedrooms. From £25 to £55 a night. Open all day. Large bar menus and daily specials, lunches noon to 2pm, supper 6.30pm to 9pm.

Orkney Hotel: 40 Victoria Street, Kirkwall KW15 1DN (℡01856-873477; fax 01856-872767; email info@orkneyhotel.co.uk). Three-star, 17th century hotel in the heart of Kirkwall. 30 en suite rooms. *Victoria* restaurant offers local produce, daily harvested seafood, Angus beef and Orkney lamb. Open all year round.

St Ola Hotel: Harbour Street, Kirkwall KW15 1LE (℡/fax 01856-875090; email enquiries@stolahotel.co.uk; www.stolahotel.co.uk). Four-star, small, family-run, on harbour front. Two popular bars. From £28.

The Shore: Shore Street, Kirkwall KW15 1LG (℡01856-872200; fax 01856-873871; email eatandstay@theshore.co.uk; www.theshore.co.uk). 9 bedrooms, family-owned hotel conveniently situated on harbour front. Good food served in the *Shore* restaurant and bar. From £39 a night.

West End Hotel: Main Street, Kirkwall KW15 1BU (℡01856-872368; fax 01856-876181; email west.end@orkney.com; www.westendhotel.org.uk). Two-star, family-run hotel in quiet side street in centre of Kirkwall, private car park. From £37 a night.

Guest Houses

Brekkness Guest House: Muddisdale Road, Kirkwall KW15 1RS (℡/fax 01856-874317; email sandrabews@aol.com). Three-star, next to Pickaquoy sports/leisure centre, short walk from town centre, guest library and lounge. From £30 a night.

Lav'rockha Guest House: Inganess Road, Kirkwall KW15 1SP (℡/fax 01856-876103; email lavrockha@orkney.com; www.lavrockha.co.uk). Four-star, well-equipped rooms in large modern house, a mile (1.6km) from the town centre. Assisted wheelchair access. Private car park. From £23.

Polrudden Guest House: Peerie Sea Loan, Pickaquoy Road, Kirkwall KW15 1UH (℡01856-874761; fax 01856-870950; email linda@polrudden.com; www.polrudden.com). Three-star, within walking distance of town centre, sports complex, golf course and harbour. Large walled car park. All rooms en suite. From £30. Broadband internet access.

Royal Oak Guest House: Holm Road, Kirkwall KW15 1PY (℡/fax 01856-877177; email info@royaloakhouse.co.uk; www.royaloakhouse.co.uk). Three-star, all rooms en suite. Views of Scapa Flow, private parking. From £25 a night.

Sanderlay Guest House: 2 Viewfield Drive, Kirkwall KW15 1RB (℡01856-875587; fax 01856-876350; email enquiries@sanderlay.co.uk; www.sanderlay.co.uk). Three-star on the outskirts of the town, three self-contained flats upstairs with kitchenette, cooker and fridge. Ground floor rooms share bathroom and lounge. From £16 to £24 a night.

Bed & Breakfast

Bellavista: Mrs L Davidson, Carness Road, Kirkwall KW15 1UE (℡01856-872306; email bellavista_orkney@yahoo.co.uk; www.bellavistaorkney.co.uk). Three-star, one mile (1.6km) from Kirkwall, private car park. From £25 a night.

Berstane House: Mr C Reid, St Ola KW15 1SZ (℡01856-876277; email collinreid@ btinternet.com; www.berstane.co.uk). Three-star, set in private woodland, seaviews. Private parking, rooms en suite, from £25.

Crossford: Mrs H Herbertson, Heathery Loan, St Ola KW15 1SY (℡01856-876142; email crossford@bushinternet.com). Three-star, one double en suite. Quite, rural location. Private parking. Open all year, from £25.

Lerona: Mrs S Delday, Cromwell Crescent, Kirkwall KW15 1LW (℡01856-874538). Three-star, easy walking distance from town centre. Comfortable and friendly. Well-prepared, tasty breakfast. Open all year. From £25 a night.

Mr Peter McKinlay: 13 Palace Road, Kirkwall KW15 1PA (℡01856-872249). 19th-century house, opposite cathedral in centre of town, family-run. From £25.

Four Seasons: Carness, Kirkwall KW15 1UE (℡01856-875514; email helenmac@global-net.co.uk). Four-star, 1½ miles (2.4km) from harbour. Views over Kirkwall Bay, no smoking throughout, en suite and private bathroom, private parking. From £25 a night.

Mrs M Muir: Arundel, Inganess Road, Kirkwall, KW15 1SP (℡01856-873148; email ro-nald.muir@talk21.com). Four-star, a mile (1.6km) from town centre. Private parking. From £18 a night.

Self-Catering

The Auld Smokehouse: Stewart and Diane Gray, Resolution, Tankerness KW17 2QT (℡01856-861385; email stu@orkneyholidays.com). Four-star, two apartments in complex, 'The Gable End' and 'The Turret,' each with living area and kitchen on first floor, and one double and one twin bedroom on the ground floor. Off-road private parking. Open all year. £200 to £500 a week.

Mrs A Cant: 10–12 Clay Loan, Kirkwall KW15 1EB (℡01856-875556; email alice@kirk-wallselfcatering.com; kirkwallselfcatering.com). Two three-star, terraced houses in central Kirkwall. Three bedrooms, sleeps five. Open all year. From £175 to £450 a week.

Craigiefield Apartments: Lynne and Craig Spence, Craigiefield House, Craigiefield, Kirk-wall (℡01856-878477; email info@orkneyvillage.com; www.orkneyvillage.com). Three- to four-star apartments in Victorian mansion, minutes' walk from town. Private parking, WiFi internet. Two bedrooms, sleeps four, from £200 to £500.

Crantit House: Mr J Cowie, St Ola KW15 1RZ (℡01856-872899; email crantit@aol.com). Three-star apartments adjoining 1850 country mansion, one, two and three bedrooms, sleep four and six. 15 minutes' walk to town centre, near Scapa beach. From £280 to £350 a week.

Eastmount Apartment: Eileen Tobson, East Road, Kirkwall KW15 1LX (℡01856-874391; email eileenr@freenetname.co.uk). Three-star, modern apartment. Within easy walking distance to town. One bedroom, sleeps two, from £180 to £380.

Jo Girvan: 65 Albert Street, Kirkwall KW15 1HQ (℡01856-879051; email vicky@orkney-selfcatering.com; www.orkneyselfcatering.com). Three-star, restored bank manager's house, centre of town, large Victorian rooms. Private parking, sleeps six. From £195 to £420 a week.

Greenfield Cottages: Mr D Work, Greenfield, Carness Road, St Ola KW15 1UE (℡/fax 01856-873235; email david_work@tiscali.co.uk; www.selfcateringorkney.co.uk). Three- to four-star cottages, on a former farm cottage and the other converted stables, fully modern-ised. Open all year. Ample parking. From £200 to £500 a week.

Soulisquoy Barn: Karen Leask, Carradale, Weyland Bay, Kirkwall KW15 1TD (℡01856-874425; email karen@soulisquoy.com; www.soulisquoy.com). Four-star, converted stone barn, fully equipped. Two bedrooms, sleeps six. From £200 to £400.

The Scapa Lodge: Stewart and Diane Gray, Resolution, Tankerness KW17 2QT (℡01856-861385; email stu@orkneyholidays.com). Two four-star, detached bungalows by the beach.

Jacuzzi bath, shower, and one double and one twin room. Large garden area, private parking. Open all year. £220 to £550 a week.

Further Afield

Commodore Chalets: Louise Scott, St Mary's, Holm KW17 2RU (✆01856-781319; email scott-louise@commodorechalets.co.uk; www.commodorechalets.co.uk). Three-star, self-catering chalets and overnight lodges, view over St Mary's Bay and Churchill Barriers. From £110 to £315 a week.

Deersound Cottage: Eric Coates, Halley Road, Deerness KW17 2QL (✆01856-741331; email eric.coates@ukgateway.net). Four-star, self-catering stone-built cottage, former farmhouse, sleeps four. Views of Deer Sound, near to beaches, local shop and post office. Assisted wheelchair access. From £185 to £385 a week.

Murray Arms Hotel: Back Road, St Margaret's Hope KW17 2SP (✆01856-831205; email murrayarms@freeuk.com; www.murrayarmshotel.com). Two-star inn, five en suite bed-rooms, home cooking served daily. From £33 a night.

Noust: West End, St Margaret's Hope (✆01856-831456; fax 01856-831861). Self-catering – two flats sleeps two to four people, while the house sleeps five to seven. From £200 a week.

Roeberry House: St Margaret's Hope KW17 2TW (✆01856-831228; fax 01856-831838; www.roeberry.com). Four-star guest house. Open all year, from £55.

Sands Hotel: Burray KW17 2SS (✆01856-731298; email info@thesandshotel.co.uk; www.thesandshotel.co.uk). Newly modernised, in former 19th herring station on the shores of Scapa Flow. Sea views, from £40.

Hostels

Backpackers' Hostel: Back Road, St Margaret's Hope KW17 2SP (✆01856-831205; email murrayarms@freeuk.com; www.hostel-scotland.co.uk). Centrally situated for shops and buses, well-equipped kitchen, hot showers, no curfew. From £11 a night. Member of *Scottish Independent Hostels.*

Kirkwall Youth Hostel: Old Scapa Road, Kirkwall KW15 1BB (✆0870-004 1133 hostel, ✆0870-155 3255 central reservations; email reservations@syha.org.uk; www.syha.org.uk). Two-star, on outskirts of Kirkwall close to Scapa Flow. Open April to October. 90 beds, 13 rooms with four beds, 10 rooms with three beds, three with two beds and two with one bed. Access for disabled visitors, laundry, shop nearby, bus stop ½ mile away. From £10 a night.

Peedie Hostel: 1 Ayre Houses, Kirkwall KW15 1QX (✆01856-875477; email kirkwall peediehostel@talk21.com; www.hostel-scotland.co.uk). Accommodates eight people in three rooms, two minutes' from town. Open all year, from £10. Member of *Scottish Independent Hostels.*

Wheems Bothy: Eastside, South Ronaldsay KW17 2TJ (✆01856-831537; www.hostel-scotland.co.uk). Overlooks, sandy bays and cliffs, simple, inexpensive summer hostel for up to eight people, £8 a night. Open April to October. Member of *Scottish Independent Hostels.* Camping £3.

Camping

Kirkwall Campsite: ✆01856-873535.

Pickaquoy Centre: Muddisdale Road, Kirkwall KW15 1LR (✆01856-879900; fax 01856-879901; enquiries@pickaquoy.com; www.pickaquoy.com), caravan and camping site, a short walk from town. The complex has a range of leisure facilities, as well as a cinema, café, and bar. About £7.90 a night for caravan and motorhomes, and £7.60 for tents; electric hook-up £2.30.

Contact the tourist office or check out their website at www.visitorkney.com for more information on accommodation.

EATING AND DRINKING
Kirkwall

The Auld Motor Hoose bar/pub, diagonally opposite the main Kirkwall post office at 26 Junction Road (✆01856-871422) is crammed with fascinating motoring memorabilia and attracts both buffs and a young crowd.

Ayre Hotel: Ayre Road, Kirkwall (✆01856-873001; fax 01856-876289; email ayrehotel@ btconnect.com; www.ayrehotel.co.uk). Sea front hotel. Restaurant open 6pm to 9pm for dinner, also bar meals. Fresh produce and seasonal specialities. Suitable for the disabled.

The Shore Restaurant: Shore Street, Kirkwall (✆01856-872200; fax 01856-873871; eatandstay@theshore.co.uk; www.theshore.co.uk). Recently refurbished, busy restaurant on the waterfront with a good reputation for home-cooked food using fresh local produce.

Busters Diner: 1 Mounthoolie Place, Kirkwall (✆/fax 01856-876717). Serves hundreds of different pizza combinations as well as a large selection of local food. Suitable for disabled. Open Monday to Friday 4.30pm to 10pm, Saturday midday to 10pm, Sunday 12.30pm to 7.30pm.

Internet Café: 2 West Tankerness Lane, Kirkwall KW15 1AR (✆01856-873582; fax 01856-870028). Surf the internet, £1 for 10 minutes, while enjoying soup, filled rolls, tea and coffee. Open Monday to Friday 9am to 7.30pm, Saturday 10am to 4pm.

Kirkwall Hotel: Harbour Street, Kirkwall (✆01856-872232; fax 01856-872812; email enquiries@kirkwallhotel.com; www.kirkwallhotel.com). Fully licensed *Tudor* lounge and restaurant serves teas and coffees, homebakes, snacks, lunches and dinner. Open midday to 2pm, 6pm to 9.30pm.

Lynnfield Hotel: Holm Road, St Ola, Kirkwall (✆01856-872505; fax 01856-870038; email office@lynnfieldhotel.co.uk; www.lynnfieldhotel.com). Next to Highland Park Distillery, open all day for coffee, snacks, lunches, evening meals and suppers in a choice of venues. Vegetarian meals.

The Mustard Seed: 86 Victoria Street, Kirkwall (✆01856-871596). Homebakes and light lunches. Browse developing world crafts and Christian books while you relax. Open Thursday to Tuesday 10am to 5pm.

Orkney Auction Mart: Grainshore Road, Kirkwall (✆01856-872520). Meals, snacks. Open Monday to Friday 9am to 3pm, lunches served 11.45am to 1.45pm. Evening bookings on request. Suitable for disabled.

Pomona Café: 9 Albert Street, Kirkwall (✆/fax 01856-872325). Serves soup of the day, pizzas, toasties, fish and chips, pies, cakes and homebakes. Sit in or take away. Open all year, seven days a week 7am to 5.30pm. Suitable for disabled.

Skerries Restaurant: Merkister Hotel, Harray (✆01856-771366; fax 01856-771515; email merkister–hotel@ecosse.net). A la carte, table d'hôte and vegetarian meals. Extensive wine list. Suitable for disabled.

Stables Restaurant: Albert Hotel, Mounthoolie Lane, Kirkwall (✆01856-876000; fax 01856-875397; email enquiries@alberthotel.co.uk; www.alberthotel.co.uk). Offers table d' hote and à la carte menus. Traditional 'Bothy Bar' serves bar lunches or suppers, live music, real ales. Lounge bar 'Matchmakers' offers lunches and suppers in a family environment. Vegetarian meals available. Open for lunch midday to 2pm, bar suppers 5pm to 9.30pm, dinner 6pm to 9.30pm.

Trenabies Cafe: 16 Albert Street, Kirkwall (✆01856-874336). Refreshments, ice cream, homebakes, pizzas, baked potatoes, toasted sandwiches, snacks and meals.

West End Hotel: Main Street, Kirkwall (✆01856-872368; email westendhotel@orkney. com; www.westendhotel.org). Within five minutes' walk of town centre. Lounge bar/restaurant serves the best of Orkney beef, seafood and vegetables. Private car park.

The *Victoria Restaurant* at the Orkney Hotel, 40 Victoria Street, Kirkwall (✆01856-873477; fax 01856-872767; email info@orkneyhotel.co.uk), local cuisine meets traditional Orcadian hospitality. This Taste of Orkney restaurant offers daily landed seafood, Angus beef and Orkney lamb. Daily à la carte meals from 6pm to 9pm; bar suppers available 5pm to 8.30pm.

Further Afield

Regarded as a place of pilgrimage for gourmets, the *Creel Restaurant*, Front Road, St Margaret's Hope KW17 2SL (℡01856-831311; email alan@thecreel.freeserve.co.uk; www.thecreel.co.uk), is open May to September. It is advisable to book. Celebrity chef Alan Craigie specialises in modern cooking with island influence. Pot roast North Ronaldsay lamb (actually mutton, whose diet of seaweed gives the meat its unique flavour) with baby haggis, pearl barley and caper sauce is a speciality. Fresh fish is always on the menu, including wolf-fish, megrim, torsk and sea-witch. Dinner about £32 for three courses. Vegetarians welcome. Member of the Scotch Beef Club. The restaurant also offers B&B from £50–60 per person.

Murray Arms Hotel: Back Road, St Margaret's Hope (℡01856-831205; email murra-yarms@freeuk.com), morning coffee, lunches, and afternoon tea. Dinner table d' hôte and à la carte menu. Local seafood a speciality. Suitable for disabled with assistance.

Quoyburray Inn: Tankerness (℡01856-861255), specialises in local produce. Two minutes from Mine Howe. Lunch and snacks from midday to 2pm, evening meals from 6pm to 9pm. Self-catering chalet also available.

SPORT AND RECREATION

Walking

The following are a few of the easy walks recommended by the Tourist Office:

Covenanters' Memorial. Coastal monument at Deerness recalls the drowning in 1679 of more than 200 Presbyterian prisoners from the Battle of Bothwell Brig. Straight track of 1.3 miles (2.1km) to the monument is a riot of wild flowers in summer.

Hoxa Head. This is a must for military buffs, a 1½-mile (2.5km) waymarked coastal footpath on South Ronaldsay exploring coastal battery sites from two world wars; noted for its wild flowers. Look out for tankers in Scapa Flow. Park at Bow.

Mull Head. Park near the Gloup, an enormous blow-hole, to start this 3.7-mile (6km) circular walk. The Orkney Islands Council's **Mull Head Nature Reserve** in this area has plenty to interest, with cliff and heath nesting birds, and an early Celtic Christian monastic site at Brough of Deerness with an Interpretation Centre. To get to the Gloup drive east from Kirkwall as far as you can go on the A960/B9050.

Sands o' Wright. Interesting 3½-mile (5.7km) coastal walk on South Ronaldsay passing through an area of high quality wetland; unusual section along an ayre. Look for cobble beach, plants and animals.

Wideford Farm. Near the airport. Variety is the keynote on this 3½-mile (5.6km) walk, partly through rare Orkney native scrub woodland of willow and hazel; migrant and wetland birds in abundance. Look for silver sands.

Golf

Orkney Golf Club: Grainbank, Kirkwall (℡01856-872457; email orkneygolfclub@grainbank.freeserve.co.uk; www.orkneygolfclub.co.uk). This is a challenging 18-hole, 5,411-yard (4,948m), par 70 golf course. Visitors welcome. Green fees £20 per day, £60 per week, £80 for a fortnight. Clubs for hire at £8 per day per round, trolley £2.

St Margaret's Hope Golf Club: Mr B Thomson (℡01856-831395). New nine-hole course.

Other Activities

The Pickaquoy Centre: Muddisdale Road, Kirkwall KW15 1LR; ℡01856-879900; fax 01856-879901; email enquiries@pickaquoy.com, www.pickaquoy.com) is a complex offering a wide range of leisure activities, fitness suite, sauna, jacuzzi, steam room, cinema, café, bar, adventure play area and sports arena. Full-size athletic track. Open Monday to Friday 10am to 10pm, Saturday and Sunday 10am to 8pm.

SHOPPING

These are all on the signposted **Orkney Craft Trail:**

Aurora: The Workshop, Old Finstown Road, St Ola KW15 1TR (✆/fax 01856-871861; email info@aurora-jewellery.co.uk; www.aurora-jewellery.co.uk). Design-led jewellery drawing inspiration from Orkney's environment and heritage, available in silver and 9ct gold. Open all year, 10am to 5pm Monday to Friday, and 11am to 4pm on Saturday (June to September).

Sheila Fleet Jewellery: Old Schoolhouse, Tankerness KW17 2QT (✆01856-861203; fax 01856-861204; email info@sheilafleet-jewellery.co.uk; www.sheilafleet-jewellery.co.uk). Gold, silver and enamel jewellery in contemporary designs. You can have a ring made to measure and watch jewellery being made. Open all year Monday to Sunday from 9am to 5pm. Other times by appointment. Also has a gallery at 30 Bridge Street, Kirkwall, open daily 9am to 5pm. Seasonal Sunday opening 10am to 4.30pm.

Hoxa Tapestry Gallery: Leila Thomson, Neviholm, Hoxa, St Margaret's Hope KW17 2TW (✆/fax 01856-831395; email neviholm@gmail.com; www.hoxatapestrygallery.co.uk). Large and small hand-woven tapestries, samplers, cards and prints for sale. Open April to September, Monday to Friday from 10am to 5.30pm, and Saturday and Sunday from 2pm to 6pm.

Ortak Jewellery: Hatston, Kirkwall KW15 1RH (✆01856-872224; fax 01856-875165; email ortak@ortak.co.uk; www.ortak.co.uk). One of the UK's leading designers and manufacturers of gold and silver jewellery, inspired by a blend of Orkney's Norse and Scottish cultures. Attached to the workshop is a Visitor Centre, with a permanent exhibition and video presentation, and a shop. Open all year, Monday to Friday from 9am to 1pm and 2pm to 5pm, Saturday and Sunday are seasonal.

Scapa Crafts: 12 Scapa Court, Kirkwall KW15 1BJ (✆/fax 01856-872517; email jackie@scapacrafts.co.uk; www.scapacrafts.co.uk). Orkney chairs and straw work. Deliveries worldwide. Workshop and showroom open to visitors April to October, Monday to Saturday from 10am to 5pm.

Stéphane Jaeger: Littlequoy, Burray (✆/fax 01856-731228; email stephjaegerknitwear@yahoo.com). Wide range of knitwear with a French look. Open mid-May to mid-October Monday to Saturday from 10am to 6pm.

Traditional Orkney Crafts: Mariveg, Rope Walk, Kirkwall (✆01856-875110; email enquiries@orkneychairs.co.uk; www.orkneychairs.co.uk). Orkney chairs, stools and other hand-crafted furniture. Open all year, Monday to Friday from 9am to 5pm.

Other arts and craft outlets include:

John Kemp Embroidery: 28 Albert Street, Kirkwall KW15 1HL (✆/fax 01856-873190; email info@johnkemp.co.uk; www.johnkemp.co.uk). Orkney designs such as puffins, longships, diving designs embroidered on garment, as a memento of your visit. Open 9am to 5pm, Monday to Saturday.

Elli Pearson Pottery: Church Road, St Margaret's Hope, South Ronaldsay KW17 2SR (✆/fax 01856-831811). A working pottery in the picturesque village of St Margaret's Hope. You are welcome to watch Elli at work or browse in the showroom. Open Monday to Saturday 10am to 5pm.

Soli-Deo: Anchor Buildings, Bridge Street, Kirkwall (✆/fax 01856-873356). Has figurines and collectables made in Orkney; *Robert H Towers:* Rosegarth House, Orphir Road, St Ola, Kirkwall KW15 1SE (✆/fax 01856-873521; email sales@orkney-chairs.co.uk; www.orkney-chairs.co.uk). Orkney chairmaker, welcomes visits to workshop Monday to Friday but telephone first. The workshop is on the A964 Orphir Road, 1½ miles from Kirkwall, next to the entrance to the Scapa Distillery.

The main book stockists are:

Leonards Bookshop: The Bridge, Kirkwall KW15 1HP (✆01856-872014/876156; fax 01856-876198).

ME McCarty Bookseller: 54 Junction Road, Kirkwall (✆01856-870860). For second hand books. Open Monday to Saturday 10.30am to 1pm, 2pm to 5pm.

The Orcadian Bookshop: 50 Albert Street, Kirkwall (✆01856-878888; fax 01856-878001; email bookshop@orcadian.co.uk, www.orcadian.co.uk). Open Monday to Saturday 9am to 5.30pm.

HELP AND INFORMATION

Kirkwall Tourist Information Centre is housed at Visit*Orkney* (6 Broad Street, Kirkwall KW15 1NX; ℂ01856-872856; fax 01856-875056; email info@visitorkney.com; www.visitorkney.com). It is open in May, every day 9am to 6pm; June to October, Monday to Sunday from 8.30am to 8pm; and October to April, Monday to Friday from 9am to 5pm, Saturday 10am to 1pm and 2pm to 4pm.

Kirkwall Bus Station: Great Western Road, Kirkwall, has a left luggage facility from £1 and £2 depending on size. Open Monday to Friday 8am to 6pm, Saturday 10am to 4pm.

Kirkwall Swimming Pool & Sports Centre: ℂ01856-872364.

Police Station: Watergate, Kirkwall (ℂ01856-872241).

Banks

Bank of Scotland: 56 Albert Street, Kirkwall (ℂ01856-682000). Open Monday, Tuesday, Thursday and Friday 9am to 5pm, Wednesday 9.30am to 5pm.

Clydesdale Bank: 3 Broad Street, Kirkwall, KW15 1DH (ℂ01856-873237). Open Monday, Tuesday, Thursday and Friday 9.15am to 4.45pm, Wednesday 9.45am to 4.45pm

Lloyds TSB: Broad Street, Kirkwall (ℂ01856-872174). Open Monday, Tuesday 9.30am to 4pm, Wednesday 10am to 4pm, Thursday 9.30am to 5.30pm, Friday 9.30am to 5pm.

Royal Bank of Scotland: 1 Victoria Street, Kirkwall (ℂ01856-872718). Open Monday, Tuesday, Thursday and Friday 9.15am to 4.45pm, Wednesday 10am to 4.45pm.

Stromness & the West Mainland

Nearly all the jewels of Orkney lie in the green casket that is the West Mainland, the richest archaeological area in Britain with an average of three recognised sites of antiquarian interest to every square mile. Stromness is the port and main town, the second largest after Kirkwall, with a population of around 2,000. Deerness, nearly 27 miles (44km) distant in the extreme east, is the greatest distance you can go in any one direction and Kirkwall is 15 miles (24km) away. Stromness gets its name from the descriptive Old Norse words *strom*, a stream, and *ness*, a point or promontory. It is situated round the shore of the landlocked bay of Hamnavoe at the western entrance to Scapa Flow. The sheltered harbour is known as one of the safest in Scotland. The gently sloping east Cairston shore was the area most likely to have attracted the earliest settlement, but records begin only in September 1152, when the *Okneyinga Saga* notes that Earl Harald Maddadarson took refuge in the Castle of Cairston from his cousin Erlend and the brigand Svein Asleifarson. Other records show there was a house at Garson, on the Cairston shore, in 1492 on the site of an earlier settlement. In the 1620s the Bishop of Orkney issued *feus*, or conditional rights to build, on the west side of the harbour, where Stromness now stands. By the late 17th century. landowners in Cairston and Hoy were notable shipowners and from then on wars and shipping underpinned the prosperity and growth of the town. Between 1688 and 1815 wars made the English Channel unsafe for merchant vessels and the route round the top of Scotland was the alternative, with obvious spin-off for Stromness. An important source of employment was the 'Nor-Wast,' the Orcadian nickname for Canada's Hudson Bay Company. Stromness was the company's prime recruiting outpost from 1702 onwards and in 1791 a resident merchant was appointed to round up recruits. The company's ships were watered and provisioned in Stromness until the early 1900s.

At one time Stromness was a haven for vessels of all nations and hundreds a year called, many of them whalers in search of crews and bound for the Arctic. In one year alone 800 men signed on. Ship repair flourished and soon developed into boatbuilding. By 1824, there were four boatyards in Stromness. In 1856 a local yard built the *Royal Mail*, which made the first regular crossings of the Pentland Firth. From 1888 onwards Stromness harbour was jammed with fishing vessels during the herring season, often more than 400 of them. For a couple of months the town was swollen with up to an extra 5,000 fishermen and the women who followed the boats as gutters and packers. The herring boom petered out before World War I. During two World Wars Scapa Flow became the base for the Royal Navy's Home Fleet and Stromness became a naval HQ. The town's prosperity is still closely linked with the sea. The NorthLink Ro-Ro (roll-on roll-off) ferry terminal is here, and the fishing fleet comprises one of Britain's largest purse-netters, several large seine net boats and smaller lobster boats. Crabs and lobsters are marketed through the Orkney Fishermen's Society and processed locally. Tourism is rapidly growing in importance and has added sea anglers and scuba-divers to the visiting archaeology, birdlife, and walking fraternities.

Stromness has many literary associations. Sir Walter Scott found the originals of several of his characters here: Orkney pirate John Gow, who became the fictional Captain Cleveland of *The Pirate*, was born on the Cairston shore, and spent his schooldays in Stromness, while Bessie Miller of Back Road, the last Orkney woman to sell fair wind to sailors, provided Scott with his model for *Norna of the Fitful Head*. 'Torquil' of Lord Byron's poem *The Island* drew on the life of George Stewart of Massater, a young man who passed his early days in Stromness. The **Whitehouse** (1680), so called because it was the first local dwelling to be built with lime mortar instead of clay, saw Captain William Bligh dining here with the Stewarts in 1780 on his return with Captain Cook's ships from their fateful last voyage. George Stewart served as midshipman on *HMS Bounty* with Bligh during the famous mutiny of 1789. In more recent times Stromness was the home of the poet George Mackay Brown (1921-1996).

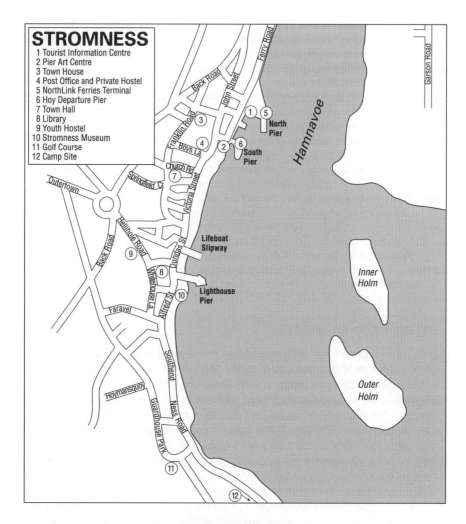

STROMNESS

STROMNESS
1 Tourist Information Centre
2 Pier Art Centre
3 Town House
4 Post Office and Private Hostel
5 NorthLink Ferries Terminal
6 Hoy Departure Pier
7 Town Hall
8 Library
9 Youth Hostel
10 Stromness Museum
11 Golf Course
12 Camp Site

STROMNESS

The distinctive architectural character of Stromness is a delight. The main street is flanked on both sides by tightly packed stone houses and shops, two or three storeys high and often with gable ends to the street and harbour. Buildings are meant to withstand harsh weather. Windows are small and set in thick walls, which provide good insulation. The streets and square are paved with local flagstone, which weathers to a warm ochre and blends well with the houses. The result is the Stromness Conservation Area which contains 70 buildings of historical and architectural interest. The quaint wynds and narrow old streets that you might find picturesque upset Sir Walter Scott when he visited Stromness in 1814. He complained that the town 'cannot be traversed by a cart or even by a horse, for there are stairs up and down even in the principal street... whose twistings are often caused by a little inclosure before the house, a sort of yard, about twenty feet square called a park.' Nothing has changed since then, except that the narrow, twisting passages reminiscent of a Norwegian fishing village now also link newer houses high on Brinkie's Brae – a hill capped by the oldest known rock in Orkney – with the old harbour-side buildings. The street, as local poet George Mackay Brown wrote, 'uncoiled like a sailor's rope from North to South and closes swarmed up the side of the hill...' By 1857 the town's little streets were paved, lit by oil-lamps, and given names. Among the name plates that still adorn the walls to tell you where you are is the **Khyber Pass**, named to celebrate Britain's imperial role in India; **Hellihole**

Road where you'll find the Youth Hostel and the Stromness Library; **Puffer's Close**, named after Town Crier James 'Puffer' Leask; and **Rae's Close**, which is named after Dr John Rae (1813–93), the Orkney-born Arctic explorer who mapped virtually all Canada's northern lands and discovered the fate of the Franklin Expedition.

The main street through Stromness runs along the water and oddly changes its name several times along its length, from Ferry Road at the NorthLink terminal to Victoria Street, through Graham Place, Dundas and Alfred streets, and into Southend and Ness Road. It's a pleasant walk and shouldn't be hurried, as there's plenty to see. At Southend there's a seat where you can sit and look across to the islets of Inner Holm and Outer Holm, with Graemsay and Hoy in the background. Near the seat is a little cannon once used to signal the arrival of a Hudson Bay Company ship and said to have last been fired in anger by *The Liberty*, an American privateer captured in 1813. The imposing house set back from the road is the former **Sule Skerry Shore Station**, built in 1892 for the families of the skerry's lighthouse keepers.

From the viewpoint above South End you get a magnificent panoramic view. To the east, in the distance, you can make out several of the South Isles, while in the west are the cliffs of the Black Craig. On Alfred Street is glassed-in **Login's Well**, with its many historical associations. Set in the wall is a slab with the inscription: 'There watered here the Hudson Bay Coy's ships 1670–1891. Captain Cook's vessels *Resolution* and *Discovery* 1780. Sir John Franklin's ships *Erebus* and *Terror* on Arctic Exploration 1845. Also the merchant vessels of former days.' The well was sealed up in 1931.

STROMNESS MUSEUM

From its earliest days men of Stromness have travelled and worked in all corners of the globe and one result has been a considerable flow into the town of foreign artefacts and curios, many of which now displayed in the Stromness Museum (52 Alfred Street, Stromness KW16 3DF; ✆01856-850025/873191; fax 01856-871560; www.orkneyheritage.com). The museum is a treasure trove of material that calls for several visits to appreciate its remarkable collections. Part of Captain Cook's South Sea collection, for instance, was left in Stromness in July 1780 when his ships Discovery and Resolution, returned after he had been murdered in Hawaii. Many of the weapons and artefacts collected by Cook were sold to local people to raise money to pay the crew. More than half a century later many of these were presented to the museum, which also has informative displays on fishing, Arctic whaling, the Hudson Bay Company of Canada, shipping, shipwrecks, lighthouses, Orkney pirate John Gow, and the German High Seas Fleet in Scapa Flow.

On display is the Halkett Air Boat, one of the earliest inflatables, which was used by Dr John Rae in his Canadian exploration and during his search for the missing expedition of Sir John Franklin. The museum also has Dr Rae's sextant. Exotica includes shells brought home by William Balfour Baikie, explorer of the Niger; an African chief's throne of ebony and ivory; grave goods from Peru; a naval dress vest worn by Scott of the Antarctic; a pipe which belonged to Robbie Burns; birds, animals, eggs and butterflies of Orkney, as well as the fossilised bones of dinosaurs. Fossil fish of Orkney include Asterolepis of Stromness, on which geologist Hugh Miller based his book Footprints of the Creator, a work that helped Charles Darwin to formulate his theory of evolution. Open daily 10am to 5pm. Access for disabled. Admission adults £3, concession £2, school age 50p.

Across from the museum on the site of the 'Old Orkney' whisky distillery is Mayburn Court where noted Orcadian poet George MacKay Brown lived from 1968 until his death in 1996. Near the Northern Lighthouse Board is **The Haven**, former premises of the Orkney Hudson Bay Company agents David Geddes (1771–1812), George Geddes (1812–19) and John Rae, father of Dr John Rae, the Arctic explorer (1819–36). Lady Franklin lived here in 1851 during Dr Rae's search for her husband's missing expedition. The RNLI Station's lifeboat is based at the South Pier.

Church Road leads up from the main street to the **Community Centre**, formerly the Parish Church of St Peter's (1814). Halfway up the north side is the Scottish Episcopalian Church and on the south side at the bottom is the former Free Church of Scotland, which now houses **Stromness Town Hall**. The Victoria Street Church is now the sole Parish Church, uniting three congregations. The **Pier Arts Centre** (Victoria Street, Stromness KW16 3AA; ✆01856-850209; fax 01856-851462; email info@pierartscentre.com; www. pierartscentre.com), once an 18th century merchant's pier and a recruiting agency for the Hudson Bay Company, is now a modern art gallery. Open all year, Tuesday to Saturday 10.30am to 12.30pm, and 1.30pm to 5pm; admission free. At the end of the main street on the way out of town is **the Lieutenant's House**, built and occupied by Lt James Robertson RN until his death in 1860. He commanded *HMS Beresford* during the attack on the American squadron at the Battle of Plattsburgh in the war of 1812.

Distances in miles/km from Stromness:

Borwick (36/58)	Rendall (12/19)
Dounby (9½/15)	Sandwick (6½/10)
Evie (17/27)	Skara Brae (8/13)
Finstown (8/13)	Standing Stones (6½/10)
Houton (7/11)	Stenness (4/6)
Kirkwall (15/24)	Twatt (10¼/16)
Maes Howe (4½/7)	Yesnaby (5½/9)
Orphir (11/18)	

FURTHER AFIELD

The West Mainland contains outstanding historic and prehistoric sites, as well as some of the best wild brown trout fishing lochs in Northern Scotland, wildlife attractions, and some fine walks. Distances are not great and locations are well signposted and served by good, surfaced roads. Free parking is available in most places.

Starting from Stromness is a 10-mile (16km) coastal walk said to be the finest on the Mainland. It goes north from **Breck Ness** and the cliffs of **Black Craig**, past the caves at **Neban Point** and the sea stacks of **North Gaulton Castle**, and **Yesnaby Castle**, just south of **Brough of Bigging**, and the ruined broch at Borwick, to the justly famous Neolithic village on the **Bay of Skaill**.

Skara Brae

You can literally take a walk back in time from the **Skara Brae Visitor Centre** (✆01856-841815; www.historic-scotland.gov.uk) along a coastal path which is punctuated by markers reminding you when some of mankind's greatest monuments were constructed: The Great Wall of China 220BC, The Parthenon 480BC, the Temple of Solomon 962BC, Stonehenge 2100BC. and the Pyramids of Giza 2500BC.

Finally comes Europe's best preserved Neolithic village, dated at 3100BC. This stunning complex, one of Britain's first farming villages, came to light in 1850 after a violent storm swept away the sand dunes covering the Stone Age village and its surrounding middens. Excavations revealed a warren of covered passages connecting stone-built houses and workshops which had survived the centuries in incredibly good condition. Even the furniture – made of stone – was still in place. It still is, and when you look down into the houses from the grassy mounds you'd think the residents had just gone off fishing. Set in the floors near the hearth are stone boxes cemented with clay to make them watertight so that shellfish could be soaked to prepare them for use as bait. There are stone bedsteads in the houses and dressers for displaying prized possessions; some even have water closets and primitive drains to carry away waste, and all this 3,000 years before the Romans arrived in Britain with their vaunted plumbing and sanitation.

You can see some of the finds made in the settlement and learn more of its fascinating story at the Skara Brae Visitor Centre. You also get to walk around a replica Neolithic dwelling to give you an idea of everyday Stone Age life. There's a café and shop at the centre. Open daily in summer 9.30am to 6.30pm, winter 9.30am to 4.30pm. Last admission 45 minutes before closing. Admission charge. A joint entry ticket, which includes nearby Skaill House, is available.

Skaill House (Breckness Estate, Sandwick KW16 3LR; ℂ01856-841501; fax 01856-841668; email info@skaillhouse.com; www.skaillhouse.com) was the home of William Graham Watt, the Breckness laird who discovered Skara Brae. In this 17th–century mansion house you can see the bed of Bishop George Graham (1620), the dinner service used by Captain James Cook on his ship the *Resolution* and a gun room full of sporting and military memorabilia. Open April to September, daily 9.30am to 5.30pm.

The road continues north from Skara Brae through rich, rolling farmland, with the RSPB reserve of **The Loons** at the Loch of Isbister to the east and the **RSPB Marwick Head RSPB Reserve** and the **Kitchener Memorial** on the coast above Marwick Bay to the west. Park and walk 1,000 yards (1km) to the crenellated square stone memorial, which stands silhouetted against the skyline overlooking the spot where Lord Kitchener of Khartoum went down with *HMS Hampshire* and most of her 665 men after the cruiser hit a German mine on 5 June 1916 and sank in 15 minutes. Kitchener, Secretary for War, was on his way to Russia at the time to discuss wartime developments with the Tsar. His body was never recovered.

Inland past Twatt and between the Loch of Boardhouse and the Loch of Hundland is **Kirbuster Museum** (℃01856-771268/411; fax 01856-871560; email museum@orkney.gov.uk). This is an Orkney-style blackhouse, the last surviving farmhouse with central hearth and stone *neuk*, or nook, beds set into the walls, where its last owners lived until the 1960s. First mentioned as an established homestead in the Birsay Parish Rentals of 1595: of northern European importance as an authentic survival. The pleasant grounds include a putting green and a Victorian garden with picnic facilities. Gift shop. Open March to October. Admission is free.

At the head of Boardhouse Loch and powered by its outflow is Orkney's only large working water mill, one of the three **Barony Mills** (Birsay; ℃01856-721439; www.birsay.org. uk). Two are in ruins but the other, built in 1873, is still going strong. There have been mills around here since Viking times. The names of millers going back to 1873 are written on the wall. Open seven days a week from May to September, 10am to 1pm and 2pm to 5pm. Admission free. Guided tours. For more information contact Johnny Johnston at the *Birsay Heritage Trust* (Springburn, Twatt KW17 2JH; ℃01856-771276; fax 01856-771751; email johnnyjohnston@talk21.com; www.birsay.org.uk).

Brough of Birsay

Off the north-west corner of the mainland is the tidal island of the Brough of Birsay where settlers and invaders have left a succession of sites and structures that are a lodestone for archaeologists. While most of the ruined buildings visible today are Norse and early medieval, artefacts discovered indicate that a Pictish community flourished here as far back as the 7th century. Traces of Pictish buildings have been found, along with the debris of a bronze workshop producing fine jewellery. The carved symbol stone just inside the graveyard is the most tangible evidence of Picts. This is a cast; the original is in the Royal Museum of Scotland, in Edinburgh. Excavation has revealed traces of Pictish settlements at several places round the Bay of Birsay, including the Point of Buckquoy.

Viking Earl Thorfinn the Mighty ruled Orkney from the Brough and its importance is underscored by the fact that he founded the first cathedral of the Northern Isles here soon after 1050, and it was here that the body of murdered Earl Magnus was buried in 1115 and only later transferred to the Cathedral of St Magnus in Kirkwall. In the 12th century the Norsemen added a small monastery to their settlement with a fine if small Romanesque church. The settlement already had the refinement of stone-lined drains to keep it dry. Today the island is about 52 acres (21ha) in area, but erosion on its coastal fringe suggests it was much bigger in the days of the Norsemen. The small lighthouse, now unmanned, was built in 1925.

On the landward side of the Brough is a modern visitor centre which displays some of the things found on the site. The Brough is accessible only around low tide by pedestrian causeway. From the car park on the Point of Buckquoy, the Brough of Birsay and its setting can be appreciated whether or not the causeway is passable. Open April to September 9.30am to 6.30pm daily. Closed between 12.30 to 1.30pm. Admission charge.

The Earl's Palace

The village of Birsay on the mainland at the head of the Bay of Birsay was the seat of 16th century nobleman Robert Stewart, Earl of Orkney. The gaunt walls of his once sumptuous palace still dominate the village. The Earl's Palace was built in about 1574 around a courtyard with projecting three-storey towers at three corners. About 20 years later his son, Patrick, enlarged it, adding a new wing on the north with rooms that had barrel-vaulted ceilings. You can see the palace well in the centre of the courtyard. The palace is regarded as a monument to Robert's royal pretensions and to his oppression of his tenantry. Earl Robert's black reputation, however, pales to a lighter shade of grey beside that of his son, Patrick, who succeeded him. Although Patrick seems not to have contributed much to the fabric of the palace it played an important role in the rebellion of his son, Robert, who seized it in 1614 and defended it against the Sheriff of Kirkwall's men. For this both Patrick and his son were executed the following year. It has been in ruins since 1700.

Orkney's Iron Age Heart

The main road (A966) running round the top of the mainland swings past the large Loch of Swannay before running south along the shore of Eynhallow Sound, with the islet of **Eynhallow** and the larger bulk of Rousay clear across the often wild strait. To the west of the road, **Burgar Hill** is the site of a group of aero-generators. The largest has a blade diameter of 197ft (60m) and a capacity of three megawatts. On adjoining Mid Hill is an RSPB reserve with a well-sited hide for red-throated divers. There is evidence of prehistoric settlement all the way along the coast, with seven brochs on the Evie coastline, mirroring the six that line the opposite shore on Rousay. This concentration seems to represent the heart of Iron Age Orkney and highlights the utility of settlements next to the sea for transport and for food.

The best preserved structure on this stretch, the **Broch of Gurness** (✆01856-751414), was discovered on the **Aikerness Peninsula** in 1929 by Orkney poet Robert Rendall, who was sitting sketching the view when one of the legs of his stool sank into the ground. He then uncovered some descending stairs and subsequent excavations revealed the broch surrounded by an impressive settlement of stone buildings. As well as round Pictish houses a rectangular longhouse, usually a sign of Norse occupation, was also uncovered.

Viking artefacts unearthed include iron shield bosses, a merchant's folding balance and a linen-smoother. A Norse grave revealed the body of a woman who had been buried in a stone-lined pit. She lay on her back, fully dressed, with two oval bronze brooches on her breast, the back of one showing traces of wool from her burial garment. She wore an iron necklet, and next to her lay an iron knife and an iron sickle. Excavations in the Gurness Broch midden revealed a more grisly reminder of the past, two severed hands in the garbage, flung there before anyone had even removed the five rings from their fingers. Vehicle access is signposted from the main road to Evie. The site is accessible at all times.

During the summer months the small **Visitor Centre** is open April to September, 9.30am to 6.30pm, closed 12.30pm to 1.30pm; and October (check opening times). Closed November to March. Last admission 30 minutes before closing. Admission charge.

Aikerness beach is probably the longest sandy stretch in the West Mainland, and it's great for bathing, picnicking or beachcombing for shells, especially *groatie buckies* (cowries). At Aikerness is one of the finest examples of a rare form of rock known as aeolianite. Unlike the ancient sandstones that make up most of Orkney, aeolianite has been formed within the last 10,000 years. Nowhere else in Scotland are there aeolianite outcrops as thick or as extensive as at Aikerness, making this one of the most important landform sites in Orkney. The **Hall of Rendall** is worth a detour to see the recently restored 'Doocot,' a fine example of a dovecote that is unique in Orkney. It's built of local flagstone and looks like a small version of an Iron Age broch. Offshore you'll see the little island of Gairsay, once the lair of notorious Viking Svein Asleifarson, who was killed by the Irish in Dublin in 1171.

There is evidence of another broch at **Tingwall**, close to the ferry terminal for Rousay, Egilsay and Wyre, and at Ingashowe, on the Bay of Firth, where human remains and red deer bones have been uncovered. At nearby Rennibister Farm in 1926 a steam thresher was trundling out of the gate when the ground caved in and it became stuck in a large hole, which proved to be the roof of a *souterrain*, or earth house. These were generally attached to settlements and used for storage, but excavation of this one revealed the bones of 12 children and six adults in the chamber.

Cut into the bedrock of **Cuween Hill**, overlooking the Bay of Firth, is a chambered tomb, known locally as the **'Fairy Knowe'**. When it was opened in 1901 evidence of eight burials was found and 24 dog skulls were lying on the floor of the main chamber. It's thought the dog skulls could have been some form of totemic protection. The tomb has been given a modern roof but it's worth crawling down the entrance passage to admire the flagstone masonry, which has been there for 5,000 years. Excavations at **Stonehall** in Firth have revealed early Neolithic houses which could date back to 3800BC and pre-date Orkney's oldest recognised dwelling at the Knap of Howar, on Papa Westray, by at least 200 years.

Finstown is a pleasant village, Orkney's third largest. It was probably named after Phin, an Irish soldier who retired here after the Napoleonic Wars and opened an inn he called 'The Toddy Hole,' now the Pomona Inn. In the area around you can visit **Langalour**, a 19th-century farm, complete with stone neuk (wall cavity) beds. It was originally a longhouse, shared alike by family and farm animals. At **Binscarth** is a stand of 7 acres (3ha) of coniferous trees and broad-leafed woodland planted more than 100 years ago. Below the woodland is the **Old Mill** on the Ouse. It doesn't grind corn any more but it is still complete, down to the overshot wheel which provided the power.

NEOLITHIC HEARTLAND

The short route back to Stromness takes you to an area of magnificent archaeological treasures that has gained a listing as a Unesco World Heritage Site, one of only three in Scotland to be awarded this global accolade. These are the chambered tomb of **Maes Howe**, the **Standing Stones of Stenness**, and the **Ring of Brodgar**, which for miles around are surrounded by a variety of less impressive but still interesting prehistoric works. Archaeologists regard the entire area as Orkney's Neolithic heartland.

Maes Howe

Orkney's superlative megalithic culture reached its zenith around 5,000 years ago and the monumental chambered tomb of Maes Howe is regarded as the pinnacle of the Neolithic people's achievement. Standing incongruously alongside the A965 road 4½ miles (7km) from Stromness and close to the Loch of Harray, Maes Howe appears as a mighty grassy mound, 24ft (7m) high and 110ft (34m) in diameter. Buy a ticket across the road from the site at **Tormiston Mill** from Historic Scotland and you can enter to marvel at the tomb's size and unsurpassed workmanship. Maes Howe consists of a large central chamber roofed by colossal slabs, some weighing up to 30 tons. Several chambers lead off to the side, in which the dead were sealed. The builders positioned the entrance so that at sunset on the shortest day of the year the sun lit the inside of the main chamber, which is supported by four square pillars positioned at the cardinal points.

In 1153, Vikings seeking shelter broke into Maes Howe by digging through the roof. Others, returning from the Crusades that year, also entered the tomb and left a message in runes saying 'Jerusalem-farers opened this mound.' Ransackers also left a tantalising runic message on the wall referring to 'a great treasure hidden here'. Other inscriptions added by visiting Vikings make up the best collection of runes outside Scandinavia. Among the 30 ancient graffiti is the longest, 'These runes were carved by the man most skilled in runes in the Western Ocean with the axe that killed Gauk Thrandilsson in the south of Iceland.' The shortest says, 'Thorfinn wrote these runes.'

Maes Howe (✆01856-761606; fax 01856-761705; www.historic-scotland.gov.uk) is open all year: summer 9.30am to 6pm, winter 9.30am to 4pm. Last admission 30 minutes before closing. Adult £3, concession £2.30, children £1. Joint entry for other Orkney monuments. The site has a winter solstice website during December and January with a live webcam every afternoon at www.maeshowe.mypage.org. Tormiston Mill has a display of Orkney's most accessible prehistoric sites and its restaurant is open from April to November.

In the field opposite the entrance to Maes Howe is a small standing stone known as the **Barnhouse Stone**. Two miles (3km) or so down the road you can't miss the grassy mound of **Unstan Cairn**, on a small promontory jutting out into the Loch of Stenness. This oval chambered tomb was opened in 1884, when about 35 Neolithic pots were found whose fine decoration and shallow deep-collared shape now characterises similar pottery as Unstan Ware. Slabs of stone divided the inside chamber of the tomb into separate compartments, where skeletal remains were found.

Standing Stones of Stenness and Ring of Brodgar

The **Standing Stones of Stenness** tower over a field on the southern peninsula between the lochs of Harray and Stenness, an area believed to have had special religious significances for Neolithic and later Bronze Age people. The Stenness Stones are the remains of a 100ft (30m) circle within a henge. Four unusually shaped stones, the tallest one nearly 17ft (5m) high, are all that remain of the original 12 stones making up the circle. Radiocarbon dating of animal bones found in a hearth indicate that the henge was built around 3000–2500BC. It's calculated that it took more than 5,000 man days to complete Stenness, time mainly spent digging a ditch 20ft (6m) wide and about 7½ft (2.3m) deep, partly through solid rock, and building a bank of similar width.

A mile away across the causeway linking it to the northern peninsula is the spectacular **Ring of Brodgar**, which once consisted of 60 stones. About 36 stones still stand, some up to 15ft (4.5m) high, while others are simply broken stumps. The circle has a diameter of nearly 114 yards (104m) and is surrounded by a deep trench. The massive ditch is the work of more than 10,000 man days and the stones would have taken about a 1,000 man days to erect. Single stones point south-eastwards to the smaller circle of Stenness. The massive monolith of the **Watch Stone** stands by the Brig o' Brodgar and there are also numerous burial mounds around, probably from the early Bronze Age.

Continue up the road and you'll reach Dounby, a small settlement where the parishes of Birsay, Harray and Sandwick meet. Within a radius of a couple of miles you'll find the **Corrigall Farm Museum** (Corston Road, Harray KW17 2JR; ✆01856-771411; fax 01856-871560; museum@orkney.gov.uk), a late 19th-century farmstead with a grain-drying kiln and native livestock. Open daily March to October, Monday to Saturday 10.30am to 1pm and 2pm to 5pm, Sunday 2pm to 7pm; and the **Click Mill**, a simple type of mill with a horizontal wooden waterwheel of early 19th-century design. This is the last of its kind in Orkney. The mill got its name from the noise it made while working. South of the main Stromness–Kirkwall road the last pitched battle in Orkney was fought in 1528 on the borders of Stenness and Orphir and you can stand on the **Battle of Summerdale** site where soldiers led by the Earl of Caithness were defeated. They had been sent by King James V to crush a rebellion of islanders who took up arms against feudalism and unfair taxes. Here, too, is **Ward Hill**, at 879ft (268m) the highest point on the Orkney Mainland.

Below the **Loch of Kirbister** – good for trout and windsurfing – is the beautiful sheltered beach of **Waulkmill Bay**, known as one of the warmest places in Orkney to swim because its broad expanse of sand heats up when there is sun. On both sides of the road above it is the 1,878-acre (760ha) **RSPB Hobbister Bird Reserve**, where there is parking and a pleasant track walk to a moorland area still actively worked for peat. The diversity of habitat here attracts a great variety of breeding birds.

Orphir

This is the scene of one of the great passages from the *Orkneyinga Saga*, more particularly the **Earl's Bu** with its remains of a Viking drinking hall and the **Round Church**, Scotland's only circular medieval church. A starting point for an exploration of Orkney's Norse heritage is the **Orkneyinga Saga Centre**, open all year, 9am to 5pm, admission free. Take the Gyre Road turn-off from the A964. The centre is situated at the Bu in Orphir, an area rich in Viking remains. Here you can sit and watch a film which introduces you to the Norse period in Orkney, and points the way to related sites throughout the islands. There are also static displays.

Alongside the centre is a footpath leading to the Earl's Bu, the remains of a Norse farmstead and in the 12th-century home to some of the Viking earls so important in Orkney's history. The Bu, or farmstead, comprised the longhouse and a group of farm buildings, a huge drinking hall for feasting, store-rooms and other chambers. The grass-grown foundations to the left of the path as you approach the church and its burial ground were excavated at the end of the last century and are believed to be the remains of the great drinking hall where in 1136 Svein Breast-Rope was murdered during a feast. St Nicholas Church is the only round church known to have been built in Scotland, and was inspired by the rotunda of the Church of the Holy Sepulchre in Jerusalem. The chronicles mention the Orphir church in 1136. It was largely destroyed in the mid-18th century to provide stones for a new church, which has since been demolished, but what's left is highly attractive. There's a pleasant **circular walk** of about an hour from the centre and the Earl's Bu to Breck, along a coastal path and returning by public road. The cliff-top is full of wild flowers and otters are occasional visitors to the old mill-pond near Orphir House.

The ferry for the South Isles and the oil terminal at Flotta goes from the pier at **Houton**, whose sheltered harbour was used by the fleet of King Haakon in 1263 and by the British Royal Navy during the First World War. The little **Bridge of Waithe** which crosses the tidal Stenness loch's outlet to the Bay of Ireland is remembered locally as the place where a stray German bomb killed James Isbister, the first British civilian to die in World War II. He was watching aircraft attacking ships in Scapa Flow when he was hit by shrapnel.

NATURE RESERVES

The Royal Society for the Protection of Birds (RSPB) owns or leases two reserves totalling 6,033 acres (2,433ha) in the West Mainland, one if which is known as **Birsay Moors** and the other **Cottascarth and Rendall Moss**. The reserve is primarily heather moorland, but with a variety of habitats ranging from dry heath through wet heath to marsh and bogs. Peat-cutting is evident on the hillsides and while there are no trails, peat cutters' tracks make access easy. Durkadale, a detached north-western section of the Birsay Moors, has a diversity of sedges and mosses, with patches of willow scrub and a reedbed. The commonest birds here are **meadow pipits** and **skylarks**, with smaller numbers of **wrens**, **wheatears**, **stonechats** and **twites. Reed buntings** and **sedge warblers** also breed. Eight species of waders, including **golden plover** and **dunlin**, breed on the moors, as well as large numbers of **curlew. Teal, wigeon** and **red-breasted merganser** are among the breeding ducks. Twitchers should try to keep clear of the small hill lochans because **red-throated divers** nest on some of them. Excellent views can usually be obtained of these shy birds from the hide at Burgar Hill. Orkney has always been a stronghold for **hen harriers**, which can be viewed from most of the moorland roads. The **Dee of Durkadale** is a prime attraction for botanists. Here, the pinks and purples of **heath spotted**, **northern marsh** and **early marsh orchids** mix with the vivid yellow of **marsh marigolds**. Some 15 species of **sedge** grow here. The reserve is always open. There is no admission charge. To reach the reserve turn off A986, 2.5 miles (4km) north of Dounby, then right along track at south end of Loch of Hundland to the ruined farm of Durkadale. The Dee lies on the opposite side of the Burn of Durkadale. Contact ℂ01856-850176.

Cottascarth Nature Reserve is always open. There is no admission charge. To get there turn left off the A966, three miles north of Finstown (just north of Norseman Village), then right along the signposted track. Park in farmyard and follow signs to the hide. Contact ℂ01856-850176. **Burgar Hill Nature Reserve**, part of Birsay Moors, is always open. There is no admission charge. There's a car park and facilities for visitors with disabilities. A hide overlooks Lowrie's Water, which gives excellent views of **red-throated divers** in spring and summer.

The RSPB has bought 219 acres (88ha) of marsh in Orkney to establish **the Loons and Loch of Banks Nature Reserve** about three miles (5km) north of Dounby and a mile (1.6km) east of Marwick Head. Known as a basin mire, The Loons can become completely flooded in winter and even in summer remains wet. Eight species of duck breed here and at Loch of Banks including **wigeon** and **pintail**. There's a high density of waders, with as many as 66 pairs of **lapwings**, 72 pairs of **curlews**, 32 pairs of **redshanks**, 30 pairs of **snipe**, 31 of **oystercatchers** and 11 of **dunlins**. There are also substantial colonies of both **black-headed** and **common gulls** and small numbers of **arctic terns**. You should not enter the Loons during the breeding period between April and July. The Loons attract several hundred wintering ducks and a flock of up to 150 **Greenland white-fronted geese**. There is no access to the marsh but good views can be had from the roadside hide on the west edge of the marsh. There is no admission charge. The Loch of Banks is viewable from the A986.

The **RSPB Marwick Head Nature Reserve** is in the north-west corner of the Mainland, about 11 miles (18km) north of Stromness. More than 10,000 **guillemots** and almost 1,400 pairs of **kittiwakes** crowd less than a mile of coastline. There are also many **fulmars** and **razorbills** as well as small populations of **ravens**, **rock doves** and **twites**. The reserve is always open. There is no admission charge.

The **RSPB Hobbister Nature Reserve** is mainly moorland, with habitats such as bog and fen, cliffs up to 98ft (30m) high and, at Waulkmill Bay, tidal sandflats and saltmarsh. Having remained virtually unburned and ungrazed for many years the reserve has a rich moorland bird community, including high densities of **meadow pipits**, **skylarks**, **wrens**, several pairs of **stonechats**, and nearly 100 pairs of **curlew**, along with some large **gull** colonies. There are usually one or two pairs of **merlin** and two of three **hen harrier** nests; as many as four pairs of **short-eared owls** also use the reserve. In winter, Waulk-mill Bay is an ideal place to spot wintering seafowl, including **black-throated divers**. On the coast look out for **red-breasted mergansers** and **black guillemots**. The reserve is always open, but access is limited to the land between A964 and the sea. There is no admission charge. There is no office at the reserve. For more information on any reserve contact *RSPB Orkney Reserves Office*, 12–14 North End Road, Stromness, KW16 3AC; ℂ01856-850176.

The *Scottish Wildlife Trust*'s (SWT) **Harray Road Ends Reserve** is a 22-acre (9ha) site at the junction of the A965/A986 roads. The reserve has a mixture of wet and dry heath together with rough grass and mire communities typical of uncultivated parts of Orkney. The **Orkney vole** is common here and the reserve is also a breeding site for several species of wading birds. Park beside the A986, 1½ miles (2½km) west of Finstown.

GETTING AROUND

Buses

The bus stop is through the car park from the ferry terminal, across the road and at the lay-by.
Stromness to Kirkwall costs £2.35. The driver will give you change.
Orkney Coaches: Scott Road, Hatston Industrial Estate, Kirkwall KW15 1GR; ℂ01856-870555;

fax 01856-877501; email info@rapsons.co.uk; www.rapsons.com). Operates a service from Stromness to Kirkwall; Birsay–Dounby–Harray–Finstown–Kirkwall; and to the Houton ferry terminal. All vehicles are non-smoking. Free timetable from the tourist office.

Taxis

There is a taxi rank outside the ferry office at the harbour.

Brass's Taxis: Terminal Building, Ferry Road, Stromness KW16 3AA (✆01856-850750; fax 01856-850491; email brass_taxis@yahoo.co.uk). Taxis and minibus hire with driver. Also tours to sites of interest.

Taxi Service: Evie (✆01856-751232). Also minibus hire.

Vehicle Rental

Norman Brass Self-Drive Car Hire: Blue Star Filling Station, North End Road, Stromness KW16 13AG (✆01856-850850; fax 01856-850985; email info@nwbrass.so.uk). Ideally situated for all the ferries. No mileage charge. Group 1 from £33 a day to £171 for a week; Group 3 from £41 a day to £196 a week.

Stromness Car Hire and Taxis: The Box, 16 John Street, Stromness KW15 1QZ (✆01856-850973; fax 01856-851777). Taxis, self-drive cars, minibus service.

Cycle Hire

Orkney Cycle Hire: 54 Dundas Street, Stromness KW16 3DA (✆/fax 01856-850255; email orkney.cycle.hire@talk21.com; www.scbf.demon.co.uk). Daily and weekly cycle hire. Shimano-equipped mountain bikes and tourers, free maps and helmets. Seven-day service.

Stromness Cycle Hire: Ferry Road, Stromness KW16 3AA (✆01856-850750; fax 01856-850491; email brass_taxis@yahoo.co.uk) mountain bikes with free helmets. Open daily.

Tours

Dragon History: 58 Dundas Street, Stromness (✆078-1505 3894; email dragonhist@hotmail.com). Entertaining history tours with qualified guides.

Five Senses: 1 Manse Lane, Stromness KW16 3BX (✆079-2138 3503; email info@allfivesenses.com; www.allfivesenses.com). Learn the art of fire making, meet craft folk, sample foods, work with natural fibres and stone. Full day £45 a person, includes homemade lunch. Two-hour session £18.

Orkney Tourist Guides Association: c/o Karisgill, 43 Hamnavoe, Stromness KW16 3JQ (✆/fax 01856-872865; email info@otga.co.uk; www.orga.co.uk). Guided tours and walks with accredited tour guides.

ACCOMMODATION: STROMNESS

Hotels

Ferry Inn: John Street, Stromness KW16 3AA (✆01856-850280; fax 01856-851332; email adrian@ferryinn.com; www.ferryinn.com). Two-star inn with nautical flavour, 11 bedrooms, restaurant and lounge bar, near harbour. From £25 a night.

Orca Hotel: 76 Victoria Street, Stromness KW16 3BS (✆01856-850447; email info@orcahotel.com; www.orcahotel.com). Two-star, seafront location within two minutes of all amenities. From £20.

Royal Hotel: 55 Victoria Street, Stromness KW16 3BS (✆/fax 01856-850342; email enquiries@royalhotel.biz; www.royalhotel.biz). Two-star, family-run, 11 bedrooms, central to ferries and buses. Lounge bar, small public bar, restaurant. From £30 a night.

Stromness Hotel: Pier Head, Victoria Street, Stromness KW16 3AA (✆01856-850298; fax 01856-850610; email info@stromnesshotel.com; www.stromnesshotel.com). Spacious three-star historic 42 en suite bedroomed hotel overlooking the working harbour and opposite the ferry terminal. Spectacular views over Scapa Flow and Hoy. Lift to all floors and private car parking. *Hamnavoe Lounge Bar* with harbour view. Only cask-conditioned

Orkney ales in Stromness. *Flattie Bar* has a local fishing theme with award-winning Orkney ales on tap. *Still Room* whisky bar offers more than 100 malt whiskies. *Scapa Flow* à la carte restaurant. Music and live entertainment. Plenty of parking at rear of hotel, where there is disabled access. Pets and children are welcome. Open all year, from £40.

Guest Houses

Harbourside Guest House: 7 John Street, Stromness KW16 3AD (℡01856-851969; fax 01856-851967; email millershouse@orkney.com; www.orkneyisles.co.uk/millershouse). Three-star guest house near ferry terminal, all rooms en suite. From £23 a night.

Bed & Breakfast

Bea House: Mrs I.Borland, Back Road, Stromness KW16 3AW (℡/fax 01856-851043; email bea.house@virgin.net). Three-star, large stone-built 1880 house on hillside overlooking central Stromness, view over the harbour. From £18 a night B&B, £15 bed only.

Ferry Bank: Mrs Venus Hourston, 2 North End Road, Stromness KW16 3AG (℡01856-851250). Four-star, en suite rooms. Opposite ferry terminal, overlooking harbour. Unusual range of breakfasts. One double and one family room, from £25.

Ferry Lodge: 15 John Street, Stromness (℡01856-850109; email neil@theferrylodge.com; www.theferrylodge.com). Family-run, from £25.

Miller's House: 13 John Street, Stromness KW16 3AD (℡01856-851969; fax 01856-851967; email millershouse@orkney.com; www.orkneyisles.co.uk/millershouse), the earliest dateable house in Stromness. From £25 per person a night.

Thira Guest House: Innertown, Stromness KW16 3JP (℡01856-851181; email info@thiraorkney.co.uk; www.thiraorkney.co.uk). Four-star, spacious, on the outskirts of town, views over Hoy Sound and Hoy Hills. From £28.

Self-Catering

Braehead Farm: Bu Road, Cairston, Stromness KW16 3JH (℡/fax 01856-851313). Four-star, on working croft, views over Scapa Flow, 1½ miles (2.4km) from town. Two bedrooms, sleeps 5–6, from £120 to £300.

Caledonia Apartment: MA Robertson, Back Road, Stromness KW16 3HA (℡01856-850136; fax 01856-851633; email info@millofeyrland.com; www.millofeyrland.co.uk). Three-star self-contained flat within Victorian villa, 3 bedrooms, sleeps 6. View over harbour and Scapa Flow. From £200 to £350 a week.

Harbour Cottage: 30 John Street, Stromness KW16 2AD (℡/fax 01856-850475; email mralan.mac@virgin.net). Three-star, recently modernised, traditional end-on Orkney house. Two bedrooms, sleeps four, from £175 to £275.

Mrs A Heddle: 54 Dundas Street, Stromness KW16 3DA (℡01856-850255; email orkney.cycle.hire@talk21.com). Four-star, overlooking harbour and Scapa Flow, one bedroom, sleeps two. Open all year. From £180 to £240 a week.

Stenigar Flat and Cottage: Stenigar, Ness Road, Stromness KW16 3DW (℡01856-850438; email christorkney@aol.com). Cottage wing and garden cottage, views of harbour. Open all year, one and two bedrooms, sleep two and four, from £150 to £350.

Mrs Charlotte Worthington: 2 South End, Stromness KW16 3DJ (℡01856-850215). Three-star 19th-century house on private stone pier overlooking harbour and Scapa Flow. Open May to October.

Hostels

Brown's Hostel: 45–47 Victoria Street, Stromness KW16 3BS (℡01856-850661; fax 01856-851775). Self-catering, two, three and four bedded rooms, all linen provided, fully-equipped kitchen. Hot showers. Centrally situated near shops, ferry terminal and bus stop. £10 per person a night, no curfew. Open all year. Member of *Scottish Independent Hostels*.

Stromness Youth Hostel: 6 Hellihole Road, Stromness KW16 3DE (✆01856-850589; email office@stromnesshostel.co.uk; www.stromnesshostel.co.uk). Three-star, one room with 4 beds, two rooms with 6 beds, both en suite; two dorm rooms with eight beds. Shop nearby, bus ½ mile away, ferry ½ mile. Cycling, fishing, entertainment, 18-hole golf course, pony trekking, sailing, swimming. En suite from £12, dorms £10.50.

Camping

Point of Ness, camping and caravan site in Stromness, situated on the shoreline, one mile west of the pierhead. About £7.35 for caravan and motor homes and £3.90 for tents. Leisure activities nearby including fishing, sea angling, sailing and boating. For booking and more information contact the *Department of Education and Recreation Services* (Orkney Islands Council, School Place, Kirkwall KW15 1NY; ✆01856-875353, ext 2404; fax 01856-876327). Contact VisitOrkney in Kirkwall, the tourist office in Stromness, or visit www.visitorkney.com for more information on accommodation.

ACCOMMODATION: FURTHER AFIELD

Hotels

Barony Hotel: Birsay KW17 2LS (✆01856-721327; fax 01856-721302; email info@baronyhotel.com; www.baronyhotel.com). Two-star, Orkney's oldest fishing hotel with views of Boardhouse Loch and Brough of Birsay. En-suite facilities. Assisted wheelchair access. Closed October to April. From £30 a night.

Smithfield Hotel: Dounby KW17 2HT (✆01856-771215; fax 01856-771494; email smithfield.hotel@virgin.net; www.smithfieldhotel.co.uk). Two-star, family-run, five en suite bedrooms. Good food. Open all year, from £30 a night.

Standing Stones Hotel: Stenness KW16 3JX (✆01856-850449; fax 01856-851262; email standingstones@sol.co.uk; www.standingstoneshotel.co.uk). Three-star, on the shores of the Loch of Stenness, all 18 bedrooms en suite, 11 miles (18km) from Kirkwall and 4 miles (6km) from Stromness. From £45 a night.

Woodwick House: Evie KW17 2PQ (✆01856-751330; fax 01856-751383; email mail@woodwickhouse.co.uk; www.woodwickhouse.co.uk). Three-star, set in 12 acres of bluebell woodland, overlooks island of Gairsay. Reputable cuisine. Vegetarians and special diets. Accessible for the disabled. Fully licensed with a selection of local ales and malts. From £34 a night. Open all year.

Bed & Breakfast

Links House: Mrs B Williamson, The Palace, Birsay KW17 2LX (✆/fax 01856-721221; email barbara@erlend.fsnet.co.uk; www.ewaf.co.uk). Overlooking bay, good food, from £35.

Netherstove: Mrs A Poke, Sandwick KW16 3LS (✆/fax 01856-841625; email ann.poke@virgin.net; www.netherstove.com). Farmhouse, overlooking Skara Brae. Closed November to May, from £18.

The Noust: Mrs A Hewison, Orphir KW17 2RB (✆01856-811348; email annatnoust@aol.com; www.the-noust.co.uk). Three-star, overlooks Scapa Flow. Handy for ferries. From £23 a night. Also has pub and one bedroom self-catering flat, from £140 to £240 a week. Short stays available from November to March.

Houton Bay Lodge: Houton Bay, Orphir KW17 2RD (✆/fax 01856-811320; email sales1esp@aol.com, www.houtonbaylodge.com). Four-star, double or twin room £25 a person, single room £35. Evening meals available.

Westrow Lodge: Mrs K Bichan, Orphir KW17 2RD (✆01856-811360; fax 01856-811737; email k2bichan@aol.com; www.rovingeye.co.uk). Four-star modern purpose built Norwegian-style timber house situated halfway between Kirkwall and Stromness, views over Scapa Flow. Two en suite bedrooms on the first floor, sitting room. No pets. From £28 a night.

Self-Catering

Buxa Farm Chalets: Mrs K Bichan, Orphir KW17 2RD (✆01856-811360; fax 01856-811737; email k2bichan@aol.com; www.rovingeye.co.uk). Three, four-star two-bedroom chalets on 20 acres of waterfront property with stunning panoramic views of Scapa Flow and the Hills of Hoy. No pets, from £275 to £450 a week.

Ms S Garson: Heatherlea, Houton, Orphir KW17 2RE (✆01856-811251; email shona-garson@supanet.com). Three-star semi-detached house, close to South Isles ferry terminal. Ample parking. Three bedrooms, sleeps six. From £150 to £350 a week.

Lochland Chalets: Mrs Phyllis Norquoy, Bigging, Dounby KW17 2HR (✆01856-771340; fax 01856-771741; email enquiries@lochlandchalets.co.uk; www.lochlandchalets.co.uk). Three-star, four modern chalets, two miles from village. Own bird hide. Assisted wheelchair access. From £80 to £340.

Raingoose: Mrs LF Francis, Outbrecks, Stenness KY16 3EY (✆01856-851223; email accommodation@outbreckscottages-orkney.co.uk; www.outbreckscottages-orkney.co.uk). New house with traditional features, superb views, set in own large garden area. Four-star, open all year, from £210 to £450.

Scottish Farmhouse Holidays has a 118-acre (48ha) beef farm overlooking the Bay of Ireland and islands of Hoy and Graemsay, four miles (6km) from Stromness. Home baking and cooking. To book contact *Scottish Farmhouse Holidays* (2 Barefoots Avenue, Eyemouth TD14 5DF; ✆01890-751830; fax 01890-751831; email info@scotfarmhols.co.uk; www.scotfarmhols.co.uk).

Skaill House: Mr Macrae, Sandwick KW16 3LR (✆/fax 01856-761200; email info@skaillhouse.com). Three-star, in wing of 17th-century mansion overlooking Bay of Skaill, Skara Brae close by. Open all year. Three bedrooms, sleeps six. From £300 to £400 a week.

Skerravoe Cottage: Norton, Stenness KW16 3HA (✆01856-851077; email lindsey.cradock@btinternet.com; www.voecotages-orkney.com). Three-star, refurbished cottage. Three bedrooms, sleeps eight, from £300 to £540.

Upper Nisthouse: Elaine Mackay, Stenness KW16 3HE (✆/fax 01856-761378; email upper.nisthouse@btinternet.com). Three-star, midway between Kirkwall and Stromness, double, twin and family rooms, sitting room. Closed November to March, from £18.

Hostels

Birsay Outdoor Centre: Birsay (c/o Department of Education and Recreation Services, Orkney Islands Council, School Place, Kirkwall KW15 1NY; ✆01856-875353, ext 2415; fax 01856-876327; email community-recreation@orkney.gov.uk). Three-star, recently refurbished, 30 beds. Bus ½ mile away, shop 1½ mile. Open April to September, from £11. Member of *Scottish Independent Hostels.*

EATING AND DRINKING
Stromness

Bistro 76: Orca Hotel, 76 Victoria Street, Stromness (✆01856-851803; email info@orcahotel.com; www.orcahotel.com), à la carte menu. Food served 5pm to 11pm, daily specials.

Ferry Inn: at the Stromness ferry terminal (✆01856-850280; fax 01856-851332; email adrian@ferryinn.com; www.ferryinn.com). A la carte dinners and bar meals, vegetarian dishes. Open for breakfast from 7.30am, lunch until 2pm, evening meals from 5.30pm. Early bird specials, three course meals from 5.30pm to 6.30pm. Live folk music on Wednesday from 9pm. Accommodation available.

Hamnavoe Restaurant: 35 Graham Place, Stromness (✆01856-850606). A licensed restaurant serving à la carte menu with daily specials fresh from the fishing boats. Dining room with open fire. Open Tuesday to Sunday from 6.30pm.

Julia's Café & Bistro: Opposite ferry terminal (✆01856-850904). Food served all day. Café open Monday to Saturday 9am to 5pm, Sunday 10am to 5pm. Bistro open Thursday to Sunday 6.30pm to 10pm.

Royal Hotel: 55 Victoria Street, Stromness (✆/fax 01856-850342). Serves lunches, bar meals in the *Hudson Lounge*, an à la carte menu is available in the *Haven Restaurant*.

Scapa Flow à la carte restaurant at Stromness Hotel (Victoria Street, Stromness; ✆01856-850298; fax 01856-850610; email info@stromnesshotel.com; www.stromnesshotel.com) has a reputation for friendly service and good food using the best of Orkney beef and seafood. Also a daily specials board. Open for lunches and evening meals every day from midday to 2pm, and 6pm to 9pm. Vegetarian dishes.

If a Neolithic-size bere bannock is too much to tackle first off, *Argo's Bakery* at 50 Victoria Street, Stromness (✆01856-850245; fax 01856-851264; email sales@argosbakery.co.uk) makes Orkney Bere Biscuits which can be an addictive introduction to the distinctive taste of this ancient form of barley. You can also try the bere and white flour bread and rolls for a lighter bere taste.

Further Afield

Barony Hotel: Birsay (✆01856-721327; email info@baronyhotel.com; www.baronyhotel.com). Views of Boardhouse Loch, fine Orkney beef, fish and shellfish from à la carte menu served in the *Hampshire* lounge and restaurant. Vegetarian and diabetic meals.

Plout Kirn Restaurant: Smithfield Hotel, Dounby (✆01856-771215; email smithfield.hotel@virgin.net; www.smithfieldhotel.co.uk). Comprehensive menu using local produce. Morning coffees and afternoon teas. Special diets on request. Suitable for disabled. Open for lunch 12.30pm to 2pm, evening Friday and Saturday 7pm to 9pm, Sunday 6.30pm to 8.30pm.

Standing Stones Hotel: Stenness (✆01856-850449; email standingstones@sol.co.uk; www.standingstoneshotel.co.uk). Dinner à la carte and table d' hôte, licensed. Vegetarian and diabetic meals available. Local produce. Bookings preferred. Bar meals served from 5pm to 9pm. Suitable for disabled.

Woodwick House: Evie (✆01856-751330; fax 01856-751383; email mail@woodwickhouse.co.uk; www.woodwickhouse.co.uk), set in woodland, candlelit dinner. Fresh seafood, Orkney beef and lamb and locally grown vegetables. Open fires. Fully licensed. Book in advance.

SPORT AND RECREATION

Walking

The following are a few of the easy walks recommended by the Tourist Office:

Binscarth. A stretch of the old drover's road, close to Finstown village. Binscarth's 7½-acre (2.9ha) wood planted last century is the site of Orkney's largest rookery. Park at Finstown.

Bu to Breck. Starting at the Orkneyinga Saga Centre at Orphir this 2-mile (3.2km) circular walk is a must for wildlife enthusiasts and students of the Viking occupation. Park at the Centre, or at Breck.

Marwick. Circular 2.4-mile (3.9km) coastal footpath walk to Kitchener's Memorial. From April to August in the RSPB reserve the 'seabird city' on Marwick cliffs is a memorable sight. Park at Marwick Bay or Midcomloquoy.

Stromness to Warebeth. Easy 1.9-mile (3km) walk along coastal footpath; area of beach internationally known for fossil fish beds; important area in defence of Scapa Flow, with coastal batteries. Walk from the town or park at Warebeth.

Swartland Drover's Road. A stretch of the former Birsay-Kirkwall road, this pleasant 1.9-mile (3.1km) walk takes you through some of the richest bird wetlands in Orkney. Look for curlews, meadow pipits and views over sparkling lochs. Botanically rich trackside.

Wideford Hill. A short 1.2-mile (2km) walk from car park to a chambered cairn, an impressive Neolithic communal tomb dating from 3000BC on an artificial platform; access to interior. Park at Wideford Hall.

Diving

Shipwrecks of many nations and of all ages lie around virtually every island in the archipelago, the majority of them unidentified. Many of the ones that are known have registered owners. Check with the Orkney Islands Council, which also issues permits to dive in certain areas, including Scapa Flow. This red tape is dealt with by the dive operator you use. Souvenir hunting is forbidden.

CLARET AND PORRIDGE

Wrecks were once regarded with indifference by islanders and, in some cases, even welcomed for the bounty they provided. Robert Stevenson, the great British lighthouse engineer, wrote of an Orkney island that he had 'actually seen a park paled round chiefly with cedar-wood and mahogany from the wreck of a Honduras-bound ship, and in one island, after the wreck of a ship laden with wine, the inhabitants have been known to take claret to their barley-meal porridge.' During the various wars with France, the English Channel was a dangerous place for ships sailing the Atlantic, and vessels often chose the northern route around Orkney and Shetland instead. This put them in peril from natural hazards, which resulted in Orkney winding up with 11 major lighthouses, far more than any other single area of Scotland. The last was built on the island of Copinsay in 1915, 127 years after the first Stevenson light was first lit on North Ronaldsay.

The waters of Scapa Flow have provided a safe haven for ships from the times of the Vikings – who called it *Skalpeid-floi*, or 'Bay of the Long Valley Isthmus' – to the present day. Among divers the Flow is famed for the wrecks strewn across its even bottom of mud and sand in depths of around 66–151ft (20–46m). Lack of strong currents and the Flow's natural shelter means that it can be safely dived in a wide range of weather conditions. The diving season is usually from mid-March to late October/November. Best shore dives around Scapa Flow are on the wrecks of the Churchill Barrier blockships, which lie in shallow water within easy swimming distance from the shore. This makes them ideal for 'try a dive' visitors, as training sites for the novice, or for those inexperienced with drysuit diving.

Most of the dive shops and centres catering for the 20,000 who dive here every year are concentrated in Stromness, although there are a couple in South Ronaldsay. About 15 dive boats are available to visiting divers. Look for a dive company which is a member of the Orkney Dive Boat Operators' Association (5 Ness Road, Stromness; ℭ01856-850879; email bon@mvhalton.co.uk; www.odboa.co.uk):

The Diving Cellar: Leigh Caldwell or Dougie Snape, 4 Victoria Street, Stromness KW16 3AA (ℭ01856-850055; fax 01856-850395; email leigh@divescapaflow.co.uk; www.divescapaflow.co.uk). Fully equipped diving centre, boat charters with diving from a 65ft (20m) hard boat. Accommodation in two adjoining houses in Stromness centre with rooms sleeping 12 comfortably. Dry, semi-dry and wetsuits and full diving equipment can be hired. Most diving weeks run from Saturday to Saturday, with diving beginning on Sunday. Package of diving, accommodation and use of a minibus from £320 per diver. The Diving Cellar is closed in winter, but if you need anything from the shop you can call Maureen (01856-850967).

Halton Charters: Bob Anderson, 3 Ness Road, Stromness KW16 3DL (ℭ01856-851532; email bob@mvhalton.co.uk; www.mvhalton.co.uk). Day or liveaboard diving charters in Scapa Flow on the 70ft (21m) *MV Halton*.

MV Valkyrie: Hazel Weaver, Northfield, Holm KW17 2RZ (ℭ01856-781769; email hazel@mv-valkyrie.co.uk; www.mv-valkyrie.co.uk). A dedicated dive charter boat with luxurious accommodation. Compressor on board, cylinders supplied, and Nitrox available. Six days diving package. Accommodation in six twin-berth cabins, catering options. Diving in Orkney, Fair Isle and Shetland. The UK's only all-female-crewed live-aboard. Workboat charters, tours of the islands and fishing trips also undertaken.

Scapa Flow Charters: Andy Cuthbertson or Ingrid Thomas, 5 Church Road, Stromness KW16 3BA (ℭ/fax 01856-850879; email enquiry@jeanelaine.co.uk; www.jeanelaine. co.uk). Dayboat and liveaboard charters in Scapa Flow and Orkney's North Isles with onboard dive facilities. Fully equipped 70ft (21m) hardboat *MV Jean Elaine*, 68ft (21m) *MV*

Sharon Rose. Both boats have berths for up to 12 divers. Prices start from £1,700 for a full group or £240 on an individual basis. Dive charters to Shetland, Fair Isle and Sule Stack are also available. Also cater for trimix/rebreathers divers.

Scapa Flow Diving Centre: Dave Wombwell, Waterview Cottage, Burray, South Ronaldsay KW17 2SS (✆01856-731566; email d.wombwell@btopenworld.com; www.scapaflow-divingcentre.com). For novice or experienced divers, onboard the 63ft (19m) *MV Crusader*. Fully-fitted galley, two below-deck heated saloons, a wet change area on deck, toilet facilities, onboard Nitrox compressors and O2 clean cylinders.

Scapa Flow Diving Holidays: Ian and Fiona Trumpess, Lerquoy, Outertown, Stromness KW16 3JP (✆01856-851110; email ian@scapa-flow.co.uk; www.scapa-flow.co.uk). Dives from *MV Invincible*, fully equipped, full central heating and luxury lounge bar.

Scapa Flow Technical: John Thornton, Polrudden, Peerie Sea Loan, Kirkwall KW15 1UH (✆01856-874761; email john@scapaflow.com; www.scapaflow.com.) Guided dives in Scapa Flow, instructor training, on board *MV Karin*.

Scapa Scuba: Ben and Sara Wade, Lifeboat House, Dundas Street, Stromness KW16 3DA (✆/fax 01856-851218; email diving@scapascuba.co.uk; www.scapascuba.co.uk). Offers a full range of PADI courses, including specialities in wreck, deep, and dry suit diving. Guided shore and boat dives in Scapa Flow are run daily. IANTD and TDI nitrox diving courses also available. If you are a beginner you can do a 'try a dive' at the Churchill Barrier Blockships wrecks. The cost is £60 per person. The full Open Water Diver Course is £395. Equipment hire, manufacture and repair of neoprene dry suits, and a well stocked dive shop.

Stromness Diving Centre: Steve Mowat, Barkland, Cairston Drive, Stromness KW16 3JL (✆/fax 01856-850624; email steve@triton.force9.co.uk; www.orknet.co.uk/scapa/triton. htm). Diving charters aboard 58ft (18m) *MV Triton*, fully equipped and professionally converted MFV. Heated changing room, a six-berth cabin and storage hold. Facilities provided free of charge include air, weights, and cylinders (if required). Onboard and shore compressors. Nitrox carried on board. Main dive site is 40 minutes' steaming from Stromness. Two deep dives a day are possible.

Sunrise Charters: Dougie Leask, Carradale, Weyland Bay, Kirkwall KW15 1TD (✆01856-874425; email dougie@sunrisecharters.co.uk; www.sunrisecharters.co.uk). Diving holidays aboard the self-contained 70ft (21m) live-aboard diveboat *Sunrise*. Nitrix and Trimix available.

Fishing

The **best trout lochs** are reached most conveniently from Stromness. They include the lochs of Stenness, 2½ miles (4km) distant; Harray, 5 miles (8km); Boardhouse, 11 miles (18km); Hundland, 13 miles (21km); Swanney, 15 miles (24km); Isbister, 10 miles (16km); Kirbister, 10 miles (16km); Skaill, 7 miles (11km); and Yelda, close to town. The Loch of Stenness is regarded as one of the best fishing lochs in the whole of Scotland and has given up some monsters. In March 1889, a trout weighing 29½lb (13.4kg) was caught, the second largest trout ever caught in Britain. The popular Loch of Harray, Orkney's largest loch, also holds some enormous fish. In 1966, it yielded a brown trout of 17lb (7.8kg).

In August and September sea trout are plentiful in Loch Stenness and fish of up to 10lb (4.5kg) can be caught on fly, although the more usual weight is 4–6lb (1.8–2.7kg). Trout from Boardhouse Loch, Birsay, average ¾lb (340g) and heavy baskets of up to 12 are regularly taken. The Kirbuster burn joins Boardhouse to Loch Hundland, where fish average around 1lb (453g). Loch Swannay is a favourite spot and baskets of 8–10 trout averaging more than 1lb (453g) are not uncommon, with occasional specimens of 2–3lb (907g–1.4kg). May, June and early July are the best times to fish.

One of Orkney's leading fishing tackle specialists is *WS Sinclair:* 25–27 John Street, Stromness (✆01856-850469). You can join the *Orkney Trout Fishing Association* here. He also lets two self-catering holiday flats.

Boat fishing is best at all the larger lochs.

Boat Hire

Barony Hotel: Birsay (✆01856-721327), Boardhouse loch.
Mr Breck: Belmont Cottage, Swannay (✆01856-721281), Swannay loch.
Stanley Esslemont: Dalmahoy, Sandwick (✆01856-771366), Harray loch.
W.M. Hay: Cursiter Cottage, Twatt (✆01856-841722), Boardhouse loch.
Mr Hourston: Mucklehouse, Swannay (✆01856-721274), Hundland loch.
Merkister Hotel: Harray (✆01856-771366; email merkister-hotel.@ecosse.net), Harray loch.
Angus Muir: ✆01857-600331, North loch.
Standing Stones Hotel: Stenness (✆01856-850449), Stenness loch.
Wings n' Things Unlimited: Graham Adamson, 25 Alfred Terrace, Stromness KW16 3DF (✆01856-850526; www.wingsandthings.co.uk). You can hire a boat with a ghillie, equipment included. Accommodation is also available.

Boat Charters

Out West Charters: Hoymansquoy, Stromness (✆01856-850621; email info@outwestcharters. co.uk; www.outwestcharters.co.uk). Sea-angling charters available all year, weather permitting. Four-hour or full-day trips. Maximum of eight anglers at one time. Rod and reels can be hired for £5.

Golf

Stromness Golf Club: Golf House, Ness, Stromness (✆01856-850772; email enquiries@ stromnessgc.co.uk; www.stromnessgc.co.uk). On the shores of Hoy Sound this may justly be termed the most picturesque and sporting 18-hole, 4,762-yard, par 63 course in the north of Scotland. You can even play at midnight in summer. The club is open to visitors throughout the year. Green fees £20 a day for adults, £60 weekly; £10 a day for juniors. No bookings necessary. Clubs available for hire, Monday to Friday. There is also a bowling green at the club.

Shooting

Light shooting has resulted in increased numbers of greylag and pink-footed geese to pro-vide wildfowlers with some spectacular flights. Shooting is organised and run by Graham Adamson, BASC-registered goose guide for Wings n' Things. Parties of up to six guns are usual and shooting is limited to one hour before and two hours after sunrise, with one hour after sunset for ducks. A bag limit of four geese per gun/flight and five ducks per gun/flight is imposed and lead-free shot is preferred for both geese and ducks. Gun dogs are welcome and kennelling facilities are available. Contact *Wings n' Things* (25 Alfred Terrace, Strom-ness KW16 3DF; ✆01856-850526; www.wingsandthings.co.uk).

SHOPPING

The following are all on the signposted **Orkney Craft Trail**:

Appie's Tea Room and Photo-Art Gallery: Pam Farmer, Lower Appiehouse, Sandwick KW16 3JD (✆/fax 01856-841562; email insights@pamfarmer.freeserve.co.uk; www.pamfarmer. co.uk). Gallery of contemporary and traditional photographic art along with modern tea room serving simple, healthy, home-made and Orkney produce. Open daily 11am to 7pm (last orders 6pm) from April to October, bookings recommended.
Belgarth Bodhrans: Eoin and Jane Leonard, Belgarth, Kirbuster, Stromness KW16 3HU (✆/ fax 01856-850127; email bodhrans@belgarth.com; www.belgarth.com). Goatskin drums, frame decoration inspired by the history and landscape of Orkney. Also turned wooden bowls decorated with runic inscriptions. Open April to September, 2pm to 5pm, or by appointment.
Fursbreck Pottery: Andrew Appleby, Harray KW17 2JD (✆/fax 01856-771419; email harraypotter@applepot.co.uk; www.applepot.co.uk). Hand-thrown pottery recreated in Orkney's Neolithic Unstan and Grooved wares, and Roman designs, shapes and finishes. Open end March to October from 10am to 6pm Monday to Saturday, and Sunday afternoon.

Island Design: Wendy Baikie, Studio Workshop at The Leigh, Stenness KW16 3HA (✆/fax 01856-850252; email baikiepics@aol.com; www.orkneydesignercrafts.com). Hand-printed textiles made up into fashion accessories and soft furnishings inspired by traditional themes. Open May–September, Monday to Saturday from 11am to 5pm.

Orkneyinga Silversmiths: Kevin and Elizabeth Allen, Holland Cottage, Marwick, Birsay KW17 2NB (✆01856-721359; email orkneyinga@talk21.com; www.orkneyinga.co.uk). Hand-made jewellery and silverware, and a separate range of designer jewellery, including gold and silver rings. Open Easter to mid-September, Tuesday to Saturday 10am to 5pm. October to Easter visits by appointment.

Stewart Moar Jewellery: Stewart Moar, Cot of Stoursdale, Stenness (✆/fax 01856-761758; email stewart@stewartmoarjewellery.co.uk; www.stewartmoarjewellery.co.uk). Produces a range of Scottish, Celtic, and Norse jewellery in a three dimensional sculptural look. Open all year, Monday to Saturday, 10am to 4pm.

The Woolshed: Benlaw, Costa, Evie KW17 2NN (✆/fax 01856-751305; email woolshed@ lineone.net; www.orkneydesignercrafts.com). A craft workshop producing traditional knitwear, hand-knitting yarn, hand-made felt goods and woven throws all in North Ronaldsay wool. Patterns and designs reflecting Orkney's heritage. Also sheepskin rugs. Open April to October, Monday to Saturday midday to 6pm. Other times by arrangement.

Other arts and crafts outlets include:

Hrossey Silver: Crumbrecks, Petertown Road, Orphir KW17 2RE (✆/fax 01856-811347). Silversmith making one-off pieces of jewellery and silverware inspired by Stone Age cave drawings, Dark Age European, as well as local ancient monuments, flora and fauna.

Hundland Gallery: Old School, Swannay, Evie KW17 2NR (✆01856-721307). Workshop-gallery displays arts and crafts. Open Easter to September, Tuesday to Sunday 2pm to 5pm. Other times by arrangement. Admission free.

Pier Arts Centre: Victoria Street, Stromness KW16 3AA (✆01856-850209; fax 01856-851462; email info@pierartscentre.com). Collection of 20th-century British art and changing exhibitions of local, national and international art. Open Monday to Saturday 10.30am to 5pm.

Selkie Clarsachs: 3 Alfred Street, Stromness KW16 3DF (✆01856-851485; email harps@shiner. co.uk; www.selkieharps.co.uk). Designs and manufactures string harps, instrument repairs.

Yellowbird Gallery: Chocolate Cottage, Birsay (✆/fax 01856-721360; email info@ yelowbirdgallery.org; www.yellowbirdgallery.org). Paintings and drawings of Orkney birds and landscape, wood and ceramics.

HELP AND INFORMATION

Stromness Tourist Information Centre: Ferry Terminal Building, Pier Head, Stromness KW16 1BH (✆01856-850716; fax 01856-850777; email stromness@visitorkney.com). Open April to May, Monday to Friday 8am to 4pm, Saturday 10am to 3pm; May to end-August, Monday to Friday 8am to 5pm, Saturday and Sunday 10am to 3pm; end-August to October, Monday to Friday 8am to 3pm, Saturday 1pm to 3pm; and October to April, Monday to Friday 1pm to 3pm.

Stromness Library: Dundas Street, Stromness (✆01856-850907). Free internet access. Open Monday to Thursday 2pm to 7pm, Friday 2pm to 5pm, Saturday 10am to 5pm.

Royal Society for the Protection of Birds (RSPB): 12–14 North End Road, Stromness KW16 3AG (✆01856-850176; fax 01856-851311; email orkney@rspb.org.uk; www.rspb.org.uk). The *ferry terminal* is open Monday to Thursday 3am to 4.15am, 7.30am to 5pm, 8.30pm to 11pm; Friday 3am to 4.15am, 7.30am to 5pm; Saturday 7.30am to 5pm; and Sunday 7.30am to 5.30pm, 8.30pm to 11pm.

Police Station: North End Road, Stromness (✆01856-850222).

Bank of Scotland: 99 Victoria Street, Stromness (✆01856-850238). Open Monday, Tuesday, Thursday and Friday 9.45am to 12.30pm, and 1.30pm to 4.45pm; Wednesday 10am to 12.30pm and 1.30pm to 4.45pm.

Royal Bank of Scotland: 3 Victoria Street, Stromness (✆01856-850217). Open Monday to Friday 9.15am to 12.30pm and 1.30pm to 4.45pm.

Stromness Swimming Pool & Fitness Centre: North End Road (✆01856-850552).

Stromness Squash Club: Orkney Sports (✆01856-850665), visitors welcome.

Orkney Fisherman's Society: ✆01856-850375.

Left luggage facility available at *Stromness Car Hire and Taxis:* ✆01856-850973.

South Isles

HOY

If you like wild Scottish Highlands-type terrain you'll love Hoy. The biggest of the 70 or so Orkney islands after the Orkney Mainland itself, it's also the highest, wettest and most rugged. Looking across from the Mainland, the twin humps of **Cuilags** at 1,421ft (433m) and Orkney's highest peak, **Ward Hill**, reaching up to 1,570ft (479m), dominate the skyline of Hoy, which is why the Vikings called it High Island, *Haey* in Norse. The mass of contour lines on an Ordnance Survey map of Hoy indicate that most of its low ground is along its coastal fringe, although fertile South Walls is flatter and holds most of Hoy's 450 people. With nearly 10,000 acres (4,047ha) the **RSPB Hoy Nature Reserve** covers nearly all the uncultivated land in North Hoy and almost a third of the island's entire area. It encompasses a spectacularly scenic area of moorland and about 4 miles (6km) of unbroken sea cliffs. The reserve is always open. There is no admission charge. For more information contact *RSPB Hoy Nature Reserve* (Ley House, Hoy KW16 3NJ; ✆01856-791298).

Hoy's hill walks are regarded as the best in Orkney. All the main hills are in the northern part of the island. There are distinct ranges, starting with the Cuilags, which begin at the **Kame of Hoy** and include all the cliffs to the north and west of Rackwick Bay, terminating in the perpendicular cliff of Black Nev, overlooking the village of Rackwick. The landward part of the range overlooks the Vale of Hoy and has four outstanding spurs – High Fea, Grut Fea, Clicknafea and Moor Fea – separated by deep glens. The glen of Berriedale is notable for its native woodland and a burn full of brown trout. **Ward Hill** is easily climbed. From its flat grassy summit every island in Orkney can be seen except for the nearest, Rysa Little. The view from the top is unsurpassed on a clear day and with a pair of binoculars you can pick out prominent landmarks as far north as Sumburgh Head, in Shetland, as far south as Kinnaird Head, and as far west as Cape Wrath. Ward Hill is a single hill that, seen from different angles, gives you the impression you are looking at three different hills. Between the spur of Haist on the south-east side and Ward Hill proper lies the dark, forbidding corrie of the **Nowt Bield**, or the 'Fold of the Oxen.' On the slope immediately above are two huge rocks which popular legend says were once the lair of a bogeyman, or giant, who waylaid lone travellers. Another legend concerns a great red carbuncle said to be sometimes seen glowing on the north slopes of Ward Hill. Sir Walter Scott refers to this in his novel *The Pirate*, saying that around midnight between May and July something visible from a long way off shines and sparkles in the dark. Scott adds, 'though many have climbed the hill, and attempted to search for it, yet they could find nothing.' On the opposite side of Ward Hill is the huge, awesome hollow of the Red Glen.

Further south are a scattering of hills similar to those in the north, but all slashed by even gloomier ravines. The highest of these is the **Knap of Trowieglen** at 1,309ft (399m), which runs down the **Dwarfie Hamars**. At the base of this natural amphitheatre of low cliffs lies one of Hoy's prehistoric marvels, the huge block of stone the Norsemen called *Dvergasteinn*, or the Dwarfie Stane.

The Dwarfie Stane

In Norse mythology dwarfs were skilled blacksmiths who liked to live in hollow boulders and this certainly fits the description of the hollowed-out 29ft (8.8m) long monolith lying here in the heather. It is, however, Hoy's only chambered tomb and the only example in Britain of a burial place cut entirely into natural rock. It dates from around 3,000BC. The entrance is a hole just big enough to crawl through to the tiny cells on either side. The laborious work must have taken untold hours to complete and the marks of the chisel can still be seen.

An eccentric Indian Army major carved his name in Latin backwards on the tomb – YESNVOM SVMLEILVG AD1850. Underneath it Major Mounsey inscribed a verse in elegant

Persian script, which translates as: *Oh God: I am pierced to the heart, and very sorrowful, I wake all night, and study and learn patience.* This is thought to refer to the voracious Hoy midges that tormented him during the several nights he slept in the tomb. Major Mounsey is remembered in local lore as a strange-looking bearded figure in curly-toed yellow Persian slippers. Other names on the tomb go back to H Rossie in 1735.

Scottish traveller Martin Martin was here even before that and summed up: 'At one of the ends within this stone there is cut out a bed and pillow capable of two persons to lie in, at the other opposite end there is a void space cut out resembling a bed, and above both these there is a large hole which is supposed was a vent for smoke. The common tradition is that a giant and his wife made this their place of retreat.' The tomb was once sealed by the blocking stone lying in front of the entrance. As it is too big to fit the entrance there is doubt that the Dwarfie Stane was ever actually used as a tomb and some archaeologists believe it is simply the work of a Neolithic eccentric.

Not far south is another unusually large stone known as the **Patrick Stane**, which has several faint cup-and-ring markings on its upper surface. The 600-yard (550m) walk from the road to the Dwarfie Stane is boggy, but there's a boardwalk most of the way.

The valley road west takes you to **Rackwick**, a virtually deserted old crofting hamlet lying on a bay between steep cliffs and heather-clad hills and considered to be one of the most secluded and beautiful places in Orkney. In the 18th century it was the busy centre of a cod and herring fishery. There's an impressive beach full of boulders which roar when rough seas roll them around. In the cliffs above the Bay of Rackwick is a stone archway known as the **Aul' Wife o' the Enegars**. It stands about 200ft (60m) above the beach, a huge perpendicular rock about 50ft (15m) high and 40ft (12m) broad. South are the grassy slopes of **the Sneuk** where Rackwick villagers once caught young shearwaters for food. They were said to be a trifle on the fatty side, but boiled with cabbage were a dish fit for an epicure. On Rora Head, Orkney's most westerly point, are a dozen small, circular mounds which are probably burial mounds.

The Old Man of Hoy

From Rackwick you can take a clearly signed cliff-top path that will bring you to the symbol of the island – the towering sandstone sea stack of the **Old Man of Hoy**. The 450ft (137m) stack is Orkney's most famous landmark and if you arrive in Orkney by ferry across the Pentland Firth this is the unmistakable rock tower that looms as you approach. The walk from Rackwick to the stack is a leisurely three-hour round trip; the stack ascent is for experienced super-climbers only, and even these are warned that there is neither suitable rescue equipment nor experienced rock climbers in the vicinity to help them if they get into difficulties. The stack was first climbed in 1966 and then re-climbed the same year for television viewers.

Walk further and you come to magnificent **St John's Head**, the highest perpendicular sea cliff in Britain, rising a sheer 1,136ft (346m) above a rocky beach. The first direct ascent was a televised assault made in 1969, followed in 1970 by two climbers who took two days to get down and then five days to climb back to the top, sleeping in suspended hammocks on the way up. Past the Kame of Hoy is the high mound covering the remains of the **Broch of Braebister** built 2,000 years ago on a promontory which gave protection to this Iron Age fort. The base of the headland is a maze of caverns and sea stacks with deep water right to the cliff face. When the sea is calm, small boats can sail quite a distance into some of the caves. From here it's a short walk down to Hoy Village, with its Outdoor Centre and the Moaness jetty.

The Scapa Flow side of Hoy is the area that saw most of the action during two World Wars. A prime attraction is near the terminal used by the Ro-Ro ferry from Houton. This is the **Scapa Flow Visitor Centre & Museum** (©01856-791300), which is housed in the former oil pumping station of the Lyness Naval Base. This was used as a base in both World Wars before closing in 1956. In front of the Centre are various guns and the propeller and shaft of *HMS Hampshire*, which sank off Marwick Head in 1916 with the loss of 653 men. The manganese bronze prop and shaft, weighing about 35 tons, were salvaged in 1985. Inside the Centre are displays of artefacts, photos, and memorabilia from both World Wars, with models of the interned German Fleet before its scuttling in 1919, and a video room with films showing rare footage. A World War II oil storage tank displays artefacts and there is an underground air-raid shelter as well as a cafeteria and a souvenir shop. The Centre is open all year. There's no admission charge. At **Lyness Naval Cemetery** are the graves of those who died while serving, among them men who perished at the Battle of Jutland (1916); in *HMS Hampshire* (1916); in the explosion of *HMS Vanguard* off Flotta (1917); in and *HMS Royal Oak*, torpedoed in Scapa Flow (1939). Also buried here are two of the first three German airmen brought down on British soil during World War II. Their plane was shot down and crashed on Hoy at Pegal Burn. On the headlands of Crockness and Hackness are relics of a still earlier war, two **Martello Towers** built between 1813 and 1815 to guard the harbour in the spacious Bay of Longhope, where ships collected while waiting to leave in convoy during the Napoleonic war. The towers were never needed, although they were used again in World War I. The Hackness Martello Tower was restored in the early 1970s and is now open to the public.

Melsetter House is largely the work of the famous English Arts and Crafts architect William Lethaby who in 1898 incorporated the original 1738 building into his plan for this striking country house. The house was once the residence of the Moodie family, which owned most of Walls parish from the late 16th century until 1820. It has one of the finest old walled gardens in Orkney. Visits by appointment, Thursday, Saturday and Sunday (✆01856-791352).

The main road to the South Walls area goes over an *ayre*, a narrow isthmus which separates the North Bay of Longhope from Aith Hope. This was once a stretch of reef and rocks which silted up enough over the years to carry the present causeway. **Osmondwall** on the inlet of Kirk Hope was a favourite Viking anchorage and it was here in 995 that pagan Jarl Sigurd the Stout was ordered by King Olaf Tryggvason of Norway to choose between the Christian faith or death (Sigurd chose baptism). The Kirk Hope burial ground is dominated by the **Longhope Lifeboat Memorial**, the bronze figure of a lone lifeboatman, erected in honour of the eight-man crew of the *TGB* which was lost with all hands on 17 March 1969 while going to the rescue of a Liberian freighter in appalling seas in the Pentland Firth – known to generations of trawlermen as 'Hell's Gate'. The men were from the **Longhope Lifeboat Station** at Brims in South Walls, which opened in 1834 and has a proud record of more than 500 lives saved. The current lifeboat is at Longhope Pier. **Cantick Head Lighthouse**, built by David Stevenson in 1858, marks the southern entrance to Scapa Flow. Nearby is the **Green Hill of Hesti Geo** a large green mound containing an unusually large broch. There are two interesting gloups close by.

THE LADY OF HOY

On the south side of the Water of Hoy, roughly halfway between Lyness and Moaness ferry piers, is a railed-in enclosure with a solitary headstone that is probably the most isolated but most visited grave in Orkney. This is the unhallowed resting place of 27-year-old Betty Corrigall, who committed suicide in the late 1770s after her lover went off whaling, leaving her pregnant. She first tried to end her life by drowning herself in the sea. When this was unsuccessful, she hanged herself in a barn. As a suicide she could not be buried in consecrated ground. The lairds of Hoy and Melsetter also refused to have her interred on their estates, so she was buried in an unmarked grave on unconsecrated moorland at the parish border and forgotten. In the late 1930s, two youngsters digging for peat came across a wooden box, in it the body of Betty Corrigall in a remarkable state of preservation, with her long dark hair still cascading round her shoulders. Her remains were re-buried and lay undisturbed until the outbreak of World War II, when a military working party digging in the peat to erect telegraph poles for a searchlight unit also found the coffin. From then on newly arrived servicemen had the macabre habit of digging up the coffin to view the body. Continual exposure to the air quickly caused Betty Corrigall's remains to deteriorate and officers eventually had her grave moved to its present site and placed a heavy concrete slab on top of the coffin. On the seaward side of Betty Corrigall's grave is the Scad Head Viewpoint, *where you get a wonderful panoramic view of Scapa Flow and the Orkney Mainland.*

FLORA AND FAUNA

Flora

Botanists say that North Hoy and its tailpiece South Walls are host to some of the most varied plantlife in Orkney. Conditions on the uplands of North Hoy and the island's northern latitude have given rise to a plant community that's normally found only in higher mountainous areas. More than 250 different mosses grow here, along with **white heather** and arctic-alpine species such as **yellow mountain** and **purple saxifrage**, **alpine meadow rue** and **sea-wort**, all of them flourishing at much lower altitudes than on mainland Scotland because of their exposure to severe conditions. On the tops, wet heath is dominated by heather and **deer grass** with montane dwarf shrub heath rising to a sub-arctic habitat on the highest ground. According to some geologists, the hilltops of Hoy were once part of a vast plateau, extending across the Pentland Firth, southward into Caithness and Sutherland. A general lack of grazing has encouraged indigenous tree growth and in the sheltered valley of **Berridale** you'll find Orkney's only surviving native woodland of **aspen**, **birch**, **willow** and **rowan**.

Common blue and **large heath butterflies** are frequent flutters and the Berriedale woodland is the most northerly British location for some 19 species of **moth**. Seven species of **dragonflies** and **damselflies** occur on the RSPB's North Hoy Nature Reserve, four of which are found nowhere else in Orkney.

Fauna

The fauna of Hoy is fairly limited. **Rabbits** and **brown hares** abound and there are numerous and conspicuous **mountain hares** whose coats turn white in winter whether or not there's snow. The abundance of mountain hares is probably explained by the fact that there are no predators. **Otters** are common along the Scapa Flow coastline and are also found in the vicinity of freshwater lochs and hill tarns. They tend to be wary and difficult to spot, although they have been seen in Rackwick Burn. The little Orkney vole has not yet made it to Hoy, although **hedgehogs** are spreading in the island, which bodes ill for the eggs of ground-nesting birds. **Seals** can be seen hauled out on sandy beaches and skerries and in summer you might spot an occasional **dolphin** or **porpoise**.

Bird-watching

Commonest seabirds are **fulmars** along with clouds of **guillemots** and **kittiwakes** and smaller numbers of **razorbills**, **shags** and **herring gulls**. **Puffins** nest in large numbers in May and June, to the south of the reserve at the Burn of Forse on the Atlantic coast is a large colony of **great black-backed gulls**. Another large colony can be seen near the Loch of Stourdale on the way from Rackwick to the Old Man of Hoy. There is also at least one small colony of **Manx shearwaters**. There are close to 2,000 pairs of **great skuas** on Hoy but the colony of **Arctic skuas** has declined drastically in recent years.

Lack of prey species, especially the Orkney vole, means that **hen harriers** and **short-eared owls** are scarce, although there are **peregrines**, **merlin**, **kestrels**, several pairs of **ravens**, and up to three pairs of **buzzards**. Breeding waders include the **golden plover**, **snipe**, **curlew**, and **dunlin**, while **red-throated divers** breed on the hill lochans, and smaller species such as **wheatears**, **twites** and **stonechats** can be seen on the moors.

GETTING THERE

The ferry *MV Graemsay* (73 passengers) carries foot passengers and bicycles only from Stromness to Moaness Pier, North Hoy, seven days a week in summer, week days in winter. The crossing takes about 25 minutes. All enquiries must be made through Steve Mowatt (✆01856-850624).

There is also a Ro-Ro ferry, the *MV Hoy Head* (125 passengers and 16 cars) to Lyness from the Houton ferry terminal in Orphir from Monday to Sunday which takes 35 minutes. The first ferry leaves at 8am, then 10.15am, 11.45am, 1.20pm, 3.15pm and 5.30pm Monday to Friday; 9.50am, 2.15pm, and 4.15pm on Saturday; and 9am or 9.45am, and 4.50pm or

7pm on Sunday. The return adult fare is £6.60, cars and mobile homes £19.70, motorcycles £13, and bicycles £1.60 return. All bookings should be made at the Houton Terminal (✆01856-811397; fax 01856-811701; email info@orkneyferries.co.uk).

Vehicle and passenger tickets are issued by the purser and paid for on board the ferry. Purser takes cash or cheques or pre-paid vouchers. Pre-paid vouchers can be obtained in advance from the Ticketing and Booking Office at the terminal, no later than 15 minutes before sailing.

GETTING AROUND

Bu Farm: Mr T.Thomson (✆01856-791263). Minibus and taxi.

Glen Rackwick: Mr J. Rendall (✆01856-791262). Taxis.

North Hoy Transport: Albert and Fay Clark, Quoydale (✆01856-791315; fax 01856-791001; email quoydale@supanet.com). Taxi, minibus, and island tours.

Cycle Hire: Greenhill, Whaness, North Hoy (✆01856-791225). Mountain bikes for hire at Moaness Pier, Hoy, from £7 a day; 24 hour or weekly hire available. Free helmets. Seven-day service.

Tour Operators

Arthur and Louise Budge: Upper Settir, Lyness KW16 3NY (✆01856-791234; email uppersettir@freeuk.com). Operate tours around Hoy for private groups. They speak Dutch and German.

Hills of Hoy: Billy Hill, Halyel Garage, Lyness, Hoy KW16 3NY (✆01856-791240; email hillsofhoy@btopenworld.com). Minibus tours, taxi service. Island tours by arrangement. Seven and eight-seat minibuses, and 24-seat coach.

Hoy Ranger: RSPB Warden, Ley House, Hoy KW16 3NJ (✆/fax 01856-791298). Free guided walks every Wednesday and Friday from April to September through rich natural heritage places such as Rackwick, Ward Hill and Berriedale.

ACCOMMODATION

Hotels

Hoy Inn: North Hoy (✆01856-791313). Closest accommodation to Moaness jetty.

Stromabank Hotel: Longhope, South Walls KW16 3PA (✆01856-701611; email stromabankhotel@btconnect.com; www.stromabank.co.uk). Three-star, small family-run hotel, with four en suite bedrooms, one suitable for disabled. From £30 B&B. Evening meals available in summer months.

Bed & Breakfast

St John's Manse: Mrs Fiona Hill, Lyness KW16 3NY (✆01856-791240; fax 01856-791240). Between Lyness and Longhope. Three-star, rooms in former manse, centrally heated. From £20 a night.

Quoydale: Mrs F Clark (✆01856-791315; fax 01856-791001; email quoydale@supanet.com; www.orkneyaccommodation.co.uk). On working farm overlooking Scapa Flow. One mile from ferry. From £18.

Self-Catering

Burnhouse: Mr and Mrs Mackay (✆/fax 01856-870058; email melfea@supanet.com; www.burnhouse-selfcatering.co.uk). Three star, luxurious bungalow. Three bedrooms, sleeps five, from £300 to £500 a week.

Cantick Head Lighthouse Cottages: Christine Willers, Cantick Head Lighthouse, Longhope KW16 3PQ (✆/fax 01856-701255; email cantick@gmail.com; www.cantickhead.com). Four-star, panoramic sea views, private and secluded. Two bedrooms, sleeps three to four, from £310 to £520.

Cliffgate: Lorraine Buchan, Rackwick (✆01856-850253; email info@cliffgate.co.uk; www.cliffgate.co.uk). Four star, four bedrooms, sleeps eight. Close to reserve and beach. From £500 to £600.

Lower Rumin: Mrs Dorothy Rendall, Rackwick KW16 3NJ (✆01856-791262). Two-star stone cottage, views over Rackwick Bay, near Old Man of Hoy. One/two bedrooms, sleeps two/four. From £200 to £300.

Onedin Cottage: Mrs L. Kirkpatrick, Brims School House, Longhope KW16 3NZ (✆01856-701206; email garyhas206l@aol.com). Three-star cottage, sleeps five, all amenities. Within walking distance of shop, hotel and post office. Open all year. From £150 to £275.

Nether and *West Linksness:* Mrs F Matheson, 90 Dundas Street, Stromness KW16 3DA (✆01856-851116; email fioneil@fioneil.force9.co.uk; www.orkneycroft.co.uk). Two three-star cottages, traditional croft house with two bedrooms, sleeping four, and stone-built croft house with two bedrooms, sleeping six. Both from £350 a week in June, July, August and September; £300 a week, May to October.

Quoydale: Mrs Fay Clark, North Hoy KW16 3NJ (✆01856-791315; fax 01856-791001; email quoydale@supanet.com; www.orkneyaccommodation.co.uk). Three-star cottage on working farm, views of Scapa Flow, two bedrooms, sleeps four. All amenities plus linen. One mile (1.6km) from Moaness Pier on edge of RSPB reserve. Open all year. From £180 to £280 a week. Also B&B at £18 for double or twin, £20 for single, evening meals extra.

Snelsetter Farm: Mrs E Davidson, Longhope KW16 3PA (✆/fax 01856-701244; email snelsetterhols@btconnect.com). Three-star accommodation in 300-year-old barn, three bedrooms, sleeps six. From £150 to £400 a week.

Hostels

Hoy Centre: Moaness KW16 3NJ (c/o Orkney Islands Council's Department of Education; ✆01856-873535; fax 01856-876326; email recreation@orkney.gov.uk; www.orkney.gov. uk). Refurbished, all rooms en suite, 32 beds. Open all year, from £12. Ferry ¾ mile (1km) away, shop 10 miles (16km). Member of *Scottish Indpendent Hostels.*

Rackwick Outdoor Centre: North Hoy (c/o Orkney Islands Council's Department of Education; ✆01856-873535; fax 01856-876326; email community.recreation@orkney.gov.uk; www.orkney.gov.uk). Two-star, eight beds, pre-book only. Shop 15 miles (24km) away.Open April to September, from £945.

EATING AND DRINKING

Hoy Inn: North Hoy (✆01856-791313). Five minutes from Moaness Pier, idyllic setting for lunch. Seasonal opening times.

The RSPB Information Centre: (✆01856-791313). Has good pub grub, lunches, evening meals and bar suppers. Seasonal opening times.

Scapa Flow Visitor Centre: Lyness (✆01856-791313), has a café open in summer for hot and cold snacks.

Stromabank Hotel: (✆01856-701494). Evening meals available. Phone to book.

HELP AND INFORMATION

Scapa Flow Visitor Centre & Museum: Lyness, Hoy KW16 3NY (✆01856-791300; email museum@orkney.gov.uk). Interprets the role of Scapa Flow as the base for the British Royal Navy in the Napoleonic and both World Wars. Museum is housed in authentic wartime buildings, including an impressive audio-visual show in a huge oil tank. Open all year.

Doctor: Dr P Kettle, Health Centre, Longhope (✆01856-701209).
Nurse: Health Centre (✆01856-701224).
Lyness Post Office: (✆01856-791387).
Hoy Post Office: (✆01856-791261).
North Walls Centre: Mrs M. Besant (✆01856-791359). Swimming pool and various sports activities.

There is a shop in Longhope, *J M F Groat & Sons* (✆01856-701273), which is also a post office and where you can get petrol. Early closing on a Thursday and Saturday.

FLOTTA

Unless you are interested in oil, old naval and military installations, or are simply a curious island-bagger, it is unlikely you'll be attracted to Flotta (flat) Island in the Scapa Flow. The island is perhaps the only place in Orkney where you can see Stromness and Kirkwall at the same time and it does have a certain oddity appeal. The first European to be buried in Australia, for instance, was a Flotta man, Forbie Sutherland, a member of Cook's *Endeavour* expedition, and one of Flotta's most famous sons was island poet James Hay, who died in 1950. Hay's published works are now cherished by connoisseurs of lousy poetry written in the style of the legendary bad Scottish poet William McGonagall, the Dundee 'Ossian of the ineffably absurd' who spent some of his boyhood years just across the water from Flotta on South Ronaldsay. In *The Famous Tay Whale* McGonagall offered:

> *Then hurrah! for the mighty monster whale,*
> *Which has got seventeen feet four inches from tip to tip of a tail!*
> *Which can be seen for a sixpence or a shilling,*
> *That is to say, if the people all are willing*

A sample verse from Hay's *Roon Flotta's Isle:*

> *At Quoy o' Weddel, then to shore*
> *Where scent of ware's felt more and more;*
> *This part is called the gutter rotten,*
> *One whiff of it is ne'er forgotten.*

In 1725 came what Orcadians regard as Flotta's most sensational event. The Laird of Flotta, Sir James Stewart, murdered Captain James Moore of Melsetter, in Broad Street, Kirkwall, in broad daylight. Stewart took to his heels and fled after the crime. He stayed away from Orkney for 20 years, during which time he fought at the Battle of Culloden with Bonnie Prince Charlie's rebel army. Having survived that bloody conflict he thought it was safe to return home. The first person he saw was the son of the man he had killed, who turned him over to the authorities. The 'irascible and belligerent Jacobite' subsequently died in a London jail. From a population of around 500 in Stewart's time the number of Flotta's residents inexorably dwindled to reach its lowest point in the early 1970s, although two World Wars bumped up the population artificially during the hostilities.

At the Imperial War Museum, in London, is a remarkable photograph of a Flotta boxing match in World War I complete with 10,000 onlookers, presumably servicemen. Not until the island was chosen as the site for an oil terminal did the local economy and population pick up. The terminal became operational in December 1976 when the first crude oil arrived from the Piper platform in the North Sea and in 1977 the first oil tankers were loaded at Flotta. About 10% of Britain's oil production now passes through the island terminal, whose gas flare at the top of its 223ft (68m) stack can be seen for miles around burning off surplus methane gas. The terminal generates its own electricity and some gas is piped to an electricity sub station which generates enough power for the grid to keep Orkney supplied offpeak. Hundreds of people who work at the terminal commute by fast launch every day to the island from the Orkney Mainland.

The island bore the brunt of German air raids on Scapa Flow in World War II. Ground and ship-based anti-aircraft defences often threw up such an incredible hail of flak that the German planes turned tail, dumping their bomb loads on the nearest island, which happened to be Flotta, gateway to the Flow. Lots of derelict buildings and installations all round the island hark back to those days. Wartime relics can be found all over **Golta**, the long leg of land in the north, but access must be arranged with Flotta terminal security on arrival. Sticking out of the water between Golta and the **Calf of Flotta** are some of the hundreds of tons of anti-submarine cable dumped here at the end of World War II. A narrow channel allows boats to pass between the two islands. Around Roan Head are reminders of World War I, including part of the wall and huge fireplace of a once magnificent stone-built YMCA and **St Vincent Pier**, built by men from HMS St Vincent in 1915 and used to land personnel at the YMCA to play golf. The **Rocket Batteries** were there to protect important targets from low-flying enemy aircraft in the 1940s. They were never fired in anger. More than 130 shelters built to protect gun crews and store ammunition for the 66 rocket projectors are slowly crumbling away. In the south-west corner of the island is the **Neb Battery** where you'll find the remains of many buildings and huts along both sides of the road. The pump house that once supplied water from the burn stands at the edge of the road. There are two dams, the higher dam built in World War I and the lower built in World War II. The battery and ammunition stores are worth a visit.

At **Stanger Head** you can look out from the cliffs to the stone stacks known as the **Cletts**, but be careful. This headland can be dangerous for the unwary as there are *gloups*, or blowholes, in the area. Leading to Stanger Head is **Magnificent Lane**, a steep, winding road built by men from *HMS Magnificent*. In July 1915 King George V landed at **King's Hard** to inspect troops at Stanger Head. The remains of this jetty can still be seen. Well-preserved **Buchanan Battery** was built as part of a chain of coastal defence batteries to guard the main entrance to Scapa Flow. You can explore the many shelters, but remember to be extremely careful.

Flotta Kirk and War Memorial. The kirk is open to visitors with access through the vestry. Across Kirk Bay is the uninhabited island of **Switha**. Unfortunately, you can no longer visit the cinema built around 1940 to seat 1,500. The cinema roof now covers a garage in Kirkwall, and after the end wall was removed in the 1970s, the building was used as a sand store. You can, however, join friendly locals in the **Community Centre** where there are sporting or social activities on most evenings. The licensed bar is open on Friday evenings.

At Stanger Head and at Quoy Ness on the southern point of Pan Hope, the huge bay that almost cuts Flotta in two, men with earphones sat in hydrophone huts around the clock throughout World War I listening for submarine activity. From one of these huts the approach of a so-called German 'suicide mission' submarine was tracked. The UB116 managed to slip into the Flow under the boom defences but blew up in the minefield and sank in 82ft (25m) of water. This wreck and that of a German destroyer in deep water just off the Buchanan Battery regularly attract divers. The wreck of *HMS Vanguard*, the 19,560-ton battleship which accidentally blew up at her moorings with the loss of more than 1,000 men in July 1917, lies on the bottom 112ft (34m) down, only one nautical mile from the Flotta Terminal.

The **Flotta Stone**, the island's main archaeological artefact, is a sculptured slab found on the site of a ruined ancient church and thought to date from the 10th century. It can be seen in the Royal Museum of Scotland, in Edinburgh.

FLORA AND FAUNA

The industrial clamour on the north side of the island has not stopped birds nesting on cliffs and moorland and there's even a colony of **seals** to be seen from the south-east corner, overlooking the Sound of Hoxa. In the vicinity of the old World War II cinema the Royal Navy planted 1,000 trees at the time and about 10% survived. A further 40,000 trees and shrubs have also been planted by the oil company. An island story says many of the wartime trees disappeared because they made perfect Christmas trees as they had no branches on their weather side and thus fitted flush against the wall.

GETTING THERE

Flotta is served by the Ro-Ro vehicle and passenger ferry that goes to Hoy, the *MV Hoy Head* (125 passengers and 16 cars). All bookings should be made at the Houton Terminal, in Orphir on the Orkney Mainland (✆01856-811397; fax 01856-811701; email info@ orkneyferries.co.uk). The ferry leaves Houton three times a day Monday to Friday, with two sailings on Saturday. There is an additional sailing on Sunday during May to September. The trip takes 55 minutes. There are 'no show' charges, which means all cancellations must be made not less than 24 hours before the intended day of travel or you pay the full charge. The return adult fare is £6.60, cars and caravanettes £19.70, motorcycles £13, and bicycles £1.60 return. Gibraltar Pier, built during World War II, is the ferry terminal on Flotta.

There's a 2,000ft (610m) long **airstrip** along the south-west coast below Rotten Gutter. It was built to fly in labour during the construction of the oil terminal and can be used for charter flights.

ACCOMMODATION

Mr Flett (Roadside; ✆01856-701496) has a self-catering **caravan**.

For **hostel** accommodation a three-bedroom house (sleeps 5), or **self-catering**, one double and two twin bedrooms, contact Marina Sinclair (✆01856-701252). There's a small basic **camping site** with toilet facilities at the Visitor's Centre, near the post office.

HELP AND INFORMATION

Doctor: (✆01856-701246).
Post Office, general merchants, and Calor Gas supply (✆01856-701252). For transport on the island enquire at the post office.

GRAEMSAY

A 15-minute ferry ride from Stromness (45 minutes via Hoy) brings you to the small lush green island of Graemsay lying between Stromness and Hoy at the northern entrance to Scapa Flow, where the tidal race in the narrow strait attains speeds of up to 8 knots, sufficiently strong to retard even the largest vessels. The island boasts two small hills and two lighthouses, **Hoy Low** at the Point of Oxan and **Hoy High** on the Taing of Sandside. Smaller Hoy Low still has it own twin gun battery, set up in World War II; Hoy High's white 108ft (33m) tower tapers to a balcony supported by Gothic arches. At the foot of the tower are lightkeepers' houses, built in a style reminiscent of Assyrian temples. While Orkney's celebrated Arctic explorer, Dr John Rae, was off on an expedition in search of missing Sir John Franklin, Lady Franklin called in on Graemsay while visiting the Rae family in Stromness in June 1851.

The island is barely 1,000 acres (405ha) in size, so it doesn't take long to explore. The virtual absence of traffic on the island's one main road makes walking pleasurable and enables you to enjoy the abundant wild flowers and appreciate the views of Stromness and North Hoy. You can relax on the safe coral and sandy beaches at Sandside, within comfortable walking distance of the ferry pier, or scout the rocky shore where broken pieces of crockery are still washed up from the *Albion*, shipwrecked off the Point of Oxan on New Year's Day 1866. Picnic benches are dotted around the island. Sit and watch **seals**, **terns**, **oystercatchers**, **ringed plovers**, **redshank**, **curlew**, **lapwing**, **fulmar** and **skuas**. Graemsay has a post office at Clett (✆01856-851228). Open Monday to Friday morning, where you can also buy soft drinks and confectionery.

GETTING THERE

The *MV Graemsay* (73 passengers) carries foot passengers and bicycles to Graemsay Pier seven days a week in summer, week days only in winter. Crossing time is 15 minutes direct, 45 minutes via North Hoy. All enquiries to Steve Mowatt (✆01856-850624).

North Isles

SHAPINSAY

The story of Rip van Winkle, the fabled character of one of the world's most famous tales, has its roots in Shapinsay. The family of American author Washington Irving, creator of the story, originated here and their old traditional stone crofthouse of Quholme can still be seen. The writer's father was born at Quholme in 1731 and later settled in America. Experts believe that the Rip van Winkle in *Sketch Book* (1819) was based on an old Orkney fable Washington Irving would have heard as a child.

On the archaeological front, Shapinsay has its share of mounds, cists, underground structures and brochs, but most have yet to be excavated. One that has been is **Burroughston Broch**, which was originally excavated in 1862 by Colonel David Balfour, laird of the castle. Now reconstructed, it is a good example of an Iron Age broch. In the interior is a well 10ft (3m) deep. The site is open throughout the year. There is a small car park there, which is also a good viewpoint for seals. Nearly all other archaeological sites are on privately owned land and you need permission to visit them. A feature of the fertile island is its square 10-acre (4ha) fields and straight roads. These are also the result of work carried out by Colonel David Balfour, who changed the face of island farming in the 1850s. From 1848 to 1874 he saw the area under cultivation increase from 700 to more than 6,000 acres (283 to 2,428ha). Shapinsay farmers specialise in quality beef and lamb, annually exporting more than 1,500 cattle and 2,000 sheep. The Balfour family had owned their island estate for 400 years when the last laird died in 1961, leaving no heirs. He had already sold the farmland to the Zawadzki family and on his death they also acquired the castle they now run as an exclusive hotel.

Balfour Castle (Shapinsay KW17 2DY; ✆01856-711282; fax 01856-711283; email info@ balfourcastle.com; www.balfourcastle.co.uk) is a Victorian castle in baronial style, completed in 1848, but built around a mid-18th century house called Cliffdale. The interior of the castle is unspoilt and little changed from the days of Col David Balfour. Among the treasures in the castle is one half of a richly inlaid stone table; the other half is in the Vatican. Open Sunday only, May to September. Admission charge. Guided tour of walled Victorian garden and main rooms. Take tea in the castle staff dining-room. Booking essential. Accommodation available. **Balfour Village**, originally Shoreside, sits along sheltered Elwick Bay where the ferry berths. Balfour Village was built in the late 1700s to house the smiths, carpenters and masons employed on the Balfour estate. In 1263, Elwick Bay was the anchorage for the 120-strong Viking fleet of King Haakon, who called on his way to the fatal Battle of Largs. Legend says one of his longboats sank when leaving Shapinsay, off **Haco's Ness**, near Dead Wife's Geo. There's a ruined stalled cairn close by. The **Shapinsay Heritage Centre** (✆01856-711258) in the old smithy in Balfour village has an impressive display of photographs, documents and artefacts relating to the island's history. There's a café and craft shop in the same building. Near the village school are the remains of a mid-19th century gasworks and a water-powered grinding mill that is one of the largest of its type. The mill houses pottery workshops and a gallery.

Off the southern coast road is the **Old Church** and **Kirkyard** which contains the Balfour family graves. An easy walk takes you to the beach at the **Bay of Sandgarth** and the southern point of the island. **Castle Bloody** is not a castle at all, but a chambered cairn on Shapinsay's only remaining heather moorland, and an ideal site to spot birds and wildlife. Inland is the 10ft (3m) tall megalith known as the **Standing Stone of Mor Stein**, which supposedly landed here after being thrown by a giant at his errant wife. On the beach below Lairo Water is another large stone, **Odin's Stone**. It is unlike any other found on the beach and is believed to be associated with Viking offerings to this Norse god.

Linton Chapel probably dates from the 12th century and is dedicated to St Catherine. Folklore says that a lintel from the chapel was used by a local farmer to build a byre on his farm in the early 1900s. When he found two of his cattle hanged in the byre the next morning he promptly returned the lintel to the chapel.

The highest point on the low-lying red sandstone island is **Ward Hill** at 210ft (64m). The island is six miles (10km) long and among its interesting features are its storm beaches, or 'ayres' as they are known locally, an Old Norse word for a stretch of seawater completely barred from the ocean by a narrow gravel beach. You can see good examples at Vasa Loch on the west coast's Bay of Furrowland, and at the coastal loch of Lairo Water on sandy Veantrow Bay. This natural process is also taking place next door at the Ouse.

FLORA AND FAUNA

The island is particularly noted for its **gull** and **tern** colonies, courting **shelducks**, hunting **hen harriers** and **Arctic skua**. Most of the locally abundant waders can be seen at close quarters. Although it covers only 40 acres (16ha) the **RSPB Mill Dam Nature Reserve**, one mile (1.6km) north-east of Balfour village, has six species of breeding ducks. **Pintails** have their British breeding stronghold in Orkney, and a few pairs nest on and around the Mill Dam. Five species of wading birds, including the **redshank**, nest on the reserve. **Water rails** are more often heard than seen. In winter, the reserve attracts visiting wildfowl. **Whooper swans** graze Shapinsay's fields and often use the reserve, along with **greylag geese**. The RSPB maintains a hide overlooking the Mill Dam and it is always open, providing excellent views of the reserve. For more information contact the part-time warden at *RSPB Mill Dam Nature Reserve* (Furrowend, Shapinsay KW17 2DY; ✆01856-711373).

On the east coast is Scottish Wildlife Trust's **Holm of Burghlee**, a 27-acre (11ha) reserve lying on coastal hill ground. The reserve is ungrazed maritime heathland which supports an interesting bird community of breeding **gulls, terns, skuas** and **waders**. A more unusual habitat is the wood in the grounds of Balfour Castle, where such common songbirds as **blackbirds**, **thrushes**, **robins**, **dunnocks**, **chaffinches** and **willow warblers** breed. The craggy east coast is the place to look for **Atlantic grey** and **common seals**, and **otters**. The lochs of Lairo Water, the Ouse, and Vasa Loch are also good spots for wildlife. It was the island's minister who, in 1805, was the first to notice that the little resident vole was a unique sub-species of its European relative.

GETTING THERE

Shapinsay is a 25-minute ferry ride from Kirkwall. As you leave the shelter of Kirkwall Bay, old gun placements can be seen along the mainland Point of Carness; on the left lies Thieves Holm. Thieves and witches were once banished to this islet, now home to cormorants, kittiwakes and seals. Crossing the deep-water exit from Kirkwall Bay known as the String, the Victorian turrets of Balfour Castle loom ahead. To the right is the uninhabited island of Helliar Holm with its automatic lighthouse.

The vehicle and passenger Ro-Ro ferry *MV Shapinsay* (91 passengers and 11 cars). It departs from Kirkwall at 8.15am, 9.45am, 11.30am, 2,15pm, 4pm and 5.30pm Monday to Friday. On Saturday and Sunday the ferry leaves Kirkwall at 9.45am, 11.30am, and 2.15pm, with an additional 4pm on Saturday, and 6.15pm on Sunday. The return adult fare is £6.60, cars and mobile homes £19.70, motorcycles £13, and bicycles £1.60 return. Bookings at the Kirkwall Terminal of Orkney Ferries (✆01856-872044; fax 01856-872921; email info@orkneyferries. co.uk). The sailings from Kirkwall at 2.15pm and Shapinsay at 5.30pm on Sunday (May to August) are principally used for passengers on the Balfour Castle Package Cruise (✆01856-711282). The cruise costs £20 for adults, £10 for children under 15, £2 for children under five, and children under two free, and includes a close-up view of Helliar Holm's seal colony.

ACCOMMODATION
Guest Houses

Balfour Castle: Shapinsay KW17 2DY (✆01856-711282; fax 01856-711283; email info@ balfourcastle.com; www.balfourcastle.com). Three-star, claims to be the most northerly castle-hotel in the world. 10 miles (16km) of private coastline. Listed Victorian baronial mansion built in 1848. Seven rooms from £85-£120 per person a night, including a three-course dinner. Castle has a small chapel and drawing room available for wedding ceremonies. Open all year except Christmas and New Year.

Bed & Breakfast

Girnigoe: Jean Wallace, Girnigoe, Shapinsay KW17 2EB (✆01856-711256; email jean@girnigoe.f9.co.uk). Four-star Orkney farmhouse in the north of the island. Pick up from the ferry arranged. One ensuite twin room with shower and one double with private bath/shower, lounge, no smoking. Near beach and seal colonies. From £20 a night.

Harroldsgarth: Janice Evans, Shapinsay KW17 2EA (✆01856-711262). Three-star, three bedrooms. Quiet location near beach overlooking Sandgarth Bay. Free transport from ferry terminal. Evening meal available. Open all year, non-smoking. From £20 a night.

Hilton Farm House: Catherine Ann Bews, Shapinsay KW17 2EA (✆/fax 01856-711239; email info@hiltonorkneyfarmhouse.co.uk; www.hiltonorkneyfarmhouse.co.uk). Farmhouse accommodation, a mile (1.6km) from ferry terminal. Ensuite and all facilities. Near RSPB reserve and beaches. Courtesy transport. Home cooking, evening meal available. From £25 a night.

Monquhanny: Stu and Judi Wellden, Shapinsay KW17 2DZ (✆01856-711276; email enquiries@orkneystainedglass.com). Twin and double ensuite. Middle-eastern and traditional home cooking. Children welcome.

EATING AND DRINKING

Balfour Castle (✆01856-711282; fax 01856-711283; info@balfourcastle.com; www.balfourcastle.com) sells homely food made with produce from its walled kitchen garden, served in Victorian surroundings. *The Gatehouse* at the former estate entrance to the castle is now a bar. Open to residents only and parties who book a special occasion.

Hilton Farm House (✆/fax 01856-711239; email info@hiltonorkneyfarmhouse.co.uk; www.hiltonorkneyfarmhouse.co.uk) is open daily for teas, coffee, homebakes, snacks and light lunches.

The Smithy, Heritage Centre, Craft Shop and Restaurant: Balfour Village (✆01856-711258) offers coffee, tea, homebakes, and snacks. Open daily May to September.

SHOPPING

Cottage industry knitting thrives, along with old and modern crafts such as wood-turning, painting and jewellery making. There's a gift shop at the castle, and a craft shop and café at the *The Smithy Heritage Centre* (✆01856-711258), open every day in summer. You can buy preserves, chutneys, jams and marmalade, hand-made on the island, from Glynis Leslie (Odinstone; ✆/fax 01856-711389).

Lovatt Textiles: Fiona Lovatt, The Gardener's Cottage, Shapinsay KW7 2DY (✆01856-711269; www.lovatt-textiles.co.uk), cushions, throws, bags, and stoles in Orcadian and Scottish designs. Open May to October, Friday 2pm to 6pm, Saturday and Sunday 10am to 6pm, and Friday 10am to 2pm.

Orkney Stained Glass: Stu and Judi Wellden, Monquhanny, Shapinsay KW17 2DZ (✆01856-711276; email enquiries@orkneystainedglass.com; www.orkneystainedglass.com). A glass and fine art studio specialising in contemporary and traditional glasswork, and a range of celebration or decorative standing stone and glass sculptures. Residential or day workshops in stained glass crafting and painting are offered between May and December.

David Holmes Ceramics: Elwick Mill, Shapinsay KW17 2DY (✆01856-711211; email david.holmes25@btopenworld.com; www.davidholmesceramics.co.uk). Pottery workshop and gallery, former cornmill. Hand-made pottery, porcelain, and lustreware. Crafts for sale. Open daily, 10am to 4pm. Short walk from the ferry.

HELP AND INFORMATION

General merchants: T Sinclair, Balfour Village (℃01856-711300); and L&H Robertson, Astley Cottage (℃01856-711208) also sell petrol.

Balfour Post Office: Mrs S. Sinclair (℃01856-711300).

Shapinsay Community Enterprise: Balfour Village (℃01856-711258/271).

Doctor: (℃01856-711284).

Orkney Island Holidays: Paul and Louise Hollinrake, Furrowend, Shapinsay KW17 2DY (℃01856-711373; email holidays@orkney.com; www.orkneyislands.com). Offer a week of guided bird-watching, wildlife, flora, archaeology and local history. Ensuite accommodation and good food.

Jean Wallace: (℃01856-711256). Will take you on the Girnigoe Coastal Walk where you can see seals, birds, wild flowers, and boat nousts.

Sea fishing, diving, and island trips: Groat's Charters, Harvey Groat, Housebay, Shapinsay (℃/fax 01856-711254; email groats@orkneyangling.co.uk; www.orkneyangling.co.uk).

ROUSAY

Rousay ('Rolf's Island') has a population of 200 and is the largest of a group of close-lying islands all serviced by the same ferry. The others are Egilsay and Wyre. Between them the three have more than 166 of the richest and best preserved archaeological sites in Orkney and Rousay, with most of them, is known as the 'Egypt of the North'. Only the rich dark soil of the island's coastal fringe and the Sourin valley are farmed, and the rest of Rousay must look much as it was during the formation of its overlying blanket peat more than 3,000 years ago. Rousay is only 5 miles (8km) in diameter and is unusually hilly for an Orkney island, with high point **Blotchnie Field** rising to 820ft (250m). The island is surrounded by a shallow underwater shelf. The most accessible stretches of shore are along the western side of the island.

A road 13 miles (21km) long circles the island and will take you to or near every prehistoric monument of note. That much of Rousay's archaeological heritage has been excavated is due to the efforts of Walter Grant, who owned Trumland House in the 1930s. Profitable investments in whisky allowed Grant to invite some of the leading archaeologists of the day to work on many of the sites that are now in the care of Historic Scotland. The best preserved are signed and readily accessible but many more lie on privately owned land and permission to visit them should first be sought from the landowner.

In a sense, Grant made up for the excesses of the original owner of **Trumland House**, General Sir Frederick William Traill-Burroughs, who built the Jacobean-style mansion above the ferry pier in 1876. This laird's contribution to local history is still vilified. The man known as 'The Little General' gained a reputation as Orkney's worst landlord for the way he treated local crofters. He followed in the footsteps of his uncle, George William Traill, who carried out Orkney's only major Clearances in the mid-19th century. He evicted 210 people from Westness and Quendal and you can still see some of their ruined crofts, including the ruin of **Tofts**, which is all that remains of the oldest known two-storey building in Orkney.

Archaeological Sites

The best preserved of Rousay archaeological sites lie along the west coast and the **Westness Walk** is the recommended introduction to them. It was in this area while hunting otters that Earl Paul Hakonarson was kidnapped in 1137 by Svein Asleifarson. The Earl then vanished from Orkney; otters are still found along the shore. The Westness area was the major power centre in Rousay from the Iron Age to the 19th century, with the brochs in the area representing it at its height. You can start from the north end, after taking the path from the car park to Midhowe Cairn and Broch, or you can start from the track which leads to Westness Farm from the main road, at the south end. Waymarkers show arrows for both directions. The stretch from Midhowe to Westness Farm is around a mile and is often described as 'the most important archaeological mile in Scotland'.

The **Pict and Viking Graves** at Moaness promontory are an unusual example of a common burial ground shared by Christian Picts and pagan Vikings, dating from the fifth to the ninth centuries. The first Viking grave was found by accident in 1963 when a farmer was digging a hole to bury a dead cow. The excavated grave revealed the remains of a young woman and a baby. Two oval brooches and a magnificent, ornamental ringed pin now known as the Westness Brooch were found among the grave goods. The brooch is now in the National Museum of Scotland, in Edinburgh, although you can buy silver replicas in many craft and jewellery shops. Pictish burials show that the Vikings respected their graves as they were untouched. The Picts did not bury grave goods with their dead, who were laid in narrow full-length shallow graves. About 77 yards (70m) east of the waymarker post at Moaness is a Viking *noust*, or boat shelter, where they could haul their boats into a depression in the rock.

The **Knowe of Swandro** (Norse for 'pig-run') mound contains the remains of a broch. This was probably used as a quarry for building stone during the construction of the adjacent Norse farmstead. The excavated farmstead probably dates from the late Norse period of the 11th and 12th centuries. There are two parallel longhouses, one a 121ft (37m) long dwelling house of two large halls with benches and a central stone hearth, and the other divided into two smaller houses, which might have been used as byres for cows and sheep. The **Knowe of Rowiegar** is a stalled chambered tomb, a smaller version of the Midhowe chambered tomb.

St Mary's Church, beside the Wirk, is the former parish church of Rousay. It was abandoned in 1820 and the standing ruin probably dates from the 16th–17th century, although it is on the site of an earlier medieval church. Some elaborately carved medieval stonework fragments have been built into the exterior wall faces at the east gable and the east end of the south wall. Many similar fragments found here form an ornamental archway in the kitchen garden of Trumland House, although the house is not open to the public.

The Wirk is a square tower on the seaward side of the dyke, which is attached to a massive rectangular structure which extends into the field behind. The building is a great ceremonial hall, dating from the 13th or 14th century, and is similar in status to the Bishop's Palace in Kirkwall.

The ruined farmstead of **Brough** probably belongs to the 18th century, and has been empty since 1845, when the Traills, the landowners at that time, created Westness Farm out of the lands of three ancient townships. The eviction of the inhabitants was Orkney's one major example of Highland-style clearance.

South Howe Broch. The remains of this broch lie between Brough and the coast. You can see the broch from the wave-cut platform on the shore. It has been cut into by the sea and appears as a 328ft (100m) long section, with the stonework of the central broch tower in the middle and the surrounding houses represented by slabs in the grassy slopes. The grouping in one area of North Howe, Midhowe and South Howe, is only part of a remarkable concentration of brochs along both shores of Eynhallow Sound. There are another four between here and Trumland Pier, and seven on the facing Mainland coast.

Midhowe Cairn. This stalled chambered tomb is the longest in Orkney. It is known as the 'Great Ship of Death,' probably because the bones of 25 people were found in the compartments formed by the upright slabs. Such tombs were the collective burial-places of communities of the Neolithic farmers, who settled in Orkney more than 5,000 years ago. Midhowe is one of the earliest types. **Midhowe Broch**. Stands on a narrow cliff promontory, with the landward side barred by a formidable triple line of defence consisting of two ditches with a massive stone wall in between. Within and around the circular broch tower are small chambers formed of masonry and large upright slabs, the living quarters of a sizeable community. There is a spring-fed water tank in the floor and a hearth with sockets for what might have been a roasting spit. In the next field to the north-west is a large mound which covers **North Howe Broch**.

Attractive **Wasbister Loch** is the site of two *crannogs*, or fortified Iron Age settlements built on man-made islands. There is no access but the two sites can clearly be seen from the road running round the loch. Near the farm of Bigland is the Neolithic settlement of **Rinyo**, notable for its clay ovens, which have been found nowhere else. The settlement is similar in date and character to Skara Brae, on Orkney Mainland.

The **Faraclett Head Walk** is a circular 2-mile (3½km) coastal route covering several different habitats and early settlements passing through maritime heath in the north-east corner of the island. Access is from Faraclett Farm, where there is parking. Cliff scenery and still unexcavated chambered cairns mark the way. Look out for the enormous **Yetn-asteen** standing stone near the Loch of Scockness. This is reputedly a petrified giant who is supposed to celebrate the pagan Yule festival every year by striding over to the loch for a drink.

Eynhallow

From the west road, the beautiful uninhabited islet of Eynhallow ('Holy Isle') can be seen to the south-west in the middle of the tidal race of the sound. Folklore says it's an enchanted isle which can vanish before you reach it. Its soil is said to be magical and keeps rats and mice at bay. There are certainly none on Eynhallow. The islet is the site of a small but grandly conceived church with outbuildings which have been identified as a Benedictine monastery. The church dates from the early 12th century; all records of it end in the 16th century. A number of elaborately carved red sandstone fragments lie inside one of the buildings and have long puzzled archaeologists. The stones are similar to those used in St Magnus Cathedral and it may well be that they were given to the monks on Eynhallow to decorate their monastery in the same style as the cathedral, which was being built at the same time. Also on the islet are the remains of prehistoric dwellings at Monkerness, and **the Lodge**, a building that is the base for a long-term research project studying fulmars. The island is owned by the Orkney Islands Council and you need OIC permission to land.

FLORA AND FAUNA

Much of Rousay is a proclaimed Site of Special Scientific Interest (SSSI) for its archaeology, natural features, flora and birdlife. A nature trail starting at the entrance to Taversoe Tuick Cairn takes you around one of the wildest parts of the island, where you'll find the 1,070-acre (433ha) **RSPB Trumland Reserve**, 80% of which lies within the SSSI. The reserve is in the south of the island and is open all year round. There is no admission charge. Terrain is primarily heather moorland. There are two walks around the reserve, a one-hour ramble and another of three hours. A leaflet is available from a dispenser at the start of the trail. This is twitcher country, with 74 species of bird recorded on the reserve, 35 of them known to be resident breeders. Look for **red-throated divers** (also known as **rain geese**) on the moorlands, as well as **merlins**, **hen harriers**, **golden plovers**, **short-eared owls**, and both **great** and **Arctic skuas**. If you follow the nature trail there is a good chance you'll see all these species. There is no office at the reserve. For more information contact the *RSPB Egilsay Nature Reserve* (Onziebust, Egilsay KW17 2QD; ✆01856-821395).

There are colonies of **guillemots**, **kittiwakes** and **fulmars** on the cliffs of the western coast; **razorbills** tucked in the cracks and crannies, and **puffins** wheeling and waddling around their burrows. The Loch of Wasbister holds a variety of nesting ducks and Trumland Wood shelters birds such as **robins**, **chaffinches** and **willow warblers**. In the west of Rousay the maritime heaths of Quandal and Brings host **Artic terns** and **skuas**, **great black-backed** and **common gulls**, **oystercatchers**, **ringed plovers** and **snipe**.

There are 154 plant species on the island. One of the central lochs, Muckle Water, is particularly rich in water plants, among them such rarities as **shining pondweed** and **quillwort**. **Alpine bearberry**, two species of **wintergreen, alpine saw-wort** and **Wilson's filmy fern** all grow on the island. In the north-west and at Faraclett Head in the north-east, **crowberry** and **heather** share the maritime heathland habitat with the tiny and rare **Scottish primrose**. The valleys display typical Orkney dale vegetation, with greater woodrushes, rushes and ferns, forming a community often called 'treeless woodlan'.

GETTING THERE

The *MV Eynhallow* (95 passengers and 9 cars) serves Rousay on a daily basis. It leaves Tingwall terminal at 8.20am Monday to Friday, and 8.40am on Saturday; followed by sailings at 10.40am, 11.50am, 2.45pm, 4.05pm and 6.05pm Monday to Sunday (no 8.20am sailing on Sunday). The crossing takes about 30 minutes. The return adult fare is £6.60, cars and mobile homes £19.70, motorcycles £13, and bicycles £1.60 return. Booking must be made at the Tingwall terminal in Evie (*C*/fax 01856-751360; email info@orkneyferries.co.uk). The terminal is about 6½ miles (11km) from the A966 main road. *Orkney Bus* meets arriving ferries at Tingwall Monday to Saturday.

GETTING AROUND

There is a **Postbus** service, operated by *Royal Mail* (*C*08457-740740; www.royalmail.com/postbus), from Rousay Pier to Frotoft, Westness, Langskaill, Rousay post office, and Rousay School every day Monday to Saturday. Contact the post office at Tou Cottage (*C*01856-821352) for more information.

Taxi (*C*01856-821234), fare to Midhowe £8; taxi tour of the island £16 (for up to four people).

Tours

Rousay Traveller Guide: Andy and Rosie Beskaby, Bellona KW17 2PU (*C*/fax 01856-821234). Offer minibus tours, taxis and field trips. For a guided tour of the island during summer from June to August on Tuesday, Wednesday and Thursday a minibus meets the 10.40am ferry from Tingwall and returns you to the pier in time for the 5.30pm ferry (or earlier). The tour costs £16.50 for adults, senior citizens and students £13. Prices do not include ferry fare.

ACCOMMODATION

Taversoe Hotel: Rousay KW17 2PT (*C*01856-821325; email taversoe@hotmail.com). About 2 miles (3.5km) along the road west from Trumland Pier. From £25 in winter, £30 in summer. It has a public bar and restaurant, open all year.

Bellona: Andy and Rosie Beskaby (*C*01856-821234). One bedroom self-catering (from £315 a week) or B&B (from £34).

Ervadale Cottage: Christine (*C*01856-821351). Renovated croft house within an acre of gardens. Cottage sleeps 2–4.

Faraclett: Barbara (*C*01856-821228; email rickandbarbaracass@farming.co.uk). Renovated farm cottage, sleeps 2–3, from £200 to £300 a week.

Maybank: Dianne (*C*01856-821225; email maybank.guesthouse@btinternet.com). Views over Eynhallow Sound. Two miles (3.2km) from pier. Family room, double room and one single room, from £21.

Trumland Farm: Carol Rae, Rousay KW17 2PU (*C*01856-821252; fax 01856-821314; email trumland@btopenworld.com). One-star, self-catering semi-detached cottage on working farm, one bedroom, sleeps three. Close to ferry. Open all year. From £60 to £100 a week.

Rousay Hostel: Trumland Organic Farm, Rousay KW17 2PU (*C*01856-821252; fax 01856-821314; email trumland@btopenworld.com; www.hostel-scotland.co.uk). Has two dormitories which sleep 13, camping area. Within walking distance of pier, shop, restaurant, and bird reserve. Open all year. Member of *Scottish Independent Hostels*. From £8 a night.

HELP AND INFORMATION

Visit Rousay: Tourist group, c/o Dianne Hull, Maybank (*C*01856-821225; www.visitrousay.co.uk).

Above Trumland Pier is the **Trumland Visitors Centre** and waiting room.

The *Pier Restaurant* (*C*01856-821359) at the ferry terminal serves food all day from 11am. Dinner from 5.30pm to 9pm. Music evenings and weekends with the local Wyre Band. Arts and crafts. In the north-east is *Marion's Shop and Filling Station*, licensed general

merchant, Calor Gas, and picnic site (✆/fax 01856-821365). Many visitors like to get their **postcards** franked with the Rousay stamp at the *Sub-post office*, Ton Cottage (✆01856-821352). Open Monday, Tuesday and Thursday 2pm to 3pm, and Wednesday and Friday 9am to 10am.
Doctor: Brinian (✆01856-821265).

EGILSAY AND WYRE

Across the narrow sound from the ferry pier at Rousay are the smaller islands of Egilsay and Wyre, both with attractions that far outweigh their size.

EGILSAY

Egilsay is notable for its violent niche in Orkney history and for the church which arose as a result. Early in the 12th century Earl Haakon and Earl Magnus were joint rulers of Orkney. Their constant feuding led to a meeting on Egilsay to discuss peace terms. The **Orkneyinga Saga** tells how Magnus was praying when Haakon arrived with more than the agreed number of ships and men. Lífólf, Haakon's cook, was given the task of killing Magnus, which he did with an axe blow to the head 'so his soul passed away to Heaven.' After his canonisation Magnus became the patron saint of Orkney and Egilsay became an important shrine for pilgrims. **St Magnus Church** built shortly after his death on the rise in the middle of the island is today roofless but otherwise intact and its distinctive round tower still rises 49ft (15m) from the nave at its west end and is visible from afar. It is one of only two remaining examples of round-towered churches built by the Vikings and reflects the 11th century church architecture of Viking Ireland. A stone **cenotaph** marks the spot in the churchyard where the Earl was killed. It was erected in 1937 by the congregations of St Magnus Cathedral, Kirkwall, and the church of St Magnus the Martyr, London Bridge.

Egilsay's lochs and lochans provide a rich wetland habitat for a large number of breeding waders, such as **redshank** and **snipe**, a number of duck species and a large **black-headed gull** colony. The fields and wetlands have a wide range of wild flowers because the land has never been intensively used. Egilsay is one of the few islands where you can find the rare **corncrake**, whose rasping double-note call is a sound that is rapidly vanishing from the islands. The RSPB acquired farmland to establish a 358-acre (145ha) nature reserve on the island as part of its drive to protect and encourage the species. Recent purchases have brought the total holding to more than 672 acres (272ha). The aim is to create cover for corncrakes as soon as they arrive in spring from Africa. The reserve also provides late-cut hay for nests and chicks, and more cover late in the season for the birds to forage and shelter in. **Otters** are occasionally seen in the reserve and **common seals** pup along the shore in June. The reserve is always open. There is no admission charge. The Senior Site Manager must be contacted before you visit. A summer warden covers both Trumland Reserve, on Rousay, and Egilsay. Contact the Senior Site Manager (✆01856-721210). In winter more than 1,000 waders, mainly **purple sandpipers** and **turnstones**, frequent the island's coastline. The Loch of the Graand at the southernmost tip of Egilsay is a quiet spot to watch waders and seals. There have also been sightings of killer whales on the west coast. On a nearby hillock is a Neolithic chambered cairn.

Getting There

The Ro-Ro ferry *MV Eynhallow* (95 passengers and 9 cars) to Rousay also serves Egilsay and Wyre from the Tingwall terminal. The first ferry from Tingwall leaves at 8.20am Monday to Friday, 8.40am on Saturday, and 10.45am on Sunday and plies regularly throughout the day. Not all the trips call at Egilsay, although the ferry will take passengers there on demand. To avoid getting stuck on the island check departure times with the ferry office and in all cases book in advance. Vehicles must be ready for boarding 15 minutes – passengers 5 minutes – before departure. Bookings at the Tingwall terminal (✆/fax 01856-751360; email info@orkneyferries.co.uk).

Accommodation

There is bothy accommodation (£3.50 a night) and camping (£1.50 a night) at the *Egilsay Science Club,* Netherskill (✆01856-821357), and B&B at Kirbuist (✆Debbie Corrigan 01856-821303/308).

WYRE

The pride of the island and evidence of its former Norse importance is **Cubbie Roo's Castle**, variously described as the first recorded stone castle in Scotland or its oldest square-towered castle. Wyre was the stronghold of the Viking Kolbein Hruga who built the keep in the centre of the island in the mid-12th century. He is mentioned in the *Orkneyinga Saga* as having built a 'fine stone fort... a really solid stronghold' before 1150, one of the earliest to be documented. Whatever the date of the building, the well-preserved structure comprises a square tower surviving to a height of 49ft (15m) and substantial outer walls, thought to be the foundation of a hall and additional domestic accommodation. The sole entrance to the tower was on the first floor. The ground floor was accessed internally by ladder and was probably used for storage. A water tank cut into the bedrock is still visible in the floor. Kolbein Hruga first passed into local folklore as the giant 'Cubbie Row' and then as 'Cubbie Roo.'

Twelfth-century Norse churches were usually small and simple in design, and **St Mary's Chapel**, close to Cubbie Roo's Castle, is a beautifully preserved example. This was founded by either Kolbein or his son Bjarni Kolbeinsson, who was Bishop of Orkney at the time. There is access to the chapel from the road and a signed path leading to the castle.

The Taing, at the extreme western point of the island, is a good place to watch **seals**, both common and grey. Noted Scottish writer Edwin Muir was born on the island and the farm of **the Bu**, north-east of the castle, was his boyhood home. It is thought likely that the farm stands on the site of Kolbein Hruga's original farmhouse. Wyre attracts large numbers of seabirds in winter, including **eider** and **long-tailed ducks**, with smaller numbers of attractive **velvet scoters** and **red-breasted mergansers**. **Great northern divers** which have travelled from their breeding grounds in Iceland and Greenland can often be seen from the inter-island ferry.

The **Wyre Heritage Centre** has an informative historical exhibition, with special displays on Cubbie Roo and Edwin Muir. There's also a craft area.

EDAY

The island and the Calf of Eday, its offshore snippet, are best remembered for the capture in February 1725 of Orkney's most notorious character, John Gow the Pirate. Gow set out in his ship *Revenge* to raid Carrick House on Eday, the home of old school friend and island laird James Fea. After Gow ran his ship aground on the Calf, he sent five armed crewmen ashore to force the islanders to help him refloat the *Revenge*. The pirates were taken to the local inn where they were plied with drinks and overpowered. Gow was also captured and held prisoner by Fea in Carrick House until he was sent to London to stand trial. Gow and his pirate crew were hanged at Execution Dock, Wapping, on 11 June 1725. Gow had to be hanged twice; the rope broke the first time after the hangman obligingly swung on Gow's legs too heavily in response to his request for 'a speedy dispatch'.

Gow's body was afterwards washed by three tides before being tarred and hung in chains. Locals will tell you that Gow had become engaged to a girl from his home town of Stromness after exchanging binding vows at the Stone of Odin. After his death she travelled to London to dissolve the ritual vow the only way she could – by touching Gow's tarred hand. Sir Walter Scott used the tale of John Gow in his novel *The Pirate*, published in 1821. It is likely that he drew on an account of Gow's 'murther and piracy' written by Daniel Defoe a century earlier.

Eday is centrally situated among Orkney's 'North Isles', 14 miles (23km) north-east of Kirkwall. It is 8 miles (13km) long and blends peat-covered hilly moorland with a fertile coastal strip. The population is around 160, but numerous derelict houses indicate that the population was once much greater. The early settlers were farmers who have left their chambered tombs around the island. It is believed that each tomb served as a communal burial place for a small community. Various types of tomb cover funerary styles over a period from well before 3000BC until some time after 2000BC. Most of the island is made up of the red and yellow rocks of the Middle Old Red Sandstone. Red sandstone gives the northern cliffs of Red Head their name and much of the stone used to build St Magnus Cathedral and the Earl's Palace in Kirkwall was quarried on the eastern horn of Fersness Bay.

ARCHAEOLOGICAL SITES

Apart from the wealth of tombs there are numerous other archaeological sites, including standing stones and Iron Age houses. To see the best of these and other interesting spots follow the 4¾-mile (7.6km) route of the **Eday Heritage Walk**. The route is marked by signposts and waymarker posts with distinctive yellow hexagons and arrows. The walk starts at the Eday Community Enterprises shop and Interpretive Display and you'll first see **Mill Loch**, whose concentration of **red-throated divers**, the largest in Britain, has made it a Site of Special Scientific Interest. The **Stone of Setter**, overlooking Calf Sound, is arguably the finest prehistoric single standing stone in Orkney and at 14.8ft (4.5m) high is the tallest. It looks like a hand reaching up from the moor. In the area are indications of other structures which may relate to the ritual use of this site. The stone is covered by at least seven species of lichen. This says much for Eday's clean air, as lichens cannot tolerate polluted air; if pollution increases the number of species diminishes. The **Fold of Setter**, a massive circular enclosure some 262ft (80m) across with a 7ft (2m) thick wall, was probably used to pen cattle more than 3,000 years ago. In summer, heather covers up a lot of the stonework.

The roof of the **Braeside** chambered tomb has been removed and its centre dug out, but the internal layout can still be made out; **Huntersquoy** tomb has two chambers, one above the other, reached by separate passages. The only other island example of this is on the island of Rousay. **Vinquoy Hill Chambered Tomb** consists of a splendid central chamber with four small connecting compartments. The tomb is of the Mayes Howe type and is one of the finest in Orkney. It dates before 2,000BC. A modern acrylic dome over the roof provides light in the main chamber, which is entered by a narrow subterranean passage.

At the summit of **Vinquoy Hill** (249ft/76m) there is a cairn and a view indicator, with a magnificent panorama encompassing the North Isles, the Mainland and on a clear day, Fair Isle, in Shetland. Below Vinquoy Hill are some of the best preserved ancient field boundaries in Orkney. They can be picked out around a large unexcavated prehistoric roundhouse at **Linkataing**, where a saddle-quern, or stone for grinding grain, can be seen in the ruins.

From Vinquoy Hill you can follow the coastal route to the 230ft (70m) high cliffs of **Red Head** and return along the hilltop path over **Noup Hill** and down to **Carrick House** (Eday KW17 2AB; ℂ01857-622260), which is a fine example of a 17th-century laird's residence. It was built in 1633 by John, Earl of Carrick and younger son of Earl Robert Stewart and brother of the infamous Patrick Stewart, Earl of Orkney and Shetland. In the house the unsqueamish can view the bloodstains left by captured pirate John Gow; the squeamish can see the bell from his ship and admire the flowered silk dress of Miss Riddoch, who lived in Kirkwall more than two centuries ago. Carrick House is open by appointment only.

The circular **Warness Walk** starting from Backaland Pier in the south takes about an hour and is easy, flat walking, with views of the offshore Green Holms, Mainland and distant Hoy. There is a Bronze Age burnt mound in the area and above the bay of Greentoft is the **Castle of Stackel Brae**, a small Norse construction dating from the 12th or 13th century and buried under a large green mound. A longer walk takes you past the highest point on the island, **Ward Hill**, at 331ft (101m) and along the west side, past the sand dunes and beaches of **Mussetter** and **Doomy**, not far from the airfield.

Across the sound is the **Calf of Eday** which is part of the home farm of Carrick. It has not been occupied since the early Iron Age, probably because of the growth of peat and loss of arable land. This means that you are looking at a landscape as it was more than 2,000 years ago, when the last people left. It has been used only to graze sheep since the early 18th century. North Ronaldsay islanders used to come here to cut peat, as there was none on their home island. The early farmers used a stone point known as an *ard* to plough. Many of these have been found on the island and a model of a plough with such a point can be seen at Carrick House. The islet is rich in archaeological sites and a long, stalled tomb dating to 4,000BC and an adjoining Iron Age farmhouse from about 600BC have been excavated. Earlier Neolithic tombs contained fragments of Unstan ware, the earliest prehistoric pottery in Orkney, and a glass bead of Syrio-Egyptian type, carbon dated to about 1500BC. Some of the finds are in the *Royal Museum of Scotland* (Chambers Street, Edinburgh), the remainder are on display in Carrick House. Immediately to the north of the sandy bay called **the Graand** are the remains of a possible religious structure. The Graand itself is thought to be one of the places where the Norsemen pulled up their longships for the winter. Grey seals now haul out here to bask. The remains of two rectangular buildings of a 17th-century salt works can be seen along the southern shore. Kilns were used here to dry sea salt which was used to cure the fish which was a staple winter diet of the islanders.

FLORA AND FAUNA

Eday's landscape is largely heather moorland where peat is still cut for fuel. Almost 70 pairs of **Arctic skuas** and several pairs of **great skuas** breed on the moors, which are hunting grounds for **kestrels**, **short-eared owls**, **hen harriers** and **merlin**. May to July sees an abundance of birdlife on the island, including **guillemots**, **razorbills**, **puffins**, **fulmars**, and **red-throated divers**. Several **whimbrels** used to nest on the moorland at Whitemaw and Flaughton Hill and unusual migrants often make landfall in autumn.

Early in June and July you might see the dark, newly born **common seal** pups. The heavier **Atlantic grey seals** pup in October. Common seals and **otters** can sometimes be seen from the cliffs, especially round War Ness, the southern tip of the island, and **porpoises**, **dolphins** and **whales** are also periodic visitors.

Sea pinks, **sea campion** and **sheep's bit scabious** are among the wild flowers blooming in May and June. A 1996 survey recorded 120 species of wild plants on the island. One of the rarest, in an Orkney context, is the **bog myrtle**.

The offshore uninhabited islet of the **Calf of Eday** is a designated Site of Special Scientific Interest (SSSI) where 32 species have been recorded. **Puffins**, **guillemots**, **black guillemots**, **razorbills** and **kittiwakes** nest on Grey Head in May–June, leaving towards the end of July. 675 pairs of **great black-backed gulls** and some **herring gulls**, **skuas** and **eider ducks** nest on the heather moorland, **fulmars** on the shallow cliff ledges, and **Arctic terns** along the shore. **Cormorants** nest at the southern end and are so numerous that Eday islanders are known to other Orcadians as *Scarfs*, the local name for a cormorant or shag. Visitors are welcome on the Calf but prohibited during the lambing season in May. Dogs are not allowed. Large parties (over 10 people) should ask permission to land (✆01857-622260 or boatman 01857-622218).

GETTING THERE

By Air

You can take a ferry to **London Airport** as well as fly in. Eday's airfield is named after the nearby Bay of London and should provide you with a 'guess what?' story when you get home. *Loganair* (✆01856-872494/873457; www.loganair.co.uk), flies to Eday from Kirkwall on a Wednesday at 10.25am and 5pm, returning at 10.58am and 5.15pm. Departure times vary during winter. **Orkney Adventure Ticket,** round trip sightseer fare of £31; and senior citizen discount available.

By Sea

Three ferries sail to Eday from Kirkwall. They are *MV Earl Thorfinn* (190 passengers and 25 cars); *MV Earl Sigurd* (190 passengers and 25 cars); and *MV Varagen* (144 passengers and 32 cars). The ferry operates Monday to Sunday and leaves Kirkwall at 10.30am and 3pm on Monday; 7.40am and 4pm on Tuesday; 7am, 10.10am and 4pm on Wednesday; 7am on Thursday; 10.10am and 4pm on Friday; 7am and 4pm on Saturday; and 9.20am and 8.05pm on Sunday. It goes via Sanday on some days. The trip takes about 35 minutes on the direct route and about two hours on the Sanday route. The return adult fare is £13.10, cars and mobile homes £29.30, motorcycles £19.60, and bicycles £2.60 return. Bookings at Orkney Ferries, Kirkwall (✆01856-872044; fax 01856-872921; email info@ orkneyferries.co.uk).

GETTING AROUND

Car Hire. Self-drive or private hire available on daily or weekly rates, contact Alan Stewart, Stackald (✆01857-622206).

Bicycle Hire. Cycles for adults and children at daily and weekly rates, contact Mr Burkett, Hamarr (✆01857-622331).

Tours

There is an **Eday Explorer Tours** on Monday, Wednesday and Friday from May to August. The ferry leaves Kirkwall at 10.10am and arrives at Eday at 12.05pm (via Sanday) on Monday, 11.25 am on Wednesday and Friday. The minibus tour takes about 2½ hours. You can be dropped at the Mill Loch bird hide to watch waterfowl or walk to nearby archaeo-logical sites. The return ferry leaves at 4.30pm on Monday and Wednesday and 5.30pm on Friday. Packed lunches are available. Tour costs £7.50 per person, plus the ferry fare which you pay direct to the ferry operator. Contact Alan Stewart (Stackland, ✆01857-622206; email alan.stewart9@btinternet.com).

The **Eday Heritage Tour** on Sunday from July to September is for visitors with their own vehicle. Meet the guide at Eday pier at 10.35am for a tour around the major archaeological monuments and sights, or take a guided walk along the **Eday Heritage Walk**. Cost is £15 (no concessions), excludes ferry fare. Book at least two days in advance through Visit Orkney, Kirkwall (✆01856-872856, or contact 01857-622248/60).

ACCOMMODATION

Bed & Breakfast

Sara Cheesman: Newark Farm (✆01857-622224). One twin room ensuite, evening meal.
Mrs D. Cockram: Skaill (✆01857-622271). One twin, one double room, packed lunches and evening meal. Closed during lambing (April/May).
Mrs E. Hewison: Groatha (✆01857-622338). Packed lunches and evening meal available.
Sherry Kerr: Redbanks (✆01857-622219). Double room with shower in croft, five minutes' walk from ferry terminal, evening meal.
Emma Popplewell: Blett, Carrick Bay (✆01857-622248). One double and one single room, packed lunches and evening meal available.

Self-Catering. *Dr W.J.Cormack:* (✆020-8941 5291). Three-star, sleeps four.

Hostels

Eday Youth Hostel: London Bay, Eday KW17 2AB (✆01857-622206/311). Operated by Eday Community Association, open April to September. Available to SYHA members. 24 beds, two rooms with 9+ beds, shop 1½ miles (2.4km) away, ferry 4 miles (6km). Bed linen provided. Campers, walkers and cyclists welcome. From £8 a night.

Camping

Most farmers will let you camp on their land if you first ask permission. Contact *Eday Com-munity Association* (✆01857-622206/311) for help.

SHOPPING

Sui Generis Gallery: Redbank, Eday KW17 2AA (✆01857-622219; email enquiries@sui-generisfurniture.co.uk; www.suigenerisfurniture.co.uk), near the ferry terminal. Woodwork, including making and designing fine furniture, bookbinding, and carving. Charge for tour that takes up to one hour. Visits are preferred by arrangement. Open all year.

Emma Popplewell at *Blett Boathouse*, Calf Sound (✆01857-622248), sells island fleeces, hand-spun knitwear, and gives carding and spinning demonstrations. Coffee, snacks and meals available. Open all year.

HELP AND INFORMATION

Eday Tourist Association: Stackald KW17 2AD (✆01857-622206).
Doctor: Dr L. Fortune, Heatherlea (✆01857-622243).
Nurse: Mrs H. Bremner, Galthya (✆01857-622231).
Post Office: Mrs C. Kerr, Redbanks (✆01857-622339).

There is a general store and off-licence at *Eday Community Enterprises* (✆01857-622283) and an **island information** board at the ferry pier car park.

STRONSAY

Stronsay is about 7 miles (11km) from north to south and looks like the three-legged symbol of the Isle of Man as a result of the three large bays which have bitten chunks out of it – St Catherine's Bay, the Bay of Holland, and Mill Bay. Dotted around it are the islets of Papa Stronsay, Holm of Huip, Little Linga, Linga Holm, noted for a splendidly preserved Pictish house, and Auskerry, which is also rich in prehistoric remains. Stronsay is low-lying, the highest point being Burgh Hill at 154ft (46m).

Along its east coast between Lamb Ness and Odiness is a magnificent stretch of coastal cliffs which includes the famous **Vat of Kirbister**, a dramatic opening or *gloup* spanned by what many consider the finest natural rock arch in Orkney. Fishing boats can sail under this with ease. The east coast is also notable for the structures perched on top of three sea stacks which are thought to be the remains of mini-monasteries or the sites of hermitages dating back as early as the eighth century. The largest of these sites is at the **Broch of Burgh Head**, originally joined to the mainland by a rock bridge. Along the landward side of the stack is a stone wall erected as a symbolic barrier against the sinful outside world. A small ruined hermitage nestles inside a high parapet wall on **Tam's Castle**, the southern and larger of two stacks in Odin Bay. The other stack **the Malme**, is the site of the third early hermitage, now just a grass covered mound.

Near **Bluther's Geo** on the bay is a natural rock swimming pool, which is ideal for a dip and a picnic. A signed nature walk gives easy access to the Vat of Kirbister and cliff scenery in the area. From Whitehall the full circular walk covers 10 miles (16km), although you can vary the length to suit your fitness level. The walk takes in **Burgh Hill**, an area full of the interesting plantlife associated with northern maritime heath. South of Burgh Head the peninsula of Lamb Ness, on the east side of the Bay of Houseby, is a maze of prehistoric sites, including the remains of a broch which was partly excavated in the middle of the 19th century. Two of the cells on either side of the entrance passage can be seen through holes in the roof. Nearer the shore are a number of unexcavated mounds thought to be covering chambered tombs.

The **Dane's Pier**, frequented by seals, rather than boats, is a stony spit regarded as the site of a Norse harbour; **the Pow** at the head of the bay is a pool which provides local fisher-men with a safe anchorage. It dries out at low water. Along the coastal track to the Pow are clumps of unusual **white thistles**, as well as **Patagonian ragwort**, a naturalised plant from Patagonia and southern Chile. This is a round trip of 12 miles (19km) from Whitehall. Archaeological digs have revealed the presence of several intact prehistoric settlements and field systems on the island. Near the **Hillock of Baywest** is a chambered tomb dating from around 3,000BC. Just above the shoreline is an elongated mound containing a burial chamber of the stalled type, the earliest type found in Orkney. To the north another mound contains a broch tower and a broad platform which conceals the remains of what must have been an extensive Iron Age village.

The Ro-Ro ferry berths at **Whitehall**, which was once one of Scotland's major herring ports. In its heydey the harbour skyline was criss-crossed with the masts of up to 300 drifters and old men say that on Sundays it was often possible to walk to the neighbouring islet of Papa Stronsay across the decks of the anchored fishing fleet. Whitehall was so busy during the seasonal herring boom that it had a cinema, an ice-cream parlour and, in the original Stronsay Hotel, a bar which was said to be the longest in the north of Scotland (it burnt down in 1937). The industry which once employed hundreds of men, women and children declined in the 1930s and apart from the memories only the old **Stronsay fish market** remains. This has been renovated and is now a café, a hostel, and an interpretive centre where you can learn all about the days of the silver herring and other facets of island life. **Lower Whitehall**, built to house the community of herring fishermen and their families, is now virtually deserted.

Kelp production began in Orkney in 1722 and was a major industry in Stronsay during the 18th century. It was prepared by burning dried *tangle* (seaweed) in the circular stone-lined pits of kelp kilns to produce soda and potash for use in the production of glass, soap and iodine. On **Grice Ness**, beyond Lower Whitehall, well preserved kelp kilns and drying areas share the promontory with a prehistoric chambered cairn. Like the herrings, kelp is no longer a mainstay of the Stronsay community, although some is still gathered.

The **Ayre of Myres** behind Whitehall Village has a sandy beach where you can swim, picnic or watch seals. **Mill Bay** has the longest of the island's beaches, 1½ miles (2.4km) of dazzling white sand along its horseshoe shape. In the middle is the **Mermaid's Chair**, a rock which is said to give any girl sitting on it the power to predict the future. Above the bay is **Stronsay Meal Mill**, a three-storey early 19th-century mill which stands at the foot of Mill Brae on the burn which runs down to the bay from the loch of **Meikle Water**. The spring known as the **Well of Kildinguie**, just below high-water mark on Mill Bay, was once a famous holy well and a resort of pilgrims. When Orkney belonged to Denmark as a result of its union with Norway people came from Scandinavia to Stronsay to drink the water which, mixed with dulse, an edible red seaweed, gathered further along the shore, was reputed to be a sovereign cure for all known ailments – except the Black Death. **Rothiesholm Sand** has more than a mile of splendid beach, where some of the rarest shells in Orkney wash up. **St Catherine's Bay** has a fine 1¼ mile (2km) stretch where patches of blue-flowered **oysterplants** enliven the shingle to the south. This is a popular beach to dig out *spoots*, or edible razor shells. Near the shop and post office in the middle of the island is Stronsay's only church, the **Moncur Memorial Church**, which was built in 1955. It is architecturally unique in Orkney, although it embodies many traditional Orcadian features.

FLORA AND FAUNA

Flora

Well farmed Stronsay has only one remaining area of moorland, in the south-west peninsula of Rothiesholm (pronounced 'Rowsam'), where local crofters have traditional peat rights. This is purple with **heather** and **bell heather** during the late summer and the wetter areas are full of **rushes**, **sedges**, **cotton grass** and **cross-leaved heath**. On the opposite side of the island Burgh Hill is a good example of northern maritime heath in which **shrubby heather**, **bell heather**, **crowberry** and **creeping willow**, together with a variety of **mosses** and **lichens**, have produced springy carpet. The **heath spotted orchid** is common here and in the wetter flushes **spring scilla**, **lesser club moss**, **bog pimpernel**, **bog asphodel** and **spearwort** are among the more interesting plants. Around the large loch of Meikle Water marsh plants include **bog bean**, **ragged robin**, **mare's tail** and the spectacular purple **northern fen orchid**. In the loch and smaller pools water **crowfoot** is often abundant and in wetter hollows along the shore there are dense swathes of **yellow iris**. The loch is stocked with **brown trout** and the fishing is free. The attractive blue-flowered **oysterplant** grows in profusion in the south along the Sand of the Crook.

Fauna

Grey seal numbers increase during the autumn when they come ashore for breeding. They can be seen hauled out on Linga Holm, the Holms of Spurness and Huip, and on Auskerry to the south. Favourite haul-out sites for **common seals** – not so common as greys – are Papa Stronsay, Linga Holm and the Bay of Holland. **Linga Holm** is a 140-acre (56ha) uninhabited island off the coast of Stronsay which has the third largest single island breeding population in the world for grey seals. Nearly 2,500 grey seal pups have been recorded here, some 7% of Britain's entire grey seal breeding pool. Linga Holm is not just important for grey seals; other wildlife includes common seals, **otters**, 73 plant species, a small **Arctic tern** colony, **ringed plover**, a few pairs of **Arctic skuas**, **meadow** and **rock pipits**, **snipe**, **skylark** and a few **gulls**. On the island is a brackish lagoon, freshwater lochans, grassland, heathland, an old croft house and three listed ancient monuments, as well as eleven other archaeological features. It is a low island, rising to 59ft (18m) above sea level, surrounded by largely rocky shores. For more information contact Scottish Wildlife Trust (Cramond House, Cramond Glebe Road, Edinburgh EH4 6NS; ✆0131-312 7765; fax 0131-312 8705; email enquiries@ swt.org.uk; www.swt.org.uk).

Bird-watching

Stronsay Bird Reserve (✆01857-616363) on the shore of Mill Bay has lots to offer at any time of the year, but especially during the breeding season from late April to mid July. The reserve is owned and run by bird artists John and Sue Holloway and their family and is open all year round. Entry is opposite the Old Mill. The island is a good place to see migrant birds in spring and autumn. Unusual species such as **semi-palmated sandpiper** from America, **White's thrush** from Russia, **tawny pipit**, and the rare **yellow-breasted bunting** have been recorded in recent years. Large colonies of seabirds populate the cliffs in the south-east and south-west of the island and the lochs and marshes are havens for ducks and waders, such as **shoveler**, **red-breasted merganser**, **redshank**, **golden plover** and even **pintail**. The wreckage-strewn islet of **Auskerry** with its 112ft (34m) lighthouse, is a breeding site for **puffins**, **Arctic terns** and **guillemots** and has a large colony of **storm petrels**. There's no regular access to this uninhabited islet, about 3 miles (5km) south of Stronsay. Enquire among the fishermen at Whitehall Village for boat hire.

GETTING THERE

By Air

Loganair (✆01856-872494/873457; www.loganair.co.uk), flies to Stronsay from Kirkwall at 10.15am and 5pm on Monday; 9.15 am and 4pm on Tuesday and Thursday; 9.20am and 3.55pm on Wednesday; 10.15am and 3pm on Friday; and 8.15am and 3.45pm on Saturday. The winter schedule differs so check with Loganair. **Orkney Adventure Ticket,** round trip sightseer fare of £31; and senior citizen discount available so check with the airline.

By Sea

Three vehicle and passenger ferries, *MV Earl Thorfinn*, *MV Earl Sigurd* (both taking 190 passengers and 25 cars), and *MV Varagen* (144 passengers and 32 cars), serve Stronsay, leaving Kirkwall at 10.05am and 3pm on Monday; 7am and 4.20pm on Tuesday; 7am, 11.10am and 4pm on Wednesday; 7am and 4pm on Thursday; 4pm on Friday; 7am on Saturday; and 9am and 7.45pm on Sunday. The trip takes 1 hour 35 minutes. The return passenger fare is £13.10, cars and mobile homes £29.30, motorcycles £19.60, and bicycles £2.60 return. Bookings at Orkney Ferries, Kirkwall office (✆01856-872044; fax 01856-872921; email info@orkneyferries.co.uk).

GETTING AROUND

Hire cars and minibus service: Mr M Williamson, Olivebank (✆01857-616255).
Self-drive and **taxi service:** D S Peace, Samson's Lane (✆01857-616335).
Cycle hire from *Stronsay Hotel* (✆01857-616213).

ACCOMMODATION

Stronsay Hotel: Allen and Carol Cooke, Whitehall Village (℡01857-616213; fax 01857-616465; email stronsay.hotel@stronsay.co.uk). Three-star, four bedrooms with en- uite facilities, licensed, resident's lounge. All meals provided, including picnics. From £30 a night.

Bed & Breakfast and Self-Catering

Airy: Mrs Shearer (℡01857-616231). Evening meal available.

Claremount: Mr and Mrs Abrams (℡01857-616478). Full board available.

Clestrain: Mrs Harcus (℡01857-616340). Full board available.

Mrs G. McCarthy: Helmsley (℡01857-616369). B&B and DB&B available. Open all year.

Stronsay Bird Reserve: John and Sue Holloway, Castle, Mill Bay (℡01857-616363). Full board also available. Camping (booking essential).

Hostel

Stronsay Fish Mart: Madelaine and Clive Martin, Whitehall Village, Stronsay KW17 2AS (℡01857-616367; email stronsayfishmart@yahoo.co.uk). Café, interpretation centre, and an hostel with bunk beds sleeping 10 people. £14 a night, including bedding. Fully equipped kitchen for self-catering, shower and washing facilities. Fully heated throughout by eco-logically-friendly ground source.

Camping

Torness Camping Barn: Mr and Mrs Cotterill (℡01857-616314).

Most landowners will allow you to camp on their land, but first ask permission.

EATING AND DRINKING

Stronsay Fish Mart: Madelaine and Clive Martin, Whitehall Village, Stronsay KW17 2AS (℡01857-616367; email stronsayfishmart@yahoo.co.uk). Former fish mart, now café, in-terpretation centre, which charts the history of the herring industry, and self-catering hostel. Café serves hot meals, light snacks, hot and cold drinks, delicious homebakes. Café and interpretation centre open every day in the high season, except Tuesday. Near ferry terminal. Opposite hotel and shop.

Stronsay Hotel: Whitehall Village (℡01857-616213; fax 01857-616465). Home cooking and seafood specialities. Fresh local seafood in a variety of dishes. Wide vegetarian and vegan menu.

Woodlea: Mrs Shearer (℡01857-616337). Take-aways, open Wednesday 9.30am to 11pm, Friday, Saturday and Sunday 4.30pm to 6.30pm and 9pm to 11pm.

SHOPPING

Auskerry Sheepskins: (℡077-7835 8029). Hand-cured North Ronaldsay sheepskins and rugs in natural colours.

John Holloway: (℡01857-616363). Bird paintings and landscapes by John Holloway are on display at *Stronsay Bird Reserve.*

HELP AND INFORMATION

Stronsay Tourist Association: c/o Mr C Wilde, Millbank, Stronsay KW17 2AG (℡01857-616352).

Doctor: Dr G McKay, Geramount House (℡01857-616321).

Nurse: Mrs R Stevenson (℡01857-616251).

Royal Bank: every Thursday.

Post Office: Sue Fairbrother (℡01857-616217). Open Tuesday, Wednesday, Friday and Saturday 9am to 1pm, and Monday and Thursday 9am to 4pm.

Community Centre: Mrs S Miller (℡01857-616256).

There is a **petrol station** at Boondatoon (Mr Caithness; ℡01857-616248).

Swimming pool (℡01857-616331), details of opening times available in local shops.

General merchants:
Ebenezer Stores: Mike and Viv Erdman (✆01857-616339) and off-licence.
Kelp Stores: Mr J Fiddler (✆01857-616210).
Olivebank: Mr M Williamson (✆01857-616255), where you can also buy petrol.

PAPA STRONSAY

Not since 1046, when Earl Thorfinn the Mighty had his rival Earl Rognvald Brusason killed on this tiny island while Rognvald was looking for barley malt to brew his Christmas ale, had so much attention been focused on Papa Stronsay as in mid–1999. This was when monks of the Transalpine Redemptorists moved from their monastery in France to seek peace and solitude on the uninhabited 185-acre (75ha) island lying off Stronsay, thought to be one of the earliest locations of Christianity in the Northern Isles. When the Vikings first arrived in Orkney during the eighth century, Papa Stronsay already had a religious presence. It was one of the island homes of the mysterious Celtic clergy known to the Norsemen as *papar*. The pagan Vikings called the islet *papo[ob]y hin litli* ('little island of the priests') then left its occupants more or less alone. The return of the monks coincided with the excavation of a pre-Norse church on the island, **St Nicholas Chapel**, which was originally consecrated more than 1,000 years ago. Excavations on the site of the chapel began in 1998 at which time foundations and floors thought to date from AD1200 were uncovered. Further excavation revealed that this medieval chapel had been built on top of an earlier, perhaps Pictish, stone building that dated from the eighth or ninth century. The monks of the Transalpine Redemptorists, who refuse to accept the modernisation of the Roman Catholic Church and continue to say Mass in Latin, were attracted to Papa Stronsay after learning of its long Christian history.

As well as the religious sites on the island you can see cairns and a burnt mound near Mill Loch. There's a 26ft (8m) high mound south of the loch known as **Earl's Knoll**, as well as the foundations of the barracks which housed fisher girls during the years when Papa Stronsay was a busy herring fishing centre with five fish-curing stations. There is also a well preserved example of a kelp kiln of advanced design from the time the collection, drying and burning of this seaweed meant prosperity for the islanders. In the north-east at **The Ness** is the white tower of an automatic light beacon. The **Point of the Graan** is a sliver of land popular with seals and is one sheltering arm of the shallow tidal flats of the **Bight of Stacka-back**. There is no regular access to the island but, by appointment and weather permitting, the resident monks offer a free boat ride to the **Mound of the Celtic Cross**, a memorial to the monks and hermits of long ago, or around the island (✆01857-616389).

SANDAY

Sanday is the largest of the North Isles group and lies 15 miles (24km) north-east of Kirkwall. Of all Orkney islands it offered settlers the best arable farmland. Medieval taxation rolls valued land here higher than anywhere else in Orkney and the island paid one-sixth of all taxes raised, these being levied in proportion to the island's agricultural yield. The population has dwindled over the years to its present 500. Only a century ago more than 2,000 people lived here and their children ticked off the days on fingers with the pet names *peediman* (little finger); *lickpot* (third finger); *langman* (middle finger); *loomikin* (index finger); and *toomikin* (thumb).

Early August brings the **Sanday Show** which gives locals and visitors alike a chance to admire island cattle, sheep, ponies and goats, and sample homebakes. Knitting, embroidery, fruit and vegetables are also displayed and sold. The annual **Harvest Home** is held in October or early November when a feast is followed by a dance. St Colm model yacht club holds a regatta at Roos Loch on Boxing Day and another at Easter, water level permitting.

There is an extraordinary density of prehistoric, Viking, and later settlement sites scattered around Sanday. Major excavations at Pool in the 1980s revealed a succession of Neolithic, Pictish and Viking deposits and striking features in areas of the flat landscape are farm mounds, little hills composed almost entirely of man-made material. The most spectacular find of all was made in 1991 on the shore at Quoy Banks, near Scar, in Burness. This was a ninth century **Viking boat burial**, one of the few to be excavated in Scotland in modern times. It contained the skeletons of an old woman, a young man and a child, along with rich ornaments, household goods and weapons. Apart from a sword, bow and arrows, bone comb, lead weights, and 22 gaming pieces lying next to the man, the woman had been buried with a gilded brooch, an iron sickle, and a stunningly carved whalebone plaque. You can see the finds in the Orkney Museum, Kirkwall. Such a burial could only have been staged for a family of enormous wealth.

At Scar is a 20-ton lump of rock known as the **Saville Stone**. It is said to have been flung from Eday by a furious witch whose daughter had eloped with a Sanday farmer. The isolated peninsula of Els Ness is peppered with cairns, a Neolithic burial complex comprising two chambered tombs and numerous burial mounds. The most complete of the tombs is **Quoyness**, built around 2900BC in a similar style to Maes Howe and one of Orkney's archaeological showpieces. You'll need a torch to explore. Nearby lies the tomb of **Edmondshowe**, or Augmund Howe, which is itself enclosed by an arc of 11 Bronze Age burial mounds connected by an earthen bank. Across the bay at Tresness you can see part of the wall of **Wasso Broch**, while at the end of the Ness is an unexcavated Neolithic tomb. Nearby is deserted **Tresness Farm** with its 19th-century horse engine house where a horse turned the machine to drive a threshing-mill in an adjoining barn.

Before the lighthouse was erected at **Start Point**, off the north-east promontory, Sanday was a magnet for shipwrecks. Between 1788 and 1802 when the lighthouse was built, more than 20 vessels were victims of the reefs and the fact that low-lying Sanday was difficult to see from the deck of a ship. The islanders seem to have regarded these as providential. When engineer Robert Stevenson, grandfather of Robert Louis Stevenson, arrived in Sanday in 1806 to fit the lighthouse with the first revolving light in Scotland, he discovered that not only did local farmers fence their fields with ship's timbers instead of stone, but that rents were higher on the side of the island that produced the most wrecks. Even with a lighthouse ships continued to founder. One was the Dutch frigate *Utrecht*, which struck on the appropriately named Holms of Ire in 1807. The lighthouse was rebuilt in 1870 and later painted with vertical black and white candy stripes in a pattern rarely seen elsewhere. This didn't stop a German destroyer going aground in 1919 and its turbines and boilers can still be seen at low water in Lopness Bay. The steam trawler *Alex Hastings* was wrecked on Outer Holm in 1939. The lighthouse has been automatic since 1962. It can be visited by arrangement with A Skea at Garbo (✆01857-600385). It stands on a tidal island, so make sure you cross the sands of Ayre Sound around low water. On the island is the Neolithic chambered tomb of *Mount Maesry*, which was long used as a potato store by the lighthouse keepers.

On **Tofts Ness** peninsula, north of Start Point, is a prehistoric funerary complex of 500 burial mounds whose potential as one of Britain's most important sites awaits confirmation by archaeological excavation. On the west side of Ottterswick Bay is **Ortie**, an abandoned 19th-century fishing village which at one time housed more than 60 people. The derelict houses line a remarkably long narrow *kloss*, or lane. Some still bear the thatch and *simmons*, or straw ropes, commonly used for roofing in poor communities.

Close to 19th century **Westowe Estate House** at Scar are the remains of a circular stone windmill used for grinding meal from the estate's steadings. At **Boloquoy** is another early 19th-century meal mill. From excavations in the 19th-century the **Sties of Brough** are known to be pagan Viking graves. A sword, spearhead, shield boss and an axe were unearthed. At the head of the Bay of Stove are the ruined buildings of the industrialised 19th-century **Stove model farm**, with a steam engine house, red-brick chimney and boiler-house that were the wonder of Sanday in their day. There is no public access.

FLORA AND FAUNA

Apart from its impressive archaeological significance, Sanday's sweeping bays with their white sandy beaches – especially at Whitemill, Backaskaill, Sandquoy, Lopness, and Tressness bays – are a marvel. At Backaskaill Bay seven whales were stranded in the 1990s.

Look for **seals** and **Arctic terns** here. A delight for beachcombers are the shells. The **cowrie** (*groatie buckies*) and the beautiful **Faroese Sunset** are the two most sought after. The long indented coastline of the island gives easy access to one of Sanday's principal wildlife attractions – seals. **Common seal** pups can be seen swimming at Otterswick Bay in June and **grey seals** are born on secluded beaches in November. The Holms of Spurness are favourite breeding spots for greys. Common seals and waders can be seen in the tidal bay of Cata Sand and in nearby Newark Bay. More elusive are Sanday's **otters**. Look out for their tell-tale five-toed tracks in the sand and their 'spraint', or droppings.

Sanday attracts most of the seabirds, terns and waders found elsewhere in Orkney but has very little in the way of seacliffs and therefore no large cliff-nesting seabird colonies. Vagrants such as **hoopoe**, **red-breasted flycatcher**, **ortolan** and **little** and **pine buntings** have also all been spotted. Nearly 100 pairs of **ringed plovers** breed on the island and its shallow lochs draw **mallard**, **teal**, **wigeon**, **shoveler, tufted duck**, **red-breasted merganser** and **eider**, and throughout the spring and summer the air is filled with the cries of **lapwings**, **curlews**, **oystercatchers**, **redshanks**, **dunlin** and **snipe**. Sanday was the last known Orkney breeding site of the **red-necked phalarope**. Arctic terns breed on the island and there are also **Arctic skuas** at the Gump of Spurness, where there are Bronze Age remains of a burnt mound. **Short-eared owls** nest in the dunes and the coastline is full of waders in winter. One count totted up nearly 8,000 birds, more than 1,200 of them **purple sandpipers**.

GETTING THERE

By Air

Loganair (✆01856-872494/873457; www.loganair.co.uk), flies to Sanday from Kirkwall on Monday at 10.15am and 5pm, Tuesday and Thursday at 9.15am and 4pm, Wednesday at 8.15am and 2.50pm, Friday at 10.15am and 3pm, and Saturday at 8.15am and 3.45pm. Winter schedule differs so check with Loganair. **Orkney Adventure Ticket** round trip sightseer fare of £31; and senior citizen discount available.

By Sea

The Ro-Ro-off vehicle and passenger ferry from Kirkwall takes less than 1½ hours and berths at Loth at the south-western tip of the island, where there is a waiting room, toilets and information board. Three vessels, *MV Earl Thorfinn* and *MV Earl Sigurd* (both carrying 190 passengers and 25 cars), and *MV Varagen* (144 passengers and 32 cars), operate between Kirkwall and Sanday at 10.30am and 4.40pm on Monday; 7.40am and 4pm on Tuesday; 10.10am and 4.40pm on Wednesday and Friday; 4.40pm on Saturday; and 9.20am and 8.05pm on Sunday. The crossing takes 25 minutes. The return adult fare is £13.10, cars and mobile homes £29.30, motorcycles £19.60 and bicycles £2.60 return. Bookings made through the Orkney Ferries office in Kirkwall (✆01856-872044; fax 01856-872921; email info@orkneyferries.co.uk).

GETTING AROUND

Dial-a-Ride Tina Flett, Marygarth (✆01857-600284). Ferry bus service.
Car and taxi hire
Kettletoft (✆01857-600321).
Marygarth Manse: Bernie Flett (✆01857-600284), for self-drive cars, taxi, cycle hire, and mini-bus tours.
Kettletoft Hotel also hires out cycles (✆01857-600217).
Little Isgarth (✆01857-600370; email lir@zetnet.co.uk).

TOURS

On Monday, Wednesday and Friday May–September you can take a **Sanday Package Tour** (minimum four people) from Kirkwall. You arrive on the island at 11.55am for a tour of historical and scenic sites, returning to the pier at about 6pm. A packed lunch is included in the fare. Booking and enquiries to Bernie Flett (Marygarth, Sanday; ✆01857-600467).

ACCOMMODATION

Hotels

Kettletoft Hotel: Mark and Julia Lawlor, Kettletoft, Sanday KW17 2BJ (☎/fax 01857-600217; email marktlawlor@btopenworld.com; www.kettletofthotel.moonfruit.com). Small one-star family-run hotel. From £25 a night. Fish-and-Chip shop open Wednesday and Saturday, take-aways available. Bar meals and snacks served daily.

Guest House

The Belsair: Elizabeth and John Sinclair, Kettletoft, Sanday KW17 2BJ (☎01857-600206). Six bedrooms overlooking the old harbour. En-suite accommodation from £30 per person. Home cooking, licensed. Homebakes, bar snacks and evening meals in dining room, bar or tea room. Local produce.

Bed & Breakfast

Bowbells: Lilian Harcus (☎01857-600281).

Ladybank: Denise Thompson (☎01857-600339; email ladybank@btinternet.com; www. sandayorkney.co.uk). Old manse, meals using local produce, From £22.

North Myre: Margaret Groat (☎01857-600396).

Garbo: Irene Skea (☎01857-600385).

Marygarth Manse: Mrs Tina Flett, Sanday KW17 2BN (☎01857-600284; fax 01857-600467; email tinaflett@marygarth.fsnet.co.uk; www.sanday.co.uk). One-star, family run, home cooking, evening meals, special diets.

Self-Catering

Castlehill: Jean Sinclair (☎01857-600361). Four bedrooms.

Quivals: Amy or Damian (☎01857-600370/418), sleeps 10, ground floor bedroom, meals available. Bicycles for hire, kayak trips.

Park: Burrian KW17 2BP (☎01857-600403; email burrian@bushinternet.vom). Former croft, close to lighthouse.

Southend Schoolhouse: Netta Bain (☎01857-600389), or Margaret Peace (☎01857-600230). Sleeps 6–8.

The Bungalow: Mrs Sandra Towrie, Odinsgarth, Sanday KW17 2BN (☎/fax 01857-600347; email towriewbf@aol.com). Two-star, three-bedroomed bungalow, sleeps six. All linen provided. From £120 to £220 a week.

Self-catering **caravan** at Tofts contact Cherrie Ellis (☎01857-600769).

Hostel

Ayre's Rock Hostel: Diane Grieve, Sanday KW17 2AY (☎01857-600410; email diane@ ayresrock.fsnet.co.uk), self-catering kitchen, within walking distance of swimming pool and shop. Two twin and one family room en suite. Sleeps 7–8. From £12. Caravan, sleeps 6. Campsite, tents from £3. Meals available on request.

SPORT AND RECREATION

There's a **swimming pool** (☎01857-600310) close to the school and community hall – see shop notices for opening times – and a nine-hole **golf course** (☎01857-600341), small charge, notice on caravan (clubhouse). **Boats** are available on Bea Loch from Ernie Groundwater (Castlehill; ☎01857-600285) and at North Loch from Angus Muir (Tofts; ☎01857-600331). Enquire locally about **pony trekking** and **sea fishing**. **Sanday Light Railway** (☎01857-600700; email charlie.sandayrailway@btinternet.com; www. sandaylightrailway.co.uk), the UK's most northerly passenger-carrying railway, offers train trips by prior arrangement. Enjoy home baking at the *Brief Encounters Tea Room* set back in time.

SHOPPING

There is not much in the way of souvenirs to be found, although you can browse among an extensive range of hand-dyed angora thermal clothing (including underwear) at *Orkney*

Angora (Upper Breckan, Sanday KW17 2AZ; ✆01857-600421; email info@orkneyangora. co.uk; www.orkneyangora.co.uk), mail order is available.

There are a number of shops on the island and at several of them you can also buy petrol (one even sells peat). *Corses Shop* (✆01857-600312); *Kettletoft Stores* (✆01857-600255); and *Roadside Shop* (✆01857-600273), all sell fuel. *Sinclair* at Kettletoft (✆01857-600455), sells meat, vegetables and has an off-licence, *Ayre's Rock* (✆01857-600410) sells crafts and local produce, and *Rendall* at Neigarth (✆01857-600327), sells fresh vegetables.

Bressigarth Tea Room June Harvey (✆01857-600439), serves tea, coffee, cakes and light snacks. Open Tuesday to Sunday 10.30am to 5.30pm.

HELP AND INFORMATION

Piermaster: ✆01857-600227.
Airfield Hut: ✆01857-600346.
Doctor: ✆01857-600221.
Minister: ✆01857-600429.
Swimming Pool: ✆01857-600310.

There are **post offices** at Kettletoft (✆01857-600206); Quivals (✆01857-600467); Rusness (✆01857-600385); and Lady (✆01857-600367). The local **Tourist Information Office** is adjacent to the post office at Lady.

WESTRAY

Ever since the Viking occupation of Orkney, Westray has played a role in the life of the isles out of all proportion to its size. Although it is not the largest of the group, Westray still holds the sceptre as 'Queen of the North Isles' because not only is it the most heavily populated, with more than 600 residents, it is also the most visibly prosperous. Westray's prosperity is based on the many fine farms on its 11,650 acres (4,715ha) and an expanding fishing fleet.

While beef cattle farming is the main contributor to the island's economy seafaring is an inherited Norse trait and the island has developed a modern fishing industry built up around the largest whitefish trawler fleet in Orkney, with smaller craft fishing inshore for crab and lobster. Velvet crabs exported to Europe are a significant part of the small creel boat fishing economy and a modern factory at Gill Pier exports processed crabs throughout Britain and Continental Europe. You can buy whole or dressed crab, cocktail claws, and white or brown crab meat at the factory (Westray Processors, Gill Pier, Westray KW17 2DL; ✆01857-677273; fax 01857-677497). Echoing a bygone industry are the tangle (kelp) dykes used to dry the seaweed stalks which are still gathered during the winter and exported in June to south-west Scotland, where they are used in a variety of products, including fertiliser and ice cream.

Westray's location and its excellent harbour in Pierowall Bay has long given it a strategic place at the sea route from Norway and Shetland. This deep symmetrical bay was considered by the Vikings to be the finest anchorage in Orkney. For a quick portrait of the island and its attractions get into your stride with a visit to the **Westray Heritage Centre**, at the Lodge, next to the hotel in Pierowall village (✆01857-677231). Originally a 19th-century school, the centre houses a permanent natural heritage display and also changing local interest and historical exhibitions. There is a huge collection of photographs and three wall panels in collage together with a 10ft (3m) high cliff complete with bird models and authentic sounds. On sale are local publications, crafts and light refreshments. Open May to September, Sunday and Monday 11.30am to 5pm, Tuesday and Saturday 2pm to 5pm; in July and August also open on Tuesday to Saturday from 10am to midday. Admission for adults £2.60, senior citizens £1.50, school children and students 50p.

Pierowall, nearly 10 miles (16km) north of the Rapness ferry terminal is Westray's largest continuously occupied settlement, and most of the island's population lives around the village, which has two shops, a post office, heritage and craft centres, a community school, and swimming pool. In late July, Westray hosts one of Orkney's main regattas, with races between Pierowall and neighbouring Papay.

Physically, Westray is about 12 miles (19km) long and four miles (6km) at its widest point. Along the west, a range of hills shields the rest of the island, falling in sheer cliffs to the Atlantic Ocean around Noup Head, with the odd beach such as Grobust further north and Maesand to the south offering peaceful walks or places to beachcomb. To the east, the land is comparatively flat and slopes to sandy beaches at bays such as Skaill, Brough, and Swartmill. Shallow sandy stretches such as the tidal flats at the head of the Bay of Tuquoy are fun places to dig for razor shells (*spoots*) above the tideline when the water is low. Offshore **Rusk Holm** is the home of descendants of the original sheep brought from Norway by the Vikings. Visits are possible; ask the Harbour Master at Gill Pier.

ARCHAEOLOGICAL SITES

The earth in Westray has literally been barely scratched by archaeologists and future years are confidently expected to give up more evidence of the impact the Norse arrival had on island life, as well as the prehistoric settlers who preceded them. The island's Norse heritage came in for a fresh look in 1999 when archaeologists uncovered the remains of a Viking settlement at the **Farm of Trenabie** on the shores of the Bay of Rackwick. A well-preserved longhouse thought to be the home of an early farmer-fisherman came to light during the dig. During quarrying work in 1981 at Pierowall a rock carving with spiral and lozenge design was found that is thought to be a lintel from a 4,000-year-old chambered tomb. Known as the Westray Stone, it is the finest of its kind in Scotland and is on display at the Orkney Museum, in Kirkwall.

In the late 1970s an area of prehistoric settlement was excavated near the golf course at the **Links of Noltland** above Grobust beach. Houses and an enormous area of uncovered midden (accumulated domestic refuse) were dated to around 3000BC, but might even predate Skara Brae, on the Orkney Mainland. These remains, unfortunately, are now once again covered over. On the cliff top not far away is the conspicuous mound of **Queen Howe**, which probably contains a broch tower. The lighthouse at **Noup Head** was built in 1898 to keep vessels off the dangerous North Shoal. It was the first lighthouse to use a system of mercury flotation in the revolving light carriage before it was automated in 1964. For impressive evidence of the island's early Christian presence visit the lonely rock stack and island hermitages such as the **Castle o' Burrian** at Rackwick Bay – also a rewarding place for puffins – nearby Stanger Head, and the Holm of Aikerness, not far from the airfield.

The ruined **Church of St Mary's**, Pierowall, is one of Westray's two medieval kirks. Most of the structure dates from the 17th century but there's a remnant of the original 13th-century building in the south wall. Look for some interesting and well-preserved carved tombstones. From the kirk and its cemetery are magnificent views over Pierowall Harbour.

Lots of Westray's past lies underground, but one impressive structure still stands watch over Pierowall village. This is **Noltland Castle**, a massive though uncompleted fortress built in the second half of the 16th century by Gilbert Balfour, who was Sheriff of Orkney and held high office under Mary Queen of Scots. The castle's 6ft-thick (2m) walls are riddled with more than 70 defensive gunloops ranged in tiers like a naval man-of-war and indicating that the Sheriff must have been a man with an uneasy conscience. He even had two cannon mounted in his kitchen. Tradition says the castle is linked by an underground passage to the **Gentleman's Cave** at Noup on the west side of the island. This cave was a hide-out for Orkney lairds who supported the failed Jacobite rebellion of 1745. The cave can be explored but should be tackled only by the unflinching and with a knowledgeable local guide. At the **Knowe o' Burristae** further down the west coast near the loch of Muckle Water is a large mound containing a broch tower being remorselessly destroyed by the sea. Part of the curved wall is still standing and you can see the entrance to a mural cell or passage.

The 2.2-mile (3.6km) **Coastal Heritage Walk** follows the Tuquoy footpath leading from the parking place on the Ness of Tuquoy to the parish church of Cross Kirk, one of the best preserved medieval churches in Orkney, and the site of Valtjhof, the farm of Thorkel Flayer, a Viking who was burnt to death in his farmhouse with eight of his followers a thousand years ago. Look out along the route for seals, settlement ruins along the shore and abandoned crofts. Netherhouse is one such deserted community. A cluster of half a dozen crofts once dotted the steep brae here overlooking the Westray Firth. The impressive **West Westray Walk** takes you along a 5.7-mile (9.3km) coastal footpath above the cliffs and their vast seabird colonies, with views of Rousay to the south. Park at Kirbist or Noup.

There are shipwreck stories aplenty on Westray, but two are of particular interest. After the remnants of the defeated Spanish Armada attempted to sail home round the top of Scotland in 1588 a small boat with survivors from a galleon wrecked off North Ronaldsay made it to port in Westray. The locals accepted the men they called the Dons and they settled, many marrying island girls and adopting Orkney names. Traces of this Spanish ancestry can still be noticed in some islanders. A century and a half later an unknown ship ran aground and sank off the Head of Aikerness. The sole survivor was a small boy who spoke no recognisable language. He was adopted by a local couple and given the name Archie Angel, after a piece of wood from the wrecked ship was picked up on the shore, bearing the name of its home port, Archangel, in Russia. Although there are still descendants of the boy around the surname has died out and can now be seen only on some old gravestones.

Church Services

The *Church of Scotland* is Westray's largest religious denomination. The kirk, built in 1845, is two miles (3km) south of Pierowall and following extensive refurbishment is now a host venue for many community events. It was the first church in the country to meet all its primary heating needs from renewable sources (Iain MacDonald; ✆/fax 01857-677357; email iain@rapnessmanse.freeserve.co.uk). Open to visitors. The *United Free Church of Scotland* had as its first church the now-ruined building known as the **Sheepie Kirk**. The present kirk was opened in 1867, nearer the manse which was finished in 1863 (Danny Harcus; ✆01857-677301). The *Westray Baptist Kirk*, in the centre of Pierowall village, was built in 1850 (Stephen Hagan; ✆01857-677216; email Stephen.Hagan@orkney.gov.uk). All three denominations meet for Sunday worship at 11.30am. Evening services are held at each kirk on a rotational basis. There is also a small *Gospel Hall* (Christian Brethren) in the centre of Pierowall (Alan Bews; ✆01857-677376).

FLORA AND FAUNA

Flora

Windborne sea spray has created unusual cliff-top salt marshes along the west coast and the hills behind support a rich mosaic of northern maritime heath. **Sea pinks** (thrift) and **spring squill** thrive on the sparse grassland of the cliff-tops and the coastal fringes. Between April and June, **lady's smock** grows in the marshy ground at the edges of the lochs and in undrained land. Around Pierowall Bay you'll find the fragrant **angelica** the Vikings are believed to have brought to the island. Nowadays used mainly candied in confectionery, it was better known in the days of the Norsemen as a healing plant, an antidote to poison, and as a specific against pestilence. According to medieval folklore these amazing properties were revealed to a sage by an angel, hence the name of the plant.

Another flower to look out for in spring is Orkney's most famous plant, the tiny **Scottish primrose** which, while very rare, is now on the increase in Westray helped by farmers agreeing to keep grazing to a minimum where it grows. Good places to look for it are on Fitty and Skea hills, which harbour plants typical of high altitudes. On the storm beach at the Bay of Kirbist, **oysterplants** and **Scottish lovage** can be found. The shores around the island's three largest lochs – Burness, Saintear, and trout-stocked Swartmill – provide a damp habitat for plants such as **marsh marigolds** and **mare's tails**. **Purple orchids**, known locally as 'dead man's liver,' grow on roadside verges and in uncut grassland. They are at their best between May and July. The yellow **kidney vetch** blossoms between June and August.

Fauna

Seals are plentiful around the coast of Westray. Large numbers of **grey seals** and a few **common seals** pup every year on the neighbouring uninhabited islet of Faray, on the Holm of Faray and on Rusk Holm. In Papa Sound, in the north-east the Holm of Aikerness is also an important breeding site. **Whales**, **dolphins** and **porpoises** are occasionally seen. The resident **otters** are shy and difficult to spot, unlike the grey seals which seem to be curious about people and will often follow you as you walk along the shore. Another resident is the **Orkney vole**.

Bird-watching

Twitchers should head for the cliffs of Noup Head, an area many rate with St Kilda as one of Europe's most important seabird breeding sites. The **RSPB Nature Reserve** here includes a 1½ mile (2.4km) stretch of cliffs where more than 25,237 **common guillemots** and 4,698 pairs of **kittiwakes** breed, along with **razorbills**, **shags**, **puffins**, and **fulmars**. Inland from the cliffs **skuas** and **Arctic tern** nest. The reserve is open at all times. There is no admission charge. To get there from Pierowall follow the minor road west to Noup Farm, then the track to the lighthouse at the north end of the reserve. There is no office at the reserve but you can contact the summer warden on Papa Westray (✆01857-644240), April to August only. For more information *RSPB Orkney Reserves Office* (12–14 North End Road, Stromness KW16 3AG; ✆01856-850176; fax 01856-851311; email orkney@ rspb.org.uk) is your best bet.

In May–June this west coast area is regarded as one of the ornithological wonders of north-west Europe. In autumn, Noup cliffs and nearby North Hill attract small numbers of migrants, among them **warblers** and **flycatchers**, **wryneck** and **black redstart**. In the past even a **little egret** has blown in. There are a dozen lochs and lochans on the island where **mute swan**, **teal**, **mallard**, **shoveler** and **tufted duck** breed. The **Loch of Burness** is the most northerly breeding place in Britain for **little grebes**. Shallow lochs provide an important habitat for w**hooper swans** and other waterfowl, and winter in Westray sees a variety of these visitors. Around the lochs **snipe**, **redshank**, **lapwing** and **curlew** are common.

GETTING THERE

By Air

Loganair (✆01856-872494/873457; www.loganair.co.uk), flies to Westray from Kirkwall on Monday at 9.15am and 4pm, Tuesday and Thursday at 8.15am and 3pm, Wednesday at 9.20am and 3.55pm, Friday 9.15am and 4pm, Saturday at 9.20am and 5pm, and Sunday at 2pm. Winter schedules change so check with Loganair. **Orkney Adventure Ticket**, round trip sightseer fare of £31; and senior citizen discount available.

People come to Westray from all over the world for an experience which usually lasts just two minutes. This is the time it takes Loganair to fly on the shortest scheduled flight in the world to Papa Westray. The distance between the two islands is shorter than the main runway at Heathrow Airport, London. The 1½-mile (2.4km) flight has been completed in less than a minute and if you don't believe this, read *Guinness World Records*. Those who travel on this shortest flight can get a certificate at the Loganair desk in Kirkwall.

By Sea

Westray is served by ferries *MV Earl Thorfinn*, *MV Earl Sigurd* (both 190 passengers and 25 cars), and *MV Varagen* (144 passengers and 32 cars). The vehicle and passenger ferry leaves Kirkwall every day. It leaves at 9.40am and 4.20pm on Monday; 7.20am and 2pm on Tuesday; 7.20am, 10.40am and 4.20pm on Wednesday; 7.20am, 1pm and 4.20pm on Thursday; 7.20am, 10.45am and 5pm on Friday; 7.20am and 4.20pm on Saturday; and 9.40am and 8.25pm on Sunday. The journey takes 25 minutes. The return passenger fare is £13.10, cars and mobile homes £29.30, motorcycles £19.60, and bicycles £2.60 return. Bookings and enquiries at the Kirkwall office of Orkney Ferries (℡01856-872044; fax 01856-872921; email info@orkneyferries.co.uk).

GETTING AROUND

Bus tours and bus hire: M&J Harcus, Pierowall (℡01857-677758; email kenneth@ westray.net). Operates service from Rapness Pier to Pierowall. £2 for adults; £1 OAPs, under 16s, and students. Also service to Gill Pier for ferry to Papa Westray. If you need this service ask the steward on boarding the ferry.

Westraak: Kathy and Graham Maben, Westraak Centre, Quarry Road, Pierowall KW17 2DH (℡01857-677777; fax 01857-677767; email info@westraak.co.uk; www.westraak. co.uk). Guided historical, scenic, cultural, bird and wildlife tours with experienced guide. Lunch and refreshments included.

Taxi service: Kathy and Graham Maben (℡01857-677777).

Ferry service: for the service between Westray and Papa Westray, contact Thomas B Rendall, Bayview, Gill Pier, Westray KW17 2DL (℡01857-677216; email tom.rendall@tiscali. co.uk). Boat hire throughout the year.

Boat charter: for bird-watching or sea angling, Inga Ness (℡01857-677395).

Cycle hire:

Mrs May Bain, Twiness, Rapnesss (℡01857-677319).

Mrs Dorothy Groat, Sand o' Gill (℡01857-677374).

Costies Island Tours: (℡01857-677355; fax 01857-677471).

ACCOMMODATION

There are two hotels on the island, as well as homes offering B&B, self-catering cottages, caravans, camping, and two hostels. The hotels are the best places for food.

Hotels

Cleaton House Hotel: Westray KW17 2DB (℡01857-677508; fax 01857-677442; email cleaton@orkney.com; www.cleatonhouse.co.uk). Four-star, built as a mansion for the Laird of Cleat in 1850, 5 miles (8km) from Rapness ferry terminal. Six en suite bedrooms. Open all year except Christmas Day, B&B from £43, facilities for disabled visitors. Try *holmie* (seaweed-eating lamb) fillet with Cumberland sauce, or baked organic Westray salmon with crispy kale and Orkney farmhouse cheese. Bar meals served between midday and 2pm and 6pm to 9pm. Dinner from 7pm to 9pm.

Pierowall Hotel: Jean Fergus, Pierowall (℡01857-677472; fax 01857-677707; email pierowall.hotel@btopenworld.com). Three-star, family-run hotel. From £22 a night. Famed for its seafood and for serving what patrons swear are the best fish and chips in the Northern Isles. Take-aways available. Lunch served from midday to 2pm, supper 5pm to 9pm.

Bed & Breakfast and Self-Catering

Bis Geos: Alena Tulloch, Westray KW17 2DW (℡/fax 01857-677420; email alena@bis-geos. co.uk; www.bis-geos.co.uk). Two semi-detached cottages; family cottage has one double room and sauna, twin room, lounge/kitchen, bathroom and spa bath. The Studio cottage has a typical Orkney box bed. From £140 to £340 a week. Open all year. Bus at ferry will take you to the hostel on request.

Daisy Cottage: Kirkbrae, Westray KW17 2DB (℡01857-677470; email netta@cubbigoe. freeserve.co.uk). Two-star bungalow in Pierowall village, two bedrooms, sleeps four. Open all year. From £110 to £150 a week.

1. Muckle Roe, linked by bridge to the Shetland mainland

2. St Ninian's Isle, Shetland, where a fabulous collection of Pictish silver bowls and ornaments was found

3. Iron Age Broch on uninhabited Mousa, Shetland

4. Shetland croft house

5. Kirkwall Harbour, Orkney

6. The Bishop's Palace, Kirkwall, Orkney, dating from the 12th century

7. Prow of a Viking boat at the Orkneyinga Saga Centre, Orphir, Orkney

8. Otters have right of way

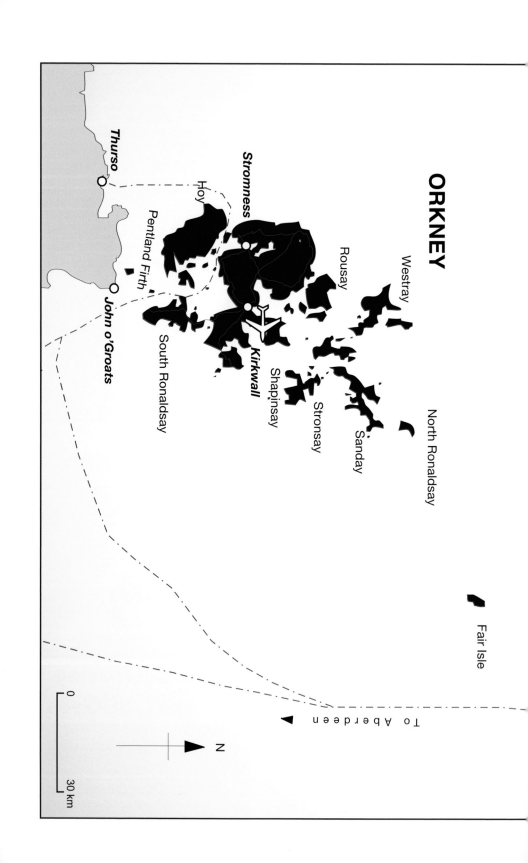

Airports, Roads and Sea Routes

Scottish mainland

○ Main town/city

✈ Airport

—— Road

— ·· — Main ferry route

NORTH

SEA

SHETLAND

Foula

Papa Stour

St. Magnus Bay

Lerwick

Whalsay

Yell

Fetlar

Unst

Herma Ness

10. Standing Stones in the snow, Orkney

11. Sheep shearing at Papil, Shetland

12. The Vallayre Burn, Shetland

13. Hamnavore bay from the beach in Stromness, Orkney

14. The sun sets over Scapa Flow, Orkney

15. Ring of Brodgar, Orkney

16. The Italian Chapel on the tiny island of Lamb Holm

Daybreak: Raymond and Suzie Rendall (©01856-876579; email raymond.rendall@ btopenworld.com). Three-star, renovated traditional cottage, two bedrooms, sleeps 4–6, from £160 to £260.

Sand o'Gill: Dorothy Groat (©01857-677374). Three-star cottage near Pierowall village, two bedrooms, sleeps four. Self-catering, from £100 to £300 a night. Also B&B.

Skaill Cottage: Mrs Linda Hagan, Skaill, Westray KW17 2DN (©01857-677226; fax 01857-677783; email lindahagan@onetel.co.uk). Three-star semi-detached farm cottage overlooking Skaill Bay, three bedrooms, sleeps six. Open all year. From £120 to £250.

Artists. Those of an artistic disposition can combine holiday accommodation with a residential course at *Seatters Studio* (Sandy McEwan, Trenabie Mill, Westray KW17 2BZ; ©01857-677447; email sandy@millwestray.com; www.millwestray.com). Self-catering accommodation, large ground floor studio surrounded by comfortable flat. Dark room, potter's wheel and kiln, spinning wheels and looms. Otherwise you can stay in an adapted and retired boat lying in a noust on the shore across the road. £220 a week. Daily rates possible. Art and craft courses held in the studio throughout the year. You can hire Seatters to run a course yourself or join one of the organised courses. Visiting artists can exhibit their work in the gallery.

Hostels

The Barn: Isabell Harcus, Chalmersquoy, Westray KW17 2BZ (©01857-677214; email info@thebarnwestray.co.uk www.thebarnwestray.co.uk). On the edge of Pierowall Village, overlooking Pierowall Bay. Five bedrooms, sleeps 12. From £12 a night. Open all year. Member of *Scottish Independent Hostels.*

Bis Geos: Westray KW17 2 DW (©/fax 01857-677420; email alena@bis-geos.co.uk; www. bis-geos.co.uk). Five-star, bothy-style hostel, sleeps 12, kitchen. From £12 a night.

Camping

Chalmersquoy Camp Site: Isabell Harcus (©01857-677214; email info@thebarnwestray. co.uk; www.thebarnwestray.co.uk). Campers and caravans, electric hook up. From £4.

Mount Pleasant Caravan Park: Mary Seatter (©01857-677229). Three caravans, sleeps 4–5 people. Linen provided. Five minutes walk to village.

Sand o'Gill: Dorothy Groat (©01857-677374). Caravans and camping.

SPORT AND RECREATION

Swimming pool (©01857-677430), Monday to Friday 9am to 11am and 2pm to 7pm, and Saturday 9am to 11pm. Football, netball, badminton, snooker, pool, darts, weight training are available at the *Community Centre*, information from Alan Drever and Alison Hutchison (©/fax 01857-677750).

Pètanque (bowls), Malcolm Stout, Cleaton House (©01857-677508).

There is a s**ailing club**, from 1 June to 31 August, Tuesday and Thursday evenings, contact Sam Harcus (©01857-677432). Nine-hole **golf course**, just before Noltland Castle. Contact Billy Tulloch (©01857-677373), adults £4 a day, £17 a week, seniors and juniors £2 a day, £8 a week. Tickets available at JC Tulloch general merchant. **Netball and football** at the Links from May to September. Monday, Wednesday and Saturday from 7.30pm.

SHOPPING

Westray is home to many artists and craftspeople. Orkney straw-backed chairs are an island speciality. Each one is hand-made, signed and numbered by its maker. The chairs are not only attractive, they are also extremely practical, because the hooded versions keep out the draughts. The Orkney Islands Council sent two of these chairs as a wedding gift to the Prince and Princess of Wales. Top quality knitwear is produced in traditional and modern designs under the island's own label, Auk Knitwear and is also a good buy. Contact *Westray and Papa Westray Craft Association* (Lizza Hume, Hume Sweet Hume, Pierowall, Westray KW17 2DH; ©/fax 01857-677259) for more information on local arts and craftwork.

Local crafts can be bought at the *Westray Heritage Centre* in Pierowall (✆01857-677414; email enquiries@westrayheritage.co.uk; www.westrayheritage.co.uk), and *Seatters Gallery* in Pierowall (✆01857-677770) who also display work by guest artists.

Other Spots on the Westray Craft Trail

Hume Sweet Hume: Jenna and Lizza Hume, Pierowall (✆01857-677259; email info@ humesweethume.com; www.humesweethume.com). Produces a range of interior textiles, individually hand-crafted and inspired by the ocean's ebb and flow. All products produced on premises and each incorporate a pebble button gathered from the local beaches. Open Monday to Friday 10am to 1pm, 2pm to 4pm, Saturday and Sunday 2pm to 4pm.

West-Ray Jewellery: George Thomson, Mid Ouseness KW17 2DN (✆01857-677400; email geordie@westrayjewellery.com; www.westrayjewellery.com). Hand-finished silver and gold jewellery. Open Monday to Saturday 1pm to 5pm, or by arrangement.

Orkney Chairs: James Fergus, East Surrigarth, Skelwick (✆01857-677323), strawback chairs.

Westray Cards: John Cable, Lightcost (✆01857-677287; email jfcable@btinternet.com). Hand-made cards, bookmarks, gift tags using wild grasses and plants from Westray. Open every day 11am to 5pm. Closed Wednesday.

Westray Knitters Society Ltd: Marlene Bews, Midhouse KW17 2DR (✆/fax 01857-677366). The society was established in 1973 to create work for the women of the island and supplement family incomes. Knitted and handframed garments produced in Shetland lace, Arran, and Icelandic wools. They've also developed an **Orkney tartan** which is incorporated in knitwear and other souvenirs. Open all year Monday to Saturday from 10am to 5pm, closed Sunday.

Westray Straw: Edith Costie, Pierowall House (✆01857-677411; email edith.costie@ btinternet.com; www.westraystudios.com). Makes traditional Orkney chairs with straw and sisal for the backs and seedgrass for the seats. Made to order. Unique to Westray is an armless straw-backed bedroom or nursing chair. The oat straw is grown locally and the woven backs each take 60 to 100 hours to make. Open every day 2pm to 4pm.

Wheeling Steen Gallery: Edwin Rendall, Bucklesberry (✆01857-677464). A working studio and gallery in a converted croft house. The name is Old Norse and means 'resting stone' and the gallery has a stone as its centrepiece. Paintings and photographs. Open all year, April to September, Monday to Saturday, 2pm to 5pm. Other times by arrangement.

The Craft Trail leaflet is available from the Orkney Islands Ferries booking office at the harbour in Kirkwall, or from the Westray Tourist Office (✆01857-677226).

HELP AND INFORMATION

Westray and Papa Westray Tourist Association: Graham and Kathy Maben, Westray KW17 2DN (✆01857-677777; email info@westraak.co.uk.co.uk; www.westrayandpapawestray. com).

Doctor: Gill Pier (✆01857-677209). Open Monday to Saturday.

Nurse: (✆01857-677706).

General merchant and **post office:** JC Tulloch, Pierowall (✆01857-677373). Petrol and diesel available. Post office open Monday, Wednesday, Thursday and Friday from 9am to 1pm, 2pm to 5.30pm, Tuesday 9.30am to 1pm, and Saturday 9am to 1pm.

Sub post office and **General merchant**: Peter Miller, Skelwick (✆01857-677351), in the south east of the island. You can also buy petrol. Post office open Monday, Tuesday, Thursday, Friday from 9am to 1pm, Wednesday 9am to 11am. Closed Saturday.

Calor and **Camping gas** is available from *WT Rendall* general merchant, Pierowall (✆01857-677389). Open Monday to Friday 9am to 6pm, Saturday 9am to 7pm, and Sunday 2pm to 4.30pm.

PAPA WESTRAY

For more than 5,000 years the people of Papa Westray have tilled the rich soil and harvested the surrounding sea for a living. The island, commonly known as Papay, or 'big island of the priests', lies roughly on the same latitude as the Norwegian town of Stavanger, and Anchorage, in Alaska, and is just over four miles (6km) long and a mile (1.6km) wide. Cars still take second place to walkers on the island's five miles (8km) of surfaced road. The land undulates along a central ridge to **North Hill**, the highest point of the island at 157ft (48m). The steep cliffs at the northern tip are eroded by pounding waves, making ideal homes for a dense population of seabirds. Off Mull Head at the extreme northern tip of the island is the Bore, a daunting tidal röst (race) where the Atlantic marries the North Sea. Under certain conditions this is a boiling cauldron with currents clashing many fathoms below the surface, presenting a challenge to even the hardiest seaman. The rocky west coast of Papay stretches almost unbroken, while the eastern and southern shores are scalloped by several fine sandy bays.

The shores in the east look out across an untroubled and remarkable azure stretch of water to Papay's little calf island, the **Holm of Papa**. This was probably a promontory of Papa Westray in Neolithic times and digs indicate that it supported a busy farming community. The holm is full of prehistoric cairns, although only two chambered tombs have been professionally excavated. One is a cairn of Maes Howe type in the south, one of the most impressive in Orkney; the other is a stalled cairn in the north, not far from intriguingly named Dog Bones. Opposite the Holm of Papa on South Wick is the **Old Pier** where the steamer from Kirkwall used to call once a week before the New Pier was built further south. It is now used only by local lobster boats and for access to the Holm. Nearby are some old kelp stores. The **New Pier** used by the ferry from Kirkwall and the service with Westray is on the **Bay of Moclett**. There is a fine sandy stretch at the head of the bay and nearby are the island's golf links.

The top third of Papay is occupied by the **RSPB Nature Reserve**, while central and south Papay are dominated by the broad expanse of **St Tredwell's Loch**, which gets its name from a medieval chapel on an artificial peninsula jutting into the water and dedicated to St Triduana. She was a nun who accompanied Boniface on his proselytising mission from Northumbria around 710. The pagan King of the Picts, Nechtan, was more interested in her lovely eyes than in tales from the Gospels so she plucked them out and gave them to him skewered on a twig. Her chapel at the loch became a holy shrine, especially for pilgrims with eye problems. Excavations at the chapel uncovered the bones of a woman, some say those of St Triduana herself, although more likely associated with the ruined Iron Age fortification on the same peninsula. The 12th-century church of **St Boniface** a couple of miles away on the west coast is not so famous, although it has been restored to the point that it can once again be used.

Brochs have been identified at several sites, one of the most notable being at **Munkerhouse**, an important early Christian site close to the church of St Boniface. For such a small area (2,270 acres/919ha), Papay has a staggering number of archaeological sites. The jewel in the crown is the **Knap of Howar**, a remarkable two-roomed stone house dating back at least 5,600 years ago, making it the oldest house in northern Europe. Like the Neolithic village of Skara Brae, this amazing dwelling was perfectly preserved under sand dunes until uncovered by a severe storm.

At the south-western corner of Papay is **Minister's Flag**. At one time the minister from Westray was obliged to land here and walk below the high-tide mark to the kirk of St Boniface because he was at loggerheads with the laird, who wouldn't allow him on his land. There is an interesting complex of agricultural buildings around **Holland House**, which was for 14 generations the seat of the Traill family lairds of Papay. The farm includes a 19th-century circular engine house where horses once provided the horse power. A farm bothy has been converted into the compact **John o'Holland's Museum**, with a range of artefacts that includes the parish handcuffs.

The opening of **Beltane House** in 1980 and the arrival of an underwater cable bringing mains electricity was a memorable year for the island. Beltane House, at the centre of the island, has the only shop on the island and its guest house-hostel complex is a focal point of community life. This building is part of a row of renovated cottages and offers magnificent views towards Fair Isle. It is run by the island's *Community Co-operative*, the first in the Northern Isles. The Co-op shop is a gathering point where gossip – known as information exchange – is retailed along with the canned food. There are regular services and get-togethers at the kirk and gospel hall. In winter there are dances, talks and concerts at the school and at Beltane House. The **Church of Scotland** congregation meet every Sunday at 2.30pm.

FLORA AND FAUNA

Papa Westray has habitats ranging from rocky foreshore and sandy beaches to marshy fields and moorland. The area of **North Hill** (157ft/48m) is an excellent example of maritime sedge heath where exposure, salt spray and grazing have combined to produce a ground cover which gradually changes from dominant **thrift**, **spring squill** and **sea plantain** near the cliff top to **heather**, **crowberry** and **creeping willow** further inland. Sizeable patches of **Scottish primrose** add to the attractions. In summer, the meadows are full of fragrant wild flowers and the golf links in the south behind the New Pier are full of **orchids**. Other flowers include **mountain everlasting**, **frog orchid**, **grass of Parnassus** and **alpine meadow rue**.

As you walk the beaches you might be surprised to see **seals** from the island's colony following you, swimming close inshore. The lovely white sand bays of North and South Wick are the best places on the island to watch common and grey seals basking on the tidal reefs. You might also catch a glimpse of **porpoises**, an **otter** or even a **whale**.

BIRD-WATCHING

The RSPB's 509-acre (206ha) **Nature Reserve** on **North Hill** at the northern extremity of the island is held under an agreement with Scottish Natural Heritage and the people of Papay, who retain communal grazing rights on the hill. The low line of cliffs on its east coast was one of Britain's last great auk breeding sites. The last of these magnificent birds was killed in 1813. Today the cliffs hold a small but densely packed colony of **guillemots**, **razorbills** and **kittiwakes**, which are particularly easy to observe at Fowl Craig, in the south-east corner of the reserve. South of Fowl Craig the land levels out and is dotted with the remains of many small stone enclosures once widely used for growing kale or penning geese. North Hill shelters one of Britain's three largest colonies of **Arctic terns**, the terminal for their 7,000-mile (11,265km) flight in May from the Southern Ocean. Up to 1,000 pairs of these elegant birds provide an incredible sound and visual spectacle, the more so because among them nest up to 70 pairs of **Arctic skuas**. These skuas get much of their food by harassing the smaller terns until they drop their catch and you can watch some of these aerobatic chases taking place over the sea. You should not, however, walk through the tern colony. The nature reserve also has **oystercatchers**, **lapwings**, **ringed plovers**, **snipe**, **curlews** and **redshanks**, and a scattering of **eiders**. To the east lies the **Holm of Papay** with many *tysties* (black guillemots), **terns** and **gulls**, and also a small colony of **storm petrels**. In autumn, and to a certain extent in spring, rare and unusual birds arrive, such as **red-footed falcon**, **red-backed shrike** and **scarlet rosefinch**. Equally interesting for twitchers are the falls of **thrushes** from Scandinavia and **snow buntings** from Iceland and Greenland. The reserve is always open, but if you arrive during the breeding season you should contact the summer warden (April–August only). Guided tours of the reserve are given by the warden on Tuesday, Thursday and Saturday afternoon. Contact the warden at Rose Cottage, close to the reserve entrance (℡01857-644240).

GETTING THERE

By Air

Loganair (℡01856-872494/873457; www.loganair.co.uk) flies to Papa Westray from Kirkwall at 9.15am, 11.15am and 4pm on Monday, 8.15am, 1.50pm and 3pm on Tuesday and Thursday, 10.25am, 12.15pm and 5pm on Wednesday, 9.15am, 1.50pm and 4pm on Friday,

Saturday at 9.30am and 5pm, and Sunday 2pm. Check winter schedule with the airline. Special overnight stay fare £12. Alternatively, a two-minute flight from Westray will get you to its sister island.

By Sea

The scheduled inter-island ferry calls twice weekly. There is a daily feeder service by boat in summer between Westray and Papa Westray. *Orkney Ferries* (✆01856-872044; fax 01856-872921; email info@orkneyferries.co.uk) operates vehicle and passenger ferries on the Westray route leaving Kirkwall at 10.45am on Friday, arriving in Papa Westray at 1pm; and at 2pm on Tuesday, arriving 4.15pm via Westray. The adult return fare is £13.10, cars and mobile homes £29.30, motorcycles £19.60, and bicycles £2.60 return. There are also Sunday sailings direct to Papa Westray on certain dates during June to August. Ferry services are complex. Best to check all dates and departure times with Orkney Ferries.

There is also a feeder service on the passenger-only *MV Golden Mariana* (40 passengers) which links Westray and Papa Westray and connects with the scheduled ferry services. This 20-minute trip is free to passengers who arrive at Rapness on the ferry from Kirkwall. All other passengers pay the inter-island fare of £10.50 return for adults. Children aged 5–16, senior citizens and the disabled travel half fare. The ferry leaves Gills Pier for Papa Westray three to six times a day Monday to Sunday. For more information, bookings, request calls, and hires contact Thomas Rendall, harbour master (✆01857-677216). A minibus meets all scheduled ferries and connects with the passenger-only feeder service.

TOURS

You can take the guided **Papay's Peedie Tour** (✆01857-644321). Departs from Kirkwall on the regular ferry service on Tuesday, Thursday and Saturday at 7.20am, arriving Rapness at 8.45am. Minibus to Pierowall for the local ferry for Papa Westray. The tour includes a visit to Knap of Howar, St Boniface Kirk, the RSPB Reserve on North Hill, Holland Farm and Bothy Museum. Costs £28 for adults, £23.20 OAPs and £13 for children, includes lunch and afternoon tea at Beltane House.

GETTING AROUND

Car hire available from Papay Car Hire (Sue Jeffery; ✆01857-644202).
Taxi. A. Davidson (✆01857-644246). Also car hire.

ACCOMMODATION

The word is, for everything you need to know contact the **Papa Westray Community Co-operative**. They can fix you up with accommodation, a meal and a drink, provisions, boat hire, guides, and virtually anything else you might need.

Guest House

Beltane Guest House: Community Co-operative (✆01857-644321). Two-star, converted farm cottages, B&B or full board. Home cooked meals. Superb views. From £25 a night.

Bed & Breakfast and Self-Catering

Holm View: Tom Hughes, Bayview KW17 2BU (✆01857-644211; email tomhughes@ scotnet.co.uk). Four-star, near the east pier. Detached cottage, two bedrooms (double and twin), sleeps four, en suite shower room.
Morven House: Community Co-operative (✆01857-644267), two-storey former doctor's house. Two large, one small bedroom, sleeps 6/7. Linen provided.
School Place: Mrs Morag Hewitson (✆01857-644268; email sonofhewitj@aol.com). Two-star B&B, from £20.

Hostel

Papa Westray Youth Hostel, in Beltane House (✆01857-644321), owned and operated by the Community Co-operative. Open all year. 16 beds, two rooms with 5–8 beds, wheelchair access, hostel store, shop nearby, ferry for Kirkwall 2 miles (3km) away. Walkers and cyclists welcome. From £10.

SHOPPING

Papay's history, isolation and natural features have inspired some of the tiny population to take up a surprising variety of crafts and a small but enthusiastic group works every Saturday at the bothy at Holland Farm turning out hand and machine-knitted garments of wool from Papay sheep, crochet, hand-made felt, turned woodwork, pictures, photographs and cards, silk scarves and much more. The full range is available at *Daybreak* (✆01857-644275) open April to September; the *Papay Co-operative* (✆01857-644321) which is open all year, 10am to midday and 3pm to 5pm Monday and Wednesday; 3pm to 5pm Tuesday and Friday; 2.30pm to 5pm Thursday; 10am to midday and 7pm to 9pm Saturday; and at *Seaters Gallery* Westray. For more information contact *Westray and Papa Westray Craft Association* (✆Lizza Hume, Hume Sweet Hume, Pierowall, Westray; ✆/fax 01857-677259).

HELP AND INFORMATION

Westray and Papa Westray Tourist Association: Graham and Kathy Maben, (✆01857-677777; email info@westraak.co.uk.co.uk; www.westrayandpapawestray.com).
Nurse: Fiona McNab, Windywalls (✆01857-644239).
Airport: (✆01857-644252).
Boat Hire Jim Davidson (✆01857-644259). To the Holm of Papa.
Co-op Shop: General merchants, and information exchange (✆01857-644321; email papay-coop@orkney.com).
Golf course: Alistair Hourston (✆01857-644238). Nine-hole links, clubs available for hire.
Papay Museum: John Rendall, Holland Farm (✆01857-644251).
Post Office: Margit and Hartmut Fassbender, Daybreak (✆01857-644275).
RSPB Warden: North Hill (✆01857-644240).

NORTH RONALDSAY

Its distance from the Orkney Mainland along with the tricky tidal races of the North Ronaldsay Firth have combined to isolate North Ronaldsay – it didn't get electricity until 1983 – and give it a distinct cultural tradition and a different flavour from the other islands. Speaking of flavour, North Ronaldsay is probably best known for the 2,000 or so sheep that live on its beaches on an almost permanent diet of seaweed, as well as for the 6ft-high (1.8m) drystone wall that runs for some 13 miles (21km) around the island and was built back in 1832 to keep them there and prevent them grazing on valuable pasture. The wall is maintained by a 'Sheep Court' of 12 islanders and the only time the sheep are allowed inside the wall is during the lambing season when the ewes are tethered on grass. The sheep have become efficient at absorbing the copper contained in seaweed but when they eat grass, which contains much more of the mineral, they often absorb too much and get copper poisoning. The sheep are a fine-haired primitive breed related to the Soay sheep of St Kilda, producing dark mutton that tastes, well, seaweedy but definitely moreish. North Ronaldsay mutton can be found on menus in some top eateries in London and the Mutton Renaissance Club, championed by Prince Charles, want to re-establish the meat in gastronomic circles. Prince Charles personally sampled the Orcadian mutton during a visit to the island and enthused about its flavour. Farming is less intensive on North Ronaldsay than on most of the other islands and this is good news for that rarity, the breeding corncrake. Croft land is used mainly to raise beef cattle such as Aberdeen Angus, Charolais and Simmental. Crops include potatoes and vegetables, barley, bere and myrtle oats, a rare seed found only in

North Ronaldsay and Sanday. There is less fishing from the island today than there used to be, when good hauls of halibut, ling and cod were made and, in the North Ronaldsay Firth, saithe, or coalfish, were frequently caught, though this was dangerous work as the fish were most prolific where the tides and currents ran strongest.

The island is only 4 miles (6km) long by 2 miles (3km) wide and lies at the north-eastern extremity of the Orkney archipelago. Beyond it's open sea all the way to Shetland and Norway. As the nearest Orkney island to Scandinavia it's no surprise that its people were the last Orcadians to give up the Old Norse language, Norn, although even today their speech is larded with words that can be incomprehensible even to other islanders. Many old traditions are still common, although the islanders no longer dance around the lone 13ft (4m) high **Standing Stone** on New Year's Day. This sentinel stone stands near Loch Gretchen beyond the pier where the ferry docks in Nouster Bay. It has a hole pierced in it which might have been used as a sighting aid, or as a primitive sundial, although locals naturally prefer the story that a giantess pushed her finger through the stone. Across the bay at Stromness Point is the **Broch of Burrian** which is the focal point of an extensive coastal Iron Age settlement. To the landward side of the broch are the buried remains of a village fronted by four massive defensive ramparts. Among the objects found during excavations in the 1870s were several relics which were distinctively Christian and placed occupation late in the Pictish period around AD800 or even later. The **Burrian Cross** found carved on a flat piece of stone at this site is now a common motif in modern Orkney jewellery.

North along the cliffs is the **Brae of Stennabreck**, a small but steep hill crowned by a cluster of stone huts. Like the mounds found beneath many of the island farms, it is probable that the Brae itself is the accumulation of deposits from prehistoric settlements. Relics found here, at **Howmae** and at **Burrian** can be seen in the Royal Museum of Scotland, in Edinburgh. At the **Knowe o' Samilands**, near Hooking Loch, is a good example of the burnt mounds found in several other places left over from the Neolithic practice of dumping heated stones into troughs of water to cook food. Dotted about at **Tor Ness**, on the west coast, are some 15 puzzling circular depressions which might indicate the site of an ancient stone circle or barrow burials. On the other hand they could simply be old kelp-burning pits.

Two earth and stone dykes, one to the south of the Community Centre and new school and the other running from Northmanse Farm to the central Ancum Loch split the island into three fairly equal parts. According to legend the southern dyke of **Muckle Gersty** and the northern **Matches** dyke were built by three brothers to divide and share the land. Little else is known about the dykes. They probably date from before 1000BC and although sections have disappeared, some parts are still impressive and must have involved the brothers in an awful amount of back-breaking toil. The Muckle Gersty dyke to the south of Newbigging is still 6ft (2m) high and 30ft (9m) across.

A dyke of a different kind lies out at sea off Bride's Ness headland. This is a treacherous group of rocks called **Reef Dyke**, which has torn the bottom out of many a ship over the past three centuries. One of the first recorded was the Swedish East Indiaman *Svecia*, which was wrecked on Reef Dyke in 1740 with the loss of some 90 lives. Four years later the Danish East Indiaman *Crown Prince* went down at Savie Geo; three German ships ran aground one after the other near Dennis Head in March 1926, where folk tales say a Spanish Armada galleon also sank in 1588; and the *Royal Oak* came ashore in dense fog at Bride's Kirk in August 1882. Her cargo of dressed timber was bought by a Kirkwall merchant, though much of it was used on North Ronaldsay for housing. The last vessel to come to grief on Reef Dyke was the coasting steamer *Mistley*, which was wrecked there in 1957. Three ancient cannon salvaged from the wreck of the *Crown Prince* still stand outside **Holland House**, the laird's residence originally built by the Traill family, who bought the island in 1727. The trees and shrubs in the gardens adjoining the house are an attraction for some species of migrant birds and for ringing studies as it is the only sizeable patch of woodland on the island.

The **Mill** and **Windmill** were provided in 1907 by the laird, Mr Traill, to grind corn, reputedly one of the last working windmills in Scotland. A previous mill was abandoned after its grindstone broke and killed the miller. The **Store House** at Noust of Howar was used in the 18th century to hold the grain given by tenants in part payment of their rents. It was also a handy hiding place for young men dodging the naval Press Gang and later used as a kelp store. Other notable buildings are the **Old Kirk**, a parliamentary church from the early 1800s with its Thomas Telford-designed manse built in 1829; and the **Old School**, which is visible evidence of an educational system going back to the late 18th century, although the benefit of a resident schoolmaster is documented only from 1837 onwards. The new **Community Centre** was opened in 1981 and adjoins the school buildings. Facilities include badminton, carpet bowls, table tennis, snooker, television and video recorder, a film projector and screen, reference library, toilets, and a cooker. Visitors are welcome, contact Miss I Bain, School House (✆01857-633224/248); or Mrs I Muir, Hooking (✆01857-633257).

The increasing number of **shipwrecks** in the 17th and 18th centuries led Parliament in 1786 to pass 'The Act for Erecting Certain Lighthouses in the Northern Parts of Great Britain' and one of the first the Northern Lighthouse Board was ordered to build was on North Ronaldsay. The island's first **fixed light beacon** was lit in October 1789. This proved unsatisfactory and a new **lighthouse** was built to replace it and is, at 133ft (42m) still the tallest land-based lighthouse in Britain. Material to build the new lighhouse was landed at the pier at nearby **Bewan Store**. One of the early lighthouse keepers had the authorities tearing out their hair when they discovered he was running a thriving black market business in North Ronaldsay and Sanday selling the oil meant to keep the light burning – an enterprise they found 'infamous'. After the first beacon light was extinguished its lantern was replaced in 1809 by an enormous stone ball and the structure still survives today as the **Old Beacon**, standing on the rocks at Dennis Head and looking for all the world, like a giant chess piece.

FLORA AND FAUNA

North Ronaldsay lies at a migration crossroads for birds flying to Iceland, Greenland and Scandinavia. Many rest here or are grounded by weather on this little isolated stretch of land. From late March to early June, and from the middle of August to early November, large numbers of migrants touch down – seabirds, wildfowl, raptors, waders, near passerines and passerines, as well as less common species and several national rarities. There are long clean stretches of sandy beaches at **Nouster**, **Haskie** and **Linklet Bay**, and these attract **sanderling**. **Ringed plover** breed here and sand and shingle are also popular habitats with **Arctic terns**. Up to 10 species of **duck** breed on the island, mostly on the wet meadow-fringed lochs which provide the most northerly breeding area for **mute swans**. **shelduck**, a hole-nesting species, often take over abandoned rabbit burrows, and **fulmar**, normally a cliff-nesting species, nest on the ground because there are no predators such as rats, stoats or foxes on the island. The skerry off the northerly tip has a few pairs of **cormorants**, as well as a summer colony of **kittiwakes**.

The **North Ronaldsay Bird Observatory** (✆01857-633200; fax 01857-633207; email warden@nrbo.prestel.co.uk) was established in 1987 to monitor migrations and populations. It does this by census and a bird ringing programme.

An extraordinarily large number of migrants pass through each year, mainly from the end of March through to November. Depending on the weather, large falls of migrants can occur in April and May. Usual April migrants include **Arctic tern**, **sparrowhawk**, **long-eared owl**, **sand martin**, **swallow**, **wheatear**, chats such as **dunnock**, **robin**, **redstart**, **whinchat**, and the first warblers – **blackcap**, **chiffchaff** and **willow warbler**. The wintering **whooper swans** usually depart around 20 April. Other April birds could include **white-billed diver**, **marsh harrier**, **snowy owl**, **great grey shrike** and **hawfinch**.

Rarities can turn up in any month, but May and June, September and October are good months for vagrants, with notable ones in recent years being **red-footed falcon**, **American** and **Pacific golden plover**, **great snipe**, **snowy owl**, **olive-backed** and **red-throated pipit**, **thrush nightingale**, **Blyth's reed** and **Arctic warbler**, **rose-coloured starling**, **Arctic redpoll**, **red-necked stint**, **collared flycatcher**, **white-throated spar-**

row, and various **buntings**. June is a common time for **crossbill** and perhaps the odd **long-tailed skua**.

As passerines finish their spring migration, waders begin to return. September is good for all migrant families from raptors to near-passerine, more chats, small numbers or thrushes, a wide variety of warblers and flycatchers, and finches. From November until March there are mainly wintering birds only, but **Iceland** and **glaucous gulls** are frequently seen and the first **shelduck** usually reappear in December. NRBO is set on the crofts of Twingness and Lurand, with land totalling 36 acres (15ha), where conservation areas include species-rich grassland and remnant coastal heath. You can become a Friend of NRBO, which gets you four newsletters a year and a copy of the *Orkney Bird Report*, which includes North Ronaldsay's records.

Common and **grey seals** breed around the island and are easily seen. **Risso's** and **white-beaked dolphins**, **pilot whales** and **killer whales** have all been recorded offshore and **porpoises** occasionally swim with the local lobster boats. The island has no reptiles, amphibians, or predators, and only a few mammals, among them **rabbits**, the **long-tailed fieldmouse**, **house mouse**, and **hedgehog**. **Otters** occasionally visit and **bats** have been sighted in summer. There are no midges or wasps but a few species of **bumblebee** and the odd horsefly. Most common **butterflies** are the **large white**, the **green-veined white**, **red admiral**, and **small tortoiseshell**. Vagrant lepidoptera include **painted lady** and the **peacock**.

GETTING THERE
By Air
Loganair (℡01856-872494/873457; www.loganair.co.uk) flies from Kirkwall to North Ronaldsay at 8.15am, 11.15am and 3pm on Monday; Tuesday and Thursday at 10.15am, 11.50pm and 5pm; Wednesday 8.15am, 12.15pm and 2.50pm; Friday 8.15am, 1.50pm and 5.15pm; Saturday at 8.15am and 3.45pm; and Sunday at 9am and 2pm. Special overnight stay fare £12. Part of your **Orkney Adventure Ticket**.

By Sea
Two vessels, the *MV Earl Thorfinn* and *MV Earl Sigurd* (each carrying 190 passengers and 25 cars), operate a service from Kirkwall to North Ronaldsay once a week on a Friday from mid-May to end-September. The crossing takes 2 hours 45 minutes. The adult return fare is £13.10, cars and mobile homes £29.30, motorcycles £19.60, and bicycles £2.60 return. Bookings at Orkney Ferries, Kirkwall office (℡01856-872044; fax 01856-872921; email info@orkneyferries.co.uk).

GETTING AROUND
Garso No 1 taxi, self-drive cars, minibus hire and tours, lunch by arrangement (T&C Muir; ℡01857-633244).

The tallest land-based **lighthouse** in Scotland is on North Ronaldsay. The 109ft (33m) lighthouse has 179 steps to the top and was first lit in 1854 and automated in 1998. Tours are organised by the *North Ronaldsay Trust* (c/o William Muir, Hooking; ℡01857-633257;email wtmuir@yahoo.com; www.northronaldsay.com) on Sunday from May to September, midday to 5.30pm. Other times by arrangement.

ACCOMMODATION
Guest Houses
Garso Guest House: Christine Muir (℡/fax 01857-633244). B&B or full board.

North Ronaldsay Bird Observatory: (℡01857-633200; fax 01857-633207; email warden@nrbo.prestel.co.uk). Has double and twin en suite guest rooms in the main house. One twin room is on the ground floor and is suitable for disabled visitors. Guest rooms cost from £26.50 per person a night B&B, £38 half-board. The *hostel* annexe is self-contained with two four-bedded dormitories, showers, and a small kitchen. Two four-bedded dormitories in the main building are also available at hostel rates. The hostel is £11 per person a night, £16.50 B&B, £26 half-board. There is a 10% discount for seven consective nights or more. Lunches are available in the *Obscafe* and packed lunches by request. An à la carte restaurant opens on Saturday nights in summer. Vegetarian option available. The observatory is licensed and stocks a good range of beers, wines and spirits. Open to non-residents.

Self-Catering

Brigg: Christine Muir (✆/fax 01857-633244). Fully equipped cottage.

Dennishill: Mrs Jennifer Smith (✆01856-874486; email dennis_hill@hotmail.com; www. island-cottage.co.uk). Three-star cottage, renovated croft, fully equipped. Two bedrooms, sleeps four. Open all year. From £210 to £250.

The Doll's House and Quoybanks: S. Mawson, Roadside (✆01857-633221). Fully equipped, self-catering and B&B, evening meals.

Neven: Miss L Forgan (✆0171-483 2391). Fully equipped, self-catering.

Camping: contact Mr I Scott (✆01857-633222).

EATING AND DRINKING

Burrian Inn and Restaurant: S Mawson (✆01857-633221). Orkney's most northerly pub, **off-licence and tea room**, also sells North Ronaldsay woollen products and jewellery. The *Bird Observatory* (✆01857-633200)is open to non-residents for meals and snacks.

HELP AND INFORMATION

Doctor: New Manse (✆01857-633226) or at home in Twingness (✆01857-633267).

Post Office: Roadside (✆01857-633221).

Bank: monthly, enquire at post office.

Community Centre (Miss I Bain; ✆01857-633224/248); or Mrs I Muir, Hooking (✆01857-633257).

Airfield Goods & Services: in Trebb (Mrs H. Swanney; ✆01857-633220) is a general merchant selling woollen products and petrol. Petrol is also available at Hooking (Mr W. Muir; ✆01857-633257). Campers can buy **Calor Gas** from *Scotsha'* (Mr T. Muir; ✆01857-633244).

There is a nine-hole links **golf course**, clubs available for hire. Enquiries to Mr P Donnelly (✆01857-633242).

SHETLAND

Background Information

Practical Information

SHETLAND
Background Information

Shetland is as far north as you can go in Britain. It is not on the normal tourist routes and this naturally adds to its magnetic attraction. You are unlikely to meet anyone who has been there. This is a destination for those with a definite purpose – although it's also great for idling – and amply rewards anyone with an interest in birdlife, archaeology, history, geology, diving, angling, sailing, walking, kayaking, cycling, music – and even knitting. Shetland is noticeably different, even from the rest of Scotland. There is no tartan and no Gaelic and the islanders still cling to many of the ways of their Norse ancestors, with some surprising results.

Shetland is still officially named Zetland, thought to have come from *Hjaltland*, the Viking name for the archipelago. This in turn derives from *hjalt*, the handle end of a sword and if you share the imagination of those sea rovers of old you'll no doubt be able to see in the string of 100 or so islands, islets and skerries a long sword being flourished with its business end pointed at Orkney and Scotland.

There is plenty to inform and entrance in this scattering of rugged islands, whose people are probably best epitomised by that truly native inhabitant, the sturdy little Shetland pony – hardy, self-reliant, enduring and friendly.

GEOGRAPHY

In her *Sketches and Tales of the Shetland Islands* published in Edinburgh in 1856, Eliza Edmonston has one of her characters ask: 'Pray, Sir, where is Shetland?' Good question. A century and a half later many people still have only the haziest of ideas of exactly where the islands of this fascinating archipelago lie. Most maps and atlases are of little help either, as for reasons of space and convenience many of them stick the islands in a box in the corner of the sheet, making their correct location largely a matter of conjecture. Shetland – never call it the Shetlands – is made up of a long, narrow archipelago of some 100 rugged islands stretching about 70 miles (113km) from Sumburgh Head in the south to Muckle Flugga and the Out Stack rock off the coast of Unst in the north. Only 14 of the islands are now inhabited. The island cluster is roughly equidistant from the north coast of Scotland, Norway and the Faroes, mostly above the 60 degrees of latitude north mark, which places them further north than Moscow, Stockholm, and the southern tip of Greenland, and level with the centre of Hudson Bay, in Canada. The 60th parallel, in fact, passes through the little island of Mousa and Shetland's southern Mainland. Lerwick, the capital, is as far from London as is Milan in Italy. Instead of regarding them as remote, as did the Romans who seem never to have set foot on what they dubbed *Ultima Thule*, think rather of the Shetland Islands in light of the fact that they lie at the hub of major maritime trading routes where the Atlantic, the North Sea and the Norwegian sea meet, a juxtaposition which has shaped much of their history. Midway between Shetland and Orkney, 24 miles (39km) south-west of Sumburgh Head, lies the island world famous for its birdlife and its intricately patterned knitwear, Fair Isle; Foula of the stupendous cliffs is about 18 miles (29km) to the west of Walls on the West Mainland. In common with their neighbours in Orkney, 50 miles (80km) to the south-west, when the people of Shetland talk about the Mainland they are referring to their main island, not the mainland of Scotland.

Geology

Not for nothing do islanders refer affectionately to Shetland as 'the Auld Rock'. Geologists believe the oldest rocks in the complex making up the islands are Lewisian gneisses which were formed deep beneath the earth's crust up to three billion years ago. They surmise that the Shetland Islands, along with the Orkney group, came into being at the end of a dramatic period in the earth's history when land masses were successively being formed and reshaped by shattering global upheavals caused by tectonic plate movement. Some 400 million years ago what is now Britain and its islands lay on the Tropic of Capricorn below the equator, an integral part of a super-continent which incorporated present-day Europe, North America, Scandinavia and Greenland. During this period enormous river systems emptied sand, silt, mud and other sediments into vast basins and one, the Orcadian Basin and its freshwater lake, held what are now Orkney and Shetland. Once the Orcadian Basin silted up completely it hardened into sedimentary rock.

Aeons of continental drift gradually nudged this southern land mass north until it collided with the great northern continent of Laurentia. The resultant buckling threw up giant mountains and the northernmost chain weathered until erosion and the grinding of successive Ice Ages revealed the Devonian sedimentary rock overlying the older gneisses and visible today in south-eastern and western Shetland. Old Red Sandstone is the name given to Devonian rocks as a whole and this is where fossils of the earliest life forms are usually found. The largest group of Shetland rocks is the metamorphic Dalradian series, formed from sediments laid down even earlier and forged by heat and pressure. This occurs on the Mainland, and on Unst and Fetlar, and is estimated to be about 8 miles (12km) thick. Rocks of eastern Unst and Fetlar comprise dense and dark fragments of the ancient ocean floor and underlying crust which once lay between the two super-continents. Where there is granite it usually forms the high ground and where it reaches the sea it has created steep cliffs, such as those of Ronas Voe, which are pinkish-red granite. By contrast, the rock at Sumburgh Head is reddish-brown sandstone and on Fetlar you'll find blue-green serpentine. Eshaness has impressive cliffs of dark basalt.

Thick sheets of ice covered Shetland many times over the past two million years and glaciation has had a more noticeable effect in the shaping of Shetland than in Orkney. After the last Ice Age, about 10,000 years ago, the archipelago emerged more or less in its present pattern as the higher sea level caused by the melt turned old mountain tops into a remarkable conglomeration of islands and skerries separated by sounds. Subsequent erosion by sea, particularly on the Atlantic side of the archipelago, further shaped Shetland and has produced some extraordinary features. The western side of Foula, for instance, has been carved into a series of cliffs more than 1,200ft (366m) high and on the island of Papa Stour the sea has tunnelled inland to produce a series of remarkable caves, arches and stacks which are without parallel in the British Isles.

Topography

Although the islands have an estimated total area of only 580 sq miles (1,500 sqkm) they are fretted with inlets and bays and are gashed by great sea lochs called *voes*, which are the most noticeable characteristic of Shetland and which give the archipelago nearly a thousand miles of stunning coastline. The fjord-like *voes* are the result of melting glaciers and a subsequent rise in sea level over the past 5,000–6,000 years which flooded the valleys they hollowed out. The steep slopes and indentations of these sea lochs have generally prevented the formation of any large, sandy beaches, although narrow spits of shingle or sand called *ayres* often cut across the landward and seaward ends of some shallow bays and lochs. Some sandy stretches known as *tombolos* join islands to the mainland or to other isles. Striking examples are those joining Fora Ness to the Mainland at Delting, and the splendid sand-capped shingle *tombolo* linking St Ninian's Isle to the south-western coast. The sea is an ever-present element in the landscape and nowhere will you ever be more than 3 miles (5km) from it.

Shetland is not a mountainous region – it's highest point is the 1,477ft (450m) summit of Ronas Hill, a mass of red granite in North Mainland – but what it lacks in peaks it makes up in some spectacularly steep sea cliffs, such as the dramatic Kame of Foula, about 18 miles (29km) off the West Mainland, with its sheer drop of 1,220ft (372m), and others in the west and north of Shetland and on Fair Isle. Some of the finest of Shetland's natural wonders are best seen from the sea, which has chiselled steep-sided, narrow *geos* into the cliffs, created

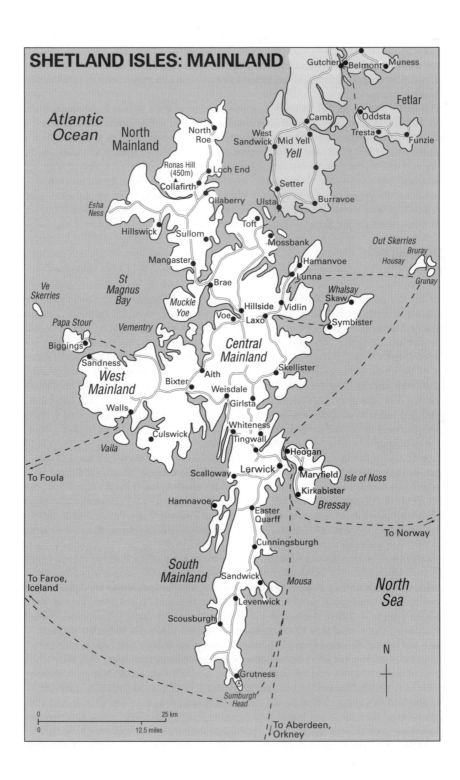

SHETLAND ISLES: MAINLAND

Atlantic
Ocean

North
Mainland

Gutcher • Belmont • • Muness

Fetlar

Camb • • Oddsta
West • • Tresta
Sandwick Mid Yell • Funzie
Yell

North
Roe

Ronas Hill
(450m)
▲ Collafirth

Loch End

Setter

Esha
Ness

Qllaberry

Ulsta • Burravoe

Out Skerries
Bruray
Housay

Hillswick • Sullom

Toft

Mossbank

Mangaster

Hamanvoe
Lunna

Grunay

Brae

Whalsay
Skaw

Ve
Skerries

St
Magnus
Bay

Muckle
Yoe

Hillside • Vidlin

Voe •
Laxo

Symbister

Papa Stour

Vementry

Central
Mainland

Biggings

Sandness

West
Mainland

Bixter • Aith

Skellister

Weisdale

Walls

Girlsta

Culswick

Whiteness
Tingwall

Vaila

Scalloway

Lerwick

Heogan
Maryfield Isle of Noss
Kirkabister
Bressay

To Foula

Hamnavoe

Easter
Quarff

To Norway

Cunningsburgh

South
Mainland

Sandwick

Mousa

North
Sea

To Faroe,
Iceland

Levenwick

Scousburgh

N

Grutness

Sumburgh
Head

| 0 | | 25 km |
| 0 | | 12.5 miles |

To Aberdeen,
Orkney

soaring rock arches and towering stacks, and gouged out labyrinths of caves and tunnels. Some of these penetrate far inland and reach the surface as pit-like openings at the bottom of which the sea foams and swirls, giving them their local name of *kirns* ('churns'). Most of the best arable land lies along the coastal belt and the green of working croft areas contrasts with barren open moorland and heath and the stretches of infertile hill land known as *scattald*. Scattered throughout the landscape like bits of broken mirror are numerous small freshwater lochs.

One of the first things that strikes you as you travel around the islands is the absence of trees. Palaeo-botanists have divined from remains and fossil pollen grains found in peat that Shetland was once forested but estimate that the islands have been all but treeless for at least the past 10,000 years. The islands once supported scrubby vegetation of mainly birch, hazel, and willow, but grazing and farming destroyed this and native trees survive only in inaccessible places. Small areas of planted woodland are mostly experimental coniferous plantations, the largest being at Kergord in Weisdale, where the trees are more than 80 years old. Small isolated stands of trees can also be seen but their contortions and stunted growth testify to a never-ending struggle against both sheep and wind.

CLIMATE

Considering its location – it's closer to the Arctic Circle than it is to Manchester or Liverpool – Shetland's climate is surprisingly mild all year round, thanks to a continuation of the Gulf Stream known as North Atlantic Drift, an oceanic current which brings relatively warm water up from the Gulf of Mexico and past the islands, sweeping as far as northern Norway. Temperatures range from an average of around 59°F (15°C) in summer to a low in winter around 41°F (5°C). This is not to say that summer days don't get any hotter. They do, up to 71°F (22°C). Long summer days are another bonus from Shetland's position on the globe and in midsummer you'll enjoy near-continuous daylight in the islands. In June, the sun can shine for up to 19 hours. The sun does set for a few hours but there is no real darkness, only what islanders poetically call the 'Simmer Dim,' a twilight that makes it possible to read the newspaper outdoors late at night without light. This is also a time welcomed by sportsmen and women and it is not unusual for a game of golf to tee-off at midnight.

Locals pay for this bonus in midwinter however when they see barely six hours of daylight. Winter temperatures are mild and comparable to the average for western Britain, although in December and January it is usually windy. Shetland holds the all-time UK record for a 169-knot (194mph/312km/h) corker on New Year's Day 1992. The warm-water fingers of the Gulf Stream mean that snow rarely lies around for more than a day or two. Rainfall averages a scant 40 inches (102 mm) a year, which is less than half the soaking the western Scottish Highlands gets annually.

'Simmermal' is the name traditionally given to the first day of the summer season, which falls on 3 April. Whatever the weather is on this day is regarded by islanders as a foretaste of what the summer has in store. Even in summer the weather can change amazingly rapidly and with little warning. Locals will tell you that if the weather is not to your liking in the morning it might well have changed to something more to your taste by lunchtime. Walkers are cautioned that even if they set out in bright sunshine it is sensible to pack waterproof gear – just in case. It is also often quite breezy. There is no definite best time to visit Shetland as far as the weather is concerned. More important considerations are such things as the timing of bird migrations for twitchers, the fishing season for sea and loch anglers, and so on. We have been in Shetland in February and spent days in glorious sunshine while mainland Scotland was being choked by blizzards. The holiday season is at its peak in July and August, but all the islands are geared up for visitors from April to September, although many facilities are open all year round. If you visit in late autumn or winter you might be lucky enough to see the sky lit up by the Northern Lights, or *Aurora Borealis*, whose shimmering arcs and streamers are known locally as *mirry-dancers*.

Fair Isle

Fair Isle has its own weather, an oceanic micro-climate which means stormy but fairly mild winters, while in summer sparkling sunshine and marvellous visibility can rapidly be followed by blankets of thick mist and low cloud. There is measurable rainfall on 216–266 days of the year. Mean annual temperature is 45°F (7.5°C). Sea temperatures do not reach their highest levels until late summer, when maximum temperatures can be around 61°–63°F (16°–17°C). In spring and summer Fair Isle can report the lowest daytime maximum temperature in Britain, even though in May and early June it might also be the sunniest place in the country. Fair Isle is one of the windiest lowland sites in Britain, with gales on an average of 57 days a year. Snow can fall on as many as 70 days in winter, but it does not usually lie for long. Stout, waterproof shoes or boots and warm, weatherproof clothing are a must, no matter when you visit.

HISTORY

The Picts

Until the first probing raids of the Vikings from Norway in the eighth century the islands of Shetland were inhabited by vigorous people whose Stone Age predecessors had been there for more than 5,000 years. Within the space of a century, as the Norsemen began to settle in increasing numbers, these shadowy islanders had all but vanished from the scene. They are mentioned briefly in the 12th century *Historia Norwegiae*, which calls the inhabitants of Scotland's northern islands the *Peti*, probably a corruption of *Picti* (the painted or tattooed people), which is what the Romans called their far northern enemies. They are known to more recent historians as the Picts.

> **VANISHING PICTS**
>
> *The Norwegian scribe says that the* Peti *were* 'scarcely taller than pygmies. Morning and evening they busied themselves to an amazing degree with the building and fitting out of their towns. But at midday, thoroughly drained of all their strength, they lay low in their little underground houses under the pressure of their fears...' *Their fears proved well founded.*
>
> *Between AD860–870, in the days of Norwegian king Harald the Hairy, the Vikings fell with a vengeance on the little islanders and, as the scribe approvingly notes, 'utterly destroyed them'. The Picts who made up their fellow tribes on the Scottish mainland also disappeared as a distinct people around the same time. First they were slaughtered by the Norsemen during a battle in AD839 in which they killed the last Pictish king, Eoganan, and then remnants of the Pictish confederation were absorbed by other warlike incomers – the Scotti, or Scots, who had moved into much of the west coast from Ireland around AD500 to found the kingdom of Dalriada. The integration under Scots king Kenneth MacAlpin of the two peoples through a mixture of force and intermarriage was unwittingly the first step on the road to a united Scottish nation.*

Tantalisingly, the Picts left little trace of their passing on Shetland apart from the outlines of some of their shattered settlements, a clutch of some superb silverwork and the carved rocks and stone slabs which can still startle with their astonishing mastery of intricate design. They left behind no chronicles or records in the Pictish language. Some brief inscriptions found incised in rock and bone use the rune-like lettering introduced in the seventh century from Ireland, and known as *ogham*, or *ogam*. It is possible that the islands of Fetlar, Unst and Yell bear Pictish names. They are not Norse placenames and do not belong to any known language. Many of today's crofts lie on the sites of old Norse steadings, which in turn often cover the remains of Pictish and even earlier Iron Age sites.

The Vikings

Once they had subdued the local Picts the Vikings established themselves in the coastal areas around the best natural ports and sheltered havens and initially used Shetland as a handy base for their raids on other islands to the west and south as far as Wales and the Isle of Man, with forays along the way into Alba (Scotland) and Britannia (England). Shetland's poor soil meant that it was not until late in the nonth century, when all the good land in more fertile Orkney had been settled, that the Norsemen began farming in Shetland with any real interest, although even then summer was traditionally the time to go 'a-viking.'

This was the time when they spread terror and were widely regarded as 'Sons of Death,' 'Stinging Hornets,' and 'Odin's Wolves' by their victims, who took to praying: 'From the fury of the Northmen and sudden death, Lord God deliver us.' The Vikings always preferred plunder to trade, for one thing they didn't have to pay for anything that caught their eye. The only trading they did seem to enjoy was slave-trading, and they anticipated the 18th-and 19th-century Scottish Clearances with their own depopulating version among all the islands and coastal reaches around Scotland. Captives usually ended up in the Viking slave market in Dublin, which was almost as notorious as the great slave emporium at Birka, in Sweden, which drew buyers from as far afield as Arabia.

The Vikings had the same roots as the Teutonic tribes that overran most of Europe and contributed to the destruction of the Roman Empire. Their ancestors came from the east and first invaded Denmark before crossing into southern Sweden. Latecomers were obliged to settle among the mountains and fjords of western Norway, an unforgiving environment that forced them to look to the sea for their living. They did not, however, become true seafarers until the eighth century, as their shallow boats lacked the keel necessary for deep-sea roving. Once they incorporated this vital feature into their design their square-sailed 100ft (30m) long, high-prowed galleys could take the Vikings anywhere they fancied on their plundering expeditions. Shetland was barely two days' sail away by longboat so its uneasy future was clear. In the latter part of the 800s the Vikings using Shetland and Orkney as bases incensed Harald Fine-Hair, King of Norway, by raiding their former homeland. Harald responded with fire and sword, reprisals which quickly brought them to heel.

The Earldom

In 880 Harald set up the earldom of Orkney and made Rognvald the Powerful its first Earl in compensation for the death of his son, Ivar, who had been killed in battle during the king's punitive expedition. Shetland also fell under the earldom and was ruled from Orkney by a succession of earls with such descriptive names as Harald Smooth-Tongue, Sigurdarson Wrye-Mouth, Halfdan Long-Leg, Havard the Fecund, Sigurd the Mighty, and Thorfinn the Skull-Splitter. Late in the 12th century this administration changed and Shetland was ruled directly from Norway. The Norse sagas are full of the exploits of the earls of Orkney during this period, but they do not have much to say about Shetland and it is assumed that, largely converted to Christianity, the Norsemen of Shetland had begun to live more peaceable lives.

Despite its strong Norse character Shetland gradually took on a distinct Scottish tinge over the years leading up to its formal annexation by Scotland in 1472, so much so that from 1236 onwards the ruling earls were Scots paying allegiance to Norway. On the eve of annex-ation came what is capitalised in island history as the Impignoration, in effect a complicated pawning of both Shetland and Orkney, with Scotland as the pawnbroker. Norway's author-ity had been seriously curtailed from 1397 by its union with Denmark and Sweden under a Danish king. A royal marriage of convenience was arranged for 1469 between Margaret, the 12-year-old daughter of Denmark's king, Christian the First, and King James III of Scotland in an attempt to patch up grievances which had almost led to war between the two countries over the huge arrears Scotland owed Norway following the 1266 Treaty of Perth. This treaty gave the Scots the Isle of Man and Hebrides in return for a payment of what was known as the 'Annual of Norway' – 4,000 marks down and £100 a year thereafter.

As a condition of the royal marriage, Scotland wanted this agreement abolished, along with the cancellation of all arrears and 100,000 crowns 'for the adornment of the bride'. Scotland also demanded possession of Orkney and Shetland. Denmark agreed to cancel the arrears and terminate the agreement but insisted that Orkney and Shetland remain fiefs of

Norway. The Danes also pledged as the bride's dowry the sum of 60,000 *Rheingulden* (gold florins of the Rhineland), which was the currency at the time throughout most of northern Europe. When the marriage contract was drawn up in 1468 Christian was, as usual, short of cash, and so pledged the islands of Orkney against the sum of 50,000 Rheinish florins, promising to pay the balance of 10,000 the following year. In the event, he was able to raise only 2,000, and so less than two months before the wedding at Holyrood Abbey, he also placed the islands of Shetland in pawn to cover the 8,000 florin deficit.

It is thought that Christian was unsure of Denmark's ability to redeem the pledges during his reign, but was swayed by the fact that the islands actually belonged to Norway. The document drawn up at the time was open-ended; no time limit was set on the redemption of the islands. Over the following 150 years the outstanding amount was raised and offered to Scottish monarchs on a number of occasions, but was always refused. Scotland had moved quickly to annex both island groups shortly after the marriage and had no intention of letting them go. In fact, diplomatic approaches with a view to redemption of the pawned islands were made by Denmark until well into the 18th century. It took until 1814 for Norway to break free of Denmark and a further 90 years before its complete independence from Sweden. Interestingly, Scotland's 1472 annexation of Orkney and Shetland has never been formally recognised by Norway.

The Scots

After the annexation, Lallans, or Lowland Scots, gradually became the language of law and pulpit but it was not until 1611, eight years after the union of the Scottish and English crowns, that legislation was passed in Edinburgh finally invalidating Norse law in the islands. In 1564 Mary, Queen of Scots, granted the revenues and control of Shetland and Orkney to her half-brother, Robert Stewart, an illegitimate son of James V. The despotic Robert built a palace at Sumburgh – the New Hall – and another in Orkney while proceeding to squeeze the islanders dry, demanding ever more in rents, dues and fines. Complaints about his overly harsh administration resulted in a spell of imprisonment for him in Edinburgh Castle, but he was soon out and up to his old tricks. Surprisingly for the times, he died peacefully in bed in 1593, but only after defeating an armed expedition sent to take him back to Edinburgh to stand trial again.

Robert's son, Patrick, succeeded him as Lord of Shetland and Earl of Orkney and built himself a palace in Orkney, a castle at Scalloway, and a fortified residence in Shetland, now known as Jarlshof. His tyrannical methods of taxation, his extravagant lifestyle and his ready resort to violence showed that he was a chip off the old Stewart block. By 1614, Earl Patrick was also in jail, awaiting trial for treason. While he languished there his hot-headed illegitimate son Robert staged a revolt. This was put down and he was hanged in Edinburgh. His father was beheaded a month later. As the centuries rolled on under Scottish rule the island crofters who under Norse law had been owners of land now became tenants under Scottish law and struggled to pay rents to the landowners – earls, lairds and church ministers – who had poured in from Scotland, buying up the land and amassing large estates.

While the croft provided staple foods the money to pay the rent came mainly from the sea and practically every crofter wound up fishing for his landlord and delivering the catch to the laird's fish-curing beaches. Others joined the Merchant Service or the Arctic whaling fleet. During the Napoleonic wars many were press-ganged and forced to serve in the Royal Navy. By the middle of the 19th century landowners had decided that sheep were more profitable than crofters and evicted their tenants from large areas of land to make way for blackface and cheviot sheep. These Clearances created hardship on an unprecedented scale, but it was not until 1886 that the British Government moved to relieve the distress of displaced crofters in Shetland and other Scottish isles by setting up a Crofters' Commission and guaranteeing security of tenure under the Crofters' (Holdings) Act. This came too late for many families. Reports of better living conditions in Canada, Australia and New Zealand led them to emigrate in their thousands, effectively depopulating many of the islands.

World Wars

Shetland's geographic position made it strategically important throughout both world wars. During World War I, a naval base was established at Swarbacks Minn, North Mainland, which was used by a Royal Navy cruiser squadron patrolling the northern waters. World War II brought an influx of servicemen to Shetland and Sullom Voe became an important Coastal Command base. Within the first two months of war Shetland came under air attack by the German Luftwaffe. Relative to its population, Shetland had suffered the highest loss of life of anywhere in Britain by the end of the war in 1945. In an operation known as the 'Shetland Bus', the Norwegian resistance movement used Shetland as a base during the war for daring trips into Nazi-occupied Norway to rescue refugees and supply arms to the underground. First Lunna, and then Scalloway became the headquarters of this cloak and dagger operation.

Post-War Changes

Unemployment was rife between and after both World Wars and was not alleviated until the 1960s brought fresh opportunities with renewed deep-sea fishing and the building of a modern fish processing industry. The tapping of North Sea oil during the 1970s brought new prosperity to Shetland – and a shortage of manpower. Today, as oil revenues start to shrink, Shetland is turning its eyes once again to the sea that has for so long sustained it.

There is no doubt that the Norsemen who were around for nearly 600 years left an indelible impression on the islands' culture and history. Most place-names are Norse, or its Shetland version, Norn, and many customs and festivals are rooted in the Vikings' pagan past. They are deeply embedded in the folk memory to this day and exercise a grip on the Shetland imagination not much stirred by either the Scottish annexation of 1472, the Union of the Crowns of Scotland and England in 1603, or the Act of Union which formally united Scotland and England in 1707. A new chapter opened in 1999 with a Scottish Parliament established once more in Edinburgh following the devolution of power from London under the Scotland Act of 1997, but this seems unlikely to change the islanders' belief that they are Shetlanders first and foremost and Scots only because of a medieval pawning gone wrong.

ECONOMY

Fishing

A long seafaring heritage going back to the time of their Norse ancestors and beyond has meant that Shetlanders have always been recognised as skilled seamen and fishing has always been the lifeblood of the crofting communities battling historically with climate, poor soil and the small size of their holdings. It became the backbone of the economy when salt and smoked fish became an important trade commodity. The trade in salted fish began in the 14th century with Hanseatic League merchants, who rented böds (booths) to barter goods with local fishermen for whitefish such as ling, cod and tusk.

This trade was eventually crippled in 1712 when the British government imposed a punitive salt tax. Displays depicting this old trading link can be seen at the Pier House in Whalsay. The early fishermen were a hardy lot who thought nothing of rowing up to 40 miles (64km) offshore in their *sixerns* (six-oared boats) to long-line the far *haaf*, or deep sea, for fish. The catch was salted and dried on open, stony beaches then, as the property of the landlord, it was exported. From May to August, men left their crofts and, when not at sea, lived in stone lodges built near the drying beaches. The ruins of some of these old lodges can still be seen. Around 1820, the fishermen took to large sailing smacks to fish for cod, which was cleaned and salted on board these deep-sea vessels and then brought back to Shetland to be dried and exported worldwide. This type of fishing flourished until the end of the 19th century, although the 1870s saw the large smacks join in the herring bonanza when untold tons of the 'silver darlings' were gutted, graded and packed in barrels of brine by locals girls and women for export. By 1905, Shetland's 174 herring stations were shipping out a million barrels a year to Europe. The ruins of many of these stations can still be seen, especially on the west side of Bressay and at Baltasound, in Unst.

Despite the problems facing the fishing industry and its world-class fleet today, Shetland remains at the centre of some of the richest fishing grounds in Europe. Recent years have seen a marked increase in the quantity of fish being processed in the islands, increasing the value of fisheries to the local economy. The local fishing fleet now uses some of the most technologically sophisticated vessels in Britain. These include many purse seiners of over 150ft (45m), with the largest 260ft (79m) long. The majority catch white fish such as ling, haddock and cod and surface shoaling fish such as herring and mackerel. The larger vessels are multi-purpose, being able to switch from one type of fishing method to another. Crabs, lobsters and shellfish are caught inshore by smaller boats. The best fishing grounds are, as in the past, about 50 miles (80km) away and fish can be processed in port less than 24 hours after being caught. Whitefish processing is based largely at Lerwick, Scalloway, Burra, Northmavine and Whalsay, where fish are filleted, skinned, graded, frozen and packaged into a wide range of high-quality products. Fish products are exported far and wide.

The Shetland Catch factory at Gremista, in Lerwick, is well on the way to becoming one of the world's largest handlers of frozen fish, with plant capable of holding up to 12,000 tons of fish. Other improvements in a multi-million-pound expansion will make the factory the most modern and largest capacity plant in Europe for deep-sea fish and this, in turn, is expected to attract more vessels to Shetland. Scalloway's long fishing tradition made it an obvious choice when the Shetland Island's Council was wondering where to site a proposed new fisheries college. An ideal location was found on the site of a 19th-century herring processing station at Port Arthur, near the mouth of harbour, and the North Atlantic Fisheries College was opened there in 1992, providing a further boost to the local economy.

The last two decades have also seen the introduction and rapid growth of salmon farming in Shetland, to such a degree that aquaculture now contributes more to the local economy than some traditional fishing enterprises. **Fish farming** is a growth, if risky, business and salmon, sea trout, shellfish, and even halibut are farmed in the voes, or sea lochs. Salmon farming and processing in Shetland employs nearly 1,000 people and pumps about £80 million a year into the local economy. With wild stocks declining at an alarming rate there is a surge of interest in the possibility of farming Atlantic cod. Scientists are even looking at ways to turn carnivorous fish such as salmon and cod into vegetarians so that they can be reared on cereals instead of fishmeal.

Britain's most northerly commercial port is in Lerwick Harbour. It is open to shipping in all weathers and operates round the clock. Lerwick is a vital pivot of the islands' economy as a major fishing port, a key ferry port, including roll-on roll-off freight and passenger traffic, and an increasingly popular port of call for cruise ships and yachts. Along with the local fleet, around 4,000 fishing vessels use the port as a base every year to cut down sailing times to the northern fishing grounds. The largest deep-sea trawlers can berth at Greenhead and Dales Voe and sheltered Bressay Sound provides a safe refuge in bad weather. The port is also a cornerstone of Shetland's comprehensive support for the oil and gas industry's operations in the North Sea and in the Atlantic to the west and north. Well-developed facilities and services and proximity to offshore operations have made it a leading support centre for exploration, development and production activities in these waters.

Oil

Shetland has been closely associated with **North Sea oil** since 1978 when the first oil flowed ashore at Sullom Voe, the site of Europe's largest oil terminal. A steady stream of supertankers still carries oil from here to refineries all over the world. The oil boom brought changes to Shetland. In particular it helped to stem the steady depopulation of the islands which had been going on for more than a hundred years. Shetland's population increased by more than one-third over just a few years to its present 22,000. Other benefits have been low levels of unemployment, improved communication links, including a first-class inter-island car ferry service, and many other welcome facilities paid for with oil money. Even local wildlife has become accustomed to oil industry activities to the point where otters are frequently seen feeding and playing around the oil terminal.

The boom years of North Sea oil are past and Shetland is looking at more traditional means to sustain its economy. Money is being invested in the fishing, fish processing and salmon farming industries and agriculture. Traditional crafts such as **knitting** are being promoted and **tourism** is regarded as another industry which can help top up the island coffers.

Agriculture

Crofters and their families historically lived a hand-to-mouth existence but modern methods have changed all that. The emphasis is now on sheep rearing. There are more than 400,000 sheep in the islands, a small, hardy breed producing fine, soft wool and good mutton. Thousands of lambs are exported every year. Some 6,000 cattle make the islands virtually self-sufficient in milk.

Knitting

For more than 500 years, Shetland wool has been knitted into uniquely patterned warm garments and what was once only a **cottage craft** is now an important industry. Most fleeces were sent to the mainland for spinning and dyeing but the advent of the Sandness Spinning Mill has enabled an ever increasing number of fleeces to be spun locally. Garments are knitted by hand or on hand-frame machines, mostly by home-based knitters. There are also a number of knitting factories.

Tourism

Like other Scottish isles, Shetland is a magnet for tourists. Magnificent scenery, an intriguing natural heritage and an abundance of wildlife draws more and more people to the islands. Most come from other parts of Britain, but 45% are from other countries, with growing numbers from Scandinavia and Northern Europe.

Energy

Shetland has also entered the age of renewable energy. Three Danish-made Vestas V47 windmills atop Burradale Hill, overlooking the Tingwall Valley, are striking landmarks which produce commercial, clean energy using something Shetland has in abundance – wind. On an average day the three windmills, known as the 'Angels of Burradale,' generate about 5%–7% of Shetland's electricity. Each 660 kilowatt turbine reaches full capacity once the wind is around Force 4 (13–18 mph), and shuts down at around Force 8 (39 mph).

LANGUAGE

You quickly realise you are in the realm of another language when you arrive in Shetland to be greeted by posters urging 'Dunna Chuck Bruck'. These are part of a 'Keep Shetland Tidy' campaign and mean quite simply 'Don't Throw Rubbish.' Not that you need to learn the local dialect. English is spoken as the mother tongue, but it was not always so and Shetland betrays traces of roots buried deep in the past in the language of the Norsemen as well as later overlays of the Lowland Scottish known as Lallans, and English. The Gaelic of the Western Isles of Scotland was never the language of Shetland and Orkney. Here a variant of the Old Norse language called Norn was commonly spoken and survived in the islands until the 17th century when it was supplanted by Lallans and eventually by English. What it does have in common with Gaelic is that it became regarded as inferior and came in for official disapproval, an attitude which almost led to its complete disappearance. It lingered on, however, in remote rural areas and in the shape of a dialect, Shetlandic, is now recognised as an integral part of the rich culture bequeathed by the Vikings and other, later, invaders.

Shetland Dialect

Shetlandic lexicons have now rescued the dialect from any danger of oblivion and to browse, for instance, through *The Shetland Dictionary* compiled by John J Graham (published by The Shetland Times Ltd, Lerwick 1999) clearly shows the preoccupation of the people with the sea, the land, and the weather, something that still holds good today.

Taking the latter first, it is obvious that the islanders were alert to every nuance of the weather, describing conditions from *weety* for damp or rainy, through *dag, grop, raag, shug, skub* and *smush* for different kinds of drizzle, and *slashy* and *speet* for heavy showers, to *vaanloop* for a downpour.

Although snow is not all that common it has still added such words and phrases to the local vocabulary as *sneeb*, meaning to snow quietly; *flukra*, which is snow falling gently in large flakes; *mell-moorie*, flurries of powdery snow; *blinnd moorie*, a severe snowstorm; and *moorie*, an all-out blizzard. These words probably found their way into the vocabulary during a time when Shetland was passing through a period that was colder than today. *Mirkab-rod* is a light, variable wind, *blashy* means it's wet and windy, *flan* is a sudden squall, *snitter* is a cold, biting wind, *gabs* is stormy weather, and *haily-puckle* is hailstone. If someone tells you the weather is going to be solemn, they mean extremely bad. Good weather gets short shrift linguistically, although *gleer* does describe sunshine of the hazy variety.

The Sea. *Haaf* refers to the deep sea, 30–40 miles (48–64km) beyond coastal waters; *fram* means out to sea; *aandoo* is to row gently against the tide to maintain a boat's position, *raem calm* means a sea as smooth as cream, *boddam* is the seabed, *baa* is a sunken rock, *skerry*, a rock at sea which is frequently covered at high tide, *noost* is a hollow at the edge of a beach where a boat can be drawn up to protect it from gales and heavy seas, and *roost* is a tidal race.

The Land. Dialect words you'll come across on Ordnance Survey and other maps include *geo*, a coastal inlet or chasm with steep rocky sides; *hamar*, a rocky hill; *holm*, an islet; *kame*, a ridge of hills; *knowe*, a hillock; *ness, noup, bard* and *mool*, a headland; *rig*, a plot or field; *quoy*, enclosed common land; *scattald*, common pasture used for grazing; *shun*, a small loch; *taing*, flat land projecting into the sea; *ayre*, a beach; *haa*, a laird's house or manor; *voe*, a sea loch or inlet; *wick*, a bay; *banks*, sea cliffs; and *gloup*, a collapsed cave which has blowholes through which the sea spouts.

As you'd imagine, time in the islands doesn't get much attention, although you might come across *da moarn*, tomorrow; *dastreen*, last night; *eredastreen*, the night before last; *dayset*, nightfall; *dim*, dusk; *dimriv*, dawn; and the picturesque *rivin o da dim* for daybreak, literally the 'tearing asunder of the darkness',

Centuries of back-breaking toil on land and sea has produced lots of words for islanders to use when they want to say they are 'doon-drappin' or exhausted, among them *debaetless, disjaskit, forfochen, forlegen, hurless, mankit, ootmaagit, pyaagit*, and *pooskered*. If they are only weary they can say they are *vyalskit, wabbit*, or *daddit*. Some things are not what they might seem. *Mud* is not mud. It means to loosen up the soil before planting seeds or potatoes. *Frugal* weirdly means very, and *odious* is the word used to mean extremely, as in 'It was an odious fine day.'

Other common words are *böd*, once used to house fishermen and their stores during the fishing season and now simple accommodation for visitors; *skeo*, a dry-stone structure which allows the wind to blow through to dry hanging meat and fish; *planticrub*, a small circular dry-stone enclosure where cabbage and kale can grow safe from sheep and gales; *muckle*, large; *peerie*, small; *penga*, money; *oor*, an hour; *ook*, week; *helly*, weekend; *munt*, month; *twartree*, two or three, several; *closs*, a narrow lane with houses in either side; and *lodberrie*, a type of 18th-century house in Lerwick which was a trader's residence combining a courtyard, store and private jetty.

You'll see from all this that Shetland dialect is very much alive and kicking and it is now taught in schools and appears in many local publications such as the literary magazine *The New Shetlander* and *The Shetland Times* newspaper, which also publishes dialect stories and poetry.

A dialect poem by the late Rhoda Bulter

Sometimes I tink whin da Loard med da aert,
An He it aa pitten tagidder,
Dan He still hed a nev-foo a clippins left ower,
Trimmed aff o dis place or da tidder,
An He hedna hert to baal dem awa,
For dey lookit dat boanie an rare,
Sae he fashioned da Isles fae da ends of da aert,
An med aa-body fin at hame dere.

If you can't decipher it here is the translation:

Sometimes I think that when the Lord made earth,
And He got it all put together,
Then He still had a handful of clippings left
Trimmed off of this place and the other,
And He hadn't the heart to throw them away
For they looked that bonny and rare,
So he fashioned the Isles from the ends of the earth,
And made everybody find a home there.

Audio recordings of traditional tales can be heard at the *Shetland Museum and Archives* (Hay's Dock, Lerwick ZE1 0WP; ✆01595-695057; fax 01595-696729; email info@ shetlandmuseumarchives.org.uk; www.shetlandmuseumarchives.org.uk), and at a number of local museums and heritage centres. For more details contact the Shetland Museum and Archives. The Shetland Library also publishes material in dialect and there is a lending section covering all aspects of Shetland life and literature. A feature of the library is its Shetland Room where, on request, you can browse among a collection of both rare and recent publications.

Practical Information

GETTING THERE

BY AIR

Traditionally you travelled to Shetland by boat. Improved air services, however, are now carrying an increasing number of visitors, especially those with time constraints or those who suffer from sea-sickness. Atlantic Airways operate a direct flight between Stansted and Shetland on Mondays and Fridays: for details see below. Otherwise, Aberdeen is the main departure point airport for the Shetland Islands from the Scottish mainland. Other Scottish air connections with Shetland are from Glasgow, Edinburgh, Inverness and Orkney. There are frequent services to Sumburgh Airport, on the southern Shetland Mainland, from these as well as connections from other airports in Britain, Norway (Stavanger, Bergen and Oslo), Holland (Amsterdam), Denmark (Copenhagen, Esbjerg), Italy (Rome) and Switzerland (Vienna, Zurich). British Airways, operated by *Loganair*, and *Atlantic Airways* operates scheduled services to Shetland.

How to get to Shetland

Atlantic Airways (www.flyshetland.com) flies from Stansted to Shetland on Mondays and Fridays at 10.15 with the return flights leaving Shetland at 12.30 between 15 June and 10 September.

British Airways (℡0870-850 9850; www.britishairways.com), operated by *Loganair* (St Andrew's Drive, Glasgow Airport, Paisley, Renfrewshire PA3 2TG; ℡0141-848 7594; fax 0141-887 6020; www.loganair.co.uk), flies to Sumburgh from:

Aberdeen: six flights a day Monday, Thursday and Friday, five on Tuesday and Wednesday, and four a day Saturday and Sunday.

Edinburgh: two flights a day Monday to Friday, and one on Saturday and Sunday.

Glasgow: one a day from Monday to Sunday.

Inverness: two a day Monday to Friday, and one on Saturday and Sunday.

Kirkwall (Orkney): two flights a day Monday to Friday, and one on Saturday and Sunday.

Fares

A return ticket on the Atlantic Airways Stansted–Shetland route costs £166 if booked on the internet, including taxes and booking fee. Otherwise, fares range from £30 one way from Kirkwall, Orkney, and £68 one way from Glasgow or Edinburgh. **Flight times** are subject to change. Check fares, times and availability with *British Airways* (℡0870-850 9850; www. britishairways.com), or *British Airways*, Sumburgh, Shetland (℡01950-460345; fax 01950-460520) and *Atlantic Airways* (www.flyshetland.co.uk).

Airports

Sumburgh Airport, at the southern tip of the Mainland, 25 miles (40km) from Lerwick, is Shetland's main airport. As well as flights to and from Scotland and England it supports scheduled domestic services and a series of oil charter operations. The airport is open Monday 7.30am to 8.45pm, Tuesday to Friday 7.30am to 8.15pm, Saturday 9am to 5.15pm and Sunday 10.30am to 8.15pm. Disabled facilities include an ambulift and staff are always available and willing to assist. There is a combined shop and café in the terminal building. There are regular inter-island flights between Sumburgh Airport and Fair Isle. The airport covers a prehistoric site. A rough chest containing human bones was uncovered by contractors during building operations and radio carbon tests dated them to around 3200BC.

Tingwall Airport, 7 miles (11km) west of Lerwick, is used by *Loganair* (℡01595-840246) for other inter-isles air services.

A taxi is the best way to get to Lerwick from Sumburgh or Tingwall although there is also a regular bus service. The trip takes about 45 minutes. In Lerwick, the Viking Bus Station is within walking distance of the NorthLink ferry terminal.

Helicopter and Charter Flights
Bristows Helicopters: (✆01851-705577).
Tayflite Executive Air Charter: (✆01738-550088; www.tayflite.co.uk).

BY SEA
The views on the approach to Shetland by sea are unsurpassable and if the choppy waters where the North Sea greets the Atlantic at Sumburgh Roost don't make you feel wobbly the voyage is an unforgettable experience.

From Scotland
NorthLink Ferries Ltd (Jameson Quay, Aberdeen AB11 5NP; Kiln Corner, Ayre Road, Kirkwall KW15 1QX; reservations ✆0845-600 0449; fax 01856-879588; email info@ northlinkferries.co.uk; www.northlinkferries.co.uk) operate a passenger and vehicle service from Aberdeen to Lerwick every day of the week (Monday to Sunday), and four times a week (Tuesday, Thursday, Saturday and Sunday) via Kirkwall, Orkney, throughout the year. Departure from Aberdeen at 7pm (Monday, Wednesday and Friday) and 5pm (Tuesday, Thursday and Saturday) will see you in Lerwick the following morning for breakfast. The *MV Hjaltland* and *MV Hrossey* can carry 600 passengers and 153 cars. Each ferry has à la carte and self-service restaurants, lounge areas, bars, a well-stocked shop, children's play areas, and comfortable cabins.

Fares
On the Aberdeen to Lerwick route, the single adult fare is £31.80 in peak season (July and August), £26.50 mid-season (April, May, June, September, October and 19 Dec – 8 Jan) and £20.80 low season (January, February, March, November, December). Additional charges are added for the following. Car is £113.80, £107.80 and £84.70 single. Motorcycles are £21.60, £19.50 and £17.80 single. An outer two-berth cabin is £86.30, £77.70, £56.10 single. An inner cabin (up to four-berth) will cost you £84.10, £75.50 and £53.90 respectively. All cabins are en suite. There are specially equipped cabins for disabled passengers. There is a 10% discount available on standard passenger and vehicle fares for senior citizens, those in full-time education and the disabled.

From Scandinavia and the Faroes
Between **19 May and 16 June** *Smyril Line* (J Broncksgöta 37, PO Box 370, FO-110 Tórshavn, Faroe Islands; ✆+298 34 59 00; fax +298 34 59 01; email office@smyril-line. fo; www.smyril-line.com), operates the 12,000-ton *MF Norrona* ferry service from Iceland on Wednesday, Faroes on Thursday, Denmark on Saturday and from Norway on Sunday. From **16 June to 29 September** it leaves for Lerwick from Norway on Tuesday, Iceland on Thursday, Faroes on Friday, and from Denmark on Saturday. This new modern cruise ferry can carry more than 1,400 passengers and 800 vehicles. Onboard facilities include swimming pool, sauna, and solarium, as well as an à la carte and a buffet restaurant, cafeteria, bar lounge, nightclub, play room and game area for children, and duty-free shops. Couchettes, two–four berth cabins, 12 de luxe cabins, a suite, and six disabled-friendly cabins are available. All cabins are equipped with toilet/shower, TV, trouser press and hair dryer. One way car packages in low season for two people in a standard size car and in a two-berth outside cabin with shower/toilet, TV, and refrigerator cost £195 from Norway to Lerwick, and Faroes to Lerwick; £390 from Denmark to Lerwick; and £436 from Iceland to Lerwick.

Cruises
Arthur Anderson, co-founder of the Peninsular & Oriental Steam Navigation Company (P&O) is credited with writing and publishing the world's first ever advertisement for a

cruising holiday. This appeared in the first edition of the *Shetland Journal* in 1836. With more than 40 visiting cruise ships a season, Lerwick is now one of Scotland's top cruise destinations. It is ideally located as a midway port on cruises between Iceland, the Faroe Islands and Norway and the Scottish mainland and Europe. Cruise ships of up to 672ft (205m) can berth alongside at the port; larger ships anchor in Bressay Sound, with passengers just five minutes by launch from a floating pontoon in a sheltered dock. Passengers disembark close to the town centre. Contact *Lerwick Port Authority* (Albert Building, Lerwick ZE1 0LL; ℂ01595-692991; fax 01595-693452; email info@lerwick-harbour.co.uk; www.lerwick-harbour.co.uk).

TRAVEL AGENTS AND TOUR OPERATORS

To get the most out of your visit try to fit in a tour with a local guide who knows the history and folklore of the island and best places for wildlife, bird-watching, walking, diving, or whatever. Contact **general guides** for large or small groups, specialist, and multilingual guides through the *Shetland Tourist Guides Association* (11 Wirliegert, Aith ZE2 9NW; ℂ077-8932 6878; email shetlandtouristguides@yahoo.co.uk).

Island Trails: Bigton ZE2 9JA (ℂ01950-422408; email info@island-trails.co.uk; www.island-trails.co.uk) undertakes guided tours from the Ness at the south end of the Mainland to Fethaland in the north and takes in just about every area with a story to tell. Archaeology, local crafts, culture and heritage are all covered by these tours and guide Elma Johnson will also arrange tours to suit your own particular interests.

John Leask & Son: The Esplanade, Lerwick ZE1 0LL (ℂ01595-693162; fax 01595-693171; email info@leaskstravel.co.uk; www.leaskstravel.co.uk). Arrange fly/drive package holidays from most major UK airports. Prices include flights, accommodation and car hire. Open Monday to Saturday 7.30am to 5pm, and Sunday 9.30am to midday. They also handle full and half-day guided coach tours from mid-May to late September.

Shetland Travelscope: Toll Clock Shopping Centre, 26 North Road, Lerwick (ℂ01595-696644; fax 01595-696446; www.shetland-travelscope.co.uk). Open Monday to Friday 9am to 5.30pm, Wednesday 10am to 5.30pm, Saturday 9am to 5pm.

Shetland Small Group Tours: 1 Carlton Place, Lerwick ZE1 0ED (ℂ01595-692080; fax 01595-696564; www.shetlandtours.co.uk). Tours in luxury eight-seater vehicle with experienced guides. Individual touring requirements can be arranged.

Shetland Wildlife: Longhill, Maywick ZE2 9JF (ℂ01950-422483; fax 01950-422430; email info@shetlandwildlife.co.uk; www.shetlandwildlife.co.uk). Operates a wide variety of excursions by sea or land to showcase the best of Shetland's flora and fauna. Expert naturalist guides will get you up close to photograph the most approachable puffins in the world, search secluded bays for otters, observe harbour porpoises, and take you whale-watching. Cruises to Noss, Hermaness and Muckle Flugga are available and the company organises tours lasting from a day to a week.

BOAT TRIPS

Cycharters John Tulloch (1 Bloomfield Place, Lerwick ZE1 0PW; ℂ01595-696598; fax 01595-690441; email john@cycharters.co.uk; www.cycharters.co.uk), will take you around the Scalloway Isles on an afternoon cruise or a full day trip to the island of Foula. Evening trips go to Hildasay, Oxna, Papa and South Havra with the chance to go ashore and explore these uninhabited islands. The *MV Cyfish*, operated by John Tulloch, is a modern, twin-engined, 12-passenger vessel. The Scalloway Isles Cruise leaves Scalloway port at 2pm and returns at about 4.30pm. The trip to Foula, 20 miles (32km) off the west coast, takes about two hours. The island is then circumnavigated to view the high cliffs and seabirds nesting. You then berth in Foula for about 2½ hours, arriving back at Scalloway at 5pm. The evening trips to either Hildasay, Oxna, Papa or South Havra leave at 6pm returning at 9pm. You can go ashore and explore each island. Private charter and sea angling trips, by arrangement, are also available. All trips leave from the Muckle Yard, next to the Old Scalloway Fish Market, Scalloway. Bookings can also be made at the tourist office.

Shetland Sea Charters (℡01595-692577) operates daily cruises around Noss, from June to August, on *MV Alluvion*. The cruise takes three hours and departs Victoria Pier, Lerwick, at 1.30pm. Cost for adults is £20, children £10 (under 14), under 5 free.

Seabirds & Seals, Dr Jonathan Wills (℡01595-693434; www.seabirds-and-seals.com) has boat excursions to Noss National Nature Reserve and Britain's northern tip.

St Magnus Bay Charters (Victor Gray, Vaara, Aith, Bixter ZE2 9ND; ℡/fax 01595-810378; email vaara@tiscali.co.uk; www.stmagnusbay.shetland.co.uk) takes trips from Aith Marina into St Magnus Bay on *MV Sceptre,* carries four–eight passengers. Afternoon trips leave on Tuesday and Thursday at 2pm; evening trips on Monday and Wednesday at 6pm, weather permitting.

Tom Jamieson (℡01950-431367; email info@mousaboattrips.co.uk; www.mousaboattrips. co.uk) provides trips to Mousa. Early-April to mid-September.

COMMUNICATIONS

MAIL

The main post office is at 46 Commercial Street, Lerwick (℡01595-693372). It is open Monday to Friday 9am to 5pm, Saturday 9am to 12.30pm. It also has a Bureau de Change. There is another post office in the Toll Clock Shopping Centre (North Road, Lerwick; ℡01595-695362), which is open Monday to Friday 9am to 5pm, Saturday 9am to 5pm. Other post offices are scattered throughout the Mainland and islands (see *Help and Information* in each section).

TELEPHONES

You'll find telephone kiosks throughout Lerwick and in most other places. Instructions are prominently displayed inside. Dialling codes for different areas and countries can be found at the beginning of the telephone book. The STD code for Lerwick is 01595.

NEWSPAPERS AND MAGAZINES

The New Shetlander is Shetland's oldest literary magazine, with prose and poetry reflecting island life past and present. It's published quarterly by the Shetland Council of Social Service (Market House, 14 Market Street, Lerwick ZE1 0JP; ℡01595-743902; fax 01595-696787; email scss@shetland.org; www.shetlandcss.co.uk).

Scottish Islands Explorer is an A4 magazine published on the first Tuesday of alternate months, starting in January, and dedicated to all aspects of the Scottish Isles. For a complimentary copy and subscription form contact Philip Welch (Auld Haa, Fair Isle, Shetland ZE2 9JU; ℡01595-693380; fax 01595-694830; email info@scottishislandsexplorer.com; www.scottishislandsexplorer.com).

i'i Shetland (Millgaet Publishing, North Ness Business Park, Browns Road, Lerwick; ℡01595-690090), is a new monthly magazine covering the stories behind the headlines.

The Shetland Times (Gremista, Lerwick ZE1 0PX; ℡01595-693622; fax 01595-694637; email enquiries@shetland-times.co.uk), is an old established weekly tabloid newspaper published every Friday at 65p. It carries news and weather, magazine section, book of the week, and CD reviews. The company also publishes the traveller's guide *Shetland Visitor*, distributed free of charge for visitors, and *Shetland Life*, a monthly publication which contains literary contributions and information on all aspects of island life. There's even a crossword in the Shetland dialect.

Shetland Today is a community-oriented website for residents, exiles and visitors. Updated daily, you can read it online at www.shetlandtoday.co.uk.

You can also read the daily news from Shetland at www.shetland-news.co.uk.

For bookworms, or just to buy the newspapers, visit *The Shetland Times Bookshop* (71/79 Commerical Street, Lerwick ZE1 0AJ; ✆01595-695531; fax 01595-692897; email shop@shetlandtoday.co.uk). Open Monday to Friday 9am to 6pm, Saturday 9am to 5pm.

RADIO
BBC Radio Shetland (92.7 FM) provides a daily news and information service and weather forecast each evening Monday to Friday at 5.30pm. Through the winter months there is an extra nightly programme highlighting topics such as local music, culture and politics. Shetland Islands Broadcasting's independent service is on the air round the clock on 96.2 FM.

GETTING AROUND

MAPS AND GUIDES
You'll find a selection of the 1:50,000 and 1:25,000 Ordnance Survey maps good for walkers and cyclists and a fully indexed 1:100,000 tourist map of Orkney and Shetland at *The Shetland Times Bookshop*, opposite the post office in Lerwick. The bookshop stocks a wide selection of guides and Shetland books, as well as postcards and souvenirs. The nearby Tourist Office in the town centre also stocks a selection of guides and maps, including its official 1:128,000 tourist map, which is ideal for motorists. This is published by Estate Publications and covers both Shetland and Orkney.

BY AIR
There are regular inter-island services from Tingwall Airport, 7 miles (11km) from Lerwick, to the islands of Foula, Fair Isle, Papa Stour, and Out Skerries and also scheduled flights from Sumburgh Airport to Fair Isle. The service is operated by *Directflight*, using Britten-Norman Islander aircraft with seats for eight people. These flights provide not only a convenient and fast means of getting to the islands around the mainland, but also afford a fascinating bird's-eye view of the archipelago. Flights are increased during the summer months to meet demand. Book as far in advance as possible and keep your baggage to a minimum. Contact Directflight at Tingwall Airport (✆01595-840246; fax 01595-840247; email lwk.ops@directflight.co.uk; www.directflight.co.uk).

BY SEA
The Shetland Islands Council runs well maintained, reliable and frequent ferry services which link the larger islands with the Shetland Mainland. Passenger fares are nominal and certainly much cheaper than those charged by council-operated inter-island ferries in Orkney. For instance, ferries from the Mainland to Unst, Yell, and Fetlar charge £3 for a car and a passenger and £1.25 for each extra passenger. If you have a vehicle it is advisable to book for all ferries, especially the small vessels.

Inter-Island Ferry Booking Offices:
Bluemull: ✆01957-722259.
Bressay: not bookable.
Fair Isle: ✆01595-760222.
Foula: ✆01595-753226.
Out Skerries: ✆01806-515226.
Papa Stour: ✆01595-810460.
Whalsay: ✆01806-566259.
Yell, **Unst**, **Fetlar:** ✆01957-722259.

Journey times:

Bressay: 5 minutes.
Fair Isle: 2½ hours.
Fetlar: from Yell/Unst 25 minutes.
Foula: 2½ hours.
Out Skerries: from Vidlin 1½ hours; from Lerwick 2½ hours.
Papa Stour: 40 minutes.
Unst: from Yell 10 minutes.
Whalsay: 30 minutes.
Yell: 20 minutes.

BY ROAD

Private bus operators cover most of the country districts of the Mainland, making it possible to explore the countryside at little cost. Bus services link Lerwick with the main villages and ferry terminals. If you use a local bus service ask the driver to advise you on the best dropping off points. Timetables are available from the Viking Bus Station, in Commercial Road, Lerwick, which is the terminus and departure point for all local bus services. It has a waiting room, toilets, and left luggage area (for information on all services telephone 01595-694100; open Monday, Tuesday, Thursday and Friday 8.30am to 5.30pm, Wednesday and Saturday 9am to 5.30pm). A smaller waiting room and left luggage facility is also provided at the Esplanade, Lerwick.

Contact the bus companies for more information or spend £1 on a comprehensive timetable for all services from the bus station or *VisitShetland* (Market Cross, Lerwick; ℂ01595-693434; fax 01595-695807). Buses leave from Viking Bus Station for places of interest every day in the summer season, including:

- **Bressay** for crossing by inflatable to **Noss** on a Tuesday, Wednesday, Friday, Saturday and Sunday.
- **Island of Trondra** (near Scalloway) and the **Croft Trail**. Every day except Wednesday and Sunday.
- The extraordinary settlement site at **Jarlshof** (Sumburgh).
- Sandwick for the ferry crossing to **Mousa Broch**. Advise bus driver to drop you at the Setter Junction for Sandsayre, which is where the ferry leaves. It is about a mile or a 15-minute walk from the drop-off point. Every day except Sunday.
- **Robins Brae**, Dunrossness to visit the **Croft House Museum**. Every day except Sunday.
- **St Ninian's Isle** (Bigton). Change buses at Channerwick junction. Every day except Sunday.
- **Scalloway Castle** and **Museum**. Every day, except Sunday.
- **Weisdale Mill** on a Friday and Saturday.

Taxis

There are at least 20 taxi operators on Shetland Mainland. Taxi fares are reasonable, with maximum charges of £2 for the first ¾ mile, each additional ¼ mile 25p (6am to midnight, midnight to 6am £2.50 and 27p respectively). Waiting time costs £15 an hour or 25p a minute. Taxis carry up to seven passengers.

Driving

Undoubtedly the best way to get around is to rent a car. Driving is relaxing and stress-free. Shetland has around 500 miles (900km) of well maintained surfaced roads and, making use of a couple of vehicle ferries, you can drive quite easily from top to bottom in a day. Such a zoom through is, of course, not the way to enjoy the islands. Some of the islands, such as Muckle Roe, East and West Burra and Trondra, are connected by road bridge and you often don't realise you are travelling from one island to another until you look at the map. Salty mist often blurs the windows so make sure the screenwash reservoir is full and in work-ing order. When it is windy park into the wind as doors can easily be damaged if opened carelessly in a strong blow. There are not many petrol (gasoline) stations outside the capital, Lerwick, and it is advisable always to keep your fuel tank at least half full.

EATING AND DRINKING

EATING

Traditional dishes in Shetland sprang from impoverished communities where two inflex-ible factors led to their creation: they were made from the most basic and readily available foodstuffs and they had to be filling enough to sustain men and women through a long day's hard work. That's not to say that they weren't tasty. Combinations dreamt up by thrifty housewives resulted in some inventive mixing of root vegetables and staple grains such as oats and bere (pronounced 'bare'), a prehistoric variety of barley, with the bounty of the sea harking back to the old links with Scandinavia. After years of being despised as low-rent food many of the old dishes are now enjoying new respectability and rubbing shoulders on local menus with curries, pasta, pizza and burgers. In the old days when islanders were *fan-tin* or *hockin* (very hungry) and in need of *maet* (food) they would *punish* (consume rapidly) such reliable fillers as *raan, krappin, krampis, stap*, and *slott* with helpings of *shappit tatties, rumbledethumps* or *brönnies* and *beremeal bannocks*.

Raan is fish roe, usually cod, boiled or fried; *krappin* is fish livers mixed with either beremeal or oatmeal and flour and used to stuff the stomach or head of a fish; *krampis* is similar except that oatmeal is kneaded into a dough with melted fat or raw fish livers and then boiled; *stap* is boiled haddock livers and meat from the haddock heads, chopped and seasoned. *Slott* combines the best of both worlds – fish livers and roe mixed with flour and oatmeal, boiled, and then browned in the oven. *Shappit tatties* are simply mashed potatoes, while the quaintly named *rumbledethumps* is a more up-market version in which buttered potatoes are 'thumped' with seasonal vegetables such as cabbage, kale, onions or leeks and then 'rumbled' or mixed together. A *brönnie* is a round, thick oatmeal scone; *beremeal bannocks* have an earthy tang and are, for visitors, an acquired taste. They keep well and like pitta bread are a great standby basic *faerdie maet* (food for a journey) for hikers. Also good backpack *errands* (provisions) are Shetland Oatie biscuits, which are also made to a traditional local recipe, but baked using techniques that imitate the old open-fire method of baking. These are made by Walls Bakery in a number of flavours: golden butter, savoury garlic, toasted sesame, wholemeal honey and bran, mature cheese and traditional.

In the days before refrigerators and deep-freezers fish and meat was salted, wind-dried or smoked to preserve it, and even today fish can still be seen drying on clothes-lines dur-ing the summer months. *Sookit* (wind-dried) whitings, *saat* (salt) herring and all types of smoked fish remain popular with islanders. *Reestit mutton* – lamb smoked, salted and dried over a peat fire – is an island speciality and is used to make the tattie soup which along with salt beef and bere bannocks is traditional New Year's Eve provender in Shetland. The name is derived from the old method of drying the meat in the space under the roof of the croft cottage, known as the *reest* from the wooden framework laid across the rafters on which the salted meat was left to cure in the peat smoke. Another local speciality is *sassermaet*, a spicy mince or sausage meat, which is eaten in the shape of patties. *Globe Butchers* (49-53 Com-mercial Street, Lerwick; ℂ01595-692819), will vacuum pack this and other meat so that you can take home a real taste of Shetland.

Hardy bere is still grown and ground in Shetland. You can buy a bag with a bannock recipe at Quendale Mill (Dunrossness ZE2 9JD; ℂ01950-460969; email info@quendalemill. shetland.co.uk; www.quendalemill.shetland.co.uk). The modern recipe you'll get is more or less the same as the traditional one, except the baking method is different. In the old days the dough was baked on a griddle and then lightly toasted before a fire; now the bannocks are usually baked in a conventional oven.

If you don't fancy these traditional delights Shetland's renowned lamb, seafood – lobster, crabs, mussels and scallops – and fish are used by local hotel and restaurant chefs to good effect in a variety of tempting dishes. You will find lamb on most menus, usually cooked plain to allow you to savour the natural taste, a distinctive and delicious flavour which comes from the animal's natural diet of herby ling and heather. Shetland salmon is equally famed for its quality. Eat it fresh, smoked or marinated. Salmon farming had become an important local industry, with some farms operating their own hatcheries and rearing salmon from smolt in sheltered sea lochs. Fresh and smoked salmon are exported, mainly to the British mainland and the rest of Europe.

DRINKING

One legacy that the Vikings definitely left their island descendants is a taste for beer and strong waters. There is one brewery in Shetland. This is the **Valhalla Brewery** in Unst which opened in 1997 and produces Auld Rock, White Wife Simmer Dim ales, and Sjolmet Stout. Another local product is Stewarts Rum. Raven Ale and Highland Park Malt, both produced in Orkney, are also sold in local hotels and bars and you'll also find a wide choice of British, Continental, American and Australian bottled and canned beers and lagers. Whisky is known in local slang as *screecham*. A small swig of alcohol is a *toot*, *slockenin* means a satisfying drink and anyone who knocks back too many can become *glafterit* (boisterously jolly) at best, or *foo, mortal, stimin, swittlin, poopin* or *paloovious* (drunk) at worst. These are useful words if you get invited to a *foy*, a party to mark a special occasion.

More homely drinks are *browst*, a brew of tea, *brocken*, a hot drink containing oatmeal and *mylk-an-mell*, an oatmeal drink made with hot milk.

ENTERTAINMENT

MUSIC

Shetland has a lively and varied music scene and you'll find many music sessions going on at local bars and clubs. Traditional sessions with fiddlers and accordionists welcome visiting musicians, and the *Shetland Jazz Club* and *Shetland Country Music Club* (35 North Road, Lerwick; ✆01595-692570) both host local musicians and visiting artists. You can find out who is playing where in the listings which appear in *The Shetland Times* every Friday. The Scots brought the fiddle to the isles, although the lively local playing style has affinities with the Hardanger fiddle music of Norway. Today Shetland music and the fiddle go together like tatties and neaps. The whaling and herring fleets of the 19th century gave Shetland a cosmopolitan air and imprinted on local music the strains of Scandinavia, Europe, Scotland and America. In the 1950s the late Tom Anderson rescued the old tunes and styles which had lost their attraction as American music swamped the air waves and at the *Shetland Museum and Archives* (Hay's Dock, Lerwick ZE1 0WP; ✆01595-695057; fax 01595-696729; email info@shetland-museumandarchives.org.uk; www.shetlandmuseumandarchives.org.uk) you can listen to the traditional music he collected along with a variety of other traditional and contemporary tunes.

With the renewed interest in recent years in all areas of island culture the high standard of old-school musicians such as Peerie Willie Johnson (guitar), Tom Anderson (fiddle) and Ronnie Cooper (piano and accordion) has been maintained by such ambassadors for Shetland music as Aly Bain, Willie Hunter and Catriona Macdonald. The programme of traditional music education in local schools has prompted the emergence of a new wave of dynamic young local musicians. Bryan Gear, Fiddler's Bid, and Filska are among those gaining international reputations. Fiddler's Bid is one of Shetland's top fiddle bands, comprising four fiddles and a Scottish harp, backed by guitar, bass and piano. Their music ranges from traditional, high-energy Shetland reels to slow, melancholy airs.

The music of the islands is still developing and there is much more to it than fiddles. In line with the times the music of the islands has diversified to include folk, traditional dance, jazz, country and rock groups. Shetland now has an active contemporary music scene and in the vanguard you'll find the country sounds of **Sheila Henderson** and the band **Shoormal**. Sheila Henderson has recorded two CDs, *Call of Fate* and *Waiting for Venus*. *Indigo Skies*, the debut CD album of **Shoormal** – the name means 'water's edge' in the Shetland dialect – showcases their talents. **High Strings** is an ever-changing school fiddle group which has toured in the UK and Scandinavia, and **Stramash** originally formed by high-school pupils, underlines the benefits of traditional music tuition at school level. Contemporary bands include Drop the Box, Rock Salt and Nails, Bongshang, and the Red Vans. Country groups like May & Mackie and folk favourites Hom Bru add excitement to the brew. Some other names to look out for are Bitumen River, Epijay, Big Thrill, Malachy Tallack, Solar Polar Bears, Stevie Hook, Sufferin' Aunties, and Suppository Business.

Local and invited musicians perform at the **Shetland Folk Festival**, held in late spring, and this is the biggest musical event of the year. Contact the *Shetland Folk Festival Society* (5 Burns Lane, Lerwick ZE1 0HE; ✆01595-694757; www.shetlandfolkfestival.com). The hub of the festival weekend is the Festval Club at Islesburgh Community Centre (King Harald Street, Lerwick ZE1 0EQ; ✆01595-692114; fax 01595-696470; email enquiries@ islesburgh.org.uk; www.islesburgh.org.uk), which also gives visitors an opportunity to hear Shetland fiddlers during the summer months. Mini-festivals, known as *foys*, take place at weekends throughout the islands. The annual **Shetland Accordion and Fiddle Festival** (Peter Leask, chairman, ✆01595-693162) is held each October and is a highly popular annual event. The highlight of this lively festival of concerts and dances is the winding up Grand Dance where up to a dozen bands play virtually non-stop accordion and fiddle music. Rock, heavy metal, experimental and avant garde music also find a place, with two major rock marquee events and the **Unst Rock Festival** staged in summer.

You can also browse www.MusicScotland.com where you can also listen to clips or download full-length MP3 tracks.

DANCE

Shetland Folk Dance gives demonstrations weekly during the summer months at Islesburgh Community Centre in Lerwick. As well as Scottish country dances you might see Shetland dances such as the Foula Reel and the Papa Stour Sword Dance, which is the only Shetland dance performed exclusively by men.

FILM

Movie-makers have been inspired by Shetland since the 1930s, when Michael Powell filmed his classic *Edge of the World* in Foula. Archival film can be seen on video at some of the local museums and heritage centres. Contact *Shetland Museum and Archives* (Hay's Dock, Lerwick ZE1 0WP; ✆01595-695057; fax 01595-696729; email info@shetlandmuseumandarchives. org.uk; www.shetlandmuseumandarchives.org.uk) for more information. There is no cinema in Shetland but the *Shetland Film Club* is active. Throughout the year film weekends are held by Shetland Arts at the Garrison Theatre in Lerwick showing the latest releases. Check the local press for details. Tickets are available from Islesburgh Box Office at Islesburgh Community Centre (King Harald Street, Lerwick ZE1 0EQ; ✆01595-692114; fax 01595-696470; email enquiries@islesburgh.org.uk; www.islesburgh.org.uk).

THE GREAT OUTDOORS

FLORA

Shetland can claim more then 800 species of flowering plants and ferns and in summer the islands offer a dazzling display of colour. In late summer the hills are pink-purple with flowering heather. Many plants common in the landscape are becoming rare in other parts of Britain. If wild flowers are your bag a visit to the **Keen of Hamar National Nature Reserve** on Unst is a must. Here on the serpentine bedrock are a number of species with restricted distribution in Britain, including **northern rock cress** and **Norwegian sandwort**. You can also see the miniscule **fairy flax**, the **dioecious mountain everlasting**, slender **St John's wort** and the **frog orchid**. One species is particularly famous here, the **Shetland mouse-ear chickweed**. Discovered in 1837, this yellow and white flower is found at only one other site in the world – and that is also on Unst.

Salt-tolerant plants such as **thrift** and **roseroot**, are common on sheltered, ungrazed sea cliffs throughout Shetland, upper reaches are often a mass of **primrose, spring squill, moss campion, kidney vetch, thyme, sea campion, bird's-foot trefoil** and **red campion**. Other habitants range from bogs and marshes to moorland, hay meadows and sandy beaches, where you'll find clumps of lilac **sea rocket**.

Damp marshes host **bog asphodel, marsh marigold** and **northern fen** or **marsh orchids**, as well as **yellow iris** and **monkey flower**, a naturalised alien from Alaska. On peat moorland you'll find **tormentil, milkwort, thyme** and the pale pink **heath-spotted orchid**.

Hay meadows and pasture land hold a variety of orchids and buttercups. **Ragged robin, marsh cinquefoil, sedges** and **lady's smock** favour wet meadows, while drier meadows shelter many grasses and flowers, among them **yellow rattle, devil's-bit scabious, autumn hawkbit, red** and **white clover, eyebright** and **common mouse-ear**. Hayfields, once a much more common feature of croftland, are further enlivened by **gentians** and **orchids**. Roadside verges are also good places to find these flowering plants.

Peat is made up of dead plants compressed over century upon century and forms a globally rare and threatened habitat. In Shetland it covers vast stretches of moorland where cotton grasses, cross-leaved heath and deer grass grow in profusion. Not many plants can cope with the constant soaking they get in this habitat. Some have adapted by becoming carnivorous. Two such insect-eating plants flourish in really wet areas. These are **butterwort** and **sundew**, which trap insects on their sticky leaves and then digest them. There are several species of arctic-alpines, particularly on Ronas Hill.

All plants are protected by law in the British Isles, including more than 150 species which have special protection. It is an offence to destroy or uproot any wild plant unless this is accidental or permission has been given by the owner or occupier of the land.

FAUNA

The only mammals native to Shetland are the **Atlantic grey** and **common seal;** all the others have been introduced by humans or are visitors. The islands have barely 25% of the mammals found in mainland Britain, but their resident **otters** and **seals**, and passing **whales** and **porpoises** are among the mammals that most delight visitors.

Otters

It is estimated that there is at least one of these endearing animals every three quarters of a mile (1.2km) along the more remote coasts, which adds up to a higher density of otters than for any other area of north-west Europe. About 14% of the UK's total otter population is found in Shetland and one of the largest concentrations occurs around Yell Sound. Their distribution is almost exclusively coastal. Look for them early or late in the day in the shallow water of sheltered bays and voes with low, rocky shorelines where they like to feed around kelp beds on fish, crabs and shellfish. Shetland's otters may be genetically distinct from those found elsewhere as they are smaller and have more clearly marked throat patches. In most of Europe otters are freshwater animals, which explains why the coats of the marine otters of the islands are not suited to prolonged immersion in the sea. To stay waterproof they have to rinse themselves regularly in fresh water.

Seals

Two species of seal breed in Shetland – the **common** or **harbour seal** and the **Atlantic grey seal**. There are about 6,000 common and 3,500 grey seals on and around the islands.

The two are not often seen together, although at Mousa and Sumburgh Head they can be spotted together on the rocks. Identification is not always easy. Size is one distinguishing factor. Greys are usually much bigger than common seals. A fully grown adult male or bull grey reaches 7ft (2.2m) in length and weighs 485lb (220kg), whereas a fully grown common male reaches 5–6ft (1.5–1.8m) and weighs 250lb (113kg). As you have to see them together to identify them like this an easier way to tell them apart is by the shape of their heads. The grey has a much larger head, with a high muzzle often referred to as a Roman nose; the common seal has a low dog-like muzzle with a relatively rounded head and distinct forehead. The nostrils of the common seal form a V-shape while the grey's are much more parallel. The old Shetlandic name for the grey seal is *haaf*, or deep-sea fish, because it prefers the open sea; the common seal is known as the *tang*, or seaweed fish, because it likes more sheltered shores and islands. Grey seal milk is 50% fat and quickly piles the pounds on pups. In three weeks they gain 33–99lb (15–45kg), which is the equivalent to eating about 70 cream buns a day. On still nights in summer you'll sometimes hear the grey seal's weird, moaning cries, which are the origin of the *selkie* legends about sea people told throughout the islands off both the north and west coasts of Scotland.

Cetaceans

This is one of the best places in Europe to see whales and other cetaceans. **Whales, dolphins** and **porpoises** are regularly sighted, especially during the months of summer and early autumn. The continental shelf is only some 30 miles (48km) to the west, so even deep water cetacean species occasionally come inshore. Twenty-two species have been recorded in Shetland, although a handful of these have been seen only on rare occasions, or as fatalities. The **minke whale** is the most commonly seen of the baleen, or toothless, whales. About 26ft (8m) long, they are frequently seen off Sumburgh Head in June, and between Fetlar, Whalsay and the Out Skerries during July and August. Sightings can virtually be guaranteed if you sit long enough on a headland with calm sea conditions during July and August. Not so obvious are **killer whales**, although as many as six pods often hunt in local waters. Killer whales, or orcas, are often seen around Sumburgh Head and in Mousa Sound. **Pilot whales** used to be a much more common and in the 18th and 19th centuries used to be driven ashore and slaughtered for their blubber and oil. Once, in Quendale, south Mainland, 1,540 were driven ashore. The last drive was in 1903 when 83 were killed at Weisdale.

Sumburgh Head is the most likely place to see **humpback whales**. One or two have been recorded every summer since 1992 and this hopefully may herald a comeback following the whaling which drastically reduced their numbers earlier last century. Peak sightings occur in June and July. This large whale – up to 59ft (18m) long – has long white-notched flippers and a notched head, which may be seen as it breaches and rolls. When diving it often shows the mottled white underside of its tail.

Harbour porpoises are the smallest and most frequently seen cetacean, although short triangular fins breaking the surface are usually all that you see. They tend to favour sheltered voes or the sounds and channels between islands. Mousa, Noss and Yell Sound are good places to look for them. The commonest dolphins are the **white-sided dolphin**, **white-beaked dolphin**, and **Risso's dolphin**. **White-beaked dolphins** are often seen late in summer from the ferry *MV Good Shepherd* as it plies between Grutness and Fair Isle.

For information on best times and places to see whales and dolphins contact the Tourist Office, in Lerwick, or *The Company of Whales*, a division of Shetland Wildlife (Longhill, Maywick ZE2 9JF; ✆01950-422483; fax 01950-422430; email info@companyofwhales.co.uk or info@shetlandwildlife.co.uk; www.companyofwhales.co.uk or www.shetlandwildlife.co.uk).

The *Shetland Sea Mammal Group* records sightings of whales, dolphins and porpoises in Shetland waters and aims to promote an interest in the sea mammals which are a growing visitor attraction. You can find out about the latest sightings in local waters by contacting general secretary Paul Harvey, Shetland Amenity Trust (Garths Pool, Lerwick; ✆01595-694688; email sbrc@zetnet.co.uk) or by checking out the group's website at www.nature.shetland.co.uk.

If you are a whale-watcher you are invited to report sightings to the group (c/o SNH, Ground Floor, Stewart Building, Alexandra Wharf, Lerwick ZE1 0LL; ℅01595-693345; fax 01595-692565). Remember to record details of the date, location, species, number of animals and supply a brief description or photograph of whales and dolphins sighted. When describing whales and dolphins the key features to note are the shape of the dorsal fin, its position relevant to the body, the head shape, general colour and pattern, length, presence and the shape of its blow.

Freshwater Fish

There are only four inland lochs with a surface area greater than a sq km, so lack of decent-size stretches of water and rivers means correspondingly few freshwater fish species. Only seven species are definitely established locally and all of them have a salinity tolerance or a marine phase. Several lochs have seen a great deal of stocking with non-indigenous fish in recent years to improve the angling. A number have been stocked with **rainbow trout**. **Brown** and **sea trout** might not be as plentiful as they once were, but they are still relatively widespread. The **Atlantic salmon** has been recorded occasionally but at only a few of the larger water systems with access to the sea. **Arctic char**, a deep-water species, have been recorded only in the Loch of Girlsta on central Mainland. **Eels** are widespread and common in most burns, lochs and other stretches of water.

Terrestrial Fauna

A relatively recent newcomer is the **hedgehog**, but it has already spread from Mainland Shetland to most of the inhabited islands, apart from the Out Skerries. The **rabbit** is also widespread, and found on the Mainland and most other islands. They have bounced back from periodic onslaughts of myxomatosis. The **brown hare** was introduced to the Mainland in about 1830 but since two were trapped at Spiggie in 1937 there have been no recorded sightings. The **mountain hare**, first introduced around 1900, is widespread. The **field** or **hill mouse** is said to be Shetland's only indigenous terrestrial mammal, although some authorities believe it might have arrived in the household goods of early Viking settlers, who also brought the **house mouse**. The mouse is found everywhere except for the Out Skerries. It is believed that the field mice found on Fair Isle, Yell and Foula are sub-species. The **brown rat**, introduced by visiting vessels, has been reported on all the large inhabited islands except Yell. There is no fox population although, oddly enough, one or two have been found dead in recent times but have been regarded as escaped imported pets. **Stoats** are widespread throughout the Mainland but are apparently not found on Yell, Unst, Fetlar and Whalsay. The widely kept hybrid ferret-polecat introduced in the 1980s and found throughout the Mainland has been targeted by an eradication programme to protect ground-nesting birds.

If you are into *Arthropoda* in any shape of form Shetland is a beckoning paradise where you might give your name to a new butterfly or moth, a bee or a wasp, or even a flea before you leave. Investigation and recording of island insect life is patchy and far from complete, even with the best known groups *Lepidoptera*, *Diptera* and *Coleoptera*. As recently as 1996, 40 new species were added to the list of the best known groups of butterflies and moths.

The common **toad** and common **frog** are the only two species of freshwater amphibians found in Shetland. Both were originally introduced and although the common frog is widespread the common toad might have disappeared; none has been seen since a small specimen was found at Tingwall in April 1982.

BIRD-WATCHING

Shetland is internationally renowned for its birdlife. The islands are ocean crossroads for migrating birds, as well as being home to vast colonies of seabirds, waders and other species. The world-famous Bird Observatory on Fair Isle has recorded more than 340 species, among them exotic rarities from Europe, Asia and America. Of the 24 species of seabirds which breed in Britain no fewer than 21 breed in Shetland, ranging from the tiny storm petrel, which is smaller than a starling, to the gannet with its wingspan of nearly 6ft (1.8m).

Peerless birdwatching draws twitchers from afar, but you don't have to be an expert to enjoy the vast and bustling bird tenements clinging to soaring sea cliffs. Much of Shetland is sandstone laid down in successive beds, one on top of the other. Wind, rain and sea have eroded the sedimentary rock to form masses of ledges and more than a million seabirds return to Shetland every summer to breed on them. **Fulmars**, **gannets**, **kittiwakes** and **guillemots** favour the open ledges, **puffins**, **petrels** and **shearwaters** nest in burrows, **shags**, **razorbills** and **black guillemots** favour boulder beaches, while **skuas**, **gulls** and **terns** nest inland. Peninsulas and islets provide sanctuary to the famous long-distance migrant, the **Arctic tern**, as well as **oystercatchers**, **ringed plovers**, **herring**, **great black-backed** and **lesser black-backed gulls** and **eiders**. A few support **Manx shearwaters**, as well as clouds of **storm petrels**, Britain's smallest seabird. Storm petrels return to their nests only at dusk and one of the best places to see them is during an evening trip to the island of Mousa.

Peat bogs are home to **common gulls**, **snipe**, **redshank** and **lapwings**, while the freshwater lochs and lochans draw **teal**, **mallard**, **red-breasted merganser**, and the **red-throated diver**. Streams attract common **sandpipers**. Most seabirds partner for life and many also return to nest at the same site or burrow each year. Seabirds can be seen at their breeding colonies for just three or four months of the year. Fulmars, shags, gulls, and black guillemots, known locally as *tysties*, stay around throughout the winter.

The largest seabird colonies are on the internationally important reserves of Hermaness and Noss, which are managed by *Scottish Natural Heritage*. At Hermaness, Noss, Fair Isle and Foula you can see **gannets** galore at their nesting sites and it is thrilling to watch them fishing, arrowing into the sea from heights of up to 100ft (30m). The distinctive **puffin**, known locally as the *tammie norie*, is one of the best-known seabirds. About one-fifth of all Scotland's puffins breed in Shetland and within easy reach of Lerwick is a colony of some 2,000 pairs on the cliffs of Sumburgh Head, a short drive from the airport. **Cormorants** can be seen breeding at only a few sites in Shetland, mainly in the west. A third of Britain's fulmars breed around the coastline. Approach their nest and you could end up covered by a foul-smelling, oily liquid which both adults and chicks squirt to defend themselves.

Best place for waders and **shelduck** are the tidal mudflats at the Pool of Virkie, in the south Mainland. On farmland you'll find **meadow pipit** and **wheatear** moorland and hill are breeding habitats for the **golden plover** and the **merlin falcon**, Shetland's only regularly breeding bird of prey, as well as such summer migrants as the **great skua**, or *bonxie*, and the **Arctic skua**. Skuas swoop and attack anything – or anyone – in their territory.

There are birds everywhere, but for some species you should visit the reserves owned and managed by the *Royal Society for the Protection of Birds* (RSPB). Fetlar, for instance, is famous for its **red-necked phalarope**, the dainty Arctic wader that is one of Britain's rarest breeding birds. **Red-throated divers** are easily seen at the Loch of Funzie on Fetlar and **whimbrel**, **golden plover**, **dunlin**, **Arctic skuas** and **Arctic terns** breed on the heathland there. In 1967, Fetlar hit the headlines by attracting Britain's first-ever breeding snowy owls, now unfortunately no longer resident. Seabirds easily seen from the RSPB reserve near the lighthouse buildings at Sumburgh Head during summer include **guillemot**, **razorbill**, **fulmar** and **kittiwake**. The Loch of Spiggie nature reserve, 2 miles (3km) north of Sumburgh Airport, is one of the most important wildfowl lochs in Shetland. Large numbers of **whooper swans** gather in autumn and winter sees many species of duck. In summer the loch attracts **kittiwakes, terns** and **skuas**. The Loch of Spiggie is a large shallow loch, renowned for its trout fishing. Both it and part of the adjacent Loch of Brow were bought by the RSPB in 1979 and form part of a Site of Special Scientific Interest.

Shetland seems to have a magnetic attraction for rare migrants and vagrants in autumn and birdwatcher's from all over Britain arrive in September and October at such migration junctions as Fair Isle, the Out Skerries and Sumburgh to watch for **lanceolated** and **Pallas's grasshopper warblers**, **yellow-breasted bunting**, the **Pechora pipit** and **great snipe**.

The best time to see most breeding birds is between late May and late July. Peak migrant season is from mid-May to early June and again from mid-September to early October.

NATURE RESERVES

The RSPB's three nature reserves cover a variety of habitats, from the imposing sea cliffs of Sumburgh Head at the southern tip of Mainland Shetland to the nearby Loch of Spiggie reserve and the reserve on the island of Fetlar. There are also three National Nature Reserves managed by Scottish Natural Heritage. SNH maintains nature reserves on the island of Noss, east of Bressay and Lerwick, and at Hermaness at the northern end of the island of Unst. The Keen of Hamar reserve, near Baltasound on Unst, is a unique botanical site. Enquiries to Scottish Natural Heritage (Ground Floor, Stewart Building, Alexandra Wharf, Lerwick ZE1 0LL; ✆01595-693345; fax 01595-692565). The famous Fair Isle Lodge and Bird Observatory is operated by a Trust. There are no admission charges to any of the reserves in Shetland.

Reserve office addresses
RSPB Fetlar Nature Reserve: The Bealance, Fetlar ZE2 9DJ (✆01957-733246).
RSPB Sumburgh Head Nature Reserve: East House, Sumburgh Head Lighthouse, Virkie ZE3 9JN (✆01950-460800; fax 01950-460801; email pete.ellis@rspb.org.uk). This is also the address for Loch of Spiggie reserve.

CONSERVATION

With such a wealth of wildlife it is not surprising that conservation is big in Shetland. Scottish Natural Heritage and other organisations such as RSPB and the Shetland Oil Terminal Environmental Advisory Group (SOTEAG) constantly monitor seabird numbers and breeding success in Shetland. Seabirds serve as good indicators of the health of the sea and this monitoring can act as an early warning system if the fine balance necessary for a healthy marine ecosystem is upset.

Many of Shetland's birds are protected by the Land Reform Act (Scotland) which states that it is an offence to disturb these birds and their young at or near their nest sites. **Special permits** are required to photograph Schedule 1 birds, which include **red-throated diver**, **merlin**, **whimbrel** and **red-necked phalarope**.

The Shetland Bird Club (Sumburgh Lighthouse, Virkie ZE3 9JN; email martinheubeck@btinternet.com) was founded in 1973 to promote, study, conserve and record the birdlife of the island. Membership is open to anyone with an interest in the birdlife of Shetland. For more information contact Roger Riddington (SBC Membership Secretary, Spindrift, East Shore, Virkie ZE3 9JS; ✆01950-460080). Postal enquiries should include a stamped and self-addressed envelope. Roger Riddington is also editor of the monthly journal *British Birds*. By supporting the *Friends of Fair Isle Bird Observatory* charity (Fair Isle ZE2 9JU; ✆/fax 01595-760258; email fairisle.birdobs@zetnet.co.uk) you will be contributing directly to ornithological research on Fair Isle and receive regular newsletters and an annual report.

Several publications available from VisitShetland are of interest to twitchers. *The Shetland Bird Chart*, by Joyce JM Gammack, provides information on practical bird-watching in Shetland, birds in their habitats and the location and composition of the main seabird colonies. Also available is an RSPB publication containing information on its reserves. The *Shetland Bird Report*, published annually by the Shetland Bird Club, contains information on all species recorded each year in Shetland. The club has also publishes six newsletters a year, and published *A Country Checklist of Shetland Birds* by Dennis Coutts (1989).

Awareness and understanding can make the difference between extinction and survival for rare or threatened species and the *Shetland Biological Records Centre* (SBRC) has been set up to address this key issue. Its aim is to create a single, comprehensive source of information about Shetland wildlife that is available to everyone. Core element of the centre is a computer database used to gather information about wildlife and habitats. The work of the Centre will further systematic biological recording and help conserve the environment by raising awareness of its biodiversity. Anyone with an interest in Shetland's wildlife, or in recording natural history, can help. If you would like to assist with wildlife surveys contact SBRC (Shetland Amenity Trust, Garthspool, Lerwick ZE1 0NY; ✆01595-694688; email sbrc@zetnet.co.uk).

WALKING

Shetland has a policy of free but responsible access to the countryside and this, with the varied and often spectacular scenery, makes it a great place for serious hiking and trekking or simply for leisurely rambles. All that is required is that you respect the Scottish Outdoor Access Code, which is set out in detail in an informative leaflet for walkers available free from the tourist office. The leaflet details 20 walks on nearly all the 14 inhabited islands. These can be undertaken by anyone who is reasonably fit, and range in length from a mile (1.6km) in the Dale of Walls to 7 miles (10.2km) in Unst Saito and Hermaness. Make sure you have the right Ordnance Survey (OS) map, which will help you to decide whether to extend, shorten or otherwise vary a suggested walk.

Walkers can make use of campsites and böds (camping barns, most with an historic connection and offering simple but adequate accommodation in a restored building) which can be booked through the Tourist Office. Look out also for the square 'Walkers Welcome' symbol on establishments. These are quality-assured by VisitScotland and make a special effort to meet the needs of walkers. For a free copy of the Walk Shetland guide contact VisitShetland (Market Cross, Lerwick; ©01595-693434; fax 01595-695807) or download the walks from www.walkshetland.com.

Guides covering different parts of Shetland are readily available and you can also join guided walks organised by the *Shetland Field Studies Group* on the first Saturday and third Sunday of each month between April and October. These SFSG outings are an ideal way for you to get to some of the more remote parts of the islands. Book in advance at VisitShetland (Market Cross, Lerwick; ©01595-693434).

Walking around the coast (or *da banks* in local parlance) is very much a part of island life and in combination with towering bird-crowded cliffs, voes, quiet inland lochs, and gently undulating heathery hills is a pleasant way to spend a day. There is no better way to visit prehistoric and more recent archaeological heritage sites, and also to get close to island wildlife. Even busy industrial areas have their share of birds and mammals. At Sullom Voe, for instance, you can see mergansers, eider ducks, and divers feeding in the sea loch and otters are frequently spotted hunting and feeding around the oil terminal. Books on walks are available at **the Shetland Times Bookshop** at 71–79 Commercial Street, Lerwick, on visitor's tickets from the Shetland Library, and from the Tourist Office in Lerwick.

CYCLING

A touring holiday on two wheels, with daily stretches of 20–30 miles (30–50km), is an attractive option. Road surfaces are good and, for most of the day, traffic is light. Many sections have a hard shoulder providing a refuge if you need to pull over. In most situations you can see and be seen a long way ahead. Minor roads may be narrow, but on most of them visibility is excellent and traffic levels are even lower. Though the islands are far from flat, road ascents in the main are long and gentle and you can pedal along at a pace which should allow you to enjoy the countryside with its wildlife, make refreshment stops, and visit various attractions en route.

It's hard to believe, looking at the map, but Shetland has 1,000 miles (1,609km) of road suitable for cyclists and even more if you add the rough tracks which are offroad mountain-bike territory. Shetlanders are hospitable people and you can be sure of help if you need it no matter where you wind up. The self-reliant islanders are practical and excellent at sorting out mechanical problems. There are lots of roadside telephones and toilets around the islands and loads of accommodation. Most cyclists opt for B&B, campsites or böds. You can get a free leaflet from the tourist office called *Cycling in Shetland* which details 20 routes to start you off, from 6 to 22 miles (10–25km). Some of the suggested routes are circular; others are linear there and back. Shetland can be breezy in the extreme on occasion and on a circular route you might experience what islanders called a 'mixture of mercies'. On a linear route, a strong following wind can sometimes be a considerable advantage. If you have the advantage of a car with a cycle-carrier long stretches of coastline can also be walked. Some accommodation establishments will even drop you off and collect you after you have cycled your chosen route. Look for an establishment with a square sign saying 'Cyclists Welcome'. The *Shetland Wheelers Cycling Club*, based at Gott, is always pleased to welcome visiting cyclists. Time trials are held at 6.30pm on Tuesdays from April to the end of August.

Shetland is part of the 3,728-mile (6,000km) **North Sea Cycle Route** (www.northsea-cycle.com) set up by Scotland (including Shetland), England, the Netherlands, Germany, Denmark, Sweden and Norway. This continuous cycle route around the North Sea is signposted with North Sea Cycle Route plaques supplementing existing signage, and there are also large interpretive boards at key points. This is the world's longest signed international cycle route, stretching from Harwich and the Hook of Holland in the south to Bergen and Shetland in the north. The detailed maps and guides you need to cycle the route are available. For more information or to contact one of the participating countries check out www.northsea-cycle.com. You can also get maps covering Britain's 9,000-mile (14,484km) **National Cycle Network**, which is the lead project of *Sustrans*. The Shetland leg of 104 miles (167km) falls in the 501-mile (806km) route down to Aberdeen via John o' Groats. If you want to support a practical charity committed to providing better routes for cyclists and walkers you should join Sustrans. As a supporter you get a free pack with information about routes already open, plus regular newsletters and invitations to openings and events. Sustrans can be contacted at the following addresses:

Sustrans: 2 Cathedral Square, College Green, Bristol BS1 5DD (✆0117-926 8893; fax 0117-929 4173; email info@sustrans.org.uk; www.sustrans.org.uk).

Sustrans (Scotland): 162 Fountainbridge, Edinburgh EH3 9RX (✆0131-624 7660; email scotland@sustrans.org.uk).

Sustrans Information Line: ✆0845 113 0065.

FISHING

Fly-fishing is the most popular form of angling, with **brown trout** providing some of the best sport. Popular lochs are stocked regularly and in autumn **sea trout** and the occasional **salmon** can be hooked in the voes and larger streams. The brown trout fishing season is from 15 March to 6 October and the sea trout season is from 25 February to 31 October. The record Shetland brown trout weighed 9lb 4oz (4.2kg) and was caught in the Loch of Huxter, on Whalsay. Spinning is permitted in most lochs, with the notable exception of the Loch of Spiggie. It is illegal to fish for sea trout or salmon on Sunday, to leave unattended cast-out tackle and for any angler to use more than one rod and line at any one time. Superb fish are can be found in the more than 300 lochs scattered all around the islands, thanks to more than 80 years of skilled management by the *Shetland Anglers' Association (SAA)* (✆01595-695903; www.troutfishing.shetland.co.uk) which has boats for hire on popular lochs.

Girlsta Loch is Shetland's largest and deepest loch, and it is full of brown trout and **Arctic char**, stranded there after the last Ice Age. The loch is a Site of Special Scientific Interest (SSSI) and the Association asks you to return to the loch any char you catch. SAA owns or rents 99% of the fishing in the islands and issues annual permits, which you can find at any tackle shop or at the tourist office. The Association has also produced an informative booklet *Guide to Shetland Trout Fishing* which has a detailed listing of more than 100 lochs and voes. A leaflet *Trout Fishing in Shetland* is available from VisitShetland, in Lerwick. The SAA's licensed clubhouse in Burns Lane, Lerwick, is open on Tuesday and Friday evenings during the season and visiting anglers are welcome to socialise there or to take part in club competitions.

It's easy to get hooked on **sea angling**. It is a thrilling sport and big catches are not uncommon among islands which lie at the centre of some of the richest fishing grounds in Europe. Record-breaking **skate** of 226.8lb (102.9kg) and **porbeagle shark** weighing 450lb (204.1kg), have been caught. Other species such as **cod**, **halibut**, **catfish**, **tusk**, **haddock**, and **mackerel** can also be taken on rod and line. You can cast from the shore, but fishing from a boat is better. Recommended standard boat-fishing equipment is a 7ft (2m) rod with a multiplying reel. Generally, lines made from nylon mono-filament, braided terylene or Dacron are suitable. However, you will need wire traces if fishing for any weighty species and enough line to hook fish in water 60 fathoms (110m) deep. For shore fishing, equipment depends on what you plan to catch. You can buy tackle locally. Expect the best shore and boat-fishing in the last three months of the sea-angling season, which is from May to October. Species regularly caught include ling, whiting, cod, herring, mackerel, turbot, halibut, flatfish, skate, eels, dogfish, hake, coalfish and tope.

John Leask & Son (The Esplanade, Lerwick ZE1 0LL; ℂ01595-693162; fax 01595-693171; email info@leaskstravel.co.uk; www.leaskstravel.co.uk) can organise an angling holiday for you. A three-night stay in an hotel will cost £412, or £552 for five nights, based on two people sharing, DB&B. Guesthouses are from £327 and £411 respectively based on two people sharing on a B&B basis. These prices include car hire based on two people sharing a self-drive car, a gillie for one day, fishing permit for the duration of the stay, and a complimentary angling guidebook. A gillie costs £50 for every extra day, and for every extra day boat hire goes up £10.

DIVING

Thanks to the Gulf Stream the sea is not as cold as you'd expect at this latitude. Temperatures round the coast vary, but a general rule of thumb is that the west is the warmer coast. Mean sea temperatures are 46°F (7.5°C) in February, 48°F (9°C) in May, 65°F (18°C) in August and 51°F (10.5°C) in November. Make sure you have a thermal semi-dry or dry suit. At this latitude visibility is usually good. Clear water is the norm in the north and west and underwater life is prolific. Diving is best done from a boat. There are plenty of wrecks to explore, with some sites dating back to Shetland's earliest maritime history. The first shipwrecks chronicled in Shetland were those of the Viking galleys *Fifa* ('Arrow') and the *Hjolp* ('Help'), which drove ashore together on the east coast one stormy winter's night in 1148. They are thought to have gone down in the region of Gulberwick. Dive charter services offer all the support, advice and local knowledge you might need to call on.

AQUA SPORTS

Sailing, kayaking or cruising around Shetland's scattered jigsaw of islands gives you a completely different but riveting perspective. It is only from the sea that many of the most spectacular cliffs, stacks, sea caves and soaring arches can be seen in all their natural splendour.

Yachting

Lerwick and Scalloway are popular summer retreats for yachts from all around the North Atlantic, which also take advantage of dozens of other sheltered jetties and anchorages around the islands. Yachts have been coming to the islands since the 19th century and around 400 now visit every year. Surrounding waters are not to be treated lightly but they are well-charted and apart from contending with changeable weather there are few navigational difficulties, apart from avoiding the growing number of fish and shellfish farms that dot the sounds and sea lochs. Visiting yachtsmen are welcomed by both *Lerwick Boating Club* (12a Commercial Street, Lerwick; ℂ01595-692407) and *Scalloway Boating Club* (Port Arthur; ℂ01595-880388) and can enjoy their facilities and take part in local sailing events. Showers, toilets, phones, and laundry facilities are available. In Lerwick, keys are available from Lerwick Port Control or the tourist office.

Canoeing and Kayaking

The *Shetland Canoe Club*, based at Bridge-End Outdoor Centre on Burra, is happy to host visitors and share useful local knowledge with anyone planning to paddle around local waters. The club runs training sessions and trips during the season, which begins in mid-March and ends early in September. Pack a fleece and a waterproof jacket no matter what time of year you intend to visit. The best time for self-powered sea trips is usually July and August. Kayakers have paddled to almost all the islands over the past few years, including Foula, 18 miles (29km) offshore, and Fair Isle, 25 miles (40km) away. Highlight of the year is the annual weekend on the island of Papa Stour, which is renowned for its caves, arches and passages. Accommodation is either B&B or camping. Visiting paddlers are welcomed and the club can arrange to pick up you and your kayak if you arrive by ferry. For more details contact *Shetland Canoe Club* (Tom Smith, Bridge-End Outdoor Centre, Bridge-End, Burra, Shetland ZE2 9LD; ✆01595-859647; email tom@seakayakshetland.co.uk; www.seakayakshetland.co.uk).

Rowing

Traditional Shetland boats are pointed at both ends, reflecting their Viking ancestry and large four or six-oared versions of these *yoals* were once mainstays of the islands' fishing industry. Competitive *yoal* rowing has become popular and smaller sailing versions, some of them very light and fast, are now built and these can be seen at regattas all over the islands during the summer months. Such regattas also feature the rod and line competitions known as *eela*.

GOLF

Golfers are well catered for, with several courses of nine or 18 holes and a floodlit driving range. No floodlights are needed around midsummer, though, when it is still light enough for a tournament which is traditionally played at midnight. At the end of Dales Voe, north of Lerwick, is *Shetland Golf Club's* (Dale, Gott ZE2 9SB; ✆01595-840369; www.shetlandgolfclub.co.uk) 18-hole, 5,562 yard (5,085m), par 68 course. The course is open daily from April to September. The 19th is open from 11.30am to 2.30pm and 7pm to 10.30pm. Green fees: adult £20, children £10. There is also an 18-hole course at Skaw, on the island of Whalsay, and a nine-hole course at Asta, next to the picturesque Asta Loch, near Tingwall (Garth Lodge, Asta, Scalloway; ✆01595-880231). There is a driving range at the *Moor Park Family Golf Centre* (✆01595-696933) in Setter, near Gulberwick, which is open all week from October to March from noon to 8pm; and from April to September from 10am to 8pm. Visitors are welcome on all courses and green fees can be paid daily. Golf clubs can be hired from *Cee & Jays* shop on Commercial Road, Lerwick (✆01595-693025). Open Monday to Saturday 9am to 5pm.

HORSE-RIDING AND TREKKING

Horse-riding and pony trekking are pleasant ways to get around. The Shetland pony – which you'll see roaming wild in some parts – is a particular favourite with children. The smallest is 28 inches (71 cm) high and the maximum height is 42 inches (107 cm). The *Shetland Pony Stud Society* was formed in 1890 to ensure the purity of these famous animals and promote their breeding. Although they are primarily bred to work, many ponies are kept as pets. Carriage-driving tuition and drives are available at *Thordale Shetland Driving Centre* in Walls, West Mainland. The Centre specialises in Icelandic and other Norse breeds, including Fjords and Shetlands. It is set on a working croft 3 miles (5km) from the village of Walls and 20 miles (32km) from Lerwick. If you don't feel like riding, carriage driving is another way to see the countryside. You can learn to drive yourself or you can sit back and have places of interest pointed out by a driver. If you are an experienced rider but have never tried the extra gaits of the Icelandic horse, tölt and pace, private tuition is available. For more information contact Thordale Shetland Driving Centre (✆01595-809799; fax 01595-809288; email fstaylor@thordale.co.uk; www.thordale.co.uk). Open Tuesday to Sunday.

LEISURE CENTRES

If the weather is not up to scratch for outdoor pursuits there are a number of leisure centres and swimming pools you can use. They are run by the Shetland Recreational Trust (✆01595-741000). The leisure centres in Unst, Yell and Whalsay all have swimming pools, as well as other sports facilities, including squash courts. Walls and Aith in the West Mainland both have swimming pools. At Brae, Scalloway, and Sandwick are swimming pools with solariums, spectator and refreshment areas. Toddler pools and whirlpools also available at Scalloway and Sandwick.

SHOPPING

Most of the little shops you'll find as you travel around are quite well-stocked and many are also post office branches. These shops are also good places to find out what's going on in the area and the shopkeepers and assistants are always happy to chat and answer questions. Generations of fishermen and outdoor workers have been thankful for the *ganseys* (jerseys) knitted by island women from the fine wool of the small Shetland sheep. Today, Shetland is probably better known for its **knitwear** than for any other of its craft products and you can buy a variety of high quality knitwear and lace which draws on skills passed down over hundreds of years. Traditionally, the finest wool was plucked directly from around the neck of the sheep and teased out ready for spinning. Dyes made use of lichen, madder, onionskin, seaweed and indigo.

The Shetland Times publishes some interesting textile and knitting books, among them *Shetland Lace*, by Gladys Amedro, *Shetland Pattern Book*, by Mary Smith and Maggie Liddle, *A Shetland Knitter's Notebook*, by Mary Smith and Chris Bunyan, *Shetland Dye Book*, by Jenni Simmons, and *Book of Fair Isle Knitting*, by Alice Starmore. You can even buy them online at www.shetland-bookshop.co.uk

Also eye-catching are **fine lace shawls**, whose delicacy can be judged by the fact that they can be pulled through a wedding ring, and the *taatit* thick worsted yarn **rugs** which were traditionally made in two halves, one half by the bride's mother and one by the groom's. The two halves were sewn together and presented to the couple on the eve of their wedding.

Look out also for *kishies*, baskets and creels, which were traditionally woven from natural materials such as oat straw and stalks of the common dock and fitted with woven handles or straps so that they could be carried by hand or toted on the back. **Basket-making** is still a rural craft, although only small numbers are produced. You should find basketwork at a craft shop or fair.

As there are next to no trees growing on the islands stone is the most widely available building material and there are some particularly fine examples of architectural stonework around. There are good examples of decorative **stone carving** and modern stone sculpture throughout the islands, often blending with mosaic, stained glass and wrought ironwork. Stone carving was, and is, used not only for decorative purposes; steatite, or soapstone, has been carved into bowls, plates, loom and fishing-weights and other artefacts since prehistoric times. Carvings and figurines from local materials make interesting ornaments. Lack of suitable fuel has limited the development of **pottery** as an art form. Ceramic artists do, however, produce painted and glazed bowls and create attractive representational or abstract designs in **tiles and mosaic**. A large-scale mosaic can be seen at the pumphouse on Victoria Pier, Lerwick. Locally designed and produced stained glass can be seen on display in many public buildings and a window at Scalloway Museum depicting a fishing boat is an example of how artists have turned to familiar Shetland themes for inspiration.

For watercolours and pen and ink drawings in two strikingly different styles look out in local galleries and gift shops for works by **artists** Nicholas Barnham and Peter Forsythe. **Silverwork** inspired by old Celtic and Norse themes and wildlife is a thriving business and **gemstones** are cut and polished and set in hand-wrought silver and enamel jewellery. Other interesting island craft items include hand-made and engraved glass, model boats, leatherwork, dolls, fine woodwork, and marquetry. Shetland is home not only to superb fiddle music, but also to some highly skilled craftsmen who can make you a traditional or even an electronic fiddle.

HELP AND INFORMATION

TOURIST INFORMATION CENTRES

VisitShetland: Market Cross, Lerwick, ZE1 0LU (✆01595-693434; fax 01595-695807; email info@visitshetland.com; www.visitshetland.com). Open April to October, Monday to Friday 8am to 6pm, Saturday 8am to 4pm. November to March, Monday to Friday 9am to 5pm. There is also a tourist information centre at Sumburgh Airport.

USEFUL ADDRESSES AND TELEPHONE NUMBERS

AL Laing Chemist: 101–103 Commercial Street, Lerwick (✆01595-692579). Situated at the Market Cross. Open Monday to Saturday 9am to 5pm.

Boots the Chemist: Commercial Street, Lerwick (✆01595-692619). Open Monday to Saturday 9am to 5pm.

British Airways: (✆01950-460345).

Gilbert Bain Hospital: South Road, Lerwick (✆01595-743000).

HM Customs & Excise: (✆01595-696166).

Lerwick Health Centre: South Road, Lerwick (✆01595-693201). Open Monday to Friday 8.30am to 5pm, Saturday 8.30am to 1pm.

Police: Northern Constabulary, County Buildings, Hillhead, Lerwick (✆01595-692110).

Scottish Natural Heritage: Ground Floor, Stewart Building, Alexandra Wharf, Lerwick ZE1 0LL (✆01595-693345; fax 01595-692565; email northern_isles@snh.gov.uk; www.snh.gov.uk).

Shetland Islands Council: Town Hall, Lerwick ZE1 0HB (✆01595-693535; fax 01595-695590; email sic@sic.shetland.gov.uk; www.shetland.gov.uk).

Shetland Library: Lower Hillhead, Lerwick (✆01595-743868; email shetlandlibrary@sic.shetland.gov.uk; www.shetland-library.gov.uk).

Shetland Museum and Archives: Hay's Dock, Lerwick (✆01595-695057; email info@shetlandmuseumandarchives.org.uk; www.shetlandmuseumandarchives.org.uk).

Shetland Taxi Owners' Association: 31 Harbour Street, Lerwick ZE1 0JS (✆01595-694617; fax 01595-695035).

Shetland Islands Tourist Guides' Association: 11 Wirliegert, Aith ZE2 9NW (✆077-8932 6878).

Sumburgh Airport: (✆01950-460654).

Tingwall Airport: Loganair (✆01595-840246).

Banks

Bank of Scotland: 117 Commercial Street, Lerwick (✆01595-732200). Open Monday, Tuesday, Thursday, and Friday 9am to 5pm, Wednesday 9.30am to 5pm, Saturday 9.30am to 12.30pm.

Clydesdale Bank: 106 Commercial Street, Lerwick (✆01595-695664). Open Monday, Tuesday, Thursday, and Friday 9.15am to 4.45pm, Wednesday 9.45am to 4.45pm.

Royal Bank of Scotland: 81 Commercial Street, Lerwick (✆01595-694520). Open Monday to Friday 9.15am to 4.45pm, Wednesday 10am to 4.45pm.

Lloyd's TSB: Victoria Buildings, Esplanade, Lerwick (✆01595-693605). Open Monday, Tuesday 9.30am to 4pm; Wednesday 10am to 1pm; Thursday, Friday 9.30am to 5.30pm; Friday 9.30am to 5pm.

CALENDAR OF EVENTS

In homage to Shetland's Viking heritage, the year's events start with a string of spectacular fire festivals, known as *Up Helly Aa*. The biggest of these takes place in Lerwick on the last Tuesday in January and sees a procession of nearly a thousand flaming torches carried through the streets of the port by *guizers* (men in disguise) led by the elected Jarl (Earl) and his squad in full Viking costume, horned helmets and all. The procession ends with the setting alight of a specially built full-size replica Viking galley. After this spectacle the squads and locals party the night away in halls and venues throughout the town. Similar festivals on a smaller scale are held throughout Shetland from January to March. A nugget for history buffs: When the western world adopted the Gregorian calendar in 1751 it was not initially adopted in Shetland and Christmas was celebrated on 6 January with Up Helly Aa following at the end of the month. Interestingly, the old Julian calendar lingers on in Foula, where inhabitants still celebrate Yule on 6 January and New Year's Day on 13 January.

Shetland's **Folk Festival** is held every April/May and attracts music lovers from all over the world. The festival features talented local performers and international visiting musicians and artists. Concerts and dances are held throughout Shetland and these are supplemented by workshops and informal music sessions. Highlight of October is the annual Shetland

Accordion and Fiddle Festival. This lively festival of concerts and dances held throughout the islands culminates in a Grand Dance, where up to a dozen bands play virtually non-stop accordion and fiddle music.

Annual Events

May   *Shetland Folk Festival* (www.shetlandfolkfestival.com).
Fair Isle Spring Migration, a bird-watching holiday on Fair Isle, famous for its seabird colonies, scenery and knitwear.
Norwegian National Day, celebration concert, supper and dance, Lerwick Town Hall.

June   *Johnsmas Foy – Festival of the Sea,* celebration of fishing heritage.
Shetland Race, 400-mile (643km) round trip yacht race from Bergen to Lerwick.
Flavour of Shetland, music, craft stalls and demonstrations, local food and drink, seafood demonstrations, stories of Shetland folklore, Viking parade, Victoria Pier, Lerwick (www.flavourofshetland.com).

July   *Noss Open Day*

August   *Abacore European Championship,* Unst Boating Club.
Shetland Fiddle Frenzy, Shetland Arts (www.shetlandfiddlefrenzy.com).
Blues Festival.

September *Viking Sea Angling Competition*, Lerwick four-day sea angling competition.
Book Festival.
Fair Isle Autumn Migration enables you to see some of Britain's rarest birds with ornithological guides on Fair Isle.

October *Shetland Fiddle and Accordion Festival* at the Islesburgh Community Centre, Lerwick, and other country venues.

November *Guitar Festival.*
Festival of Country Music.

Weekly Events

Tuesdays: May to September
Shetland Experience Evening: a coach tour followed by traditional island meal at Herrislea House Hotel, Tingwall, local music sessions, knitwear demonstrations and crafts.
Simmer n' Sessions: award-winning traditional music sessions in Douglas Arms, Lerwick. Contact VisitShetland.

Wednesdays: May to September
Islesburgh Exhibition of Shetland Crafts and Culture: a live experience of Shetland crafts and culture, including knitwear, traditional music, dance and photo displays from 7pm.
Simmer n' Sessions: award-winning traditional music sessions in the Lounge Bar, Lerwick.

Fridays: May to September
Simmer n' Sessions: traditional music sessions in Da Noost, Lerwick. For up-to-date information on Shetland's events calendar call the **events hotline** (✆01595-694200) or check out www.visitshetland.com.

EXPLORING SHETLAND

Lerwick, Bressay & Noss

LERWICK

The most northerly town in Britain, Lerwick is Shetland's capital and administrative centre and has a population of around 7,600, roughly a third of Shetland's total. It is situated on a superb natural harbour on Bressay Sound on the eastern coast of the Shetland Mainland, protected by the barrier island of Bressay. This fine harbour has always made it an important port of call for ships. When King Haakon of Norway launched his massive attack on Scotland in 1263 he rested his armada at Lerwick on his way to the battle which culminated in his defeat at the Battle of Largs. The town takes its name from the Norse *Leir-vik* which means 'muddy bay'. Lerwick grew to importance relatively late in Shetland's history, emerging from a humble fishing settlement of scattered huts in the 17th century until it superseded Scalloway as the island's capital in 1708. Lerwick built its prosperity on the shining shoals of herring and by late 1800s was recognised as the premier herring port of northern Europe.

Along the shoreline track, now bustling **Commercial Street**, the town first developed as a jumble of narrow lanes and closes (*lons* and *klosses*) behind a waterfront where merchants built their *lodberries*, warehouses where goods could be directly loaded and unloaded from boats and which eventually became residences, courtyards, offices and private jetties all rolled into one. Some can still be seen in the old part of the town at the South End, the buildings standing washed by the sea. Past Bain's Beach *The Lodberrie* is probably the most photographed house in Shetland. Smugglers found plenty of hidey-holes here and in recent times barrels, kegs, and jars have come to light in tunnels and cellars under the waterside streets of the town.

During the summer season, you can step back in time with Elma Johnson to the days of smugglers and press gangs in old Lerwick during the 18th century, Accompanied by Douglas Sinclair, dressed in traditional costume, listen to tales of romance, mystery and strife as you amble along some of Lerwick's oldest streets and absorb the atmosphere. There are a number of tours available, for more information contact *Island Trails* (Bigton, ZE2 9JA; ✆01950-422408; email info@island-trails.co.uk; www.island-trails.co.uk). At the end of your tour, or if your ship is leaving late from Lerwick Harbour, you could spend the evening with the owners, Elma and Douglas Johnson, in the comfort of their own home. Enjoy a traditional Shetland supper of bannocks and heather-fed lamb. True natives of Shetland, they have first-hand knowledge of country life and many of their stories are recalled from their own childhoods. You can also book one of their tours through VisitShetland (Market Cross, Lerwick; ✆01595-693434; fax 01595-695807; email info@visitshetland.com; www. visitshetland.com).

Town Centre

Commercial Street is the shopping hub of the town. The **Market Cross**, the place of proclamations, outside the Tourist Office, sees its most important day on the last Tuesday of January when the **Up Helly Aa** bill is placed announcing details of this famous and peerless Viking fire festival. The Up Helly Aa exhibition in the St Sunniva Street **Galley Shed**, open during the summer months, captures the mood of the festival with displays of shields, costumes, memorabilia, paintings, photographs, videos and a magnificent full-size wooden Viking longship, a replica of the one burnt to ashes each January on Up Helly Aa night. The exhibition is held from mid-May to mid-September. It's open on Tuesday and Saturday from 2pm to 4pm, and Tuesday and Friday 7pm to 9pm. Admission £3 for adults, OAPs £1, children £1.

VIKING FIRE FESTIVAL

Many Norse festivals have been absorbed into the local way of life. Most important of these were the feasts of Beltane (spring), Midsummer (June), Hallomas (end of Harvest), and Yule (Christmas). Yule was the most lengthy of all pagan feasts, lasting three weeks, but with the coming of Christianity Yule became Christmas and the 24th night after Christmas was called Up Helly Aa, or 'the up-ending' of the holy days. Possibly remembering their pagan past the Norsemen looked forward to Up Helly Aa as the end of the enforced Christian holy period and the beginning of an almighty binge and carousal.

Up Helly Aa is not a festival organised to impress tourists, but a celebration for the people of Lerwick and other communities. It is held in Lerwick on the last Tuesday in January and is announced in the morning with an elaborate proclamation ('the Bill') on the Market Cross in central Lerwick. A banner depicting a raven is flown from the Town Hall as a signal that the Guizer Jarl, or Earl, has the freedom of the town for the day. The Guizer Jarl and the magnificently costumed Jarl Squad of about 40 guizers escort the galley – a 30ft (9m) replica of a Viking longship – through the town to the harbour, where it can be admired throughout the day. The climax of Up Helly Aa comes at night, after up to a thousand colourfully attired guizers carrying flaming torches walk in procession through the town, accompanying the galley to the playing fields, near the Town Hall, where the torches are hurled into the galley and fire consumes it. Night-long celebrations then begin at venues across the town. The revelry continues until the guizers squads have visited all the halls, which is normally by daybreak. It is impossible for casual visitors to gain admission to halls on Up Helly Aa night as the all-night celebrations are run by locals for locals and it is rare for visitors to be invited. Tickets for the Town Hall party (which you can attend) usually go on sale around Christmas–New Year and can be obtained by writing to the Up Helly Aa Committee there. The day following Up Helly Aa is, sensibly, a public holiday.

Islesburgh House, Islesburgh Community Centre, on King Harald Street provides the elderly and disabled with sheltered viewing on a main procession route. There is also limited parking there in the evening for disabled drivers. Accommodation in Lerwick for Up Helly Aa is often booked years in advance, so check with Shetland Island Tourism if you'd like to see this spectacular festival. Lerwick's festival signals the start of a series of similar celebrations, held between January and March in other island communities, notably Scalloway, Nesting and Girlsta, Uyeasound, Northmavine, Bressay, Cullivoe and Brae.

The northern end of Commercial Street passes below the towering walls of **Fort Charlotte**, which was designed as a pentagonal stronghold by Charles II's master mason, John Mylne, and built in 1665–1667 to protect shipping during the Second Dutch War. It was burned by the Dutch in 1673 and lay ruined until 1782 when it was reconstructed and named after Queen Charlotte, wife of George III. The 18th-century buildings have been altered only superficially by some Victorian additions. As changes over the centuries have been minor the fort is the most complete surviving example of its type. There was no garrison in the 19th century, so the fort became accommodation for the town's bachelors. By the mid-19th century the fort housed the prison and, from 1881 to 1910, the Royal Naval Reserve. The Territorial Army Defence Volunteers and the Army Cadet force now have their headquarters here. The gunports provide good views over the harbour. The fort is in the care of Historic Scotland and open from 1 June to 30 September, 9am to 10pm, and from 1 October to 31 May from 9am to 4pm. In summer the Royal National Mission to Deep Sea Fishermen (RNMDSF) in nearby Harbour Street stages a summer **fishing exhibition** which includes photographs of the fishing fleet through the years and a display of maritime items.

By the late 19th century the wealthier locals were moving from the crowded waterfront

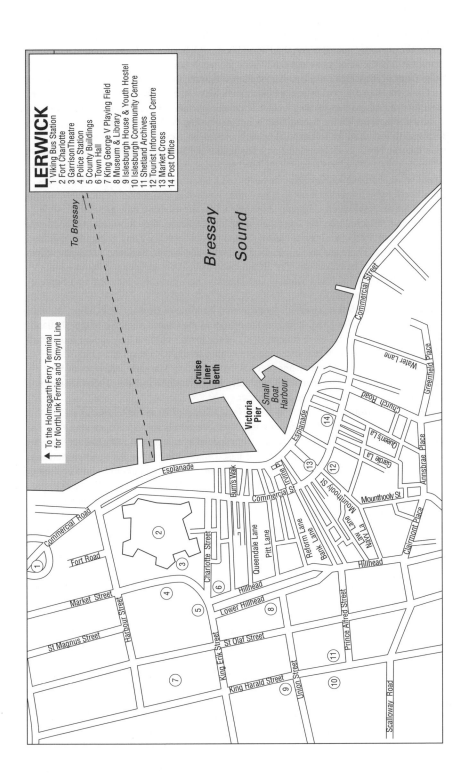

LERWICK

1 Viking Bus Station
2 Fort Charlotte
3 Garrison Theatre
4 Police Station
5 County Buildings
6 Town Hall
7 King George V Playing Field
8 Museum & Library
9 Islesburgh House & Youth Hostel
10 Islesburgh Community Centre
11 Shetland Archives
12 Tourist Information Centre
13 Market Cross
14 Post Office

To Bressay

To the Holmsgarth Ferry Terminal
for NorthLink Ferries and Smyril Line

Bressay Sound

Cruise Liner Berth

Victoria Pier

Small Boat Harbour

Esplanade

Burns Wak

Commercial Street

Esplanade

Commercial Street

Water Lane

Greenfield Place

Church Road

Queen's La.

Cairdie La.

Annsbrae Place

Mounthooly St

Mounthooly St

Clairmont Place

Reform Lane

Bank Lane

Navy Lane

New La.

Hillhead

Commercial Road

Fort Road

Market Street

Harbour Street

St Magnus Street

Charlotte Street

Queendale Lane

Pitt Lane

Hillhead

Lower Hillhead

King Erik Street

St Olaf Street

King Harald Street

Union Street

Prince Alfred Street

Scalloway Road

part of town to the flatter land west of Hillhead, which still has impressive residences and public buildings from that time. A steamer service to the Scottish Mainland began in 1868 and **Victoria Pier** was built that year. Much of the foreshore was reclaimed, including the sites of the present Thule Bar and the Peerie Shop, which were both once lodberries. Next to Victoria Pier is the small boat harbour. Above the small boat harbour is the **Old Tolbooth**, dating from 1770, which once housed the Sheriff Courts and the prison and later saw service as a Customs House, a post office, a Fishermen's Mission and a Red Cross centre. The terminal for the ferry to Bressay and to Out Skerries is further north along the **Esplanade**.

The main berthing for the fishing fleet is further north at the Morrison Dock, near the main **Holmsgarth terminal** for ferries to Stromness, Aberdeen, Bergen, Norway, Iceland and the Faroe Islands. North of Holmsgarth Ferry Terminal is the **Böd of Gremista Museum** (Gremista, Lerwick; ✆01595-695057; fax 01595-696729; email info@shetlandmuseumandarchives. org.uk; www.shetlandmuseumandarchives.org.uk), a restored 18th century böd, a fisherman's booth, which was the birthplace of Arthur Anderson, co-founder of the Peninsular and Oriental Steam Navigation Company, now P&O. It is furnished in typical Shetland style, with displays reflecting the life and times of Arthur Anderson. One room commemorates his association with P&O, with prints, paintings and models of early P&O ships and Andersonian memorabilia. There are also copies of *The Shetland Journal*, Shetland's first newspaper, which was founded by Anderson. The Böd is open from 10am to 1pm and 2pm to 5pm, Wednesday to Sunday (closed Monday and Tuesday) between the 1 May and mid-September. Admission is free.

Lerwick's **Town Hall** is a beautifully preserved building of Bressay and Orkney sandstone which was completed in 1883. It houses the offices of the Chief Executive of the Shetland Islands Council. Armorial work reflects many of the town's cultural and trading links. Rich stained glass – best seen in late afternoon or evening sunlight – shows characters from Shetland's history. A particularly fine piece is that depicting Margaret, daughter of King Christian I of Norway, who married King James III of Scotland in 1469. There are panoramic views of the town from the clock tower.

Islesburgh Community Centre in King Harald Street (✆01595-692114; fax 01595-696470; email enquiries@islesburgh.org.uk; www.islesburgh.org.uk) is open seven days a week, and offers something for everyone, from special events and recreational activities for the young to arts, crafts, cultural and leisure-based entertainment for the wider community. There's also knitwear, dancing, singers, music, historical films and photos, and a crofthouse set. The Islesburgh Exhibition is a display of Shetland crafts and culture, a living example of Shetland traditions from spinning, carding and knitting skills to live fiddle music. It is open every Monday, Wednesday and Thursday from 7pm to 9.30pm from mid-June to mid-August. Admission payable at the door, discounts for concessions. **St Magnus Episcopal Church** (1862–4) has an attractive interior with stained glass windows designed by Sir Ninian Comper. The strawberries incorporated in the design are in memory of his father, who died in Aberdeen while distributing this fruit to poor children.

The massive brass propeller blade outside the **Shetland Library** in Lower Hillhead is from the sister ship to the *RMS Titanic*, the 17,000 ton liner *RMS Oceanic*, which was wrecked off Foula in 1914. The *Shetland Library* (Lower Hillhead, Lerwick ZE1 0EL; ✆01595-743868; fax 01595-694430; email shetlandlibrary@sic.shetland.gov.uk; www. shetland-library.gov.uk) is housed in the converted St Ringans Church and has a collection of local materials on the mezzanine floor, as well as an excellent computer centre. Visitors are welcome to join the library, borrow books and use the internet. Opening hours are Monday and Thursday 9.30am to 8pm; Tuesday, Wednesday, Friday and Saturday 9.30am to 5pm.

Set in a restored 19th-century dock, the **Shetland Museum and Archives** introduces Shetland's story and provides a gateway to the island's heritage and culture. The building houses more than 3,000 artefacts and a wealth of archival material encompassing every aspect of Shetland life: industry, history, environment and culture. Highlights include the boat hall with its hanging boats, the Scatness Pictish bear discovered in 2002, a superb collection of Shetland fine lace and knitwear, documents and books from the 15th to the 21st century and the fourth largest collection of archive photography in Scotland. Other facilities include a café restaurant offering local produce and panoramic views of the harbour; a fully equipped auditorium; a temporary exhibition gallery for local, national and international exhibitions; and a shop selling local crafts and gifts reflecting the museum and archives collections. *Shetland Museum and Archives* (Hay's Dock, Lerwick ZE1 0WP; ✆01595-695057; fax 01595-696729; email info@shetlandmuseumandarchives.org.uk; www.shetlandmuseumandarchives.org.uk). Admission is free and it is open daily.

Clickimin

Lerwick's biggest open public space is around the **Loch of Clickimin**, about a mile (1.6km) from the centre of town. The loch is best known for its **prehistoric stone broch**, which is one of Shetland's major archaeological sites, as well as being notable for its waterfowl. **Mallard** and **teal** can be seen all year round, and **goldeneye**, **wigeon**, **pochard**, **tufted duck** and **whooper swans** use the loch as a stopover on their migration route. A causeway leads to the broch, which was originally built on an islet. In the 19th century the water level was lowered and as a result the broch now stands on a promontory. It was occupied from about 700BC and was first a Bronze Age farmhouse and then an Iron Age ring fort. The broch is probably not far short of its original height of 33ft (10m) and an odd feature across the original approach from the causeway is a stone slab with the outline of two footprints carved into it. The footpath from North Lochside, around the back of Clickimin Loch and joining South Road is a pleasant walk and takes you to the Safeway Supermarket. The footpath around Breiwick Bay, where **seals** and **otters** can often be seen, joins another footpath which takes you around the Knab promontory and will eventually lead you back to the town centre through the picturesque South End of the town. Walks around Lerwick are organised by the *Shetland Islands Tourist Guides Association* (11 Wirliegert, Aith ZE2 9NW; ✆07789-326878; email shetlandtouristguides@yahoo.co.uk) and start from the Tourist Office in town every Monday afternoon.

The Clickimin Leisure Complex (Lochside, Lerwick ZE1 0PJ; ✆01595-741000; fax 01595-741001; email mail@srt.org.uk; www.srt.org.uk) boasts an 82ft (25m) pool with flume rides, outdoor lagoon, health suite, four-rink bowls hall, games hall, squash suite, aerobics studio and *Horizons* café.

Cruises

The old fishing boat *Swan*, built as a drifter in 1900, has been restored and offers sail training and private charter cruises. These can range from an evening outing in Lerwick Harbour to expeditions to Norway, Orkney or even such distant destinations as St Kilda. For more information ✆01595-697406 (email skipper@theswan.shetland.co.uk; www.theswan.shetland. co.uk). Sharing Lerwick harbour with *Swan* is the 40ft (12m) *Dim Riv* galley. You can enjoy a half-hour trip around the port in this unusual replica of a Viking longship on Monday evenings in summer (subject to weather and demand). Cruises leave Victoria slipway at 7pm and 7.45pm from June to August. Adults £5, children £2.50. Contact the Tourist Office for more information, special hires by arrangement (contact Harry Jamieson; ✆01595-693097). The *MV Alluvion*, operated by *Shetland Sea Charters* (✆01595-692577), is a 12-passenger vessel with comfortable viewing from the panoramic wheelhouse and aft deck. Cruises around the island of Noss depart daily, subject to weather conditions, from Victoria Pier, Lerwick, at 1.30pm and last about three hours. The vessel is also available for sightseeing, sea angling, and diving trips, operating from May to September. Fare is £20 for adults, and £10 for children. Collect booking ticket in advance from the tourist office.

GETTING AROUND

Buses

The **Lerwick and Bressay** service bus service is operated by *John Leask & Son* (Esplanade, Lerwick; ✆01595-693162; fax 01595-693171), who also have an overland service.

Lerwick-Yell, Unst and Fetlar. Additional services are provided by *Shetland Islands Council* (Town Hall, Lerwick ZE1 0HB; ✆01595-693535; fax 01595-695590; email sic@sic.shetland.gov.uk).

Taxis
6050 Cabs: ✆01595-696050.
Allied Taxis: ✆01595-690069.
Rainbow: ✆01595-697070.
Roy's Taxi Service: ✆01595-692080.
Sinclairs Taxis: ✆01595-694617.

Vehicle Rental
Bolts Car Hire: Toll Clock Shopping Centre, 26 North Road, Lerwick (✆01595-693636; fax 01595-694646; email info@boltscarhire.co.uk; www.boltscarhire.co.uk). Are the agents for Avis and Europcar and have a fully staffed office, fuel and service facility at Sumburgh Airport (✆01950-460777; fax 01950-460666). This is open seven days a week for all scheduled and most charter flights. Bolts will have a car waiting for you if you arrive at Tingwall airstrip if you arrange it in advance, or you can call when you land and they will collect you. There is also a desk at the ferry terminal but is usually manned for only 15 minutes after the arrival of the ferry and from 8am to 8.30am for prior reservations. You get unlimited mileage on hire vehicles and there are five hire/drop off points throughout Shetland. Open Monday to Saturday, April to August: 9am to 5.30pm, and September to March: 9am to 5.30pm, Saturday 9am to 1pm.

John Leask & Son: The Esplanade, Lerwick ZE1 0LL (✆01595-693162; fax 01595-693171; email info@leaskstravel.co.uk; www.leaskatravel.co.uk); and at Exnaboe, Sumburgh (✆01950-460209), close to Sumburgh airport. Unlimited mileage in modern vehicles. International driving permit holders are accepted. Minimum charge of 24 hours. Open Monday to Saturday 7.30am to 5pm, Sunday 9.30am to midday.

Star Rent-A-Car: 22 Commercial Road, Lerwick ZE1 0LX (✆01595-692075; fax 01595-693964; Sumburgh office ✆01950-460444; fax 01950-460084; email info@starcar.co.uk; www.starcar.co.uk). Offers a free 'meet and greet' service at all airports and ferry terminals. You must produce a full valid and unendorsed driving licence which you've had for at least one year. Drivers must be between the ages of 21 and 75. Full comprehensive insurance is usually included in the rates, but check. Minimum hire period is one day (24 hours), and additional hours are charged at one-sixth of the daily rate. You can collect a car at one point and leave it at another on departure. Unlimited mileage. Open Monday to Sunday 8am to 5pm.

Parking. There are parking restrictions in Lerwick town centre. Parking discs allowing you to park along the zoned area of the Esplanade are available from most shops or the Tourist Office at the Market Cross. Free car parking is available off the Upper Hillhead (across from Shetland Museum) and at Church Road (limited spaces). Victoria pier is a pay-and-display parking area. Free car parking is available at the Toll Clock Shopping Centre, to the north of the town.

Bicycle Hire
You can hire a bicycle from *Eric Brown's Cycle Hire* (Grantfield Garage, North Road, Lerwick ZE1 0NT; ✆01595-692709; fax 01595-695017; www.grantfieldgarage.co.uk) for £6 a day or £35 a week. You pay a refundable deposit of £6 for a bike. You will find them ½ mile from the town centre and 500 yards from the NorthLink ferry terminal, Holmsgarth. Open seven days a week, Monday to Saturday 8am to 11pm, Sunday 11am to 11pm.

ACCOMMODATION

As well as the usual hotels, B&Bs, guest houses, self-catering establishments, youth hostels, and camping sites you can bed down in a böd, which offers simple low-cost accommodation in restored historical dwellings throughout the islands. A böd is a building originally used to house fishermen and their gear during the fishing season. Today it offers basic accommodation for a budget holiday, similar to English camping barns. They are a cheap alternative to camping. There are nine böds, managed by *Shetland Amenity Trust*. Four are on the Mainland, there's one on Whalsay, one on Yell and another on Fetlar. The Sail Loft at Voe has access and toilet facilities for disabled people. They are very basic and some in remote locations have no electricity or lighting. However, each böd has space for cooking, eating and sleeping. There is a cold water supply and toilet facilities. Everyone shares the same sleeping area and you should be prepared for this. Take your own sleeping bag and mat or air bed, camping stove, plate and mug, and cooking utensils. Book through *VisitShetland* (Market Cross, Lerwick ZE1 0LU; ✆01595-693434; fax 01595-695807; email info@visit-shetland.com), or try www.camping-bods.com. If you cancel your booking up to seven days before the first night booked, 50% of the fees will be refunded. Within seven days of the first booked night, no fees will be refunded. Owing to limited bed space it is essential that accommodation is pre-booked.

Hotels

Grand Hotel: 149 Commercial Street, Lerwick ZE1 0EX (✆01595-692826; fax 01595-694048; email info@kgqhotels.co.uk; www.kgqhotels.co.uk). Three-star, in the centre of Lerwick with Shetland's only nightclub, *Posers*. From £49.25.

Kveldsro House Hotel: Greenfield Place, Lerwick ZE1 0AQ (✆01595-692195; fax 01595-696595; email reception@kveldsrohotel.co.uk; www.shetlandhotels.com). Four-star, centrally situated, overlooking the harbour. Part of the privately owned Brudolff Hotels Group. From £60.

Lerwick Hotel: 15 South Road, Lerwick ZE1 0RB (✆01595-692166; fax 01595-694419; email reception@lerwickhotel.co.uk; www.shetlandhotels.com). Three-star, part of the privately owned Brudolff Hotels Group, three-star, 35 rooms with private facilities, views over Breiwick Bay and Bressay, 10-minute walk from the town centre. Try either the informal *Brasserie* for lunch and dinner or fine dining at the *Breiwick Restaurant* open from 6.30pm. B&B £50.

Queen's Hotel: 24 Commercial Street, Lerwick ZE1 0AB (✆01595-692826; fax 01595-694048; info@kgqhotels.co.uk; www.kgqhotels.co.uk). Has been a popular place since the early 1860s. It is located in the centre of Lerwick, opposite the harbour. Three-star, from £49.25.

Shetland Hotel: Holmsgarth Road, Lerwick ZE1 0PW (✆01595-695515; fax 01595-695828; email reception@shetlandhotel.co.uk; www.shetlandhotels.com). Three-star, the other hotel in the Brudolff group. Situated opposite main ferry terminal with views of harbour and Isle of Bressay, 65 rooms, non-smoking and disabled rooms. *Oasis Bistro* open from 11am every day for lunch and dinner. There's also the upmarket but informal *Ninian Restaurant*. From £50.

Guest Houses

Alderlodge Guest House: 6 Clairmont Place, Lerwick ZE1 0BR (✆/fax 01595-695705). Built in 1840 as the first bank in Shetland (Union Bank). Three-star, en suite rooms. Centrally situated, a few minutes' walk from harbour, museum, town centre and local amenities. Evening meals available on request. From £27.

Breiview Guest House: 43 Kantersted Road, Lerwick ZE1 0RJ (✆/fax 01595-695956; email enquiries@breiviewguesthouse.co.uk; www.breiviewguesthouse.co.uk). Three-star, 20 minutes' walk from the centre of Lerwick, on the main bus route, overlooking Breiwick Bay. All rooms en suite and evening meals are available on request. Double B&B from £50 a night.

Solheim Guest House: 34 King Harald Street, Lerwick ZE1 0EQ (✆01595-695275). Three-star, Victorian-style house, centrally located. Standard or en suite rooms, from £22.

Fort Charlotte Guest House: 1 Charlotte Street, Lerwick ZE1 0JL (✆01595-692140; email info@fortcharlotte.shetland.co.uk; www.fortcharlotte.co.uk). Three-star, situated below Fort Charlotte in the centre of Lerwick, overlooking the main shopping street, en suite rooms. From £25.

Glen Orchy House: 20 Knab Road, Lerwick ZE1 0AX (✆/fax 01595-692031; email glenorchy.house@virgin.net; www.guesthouselerwick.com). Three-star, built in 1904 by the Episcopalian church as a convent. En suite rooms and access for visitors with mobility difficulties. Enjoy a drink at the *Honesty Bar* before or after an evening meal.

Eddiewood Guest House: 8 Clairmont Place, Lerwick ZE1 0BR (✆01595-692772; email eddiewood@xin.co.uk). Three-star, near town centre, sea views. From £25.

Bed & Breakfast

Cee Aa: Mrs I Nicolson, 133 North Road ZE1 0PR (✆01595-693362; email inaandivor@ yahoo.co.uk). Looks over harbour, quiet area. Parking available. From £22.

Mrs Gifford: Whinrig, 12 Burgh Road, Lerwick ZE1 0LB (✆01595-693554; email c.gifford@btinternet.com). Four-star, centrally situated in small cul-de-sac off Burgh Road. Access for visitors with mobility difficulties. From £22.

Roseville: Janice Coupe, 95 King Harald Street, Lerwick ZE1 0ER (✆01595-697128; email contact@roseville.shetland.co.uk; www.roseville.shetland.co.uk). Three-star, centrally located, few minutes' walk from bus station, museum, and town centre. From £27.50.

Self-Catering

Brentham House: 7 Harbour Street, Lerwick ZE1 0LR (✆01950-460201; www.brenthamhouse.co.uk). Three, individual, en suite luxurious rooms, and one even more luxurious suite. From £35 a person, suite £120 a night.

Mrs V Crossan: 59 King Harald Street, Lerwick ZE1 0ER (✆01595-693054). Three-star, in town centre. Ground floor flat, fully equipped, sleeps six. From £180 to £350.

Mrs M Anderson: 9 Navy Lane, Lerwick ZE1 0BS (✆01595-694152). Two-star, close to shops, restaurants, harbour. Sleeps four, from £100 to £180.

Mrs L Gair: 4–6 Burns Lane (✆01595-695922). Four-star, in the lanes of Lerwick, re-cently refurbished. Sleeps four, from £275 to £350.

King Harald Apartments: 11a and 11b King Harald Street (✆01595-694014; email jean@ kingharald.co.uk; www.kingharald.co.uk). Three-star, newly built apartments, central loca-tion. Each sleeps four–eight, from £260 to £420.

Youth Hostels

Lerwick Youth Hostel: Islesburgh House, King Harald Street, Lerwick ZE1 0EQ (✆01595-692114; fax 01595-696470; email enquiries@islesburgh.org.uk; www.islesburgh.org. uk). One of the few five-star hostels in Scotland. In central Lerwick, Islesburgh House is Shetland's main youth hostel, and it is a member of the Scottish Youth Hostels Association (SYHA). The hostel is neighbour to Islesburgh Community Centre and close to the Garrison Theatre, which provides a range of activities and cultural attractions. A standard grade youth hostel offering top-quality accommodation at reasonable prices. A well-equipped kitchen is available for self-catering, while the *House Café* is a popular eating place for both tourists and local residents. Open April to September, 64 beds in dormitories ranging from rooms for two people to a 12 person group dorm, six rooms with four beds, two rooms with five–eight beds, three rooms with nine+ beds, family rooms (aged 5+), shop nearby, hostel store, bus stop outside front door, ferry one mile. Washing and drying facilities. Two floors fully acces-sible to disabled. Open from 8am to 11.45pm daily. Cycling, fishing, entertainment, 18-hole golf course, hillwalking, sailing, pony trekking, swimming. Walkers and cyclists welcome. Book-a-bed ahead facility is available.

Camping

There is a municipal campsite in Lerwick adjacent to the Clickimin Leisure Complex. *Clickimin Caravan & Camp Site* (Lochside, Lerwick ZE1 0PJ; ✆01595-741000; email mail@srt.org.uk; www.srt.org.uk). Open May to September, 20 touring pitches, 30 tents. £7.10 to £10.80 a night.

EATING AND DRINKING

For some of the more unusual places to eat try the following cafés, restaurants and hotels in Lerwick:

Breiwick Restaurant: Lerwick Hotel, 15 South Road, Lerwick ZE1 0RB (✆01595-692166; fax 01595-694419; email reception@lerwickhotel.co.uk). Menu using local produce, 10 minutes' walk from the town centre with views of Breiwick Bay. Open all year 6.30pm to 9.30pm. More informal meals are available at *The Brasserie.* Open all year Monday to Sunday midday to 2pm, and 5pm to 9.30pm.

Captain Flint's: Market Cross, Lerwick ZE1 0LL (✆01595-692249; fax 01595-694915). At the esplanade in the heart of the capital with views of the waterfront. Lunches, bar meals, children's menu. Steaks, filled baguettes, burgers, jacket potatoes, desserts, home-made soup with crusty bread. Open Monday to Saturday 8am to 1am, Sunday 12.30pm to 11.45pm.

The Fisherman's Mission Café: Harbour Street, Lerwick (✆01595-692703). At the main entrance to Fort Charlotte. Breakfast, lunches, afternoon teas, and café snacks. Home cooking at value for money prices, specialises in locally caught fish. Dish of the day and homemade soup. Open Monday to Friday 10am to 2pm.

Fort Café: 2 Commercial Road, Lerwick (✆01595-693125). At the north end of Commercial Street, below Fort Charlotte. Meals and snacks, simple good food cooked daily, speciality is fresh Shetland haddock. Open Monday to Friday 11am to 10.30pm, Saturday 11am to 7pm, Sunday 5pm to 10.30pm.

Grand Hotel: 149 Commercial Street, Lerwick ZE1 0EX (✆01595-6922826; fax 01595-694048). A la carte restaurant and bar meals, good value Sunday carvery £10.95 for two courses. Open Monday to Sunday midday to 2pm and 6pm to 9.30pm. Booking recommended.

Havly Café: Norwegian Seaman's Mission, 9 Charlotte Street, Lerwick ZE1 0JL (✆01595-692100; fax 01595-693118; email ravetvik@lineone.net). Near the town hall and Fort Charlotte. Family-friendly café with wide variety of homemade cakes and waffles, beefburgers, pizzas, pastas, soups, speciality Norwegian horns with fillings. Open Monday to Friday 10am to 3pm, Saturday 10am to 4.45pm.

House Café: Islesburgh Community Centre, King Harald Street, Lerwick ZE1 0EQ (✆01595-692114; fax 01595-696470; email enquiries@islesburgh.org.uk; www.islesburgh. org.uk). Central Lerwick opposite flower park and bowling green. Lunches, snacks, beverages. Vegetarian meals, soups, baked potatoes, filled rolls and other café snacks. Open Monday to Saturday 9.30am to 2.30pm, winter season (October to March). Open at 8am during hostel season (April to September).

Kveldsro House Hotel: Greenfield Place, Lerwick ZE1 0AQ (✆01595-692195; fax 01595-696595). The name means 'evening peace' and the hotel overlooks Bressay Sound. Lunch and bar snacks, restaurant. Fresh fish from the market. Open Monday to Sunday midday to 2pm, and 6pm to 9.30pm.

Lounge Bar: Mounthooly Street, Lerwick (✆01595-692231). Famous for its traditional music sessions on Wednesday evenings and at weekends. Open Monday to Saturday 11am to 1am, Sunday 12.30pm to 1am.

Monty's Bistro: 5 Mounthooly Street, Lerwick ZE1 0BJ (✆01595-696555; fax 01595-696955). Behind Tourist Information Centre at the Market Cross. Local products, home-made rosemary bread. Open for lunch and dinner (midday to 2pm and 6.30pm to 9pm) Tuesday to Sunday, all year. Open Monday 6.30pm to 9pm. Vegetarians welcome.

Oasis Bistro: Shetland Hotel, Holmsgarth Road, Lerwick ZE1 0PW (℡01595-695515; fax 01595-695828; email reception@shetlandhotel.co.uk). Within a two-minute walk of ferry terminal. Open all year Monday to Sunday 11am to 9.30pm. Also bar lunches/dinners, coffee shop open all day from 11am.

Osla's Café: 88 Commercial Street, Lerwick ZE1 0EX (℡01595-696005; fax 01595-695165). Bar and à la carte Bistro, take-away pizzas, soup, sandwiches, pasta. Open Monday to Sunday 9am till late. *Peerie Shop Café:* Esplanade, Lerwick ZE1 0LL (℡01595-692817; fax 01595-693320). Situated in a converted listed lodberry on Lerwick's Esplanade (behind the Peerie Shop). Hot and cold drinks, light meals and snacks all day. Good coffee/tea, homemade soups, cakes, doorstep sandwiches, quiche, beer and wine. Open 9am to 6pm.

Queen's Hotel: 24 Commercial Street, Lerwick ZE1 0AB (℡01595-692826; fax 01595-694048). Stands in Lerwick harbour with waterfront view and Bressay as its backdrop. Lunch, bar meals, à la carte restaurant. Emphasis on local produce, fish, seafood, lamb, Orkney beef and Scottish cheeses. Open Monday to Sunday midday to 2pm, and 6pm to 9.30pm. Booking essential.

ENTERTAINMENT

The **Garrison Theatre** has theatrical performances throughout the year, from lavish musicals to experimental improvisational performances. Amateur dramatics is popular, with groups even performing works in Shetland dialect. **Shetland Youth Theatre** gives performances at various venues throughout the year. Contact *Shetland Arts Trust* (Pitt Lane, Lerwick ZE1 0DW; ℡01595-694001; fax 01595-692941; email admin@shetland-arts-trust. co.uk; www.shetland-arts-trust.co.uk) or *Islesburgh Community Centre* (King Harald Street, Lerwick ZE1 0EQ; ℡01595-692114) for more information.

In the town centre the **Lounge Bar** caters predominantly for acoustic folk and country. **Captain Flint's** hosts bands from rock to jazz and caters for a variety of tastes and age groups. Further from the Market Cross other public bars, hotels, community halls and centres are used as venues by visiting and local musicians.

SHOPPING

The retail outlet in Lerwick for Jamieson's Sandness spinning mill is *Jamieson's Knitwear* on Commercial Street (℡01595-693114), which sells a distinctive collection of knitwear both hand and machine knitted, including lace and Fair Isle knits. Other outlets include Shetland Selection, at *The Spiders Web*, opposite the Queens Hotel at 51 Commercial Street (℡01595-695246; email shetland.knitwear@zetnet.co.uk; www.shetland-handknits.co.uk), which is open 9am to 5pm Monday to Saturday from 1 May to 31 August.

Try Anderson & Co, *The Shetland Warehouse* (60–62 Commercial Street, Lerwick; ℡01595-693714; fax 01595-694811; email pottingers@aol.com) for Shetland knitwear made in the knitters' own homes in traditional patterns and assorted styles. Mail order available. Open Monday to Saturday 9am to 5pm. *Ninian* (110 Commercial Street, Lerwick ZE1 0EX; ℡01595-696655; email donna@donnasmithdesigns.co.uk) also sells contemporary Shetland knitwear.

If you want to try knitting Shetland garments yourself you can choose from more than 230 shades of pure Shetland yarn, in various thickness including one-ply cobweb lace, from *Jamieson & Smith Wool Brokers* (90 North Road, Lerwick ZE1 0PQ; ℡01595-693579; fax 01595-695009; email sales@shetlandwoolbrokers.co.uk; www.shetlandwoolbrokers.co.uk). Raw fleeces are available for hand spinning. This is one of the most comprehensive source of supply for hand and machine knitters.

You can buy CDs from *Shetland Arts Trust* (Pitt Lane, Lerwick ZE1 0DW; ℡01595-694001; fax 01595-692941; email admin@shetland-arts-trust.co.uk; www.shetland-arts-trust.co.uk). Visit www.shetland-music.com for more information as well as reviews and sound bites of some of Shetland's musicians. Locally produced albums are stocked by *Clive's Record Shop* (108 Commercial Street, Lerwick ZE1 0HX; ℡/fax 01595-695864). Open Monday to Saturday 9am to 5pm.

High Level Music (1 Gardie Court, Lerwick; ©/fax 01595-692618; email sales@ shetlandmusic.co.uk; www.shetlandmusic.co.uk), specialises in all types of traditional music on CD, supplier of musical instruments and accessories. Open Monday to Saturday 9am to 5pm. At his Lerwick workshop Allan Leask (©01595-694831) makes exceptionally fine **fiddles** and repairs damaged instruments.

Taste Shetland (Shetland Rural Centre, Lerwick ZE1 0NA; ©01595-696770; fax 01595-696305; www.tasteshetland.com) will deliver much sought after Shetland lamb to your door or you can buy online. Open all year, Monday to Friday 9am to 5pm.

Merrie Dancers (59 Commercial Street, Lerwick ZE1 0AB; ©01595-693000; www. simply-shetland.co.uk) has a range of hand-made preserves and other Shetland produce. Hampers available. Open all year, Monday to Saturday 9am to 5pm, Sunday 11am to 4pm.

Shetland Arts & Crafts Association (PO Box 11674, Shetland ZE1 0ZH; ©01595-697300; email info@shetlandartsandcrafts.co.uk; www.shetlandartsandcrafts.co.uk) has information on all these and more.

LHD Marine Supplies (1 Alexandra Buildings, Lerwick ZE1 0LL; ©01595-692882) has a comprehensive selection of marine gear, waterproofs, jackets, boots, oilskins, sailing flags and charts, fishing rods, reels and flies. Shetland Anglers' Association membership available. Open Monday to Saturday 8am to 5pm.

Toll Clock Shopping Centre (26 North Road, Lerwick ZE1 0DE; ©01595-692855, fax 01595-693463, email info@tollclockshetland.co.uk; www.tollclockshetland.co.uk), indoor shopping complex with more than 20 local shops, post office, and the popular eating places *Skipidock Inn* and *The Olive Tree*. There is also an interesting, well-stocked, healthfood shop *Scoop Wholefoods* (©01595-695888). Extensive, free parking. Most shops are open Monday to Saturday.

HELP AND INFORMATION

VisitShetland: Market Cross, Lerwick ZE1 0LU (©01595-693434; fax 01595-695807; email info@visitshetland.com; www.visitshetland.com).
Police Station: County Buildings (©01595-692110).
Gilbert Bain Hospital: South Road (©01595-743000).
Doctor and Health Centre: South Road (©01595-693201).
Lerwick Boating Club: 12a Commercial Street, Lerwick (©01595-692407).
Lerwick Town Centre Association: 97 Commercial Street, Lerwick ZE1 0BD (©01595-695056; fax 01595-695306).
Lerwick Harbour Trust: Port Authority, Albert Building, Esplanade, Lerwick ZE1 0LL (©01595-692991; fax 01595-693452; email info@lerwick-harbour.co.uk; www.lerwick-harbour.co.uk).
Post Office: 46 Commercial Street, Lerwick (©01595-693372); and Toll Clock Shopping Centre (©01595-695362).

BRESSAY

The island of Bressay faces Lerwick across the Bressay Sound, providing natural shelter for Lerwick harbour. Although it's only 7 miles (11km) long and 3 miles (8km) wide the island is virtually Shetland in microcosm, with cliffs full of seabirds, quiet bays, hill and coastal walking, trout lochs – best ones are Brough, Setter, and Beosetter – and a welter of archaeo-logical sites, including a burnt mound at Cruister, a small *souterrain*, or underground earth house, at Wadbister, and the ruins of an Iron Age broch at Noss Sound.

Bressay is dominated by 742ft (226m) **Ward Hill**, the southern sandstone peak shaped like a volcano and known as Da Wart o' Bressay. The summit was chosen in 1964 as the site of Shetland's first TV transmitter mast. Views from the top can be impressive. If the weather is favourable you can see the Out Skerries to the north-east, Saxa Vord on Unst to the north, Fair Isle to the south and Foula to the west. On the east and southern coast, the sandstone has been shaped into high cliffs, with caves, natural arches and offshore sea stacks. There are a dozen freshwater lochs and many small pools among the hills. The largest, **Loch of Brough**, provides the island with water. In winter it is the venue for Sunday morning model yacht races and in summer a favourite bathing spot for **kittiwakes**. The island's 400 or so residents live on the west coast, looking across the Sound to the capital.

Many more people lived on Bressay early in the last century, mainly on the east coast, but they were evicted in the 1870s to clear the land for sheep, and on the east side there are many ruins from the era of the Clearances. The deserted hamlets of **Wadbister** and **Grimsetter** are forlorn examples. The island is virtually solid Old Red Sandstone, which has been extensively quarried and used among other things to pave Lerwick's streets and clad and roof its buildings. You'll find the **Bressay Heritage Centre** next to the ferry terminal car park, a minute's walk from the ferry. Owned and operated by the *Bressay History Group* it has entertaining displays and exhibitions through the summer months. During winter it is the venue for talks and slide shows on historical subjects. Open part-time from May to September. Contact VisitShetland at the Market Cross, Lerwick, or the Bressay History Group secretary (✆01595-820368). Above the terminal is **Gardie House**, built in 1724 from local sandstone. It is occupied by the Lord Lieutenant of Shetland.

Along the shore north from Gardie House to Heogan are the remains of several old fishing stations dating back to the herring boom years. At **Cruister**, are the concrete buildings of a World War II anti-aircraft gun battery. On the **Hill of Cruister** is a prehistoric standing stone, possibly Pictish, which is still used as a navigational marker by local fishing boats. In the north are the old crofting townships of **Beosetter** and **Gunnista**. The churchyard at Gunnista has the remains of a substantial 18th-century mausoleum and the ruins of the medieval **Church of St Olaf**, which was the parish church until 1772. On the promontory of Aith Ness the prized sandstone flags were quarried during the 18th and 19th centuries. On a hill past the old quarries is what's left of a World War I gun.

At Culbinsbrough the churchyard contains the ruins of the 10th century cruciform **Chapel of St Mary's**, the only cross-shaped pre-Reformation chapel in Shetland. In 1864, a carved Pictish slab known as the **Bressay Stone** was found in the churchyard wall. This depicts a rider and horse and is regarded as evidence that the Shetland pony roamed the islands long before the Vikings arrived. A replica of the stone can be seen in the Shetland Museum in Lerwick. The square tower prominent on Ander Hill above Noss Sound is a World War I look-out station. Below is the departure point for the summer boat service to the National Nature Reserve on the smaller isle of Noss. The Sound is a good place to look out for the **common porpoise**. There is good walking south from here, with spectacular cliff scenery from Grutwick to the Bressay lighthouse.

Another World War I gun is situated on the long southern promontory called the Bard. Off this headland is the rock arch known as the **Giant's Leg**. The lighthouse was built in 1858 by the father of Robert Louis Stevenson, Thomas. Not far from the lighthouse is the wreck of a Russian vessel, the *Lunokhod*. Just north of the lighthouse is a picturesque natural arch. Bressay's spectacular 17 miles (27km) of coastline can best be appreciated when viewed from the sea. There are daily boat trips from Lerwick around Bressay and Noss during the summer months. *Seabirds & Seals* (✆01595-693434; www.seabirds-and-seals.com) explores the coastline of Bressay on the way to Noss. The twin-engined cruise boat *Dunter III* displays live underwater video pictures from the kelp forest and inside sea caves. You can also do a package tour through *Shetland Wildlife* (Longhill, Maywick ZE2 9JF; ✆01950-422483; fax 01950-422430; email info@shetlandwildlife.co.uk; www.shetlandwildlife.co.uk). Visiting yachtsmen should contact the secretary of the *Bressay Boating Club* (✆01595-820284). The island has a public hall, primary school, shop and church which are all near the crossroads at Mail, about a mile (1.6km) south of Maryfield. The shop sells a variety of foodstuffs and other products, as well as diesel and lead-free petrol. Details of upcoming local events are usually displayed at the shop and on the ferry notice-board.

Crofting has generally become part-time work. Some islanders are employed by the modern fishmeal factory at Heogan, others commute to work in Lerwick. Farmland, pasture, moorland, lochs and coastal stretches combine to provide a wide range of habitats for wildlife. Many bird species breed here, among them **puffin**, **common guillemot**, **black guillemot**, **great skua**, **Arctic tern**, **golden plover**, **curlew**, **oystercatcher**, **red-throated diver**, **skylark**, **wheatear**, **wren** and **meadow-pipit**. Small colonies of cliff-nesting seabirds can be seen around the Bard and the Ord. The loch of **Sand Vatn** is a favourite dip for **skuas**. **Grey** and **common seals** frequent the coastline and in summer you should spot **whales** and **dolphins** inshore.

GETTING THERE

The Ro-Ro vehicle and passenger ferry to Bressay leaves Lerwick every day at regular intervals (every 40 or 60 minutes) from 7am to 11pm and later on Friday and Saturday and takes 7 minutes to cross to Maryfield. Contact *Bressay Sound Services* (✆01595-743974), or the *Shetland Islands Council* (Town Hall, Lerwick ZE1 0HB; ✆01595-693535; fax 01595-695590; email ferries@sic.shetland.gov.uk; www.shetland.gov.uk/ferries/). There's a sensible rule of the road on Bressay – traffic coming from the ferry gives way to traffic heading for the terminal.

There is a four-seater **Postbus** service on Bressay operated by *Royal Mail* (✆01595-820200). It runs Monday to Saturday from the post office to the ferry terminal, Hoegan, Noss Sound, Ham, Kirkabister and the lighthouse.

ACCOMMODATION

Maryfield House Hotel: Bressay (✆01595-820207). Two-star, one double room and one twin. Extensive bar supper menu with seafood a speciality, or you can dine in the restaurant with harbour views. Suppers and dinners served Monday to Saturday from 7pm to 9pm (booking essential), and lunch from midday to 2pm seven days a week.

Northern Lights Holistic Spa: Soundview, Uphouse ZE2 9ES (✆01595-820733; email northernlightsholisticspa@fsmail.net). Varied therapies available, good food. Five bedrooms, from £35.

Bressay Lighthouse: Two lightkeepers cottages, minimum booking three days. Three bedrooms, sleeps six, from £200 to £400. Contact VisitShetland, Market Cross, Lerwick ZE1 0LU (✆01595-693434; fax 01595-695807; email info@visitsheltand.com).

Camping. There is no official campsite on the island. Get permission from the nearest house if you plan to pitch a tent.

NOSS

The Marquis of Londonderry leased Noss in 1871 to breed Shetland ponies to replace the children then being used underground in his Durham mines to haul coal. He wanted the pit ponies bred with 'as much weight as possible and as near the ground as can be got'. In the 1870s the crofting community was evicted to clear the land for sheep farming and only a shepherd and his family were spared. The island has not been permanently inhabited since 1939. Noss is now owned by the Gardie Trust and since it was declared a National Nature Reserve in 1955 has been jointly managed by Scottish Natural Heritage (SNH). You can visit the island reserve when the summer wardens are present, from early May until end August, from 10am to 5pm, except Monday and Thursday. Admission for adults is £3, OAPs and children £1.50. Noss is closed to visitors throughout winter (September to mid-May). The ferry landing is at **Gungstie**, where a 17th-century house used as accommodation by the SNH summer wardens and staff also houses a small **visitor centre**.

Fondly known to visiting twitchers as 'Seabird City', the 774-acre (313ha) wedge of island rising to a height of 591ft (180m) above sea level at the **Noup of Noss** is home to **puffins**, **gannets**, **fulmars**, **shags**, **herring gulls**, **kittiwakes**, **guillemots**, **razorbills** and other species, all crammed on the ledges and in the crevices of the eroded horizontally bedded Old Red Sandstone cliffs.

Rumblewick, in the south-east, is an excellent vantage point for bird-watching; the geos and **Cradle Holm** are usually crowded with **puffins**. The flat top of Cradle Holm is **great black-backed gull** territory. Along the **North Croo** you'll find breeding **black guillemots**, **oystercatchers** and **ringed plovers**. **Arctic skuas** breed near the Hill Dyke while the moorland is dominated by a large colony of **great skuas**. Stay on the path which goes right round the island and do not disturb breeding skuas or other birds.

Noss has been inhabited since prehistoric times. The earliest sign of settlement is a 4,000-year-old Bronze Age **burnt mound** at Helia Cluve. Present day ruins are of 19th-century crofthouses and there are the remains of a pre-Reformation chapel near Gungstie. Stable buildings have been restored at the 19th-century pony *pund* where the Marquis once kept his Shetland mares and there is an interpretive display. A beehive grain-drying kiln has also been restored. You are bound to hear about the famous **Cradle of Noss**. Unfortunately, it has not existed since the factor removed it in 1864 and built a wall along the sheer cliff top. The cradle, erected every July and taken down each November, comprised a box on two cables, large enough to hold an egg hunter and one sheep. The contraption was used for 200 years to cross the 66ft (20m) gap to the precipitous 157ft (48m) high **Holm of Noss** so that it could be used to graze about a dozen sheep. Sections of cliff beyond the reach of grazing animals have colourful displays of **sea campion**, **scurvy grass** and **roseroot**. It should take you about three hours to walk around the island.

GETTING THERE

One way to get to Noss in summer is to take the ferry to Bressay from Lerwick, then hike or drive the 3 miles (5km) from Maryfield across to the 'Wait Here' sign on Noss Sound and wait for the Scottish Natural Heritage inflatable dinghy to cross the 219 yards (200m) stretch and pick you up. SNH (Ground Floor, Stewart Building, Alexandra Wharf, Lerwick ZE1 0LL; ℂ01595-693345; fax 01595-692565; email northern_isles@snh.gov.uk; www.nnr-scotland.org) operates this service to the reserve from 10am to 5pm (the last journey is at 4pm) daily except Monday and Thursday from May to end-August. Return fare is £3 for adults, and £1.50 for children. Take care on the slippery rocks when getting in and out the dinghy and wear sturdy shoes or boots and warm, waterproof clothing. On windy days – Force 6 and above – check with the Noss Ferry Line ℂ0800-107 7818 or VisitShetland (ℂ01595-693434) before leaving Lerwick to ensure that the service is operating. During bad weather and in adverse sea conditions a red flag is flown on Noss showing that it is closed to visitors. No dogs are allowed on the ferry. Another way to get to Noss is to join an organised tour. *Seabirds & Seals* sail to Noss between 30 April and 1 September at 2pm daily if there is enough demand and the weather is favourable. *Dunter III* departs from Victoria Pier Slipway, not far from the Tourist Office in Lerwick. Operators caution that the trip is not recommended for the frail or elderly. You can also book a package trip through *Shetland Wildlife* (Longhill, Maywick ZE2 9JF; ℂ01950-422483; fax 01950-422430; email info@shetlandwildlife.co.uk).

South Mainland & Mousa

SOUTH MAINLAND

Shetland Mainland tapers off to the south in a narrow peninsula which runs 25 miles (40km) from Lerwick down to its tip at Sumburgh Head. The first-class A970 between Lerwick and Sumburgh is joined by many side roads which lead to an extraordinary number of archaeological sites surrounded by scenic and wildlife attractions. There is excellent walking round the coastline and along the ridge of hills which forms the spine of the peninsula, with epic views from summits such as Scousburgh Hill and Fitful Head. This area has the most extensive sand dunes in Shetland, which account for the sandstorms that have helped to preserve such stunning archaeological sites as Jarlshof and Old Scatness. More than 70 Iron Age brochs, or defensive stone towers, were built throughout Shetland some 2,000 years ago but there is no doubt that the broch on the little island of Mousa (see *Mousa*) is the finest surviving example. The ferry to Mousa leaves from near the village of Sandwick and the trip is one of the best ways to see **harbour porpoises** (*neesiks*) at close range as they feed on fish shoaling in Mousa Sound.

Head south from the capital and you'll find **Hollanders' Knowe**, above the farm of Wick, where locals and visiting Dutch fishermen traded and bartered in the 17th and 18th centuries, and **Gulberwick**, where the Viking Earl Rognvald was wrecked in AD1148. A silver penannular Viking brooch was found here centuries later and you can see it in the Shetland Museum, in Lerwick.

The area around Brindister Loch is one of the best places to see **Shetland ponies**, which are bred at a nearby farm. A tiny island in the loch holds the ruins of a dun, or prehistoric fort. Easter and Wester **Quarff** – a name meaning 'the portage' in Old Norse – lie at opposite ends of one of Shetland's few east-west valleys, carved by ancient ice into a classic glacial valley. The Atlantic Ocean and the North Sea are less than two miles (3km) apart here. A remarkable ancient quarry is tucked away on the hillside above the main A970 road from Cunningsburgh to Sandwick. This is **Catpund Quarry**, where islanders once carved the soft steatite, or soapstone, into useful objects. In the rock along Catpund Burn you can still see spoil heaps and the shapes left from Neolithic to medieval times where bowls, urns and other artefacts were chipped out of the soapstone. At Cunningsburgh *Barbara Isbister* (✆01595-477241) and *Shetland Designer* (Swarthoull ZE2 9HB; ✆01595-477257; fax 01950-477499; email info@shetlanddesigner.co.uk; www.shetlanddesigner.co.uk) stocks a collection of traditional and contemporary Shetland knits, workshop and showroom. Open all year.

Further south along the main road, there are good views of the island of Mousa and its famous broch. The extensive remains of the **Broch of Burraland** still face the broch on Mousa. Both once guarded the entrance to Mousa Sound. Around the scenic inlet of Channerwick are the villages of Sandwick and Hoswick. The **Hoswick Visitor Centre** (✆01950-431406; email info@sandwick-community.co.uk) is open May to September, Monday to Saturday 10am to 5pm, Sunday 11am to 5pm. The centre provides light snacks, including local scones and bannocks, public internet access and interpretive displays on local heritage and culture, as well as a significant collection of radio and communication equipment. Local merchandise is on sale in the small gift shop, good parking. There's a small but **good bathing beach** nearby at Levenwick, on the North Sea coast.

At Voe, south of Boddam, is the **Shetland Crofthouse Museum** (South Voe, Dunrossness; ✆01595-695057; fax 01595-696729; email info@shetlandmuseumandarchives.org.uk; www.shetlandmuseumandarchives.org.uk), a straw-thatched cottage built in 1870 and restored to look as it would have appeared a century ago. Exhibits inside the cottage, barn and byre include home-made furniture, such as box bed and Shetland chairs, as well as farm implements and a spinning wheel. It is open mid-April to 30 September, Monday to Sunday 10am to 1pm and 2pm to 5pm. Admission fee. Nearby is a restored watermill of the horizontal Norse type, typical of those which ground oats and barley for most Shetland crofting townships until bigger mills became common in the mid-19th century. Close to Sumburgh Airport is the **Pool of Virkie**, sheltered intertidal mudflats forming one of the most important sites in Shetland for resident and visiting wader birds. Across the bay is **Sumburgh Airport**. Nearby Grutness is the Mainland base for the boat from Fair Isle. On a clear day, the island's distinctive profile can be seen from Sumburgh Head.

Built by Robert Stevenson, Shetland's first lighthouse, on **Sumburgh Head**, is a listed building. The **RSPB Nature Reserve** at Sumburgh Head has Britain's most accessible colony of **puffins**, which arrive between April and mid-August. Walk to the lighthouse and look over the wall and you'll see these comical little birds, along with **guillemots**, **kittiwakes**, and **shags**. On the rocks below you'll also see **seals**. In June and July, you might also see **humpback**, **minke** and **killer whales**, as well as more common **harbour porpoises**. RSPB Shetland Office (Easthouse, Sumburgh Head Lighthouse, Virkie, ZE3 9JN; ©01950-460800; fax 01595-460801; pete.ellis@rspb.org.uk). Reserve open all year, no admission charge. Guided walks are run by Shetland Amenity Trust (Garthspool, Lerwick ZE1 0NY; ©01595-694688; email shetamenity.trust@zetnet.co.uk) for a small charge.

ARCHAEOLOGICAL SITES

Alongside the Sumburgh Hotel is **Jarlshof**, which has been described as one of the most remarkable archaeological sites ever excavated in the British Isles. This long-buried settlement came to light a hundred years ago when violent storms exposed its massive stonework above the beach at the West Voe of Sumburgh. Jarlshof is unusual in that there is a succession of archaeological levels, dating from the late Bronze Age, some 2,800 years ago, through the Iron Age, 2,000 years ago, and the times of Norse occupation early in the ninth century, to the medieval layer and levels up to the 17th century. You can walk inside a 1,600-year-old house still complete to its full height. The best-preserved Iron- ge house overlies a Bronze Age dwelling and was in use at a time when the inhabitants of the village bred sheep, including Soay and other breeds similar to modern Shetland sheep. Remains in middens show that they also fished and hunted for grey seal and walrus. Some fish bones suggest they caught cod with heads more than a foot long. In their fields they grew cereal crops such as bere, a primitive form of barley with four rows of grains instead of two, and emmer, a kind of wheat. The first Norse settlers built on an extensive mound of rubble at Jarlshof which, unknown to them, already contained the debris from more than 2,000 years of human settlement. Bronze and carved bone pins used as cloak fasteners by the Vikings have been found at Jarlshof of a type also discovered with 11th century remains in Dublin.

The many spindle whorls unearthed indicate that spinning must have been a never-ending occupation at the settlement. Other finds show that evenings were passed playing games, board games for adults and for children the spinning of a *snorie-ben*, a toy consisting of a pig's leg bone or short piece of wood which, spun on a piece of string or wool, makes a snoring sound. The surrounding farmland is some of Shetland's most fertile, so it's not surprising that the notorious earls Robert Stewart and his son Patrick built residences here. By the early 17th-century parts of Jarlshof looked like a present-day southern Scottish farm; by the end of the century Jarlshof was in ruins. These buildings were all buried by wind-blown sand, preserving the artefacts you can see in the visitor centre at the site. Sir Walter Scott visited Shetland in 1814 on a cruise that resulted in his novel *The Pirate*, set around Sumburgh and Fitful Head. It was Scott who, in his novel, named the medieval farmhouse Jarlshof, the name now used for the entire archaeological site. To fully appreciate Jarlshof you should make use of the services of the official guide of the *Ministry of Public Building and Works* who is on duty at specified times. Jarlshof is open April to September, Monday to Sunday 9.30am to 6.30pm. Last admission 30 minutes before closing. Admission adult £3, reduced £2.30, child £1.

Only a mile (1.6km) away is the ongoing dig at **Old Scatness Broch**, which is uncovering one of Britain's most interesting Iron Age settlements, with many buildings standing at or near roof height and some even showing traces of interior yellow clay decoration. There are also Pictish and Norse remains on the site. Buried under sand and soil to roof height for nearly 2,000 years, the site is rich in artefacts and is remarkably well preserved. Admission for adults is £4, children £2. On-site interpretation, guides and 'Living History' demonstrations of ancient crafts and skills from May to September, 10am to 5.30pm, will help you to understand how man's earlier ancestors lived. Visitor Centre, saga telling in the wheelhouse. Contact the *Shetland Amenity Trust* (Garthspool, Lerwick ZE1 0NY; ©01595-694688; email shetamenity.trust@zetnet.co.uk).

A short walk from Scatness takes you to the **Ness of Burgi**, across the bay from Sumburgh, where an Iron Age fort stands on an exposed rock promontory high above the sea.

Beautifully restored **Quendale Mill** (Dunrossness ZE2 9JD; ©01950-460969, email info@quendalemill.shetland.co.uk; www.quendalemill.shetland.co.uk), heralded a labour-saving revolution for farmers and crofters in the late 1860s when this powerful water mill replaced 'clickmills' and hand querns for grinding cereals. The mill now houses a visitor centre with an exhibition of old farming methods, croft implements and archive photos. A video shows the original mill machinery in action. There are facilities for the disabled. You can enjoy a guided tour, video, and displays of local history. Craftshop, postcards and souvenirs. Open mid-April to mid-October daily from 10am to 5pm. Small admission charge. The beach at the **Bay of Quendale** is the largest in Shetland, with nearly a mile (1.6km) of beautiful sand. The road from Quendale to Scousburgh takes you past the **Loch of Spiggie**, an RSPB reserve for wildfowl. There are **otters** in the reserve, but you are more likely to see their 'spraints', or droppings, than you are the animals. This is one of the most productive trout-fishing lochs in Shetland and the burn leading down from the loch to Spiggie Beach is renowned for **sea trout**. **Scousburgh Sands** offer a sheltered bathing beach.

St Ninian's Isle hit the headlines in 1958 when a schoolboy helping at an archaeological dig in the ruins of the island's tiny 12th-century church discovered a fabulous hoard of 28 Pictish silver bowls and ornaments. These priceless treasures, believed to date from around AD800, are displayed in the Royal Museum, in Edinburgh, but replicas are on show at the Shetland Museum, in Lerwick. St Ninian's Isle is joined to the mainland at Bigton by the finest *tombolo*, or natural shell sand causeway, in Europe. You are not allowed to drive on the private road to the beach, but walkers have access. Take a pair of rubber boots as on occasion extra-high tides can cover the *tombolo*. The island, which was inhabited until the peat ran out in 1700, is used to graze sheep and is a popular spot for picnics, swimming and rambling. *Island Trails* (©01950-422408) offers a guided walking tour of St Ninian's Isle with hill-walker and storyteller Niall Cruickshank. The circular walk is best in May and June.

GETTING AROUND

South Mainland bus service is operated by *John Leask & Son* (The Esplanade, Lerwick; ©01595-693162; fax 01595-693171; email info@leaskstravel.co.uk; www.leaskstravel.co.uk and Exnaboe, Sumburgh; ©01950-460209). Lerwick-Sandwick-Sumburgh Airport with stops on the way, Monday to Sunday.

Taxis. Robert McPherson, Cunningsburgh (©01950-477333). *Boddam Cabs* (©01950-460111) is next to Sumburgh Airport, will take you to visit places of interest.

ACCOMMODATION

Hotels

Hoswick Bay Hotel: Hoswick, Sandwick ZE2 9HL (©01950-431226; fax 01950-431262). Situated in the historic coastal village, 15 miles (24km) south of Lerwick and 11 miles (18km) north of Sumburgh, six bedrooms with lovely views. From £25.

Spiggie Hotel: Scousburgh ZE2 9JE (©01950-460409; fax 01950-460674; email info@spiggiehotel.co.uk; www.thespiggiehotel.co.uk). Three-star, small family-run hotel, four en suite rooms. Home-cooked food, bar meals available seven days a week, licensed restaurant with à la carte menu. Overlooking Spiggie Loch and Peerie Voe, 10 minutes from Sumburgh Airport (free transport to and from hotel if required), 30 minutes from Lerwick. Good fly-fishing (permit from hotel). From £40.

Sumburgh Hotel: Virkie, Sumburgh ZE3 9JN (✆01950-460201; fax 01950-460394, email sumburgh.hotel@zetnet.co.uk; www.sumburgh-hotel.zetnet.co.uk). Built in 1867 as the home of the Laird of Sumburgh the hotel sits on the southern peninsula, where the North Sea meets the Atlantic Ocean, overlooking the archaeological site of Jarlshof. Three-star, 30 minutes' drive from Lerwick but a couple of minutes from the airport, courtesy transport from airport. 32 en suite rooms, two bars serving a range of pub grub. In the *West Voe* restaurant you can choose from a table d'hôte or à la carte menu. From £35.

Bed & Breakfast

Fiona Robertson: Wildrig, Scousburgh ZE2 9JE (✆01950-460373; email fiona@wildrig.biz; www.wildrig.biz). Three-star, Scandinavian-style, coastal and beach views. Home-cooking, from £27.

Mrs J Stove: Solbrekke, Park Road, Sandwick ZE2 9HP (✆01950-431410). Overlooking Mousa Broch, from £22 per person.

Mrs J Mainland: Spiggie, Scousburgh ZE2 9JE (✆/fax 01950-460468; email setterbrae@hotmail.com; www.setterbrae.co.uk). Four-star, overlooking Spiggie Loch, 10 minutes from Sumburgh Airport, from £24 per person.

Mr P Watts: Da Muckle Hus, Netherton, Levenwick ZE2 9HX (✆01950-422370; email info@mucklehus.co.uk; www.mucklehus.co.uk). Renovated 19th century house, between beach and cliffs, from £28.

Self-Catering

Mrs B Arthur: Longwell, Cunningsburgh ZE2 9HG (✆01950-477204). Three-star, quiet location. Two bedrooms, sleeps four, from £200 to £270.

Glover Chalets: Mrs R Inkster, Blaisdon, Cunningsburgh ZE2 9HA (✆01950-477596; fax 01950-477642; email rebecca.inkster@btopenworld.com; www.gloverchalets.co.uk). Four-star, Scandinavian-style, from £280 to £480 a week.

Mrs M Irvine: Cunningsburgh ZE2 9HG (✆01950-477350; email info@shetlandholiday-chalets.co.uk; www.shetlandholidaychalets.co.uk). Self-contained flat, coastal location, two bedrooms, sleeps four, from £200 to £260.

Sumburgh Lighthouse on Sumburgh Head has four bedrooms, sleeps seven, from £200 to £400. To book contact Visit Shetland, Market Cross, Lerwick ZE1 0LU (✆0870-199 9440; fax 01595-695807; email info@visitshetland.com; www.visitsheltand.com

Böd

Betty Mouat's (www.camping-bods.com), a stone cottage at the southern tip of the Shetland Mainland in Scatness. Once the home of a crippled woman who, in 1886, drifted alone to Norway and lived to tell the tale. The böd is handy for Sumburgh Airport and the Fair Isle ferry. Open 1 April–30 September (or by arrangement), three public rooms, two bedrooms, sleeps eight. Hot water heater, shower, solid fuel stove, electricity. Shop within two miles. Disabled facilities. Bus stop nearby for Lerwick and airport. £5 per person per night, £40 exclusive use (not July or August). Contact the Custodian, Christine Manson (9 Colonial Place, Scatness, Virkie; ✆01950-460395).

Camping

Cunningsburgh Village Club: Tow, Cunningsburgh (✆01950-477241). Youth centre in country setting, open June to August, £5 per night. Disabled facilities.

Levenwick Campsite: Levenwick ZE2 9HX (℃01950-422207; fax 01950-422460), just off A970 next to the village hall, grassy area for tents, hard area for caravans. Open May to 30 September. Warden on duty each evening from 7pm to 8pm. List showing day warden and telephone number is displayed in the local shop. From £5 a night.

EATING AND DRINKING

Spiggie Hotel: Scousburgh ZE2 9JE (℃/fax 01950-460409). 21 miles (34km) from Lerwick, five miles (8km) from Sumburgh. The hotel overlooks Spiggie Loch, Peerie Voe and out to Foula. Bar meals, restaurant dinner (not Monday and Tuesday), book in advance. Shetland home cooking with local fish, meat and veg.

Sumburgh Hotel: Sumburgh ZE3 9JN (℃01950-460201; fax 01950-460394). The *West Voe* restaurant has some spectacular views, including Jarlshof, Sumburgh Head and Fair Isle. Morning coffee, lunch, afternoon tea, bar meals and snacks, table d'hôte dinner. A variety of local beef, lamb and fresh fish is served daily. Bar lunches Monday to Saturday midday to 2pm, Sunday 12.30pm to 2pm; suppers 6.30pm to 9.30pm nightly. Restaurant open nightly 7pm to 9pm.

The Warp and Weft Visitor Centre: Hoswick, Sandwick ZE2 9HR (℃01950-431406). The tearoom is an extension of the centre where you can browse among historical and craft displays and tuck into snacks and homebakes, soup, sandwiches, filled rolls and locally baked cakes, scones and bannocks. Gift shop sells a variety of local crafts and souvenirs. Entertainment by local fiddlers and singers. Hand-knitting demonstrations can be arranged. Open Monday to Friday 10am to 5pm, Sunday midday to 5pm.

HELP AND INFORMATION

Police Station: Dunrossness (℃01950-460707).
Doctor and Health Centre: Levenwick (℃01950-422240).
Ferry booking office: Mousa (℃01950-431367); Fair Isle (℃01595-760222).
Shetland Ranger Service: South Mainland Ranger, Howard Towll, Hoswick (℃01950-460403).
South Mainland swimming pool: Sandwick (℃01950-431511; fax 01950-431586).
Petrol and public toilets available at Cunningsburgh, Sandwick and Dunrossness, and there are also toilets at Bigton and Grutness Pier.
Post Offices at Sandwick, Levenwick, Bigton, Dunrossness and Toab; and **public telephones** in most places.

MOUSA

The uninhabited island of Mousa is in line for Unesco World Heritage Site status as 'a place of outstanding universal value', principally for its archaeological wonder, an **Iron Age broch** that is the most complete and best preserved in Britain. It rests on island flagstone, the same indestructible material that provides the paving stones of Lerwick. The sandstone broch has a circumference of 158ft (48m) at its base, stands 43.6ft (13.3m) high and you can climb right to the top by way of a passage and stairs between the inner and outer walls, which have an external diameter of 50ft (15m) at the base and just over 43ft (13m) at the summit. It is so impeccably shaped and preserved that looking across the sound from Sandwick it looks like a modern power station cooling tower. Around AD200 brochs had generally outlived their defensive usefulness, but as late as AD900 an eloping couple, Bjorn and Thora, took shelter in what they called *Moseyarborg* ('bird island fort') when their ship was wrecked there on its way from Norway to Iceland. They married and holed up for the winter in the broch. In AD1153 the broch was besieged by Earl Harald Maddarson of Orkney, who tried without success to prise his reluctant widowed mother Margaret from the embraces of her lover, Earl Erland the Young. This event is recorded in the Norse sagas, with the understatement that Mousa broch was 'an unhandy place to get at'.

You might hear odd churring noises coming from deep within the walls of the broch, or from the nearby boulder beach, if it is nesting season. This is the signature tune of the **storm petrel**, the world's smallest seabird (about the size of a swallow), which makes these calls to guide its foraging mate home. These little birds return towards dusk to avoid predation and a late evening visit is the best time to see them as they return to settle for the night. The island is home to about 5,000 breeding pairs of storm petrels and many other species of birds live and breed on and around the island, ranging from the tiny **Shetland wren** to the **great skua**. Guided walks are run by Shetland Amenity Trust (Garthspool, Lerwick ZE1 0NY; ℡01595-694688; email shetamenity.trust@zetnet.co.uk) for a small charge.

Circular Walk

The walk around Mousa is only 4 miles (6km) and can easily be covered in two hours. The walk starts at the landing jetty at West Ham and follows the shore to the broch. As it swings inland around the Haa, or laird's house, you can see the ruins of croft houses abandoned when the island was cleared of people in the 19th century. No one has lived on the island since 1861. The oldest signs of human settlement are the Bronze Age burnt mounds, piles of scorched and cracked rocks surrounding a stone-lined trough. This is believed to have been a communal cookhouse where heated stones were dropped into water to boil food.

Further along over a small hill, you'll reach the tidal **West Pool** at the south end of the island. **Seals** are common and **Arctic terns** nest here. Be careful where you put your feet walking along the edge of the tidal pool or you might stand on their camouflaged nests. They might seem fragile but these terns are among nature's sturdiest travellers. Every year they fly from their breeding grounds near the Arctic Circle to spend the southern summer in South Africa or Antarctica. Terns can live up for up to 25 years and in that time it is estimated they fly the equivalent of the distance to the moon.

Mousa's seals are some of the most approachable in Shetland. Up to 120 common and 20 grey seals stay here all summer. Common seal pups are born in June and grow so rapidly they are completely independent of their mothers a month after birth. The larger grey seal pups in October. **Black guillemots** – known locally as *tysties* – nest among the boulders. A few **Arctic skuas** breed on the hill, along with great skuas. Both species defend their territories with swooping dives, so it's advisable to keep one arm in the air as you walk through this area to protect your head. Don't wave your arms or try to hit the birds as they are easily injured. At nearby **East Pool** you'll see more seals. Remember that seals carry several diseases and parasites which can be caught by humans either from their breath or from the ground where they rest. Turning north along the east of the island you reach a deep geo, or inlet, with its natural arch carved out by the sea. There is another tern colony in the north and on the Hamars you'll find skuas, and more seals offshore. Continue round the cliffs and back to the jetty.

GETTING THERE

From early-April to mid-September you can take a 15-minute boat trip on the *Solan IV* to Mousa. It sails from Leebitton Pier, Sandwick, to Mousa daily at 2pm (returning at 5pm). On Friday and Sunday there is an additional sailing at 12.30pm (returning at 3pm and 5pm). Time on the island ranges from 2½ to 4 hours. Adult fare £10, children 5–16 £5, under 5 free. All sailings are weather dependent. No dogs are allowed on the island. Evening trips to see storm petrels leave at 11pm on Wednesday and Saturday from late-May until late-July. Adults £12, children £6. The *Solan IV* has wheelchair access. For further information and bookings contact *Tom and Cynthia Jamieson* (℡/fax 01950-431367, mobile 07901-872339, email info@mousaboattrips.co.uk; www.mousaboattrips.co.uk). May to September you can take a coach tour from Lerwick to Mousa. Contact *John Leask & Son* (The Esplanade, Lerwick; ℡01595-693162; fax 01595-693171; email info@leaskstravel.co.uk; www. leaskstravel.co.uk).

Central Mainland, Burra, Trondra and Foula

SCALLOWAY

The ancient capital of Shetland lies on the west coast of the island, just over six miles (10km) west of Lerwick. It is the second largest town in Shetland (population 1,000) and is its major port on the Atlantic seaboard. Scalloway owes its importance to a fine natural harbour sheltered by the beautiful little islands of **Trondra**, **Papa**, and **Oxna**, to the south and west. Further down Clift Sound lie **East** and **West Burra**. Like most others in Shetland, Scalloway's name is Norse in origin, and is thought to derive from a word meaning 'the bay of the booths' because it was founded on the beach where the Vikings used to draw up their boats when they arrived to attend their annual parliament. The town lies at the southern extremity of the valley of Tingwall, which is where the Norse parliament, or *ting*, met on an islet or holm at the north end of Tingwall Loch.

The port is dominated by the gaunt ruins of the **Scalloway Castle** built in 1600 by Patrick Stewart, Earl of Orkney and Lord of Shetland, a man who ruled with an iron hand and is chiefly remembered in Shetland for his cruelty. The castle was built with forced labour and local folklore says the mortar for the walls was mixed with blood and eggs. After Earl Patrick's execution in 1615 the castle fell steadily into ruin although it was garrisoned for a time by Cromwell's troops during the Civil War. All that remains of the castle today is the main tower-house, containing the Earl's hall and apartment. The striking corbelled turret is pierced by false gunloops to deter the over-inquisitive. The key to the castle is available nearby from the *Scalloway Hotel* (℃01595-880444). Blacksness Pier (1830) was built around the castle.

Scalloway has a dignified old-world air. The 19th-century houses were the homes of prosperous fish merchants while the large 18th-century houses were built by lairds. Most of Scalloway's shops are on Main Street. New Street is a row of 19th-century cottages. A plaque on one explains the tidal and lunar theories of William Johnson, mason, inventor and philosopher.

Scalloway Boating Club is open Monday to Thursday 7pm to midnight, Saturday 11am to midnight and Sunday 12.30pm to midnight. Visiting yachts and yachtsmen are welcome. In summer, there is a sailing and sea-angling programme. Contact the club for details (℃01595-880388). **Scalloway Museum** presents a window on life here throughout the ages, with a strong emphasis on fishing. There's also a permanent exhibition featuring Scalloway's little-known role in a World War II operation known as 'The Shetland Bus'. From 1942 to 1945 the port was used by Norwegian Resistance members who regularly crossed the North Sea in fishing boats and US submarine chasers to land saboteurs, ammunition and radio sets and bring back refugees from German-occupied Norway. The museum exhibition details the fascinating story of this secret operation. The **Prince Olav Slipway**, built for the repair of these vessels, and **Norway House**, used as a barracks by Norwegian seamen, are reminders of those dark days. You can follow an interesting **art trail** along the Scalloway waterfront. You can play or listen to **traditional music** at the Asta Golf Club House, near Scalloway. Contact VisitShetland (℃01595-693434), for dates and times.

North of Scalloway is **Gallows Hill**, also known as Witches Hill in memory of the last two witches to be burned there in 1712.

CENTRAL MAINLAND

The **Loch of Tingwall** is known for its fighting brown trout, breeding gulls, duck and other waterfowl. Overlooking the loch is **Tingwall Church**, the 'mother church' of Shetland, which was built in 1790 on the site of an earlier church dating back to the early period of Norse Christianity. Nearby **Tingwall Agricultural Museum** is housed in the old granary of 18th-century Veensgarth Farm. There are displays of crofting, fishing and agricultural implements. The museum is open six days a week through June, July and August. Evening and Sunday visits can be arranged (✆01595-840344). To the north of the museum is **Tingwall Airport**. One of the most spectacular views in Shetland is from the top of **Wormadale Hill**, on the boundary between Tingwall and Whiteness, which gives you a view of islands and sea stretching from Fitful Head in the south to the dramatic silhouette of Foula, 25 miles (40km) to the west.

Across the voe lies Whiteness, a promontory with the largest continuous outcrop of crystalline limestone in Shetland. The ruins on the islet in the **Loch of Strom** are believed to date from medieval times, although there is also evidence of even earlier settlement. The ruins of the house where **John Clunies Ross** was born are near Sound on Weisdale Voe. After a successful career at sea, Ross settled in the Cocos Islands in 1827 and became unofficial 'king' of these Indian Ocean islands. After he died in 1854, the islands were governed by his sons but were eventually claimed by Australia.

Not far from the head of Weisdale Voe is the expertly restored **Weisdale Mill**, which houses the *Bonhoga Art Gallery* and *Mill Café* (✆01595-830400; email bonhoga-gallery@ shetland-arts-trust.co.uk). The gallery is open Tuesday to Saturday 10.30am to 4.30pm and Sunday midday to 4.30pm. Disabled access. Admission is free. The **Shetland Textile Working Museum** (Weisdale Mill, Weisdale ZE2 9LW, ✆01595-830419) is also housed in the mill, which is said to have a resident ghost. It has a collection illustrating the history of spinning, knitting and weaving in the islands. The collection includes cobweb hand-spun lace shawls and stoles, as well as richly patterned Fair Isle garments displayed in their historical context. Workshops in spinning and knitting are arranged by guild members where you can see local craftspeople demonstrating their skills. Spinning was taught in the home in much the same way as knitting, but as well as mastering the art of spinning various types of thread, the spinner had to learn how to select the right quality raw wool. Girls were taught to knit from as early as three years old. Instead of going out to play they were told to work on their *sok*, or knitting. With the introduction of mechanisation the craft of home weaving declined and textile production became an industrial process. **Shetland tweed** is also produced by machine at Aith.

Shetland Jewellery (Soundside, Weisdale ZE2 9LQ; ✆01595-830275; fax 01595-830352; email shetland.jewellery@zetnet.co.uk; www.jgrae.co.uk) has hand-crafted silver and gold jewellery. Open Monday to Friday 9am to 5pm. Closed Saturday and Sunday. From June to August also open on Saturday 10am to 5pm, Sunday 2pm to 5pm. Guided tours on request. At **Hjaltasteyn**, in Whiteness, you can buy jewellery made from silver, gold, enamel and Shetland gemstones. Open Monday and Thursday (✆01595-696224). The 19th-century house of **Kergord** was built with stones from crofthouses whose tenants were forcibly evicted during the Clearances. In 1940, the house was the intelligence and administrative headquarters for the wartime 'Shetland Bus' operation. The mixed coniferous and deciduous trees around Kergord were planted from the late 19th century onwards and make up the largest stand of trees in Shetland.

The **Loch of Girlsta** gets its name from a Viking princess, Geirhilda, who drowned here a thousand years ago. The loch is known for brown trout and rare Arctic char and is Shetland's deepest stretch of fresh water. A track from the loch leads to the shore of **Cat Firth**, which was a World War I base for seaplanes and in World War II was used as a naval anchorage. The bay is nowadays important for the ducks and divers that winter here. Around the crofting townships of South Nesting are peaceful **coastal walks** and a good chance of spotting seals and otters.

TRONDRA & EAST AND WEST BURRA

To the south of Scalloway lie the adjoining isles of **Trondra** and **East** and **West Burra**. They are all linked by road bridges and separated from the Mainland by the Clift Sound. At Burland (✆01595-880430) on Trondra, you can visit a **Shetland croft** and see traditional breeds of animals and types of crops. You can also visit a workshop overlooking the sea where hand-framed plain and Fair Isle designs and hand-knits in both traditional and contemporary patterns are available from *Spirit of Shetland* (Barbara Mitchell, 5 Cauldhame, Trondra ZE1 0XL, ✆/fax 01595-880437). Hand-crafted fiddles are available from *Tommy Isbister* (✆01595-880430), visitors welcome. From Setter, on West Burra, you get wonderful views out to Foula, Westside and the small nearby islands of Papa, Hildasay, Oxna and Langa. **Hamnavoe**, the main settlement, is a pretty fishing village of small cottages and ornate iron railings around an attractive harbour. There are pleasant coastal walks out to the lighthouse at Fugla Ness and along the **Sands of Meal**, one of Shetland's loveliest beaches. This is a good picnic spot, with a convenient car park. **Papil**, at the south end of West Burra, is an early Christian site, named from the Norse word for priests. In the Shetland Museum is the Monks Stone, a pre-Viking Pictish carved stone slab found there, which depicts a horseman and four figures with crosiers. Further south there is a splendid sandy beach, **Banna Minn**, on the way to the rugged southern headland of Kettla Ness. There is no road on this last stretch.

The islet of **South Havra**, south of Burra, was once home to eight families. They built their houses on the edge of the cliff to enable them to farm every scrap of land. Animals and children alike were tethered to keep them safe. The island has no running water, however, and they abandoned it in 1923.

GETTING AROUND

Scalloway and Burra bus services are operated by *John Leask & Son*, The Esplanade, Lerwick (✆01595-693162), Scalloway-Hamnavoe-Lerwick, Monday to Saturday; for **taxis** contact Bob Hepburn, Scalloway (✆01595-880654), or John Halcrow, Hamnavoe (✆01595-859369); James Smith (✆01595-880718).

ACCOMMODATION
Hotels

Herrislea House Hotel: Veensgarth, Tingwall ZE2 9SB (✆01595-840208; fax 01595-840630; email hotel@herrisleahouse.co.uk; www.herrisleahouse.co.uk). Four-star hotel located in the Tingwall Valley, 7 minutes' drive from Lerwick, 13 individually designed en suite bedrooms. The hotel has its own fast Searider boat, available for hire at short notice, and access to more than 300 trout lochs. From £40.

The Inn on the Hill: The Westings, Whiteness ZE2 9LJ (✆01595-840242; fax 01595-840500; www.westings.shetland.co.uk). Three-star inn, on the main road to Lerwick near Tingwall, close to the summit of Wormadale Hill. Six bedrooms overlooking Whiteness Voe. You can enjoy a drink or an informal meal in *The Palm Shack*. Cask-conditioned ales are a feature of the bar and you can sample Shetland's own brew from Valhalla Brewery on Unst. From £40.

Scalloway Hotel: Main Road, Scalloway ZE1 0TR (✆01595-880444; fax 01595-880445), overlooking harbour. From £40 a night.

Guest Houses

Hildasay Guest House: Upper Scalloway, Scalloway ZE1 0UP (✆01595-880822). Four-star, disabled access and all en suite facilities. Specialised holidays for anglers with equipment on hire from proprietor.

Bed & Breakfast

Broch House: Upper Scalloway ZE1 0UP (℡01595-880051; www.brochhouse.shetland. co.uk). Three-star, family-run, from £25.

Windward: Port Arthur, Scalloway ZE1 0UN (℡01595-880769; email beth_cummings@ hotmail.com). Three-star, family-run, sea views, from £20.

Self-Catering

Mrs J Bradley: Isleshavn, Gletness, South Nesting ZE2 9PS (01595-890342; www.isle-shavnchalet.co.uk). Three-star chalet, central location, fine views. Two bedrooms, sleeps three, from £200 to £270.

Briar Cottage: Hamnavoe, Burra (℡01595-859419; email e.laurenson@virgin.net). Two-star, lovely view. Three bedrooms, sleeps five, from £120 to £280.

Easterhoull Chalets: Mr R Williamson, Leagarth, East Voe, Scalloway ZE1 0UR (℡01595-880376; fax 01595-880987). Two-star cluster of nine chalets fitted with showers and central heating, fridges and cookers, sleep four to six. £150 to £280 per week.

Nilmurhaa: Brettabister, North Nesting ZE2 9PR (℡01595-890395; www.nilmurhaa. co.uk). Newly-refurbished, on waterfront. One bedroom, sleeps 2–4, from £175 to £280.

Bridge-End Outdoor Centre: Burra (℡01595-859647). Can be hired for group holidays.

Camping

Westings Camp Site: Wormadale, Whiteness ZE2 9LJ (℡01595-840242; fax 01595-840500). Open April to September, six tent pitches, from £4 per person and £8 minimum per tent. Cyclists, campers and hikers are welcome at the Westings and you can erect your tent on the purpose-built site which has its own access to toilets and showers. Campervans can use the inn's car park.

On **Burra Isle** you will find accommodation at *Highmount Cottage:* Hamnavoe, contact Jan and Lily Eriksen (Burland, Trondra, Scalloway ZE1 0XL; ℡01595-880647; email jan@ jferiksen.freeserve.co.uk). Three-star self-catering, semi-detached traditional cottage over-looking village of Hamnavoe, sleeps six, £150 to £250 per week.

EATING AND DRINKING

Da Haaf Restaurant: Port Arthur, Scalloway (℡01595-880747; fax 01595-880549; www. nafc.ac.uk). Part of the North Atlantic Fisheries College and gives you magnificent views over the harbour. Although it serves the college's staff and students, visitors are welcomed. The restaurant's name, *Da Haaf*, comes from the Shetland dialect for the deep-sea or ocean – *haaf* being the Old Norse word for ocean – and was also applied to the small open-boat fishery operating around Shetland in the 18th and 19th centuries. Not surprisingly, the restaurant specialises in high quality local seafood. Open daily from Monday to Friday. Teas, coffees and snacks served all day. Lunch is served from 12.30 to 2pm and dinner from 5pm to 8pm. The menu, which is changed daily, always includes a range of fish dishes, such as salmon and several types of wild fish, together with non-fish and vegetarian dishes, and a variety of sweets, all at reasonable prices. As the restaurant is a popular place, particularly in summer, it's wise to book a table.

The *Phoenix Restaurant:* Herrislea House Hotel, Veensgarth, Tingwall (℡01595-840208; fax 01595-840630; www.herrisleahouse.co.uk). Located at the east end of tranquil Tingwall valley. Specialises in using its own and such local produce as hill lamb, freshly caught fish, selection of Shetland vegetables, fruit and herbs. Open Monday to Saturday 6.30pm to 9pm. It also has an informal café bar, *Starboard Tack*, offering food all day, every day from 11am to 11pm or later.

Scalloway Hotel: Main Street (℡01595-880444; fax 01595-880440). Central Scalloway. Lunch table d'hôte, dinner à la carte, bar suppers. Seafood specialities and own herb garden.

Castle Café and Take-Away: New Street (℡01595-880270), opposite Castle. Fish and chips, hot and cold filled rolls, baked potatoes, pasta. Open Monday 8.15am to 2pm, Tuesday to Friday 8.15am to 2pm, 4.30pm to 7.30pm, Saturday 8.45am to 2pm, 4.30pm to 7.30pm.

HELP AND INFORMATION

Police Station: Scalloway (✆01595-880222).

Doctor and Health Centre: Scalloway (✆01595-880219).

Tingwall Airport: (✆01595-810460).

South Mainland Leisure Centre: Sandwick (✆01950-431511; email smp@srt.org.uk; www. srt.org.uk).

Swimming Pool: New Road, Scalloway (✆01595-880745; email sp@srt.org.uk; www.srt. org.uk).

Petrol is available in Burra and Weisdale.

There are **public toilets** in Hamnavoe, Mail Beach, and Scalloway; **public telephones** at Scalloway, Burra, Tingwall, Whiteness, Weisdale; and p**ost offices** at Hamnavoe, Weisdale and Scalloway.

FOULA

Fortress-like Foula is the most westerly of the Shetland islands. It lies 14 miles (23km) west of Wats Ness, the nearest point on the Shetland Mainland, and 27 miles (43km) from Scalloway. The island is about 3½ miles (5.6km) long by 2½ miles (4km) wide and is dominated by hills and precipitous cliffs. The Kame at 1,220ft (372m) is a breathtaking sheer cliff, the second highest in Britain and surpassed in height, but not in sheerness, only by Conachair (1,397ft/426m) on Hirta, St Kilda. The cliffs and stacks show interesting erosional features, as at the Sneck o' da Smallie, a deep fissure in the cliff face and the impressive natural arch through Gaada Stack, whose three pillars tower 130ft (40m) over a curving storm beach named Da Stanes on the rugged north coast. Early last century, one of the stacks at the northern end of Foula, Da Broch, had an old ruined stone wall on top, but it vanished with the collapse of the arch in 1965.

Norse Queen

Vikings conquered Foula around AD800 and settled in the fertile Hametoun, leaving croft names such as Norderhus, Krugali, and Guttren, and many other descriptive Norse place-names round the island. The grassy knowe called **Krukaitrin** ('Katherine's shelter') is a reminder of Katherine Asmunder, the last Norse queen of Foula, who died late in the 17th century. Traces of earlier settlement can be found on the island, with a burnt mound near Hametoun burn. Foula's Norse-based culture is evident in its traditions, folklore, music and special festivals. The last person to speak the Old Norse dialect, Norn, died in 1926 and the Lord's Prayer was still being said in Norn in the Foula kirk at the end of the 19th century. In 1752, the Gregorian calendar was adopted in Britain in place of the old Julian system. This deleted nearly two weeks from the year. The community ignored the change and accordingly whoops it up on 6 January to celebrate Yule and sees in 'Newerday' on 13 January. After the Scots took over James III's dowry lands of Shetland and Orkney in 1472, Foula became part of a west Shetland estate.

The Foula mailboat *Island Lass* was wrecked in 1962 and the population fell to 27, but the remaining islanders were so determined to stay they built their own airstrip in the early 1970s. The people of the 'island west of the sun' did not want Foula to go the way of another Atlantic island, St Kilda, whose entire population of 36 was evacuated in 1930, leaving the island uninhabited. The evacuation of St Kilda was immortalised in Michael Powell's 1936 film, *The Edge of the World*, which was made in Foula. Many islanders took part in the now classic movie. A book and video about the film are available and make good souvenirs. Contact *Scottish Islands Explorer* (Auld Haa, Fair Isle ZE2 9JU; ✆01595-693380; fax 01595-694830; email info@scottishislandsexplorer.com; www.scottishislandsexplorer.com), or Bob Thomson (Braemar AB35 5YW; ✆013397-41214). Foula's last old-style blackhouse was inhabited at Da Breckins until 1964, when the peat fire traditionally burning in the middle of the floor was at last allowed to go out.

The Peaks

The population is now around 40, concentrated in the main settlements at **Ham**, in the centre of the eastern coastal strip, and at **Hametoun** in the south. A 45kW aerogenerator, integrated with hydro-turbines, uses both wind and water power to supply them with electricity. Behind these crofting townships to the west is an expanse of peaty moorland rising steeply to Foula's five peaks. **The Noup** in the south is divided by the glacial valley of **the Daal** from **Hamnafield**, **the Sneug**, **the Kame** and **Soberlie**, which stretch west until they drop sheer to the sea in awe-inspiring cliffs. **Da Sneck o' da Smaallie** is a gloomy dark vertical chimney more than 100ft (30m) deep which drops down to the sea at the west end of the Daal, giving access to teeming seabird colonies. Legend says this is where the *trows* (trolls) brew up bad weather. The way down is hazardous and should on no account be attempted without an experienced guide. The summit of **the Sneug** at 1,370ft (418m) gives a panoramic view of the island. A little spring under the north shoulder of the hill is reputed to have healing properties. Strong winds and constant salt spray make farmsteading on the 5–6 acre (2–2.4ha) crofts difficult. The hill grazing is good, but adverse weather can prevent stock reaching market. Most islanders keep sheep, and some have Shetland ponies. Most of the 2,000 sheep in Foula are the original hardy and nimble Shetland breed, whose differently coloured fleeces are much in demand by hand-spinners. Colours range from the predominant *moorit*, or brown, to fawn, grey, creamy white and black, and many have attractive markings.

Foula is surrounded by rich fishing banks and fishing was important in the local economy in the past, when dried fish was bartered with Mainland traders. Historically, fish, birds, birds' eggs and crofting kept the islanders going. Tourism and crab and lobster fishing now provide seasonal income, along with the sale of sheepskins, hand-spun garments in natural coloured local wool, and the traditional Foula *gansy*, or sweater. At Broadfoot, there is a residential workshop for spinning, weaving and dyeing. Modern electronic communications mean that some islanders can supplement their croft income with computer work. As well as providing a service to the community, the local 'smiddy' sells wrought-iron work and useful items made from copper salvaged from the island's famous shipwreck, the *Oceanic*, a sister ship of the *Titanic*, which hit a reef and sank off Foula in 1914.

FLORA AND FAUNA

Foula has been designated a Site of Special Scientific Interest (SSSI) – for its flora and fauna, and for the geology of its dramatic coastline – and it is also a National Scenic Area, and a Special Protection Area (SPA) for birds. Foula gets its name from the Norse *Fugl ey*, meaning 'bird island'. Sea and moorland birds can be seen in many accessible habitats all over the island during summer. There are about 2,500 breeding pairs of **great skuas**, the largest colony in Britain. They compete for nesting sites with **Arctic skuas**. One of the island's sights is the great skuas taking their morning bath in **Mill Loch**. Other species include **kittiwakes**, **Arctic terns** and **eiders**. Every small loch in the island has its resident **red-throated divers**, and the cliffs teem with **puffins, guillemots, razorbills, shags, fulmars** and **gannets**. Foula was the first place outside of St Kilda to be colonised by the fulmar. The rare **Leach's petrel, storm petrel** and **Manx shearwater** have also been sighted. Migration time brings other unusual species.

Rabbits share the terrain with **hedgehogs** and there is not much variety in terrestrial fauna, although Foula can claim a unique sub-species of **field mouse**, and an island variety of the **house mouse**. **Atlantic grey** and **common seals** are both commonplace around the shore, and can be watched at close quarters in Ham Voe. Schools of **killer whales** have been seen close inshore and **porpoises** often follow arriving and departing ferries.

GETTING THERE

Foula's exposed small harbour at Ham Voe and its airstrip can be affected by crosswinds or fog, making both sea and air travel to Foula decidedly weather dependent. Delays are sometimes unavoidable, so it is advisable to first check sailings or flights with the ferry or airline.

By Air

Directflight (℡01595-840246) flies from Tingwall Airport, on the Mainland, 7 miles (11km) from Lerwick and Scalloway, once a day on Monday and Tuesday, and twice a day on Wednesday and Friday. During winter there is one flight a day Monday, Tuesday and Wednesday, and two on Friday. The adult return fare is £50 (senior citizens £28). The flight takes about 15 minutes. .

There are no taxis or public transport on Foula.

By Sea

The Foula ferry is operated by *Atlantic Ferries* (Gronnack, Whiteness ZE2 9LL; ℡078-8182 3732; fax 01595-840880; email bookings@atlanticferries.co.uk; www.atlanticferries.co.uk), twice weekly crossings all year round, on the 12-passenger *New Advance,* with an additional sailing in summer. The ferry departs Walls at 2.30pm on Tuesday and Thursday. The additional summer sailings are from Walls at 2.30pm on Saturday and from Scalloway at 1.30pm on alternate Thursdays. All crossings are subject to weather and sea conditions. You can check the voice bank at 01595-743976 for up-to-date sailing information.

Buses leave Lerwick's Viking Bus Station for Walls, Monday to Saturday, 9.05am and 12.30pm (except Wednesday) and 5.05pm. Contact *Whites Coaches* (West Burrafirth, Bridge of Walls; ℡01595-809443).

On Wednesdays during May to September you can join a full-day boat trip to Foula with *Cycharters* (1 Bloomfield Place, Lerwick ZE1 0PW; ℡01595-696598; fax 01595-690441; email cycharters@aol.com). The *MV Cyfish* leaves Muckle Yard, next to the Old Scalloway Fish Mart, Scalloway, May to September. Tuesday afternoon and Wednesday full-day, afternoon trips cost £30 and Foula full-day £50.

ACCOMMODATION

Leraback: Marion Taylor (Foula ZE2 9PN; ℡01595-753226; email marion@foula.net). Modern crofthouse bungalow, one-star, centrally situated B&B, £25 DB&B. Three-course homemade set evening meal.

HELP AND INFORMATION

There is no general store but a craft shop at Breckins, and a school tuck shop (times on door). You can get something to eat at Leraback (℡01595-753226). There is a **public toilet** at the airstrip, and a **public telephone** at the airstrip shelter and in the red kiosk at Mogle, near the pier. The **post office** is in Old Grups House, south of the pier. Resident **nurse** (℡01595-753254 or 01595-753238).

West Mainland & Papa Stour

WEST MAINLAND

Flooded by the sea at the end of the last Ice Age, more than 10,000 years ago, the West Mainland is a classic drowned coastline, with a shoreline varying from the startling cliffs of the outer Atlantic coast to the long voes, or sea lochs, which poke icy fingers far into the interior. When the east coast of Shetland is smothered in sea mist the west is usually sunny, and you can always find a pleasant sheltered beach somewhere. This is very much a traditional crofting community, as well as one of the main centres of the local seafood industry, with fish farms, mussel rafts, small inshore fishing boats and, at Skeld, a large fish processing plant.

Well-maintained roads lead to dozens of peaceful corners. Most villages have a shop, post office and fuel pumps. The sea lochs of the west are ideal for yachting and kayaking and natural harbours shelter marinas at Walls and Aith, where there are berths for visitors. The annual regattas at Walls, Aith and Skeld are major events and at the **Skeld Sheepdog Trials** and the **Walls Show** – the longest-running agricultural show in Shetland – visitors are always welcomed. The area has miles of hill and coastal walks, great bird and seal-watching, as well as otter-spotting, excellent angling and some fascinating historical and archaeological sites. Traces of ancient farmsteads and field systems are everywhere and excavated sites at the **Scord of Brouster** and **Stanydale** show that crops could grow 2,000–3,000 years ago on what is now unproductive moorland. There are also several ruined brochs dating back to the Iron Age.

Westside

This begins at the top of the hill dividing Weisdale from Aithsting and Sandsting. Just below the summit, the road leading down to Tresta crosses a fault which runs south to the secluded pebble beach at **Sandsound**, a popular picnic spot. **Bixter Firth** is one of Shetland's most sheltered sea lochs and a winter favourite with twitchers, particularly for sightings of **sea ducks, divers, grebes** and waders. Bixter village has a tourist information centre at the shop. The road branches north to Aith, a large township where there is a tweed mill, a secondary school and a fine marina. The local hall doubles as a café and camping barn in summer. Just north of Aith is East Burrafirth, where a path leads up the **Burn of Lunklet** to a waterfall and on to some challenging hill walks with some impressive views. On the west side of Aith Voe is **Vementry House**, a venue for annual summer schools in traditional music. Offshore is the uninhabited island of **Vementry**, with its ruins of ancient homesteads and burial cairns, one of which is regarded as the best preserved chambered cairn in Shetland. On the west side at Swarbacks Minn are two derelict Royal Navy six-inch gun emplacements from World War I.

On the way back to Bixter is the crofting township of **Twatt**, whose name is Old Norse for 'the clearing in the trees'. Legend says sailors from the Spanish Armada built part of **St Mary's**, the pre-Reformation chapel at Sand, in thanks for deliverance from shipwreck on offlying Kirk Holm. Only the chancel arch survives. The **haa of Sand** is a fine example of a Shetland laird's house, reputedly built of stones robbed from Scalloway Castle. Over the hill in **Skeld** the **Old Sail Loft** down at the pier holds occasional musical evenings. The village has a post office, public hall and a smokehouse which turns out a wide range of seafood. Shop online, or by mail order, for fresh seafood and smoked salmon from *The Shetland Smokehouse* (Skeld ZE2 9NL; ©01595-860251; fax 01595-860203; email admin@shetland-smokehouse.co.uk; www.shetlandsmokehouse.co.uk). A couple of miles beyond Skeld are two of Shetland's most exquisite bays – **Westerwick** and **Culswick** – with pebble beaches amid granite sea stacks, cliffs and caves. A track from Culswick chapel leads to the remains of a broch on a hill overlooking the entrance to Gruting Voe and Vaila Sound.

Just north of Scutta Voe is the largest and one of the most intriguing Stone Age structures in Shetland – the extraordinary **Stanydale 'temple'**, reached by the side road from the A971 at Hulma Water. The ruins, thought to be more than 4,000 years old, are strangely located in one of the few places in Shetland where you can't see the sea. The ferry to the island of **Papa Stour** leaves from the little fishing harbour of **West Burrafirth**. From the nearby hamlet of Brindister there is a grand walk around the rocky headland of the **Neeans**. Folklore says a cave here was the hide-out of *Da Tief o' da Neean*, a notorious sheep thief who wound up in Scalloway prison. From Bridge of Walls the road passes the prehistoric site at the **Scord of Brouster**, and winds through the hills to Sandness, a crofting township in a spectacular setting overlooking St Magnus Bay and the island of Papa Stour.

Sandness has Shetland's only wool-spinning mill. *Jamiesons Spinning Shetland* (℡01595-870285), open Monday to Friday 8am to 5pm. *Journeyman Leather* (℡01595-870243; email info@journeyman-leather.co.uk; www.journeyman-leather.co.uk) produces a range of saddlery and tack, belts and bags. Visitors welcome by appointment. There are many archaeological sites in the district including a restored watermill at **Huxter** and a number of burial cairns and brochs.

Walks

The coastal walk beyond Huxter gives you breathtaking views of the wild country on the westernmost point of the Shetland Mainland, with the silhouette of the island of Foula out on the Atlantic horizon. A maze of coves and sea stacks skirts the beautiful **Bay of Deepdale** and there is more good walking through to Wats Ness, the Voe of Footabrough and Littlure. The village of Walls makes a good base for exploring the Westside, with its camping böd, B&Bs and hotel. There is also a shop, bakery, post office and cheerful boating club which welcomes visitors. The village of Walls has a fine, sheltered natural harbour and marina which attract lots of yachts in summer. The name is a corruption of the Norse *vaas*, which means 'the place of voes'. Across Wester Sound from Walls is the island of **Vaila** where Arthur Anderson, founder of the P&O shipping line, ran a fish curing business in the early 19th century. Vaila was sold to Yorkshire mill owner Herbert Anderton in 1893. He changed the Haa, built in 1696, into a summer residence, complete with massive fireplace, baronial hall, and minstrel's gallery. At one time there was a Buddhist temple above the boathouse. The island was sold in 1993.

GETTING AROUND

West Mainland bus services are operated by *Whites Coaches* (West Burrafirth, Bridge of Walls; ℡01595-809443) with a minibus feeder service to Walls operated by Mr P Isbister (Walls; ℡01595-809268), and additional services provided by Shetland Islands Council.

ACCOMMODATION

Guest Houses

Burrastow House: Walls ZE2 9PD (℡01595-809307; fax 01595-809213; email burr.hs@ zetnet.co.uk). Four-star, B&B from £40, DB&B from £70. 18th-century haa overlooks Vaila Sound on Shetland's most westerly point, two miles from Walls. Open all year except January to March, October half-term, Christmas Day and New Year's Day. Closed Sunday night and Monday to non-residents. Facilities for disabled visitors. All food is home-cooked. Vegetarians and special diets catered for.

Bed & Breakfast

Mrs C Jamieson: Skeoverick, Brunatwatt, Walls (℡01595-809349). Three-star, quiet location overlooking village of Walls, from £15 per person.

Mrs E Leask: Snarraness House, West Burrafirth (℡01595-809375; fax 01595-809211). Three-star, tranquil location, from £18 per person.

Mrs W Sutherland: Pomona, Gruting, Bridge of Walls (✆01595-810438). Two-star, over-looking Gruting Voe, £30 per person DB&B.

Self-Catering

Gilbraes Chalets: Mrs A Nicolson, Gilbraes, Twatt, Bixter ZE2 9LX (✆/fax 01595-810222; email nicolson.gilbraes@talk21.com). Two-star, on working croft, sleeps four, £100 to £280 a week.

Mrs I Gray: Vaara, Aith, Bixter ZE2 9ND (✆/fax 01595-810378; email vaara@tiscali. co.uk; www.marshvale.shetland.co.uk). Three-star, quiet area, central heating, sleeps five. £120 to £300 a week.

The Hogan: Marion Sage, Hogan, West Burrafirth, Walls ZE2 9NT (✆01595-809216; www.westburrafirth.com). Three-star, modern apartment on farmland. One bedroom, sleeps two+two, from £150 to £200.

The Lodge: Sandsound, Bixter (✆/fax 01595-8110280; email burratoon@hotmail.com). Three-star, self-contained cottage, adjacent to beach. One bedroom, sleeps two–four, from £100 to £350.

Mrs C MacBeath: Bruntskerry, Walls ZE2 9PD (✆01595-809705; email parkwest@lineone.net). Two-star, on working croft, quiet. Three bedrooms, sleeps five, from £140 to £220.

Rocklea: Mrs Helen Mackay, Walls ZE2 9PF (✆01595-809766; www.rockleavilla@tiscali.co.uk). Waterfront house, four bedrooms, sleeps five, from £275 to £360.

Camping

Skeld Caravan Site: Harbour View, Skeld ZE2 9NL (✆01595-860287; fax 01595-860362; email scottjandj@tiscali.co.uk). On the waterfront, open all year. 12 touring pitches and 12 tent sites. Caravans £10, tents £6 to £8, including shower.

Böd

Voe House (www.camping-bods.com), overlooking the picturesque village of Walls, has been restored using recycled materials. The original building is thought to have been a 16th-century manse. The böd itself probably dates from the mid-18th century and the kitchen area was once a cycle shop. Open 1 April–30 September (or by arrangement), four public rooms, dining area, sleeps 16. Shower, electricity, solid fuel stove. Shop within two miles. Disabled facilities. £5 per person a night, £80 for exclusive use (not in July or August).

HELP AND INFORMATION

The nearest **police station** is in Scalloway (✆01595-880222).
Doctor and Health Centre: Bixter (✆01595-810202); and Walls (✆01595-809352).
Ferry booking office: Papa Stour (✆01595-810460); and Foula (✆01595-753254).
West Mainland Leisure Centre: Aith (✆01595-810444; email wmlc@srt.org.uk; www.srt.org.uk).
Petrol is available at Bixter, Aith, Sandness and Walls. There are **public toilets** at Bixter, Skeld, West Burrafirth, Melby and Walls, and **post offices** at these places and at Aith, Reawick, and Sandness. **Public telephones** can be found all over.

PAPA STOUR

A mile (1.6km) across the Sound of Papa lies the island of **Papa Stour**. Its name comes from *papi* (priest) and *stórr*, which means 'large'. The name 'big island of priests' refers to the Celtic missionary community believed to have inhabited the island in the sixth–seventh centuries. Papa Stour was designated a Site of Special Scientific Interest in 1975 for its birds and their breeding grounds and its fascinating geology – a variety of Devonian Age volcanic rocks, eroded to form an incredibly indented 24 miles (38km) of coastline carved into myriad sea caves, tunnels, arches and stacks. These are exposed to the full force of the Atlantic Ocean, which makes them and breaks them. Even on the calmest of days the Atlantic swell relentlessly crashes on the shore and one famous stack, the Horn of Papa, was swept away in 1953.

As the ferry approaches the terminal at **Housa Voe** from West Burrafirth it passes **Brei Holm**, where you will get your first glimpse of the island's impressive sea caves. At the foot of Brei Holm a large tunnel cuts right through the holm and in calm weather it is possible to sail through it. The tallest of the dramatic sea stacks that cluster around the entrance to Housa Voe is known as the **Maiden (or Frau) Stack**. It was here that a Norse lord imprisoned his only daughter in 1300 for refusing to agree to an arranged noble marriage. She was rescued by her lover, a poor local fisherman. Some of Britain's finest sea caves are found around the island. **Kirstan's (or Christie's) Hole** is on the south-west of the island, at the head of a narrow creek and is confined between 98ft (30m) rock faces. A columnar stack stands sentry beside the wide natural arch that forms the entrance to this deep cave. On the north coast is the **Hole of Bordie**, a passage which penetrates nearly ½ mile (1km) into the cliff beneath **Virda Field**, which is the highest point (285ft/87m) on Papa Stour and provides a panoramic view of the island. **Francie's Hole**, within Hamna Voe, is one of the island's most attractive caves. Inside the arched entrance smaller caves branch off. Alcoves have been sculpted in the rock and a small beach lies at the back.

Archaeological Trail

The island has considerable archaeological interest and there is a trail taking in a number of sites. As there is only one short road on the island the best way to see the sites is on foot. Prehistoric man arrived here around 5,000 years ago and Neolithic dwellings, chambered cairns and Bronze Age burnt mounds, as well as more recent remains, are evident all over the island. Excavation at **Da Biggings** has unearthed the impressive foundations of a large, early medieval Norse house. An informative board is displayed on site. Above the beach at **Housa Voe** is a circle of 46 stones, the remains of the **Ting**, the site where Vikings held their assemblies. Papa Stour was important for the Norsemen, providing both a strategic base and safe haven for their galleys. By the end of the 13th century the island had become the personal property of King Haakon of Norway. Although Shetland was pledged to Scotland in 1469 the 'Lairds of Norway' kept their estates on Papa Stour until well into the 17th century. During the 18th century two lairds from Mainland Shetland, Thomas Gifford of Busta and Arthur Nicolson of Lerwick, divided Papa Stour between them and the island remains part of these estates.

In the latter part of the 19th century the Hon Edwin Lindsay, an officer in the Indian Army, was confined at **Gardie House** for 26 years by his father, the Earl of Balcarres, who thought this an appropriate punishment for his son's refusal to fight a duel. The island was also used in the 18th century to isolate 'lepers' from a colony at Walls, in West Mainland. It was not realised at the time that these unfortunates did not really suffer from leprosy, but from a disfiguring hereditary skin disease. Past the kirk and primary school the road leads to the airstrip and the open heathland. To the south you can see the remains of several heel-shaped Neolithic burial chambers. Small stone buildings around **Dutch Loch** above Hamna Voe are good examples of horizontal water mills. Originally these were two-storey buildings with turf roofs. They were built into banks to give access to the upper floor where the millstone was sited. Many were in use here until the early 20th century.

Crofting is the main way of life for the 32 islanders concentrated on the east side of the island. In addition, some crofters fish part-time in their own boats. There is an important brown crab fishery in the waters around the island, but this is worked mainly by fishermen from the Mainland. A cultural echo of the past is the **Papa Stour Sword Dance**, which is performed at traditional festivals and gatherings. Each dancer performs in turn while a fiddler plays and the dancer's praise is sung in verse. The dance ends in a shield of interlocking swords. It was popular in the Middle Ages and known throughout Europe in different forms. Sir Walter Scott describes the dance as a Norse tradition in his novel *The Pirate*, which he wrote after his visit to Shetland in 1814.

Wrecks

Papa Stour has seen many **shipwrecks**, the most famous being the *Ben Doran*, which ran on the Ve Skerries in 1930. After three days a lifeboat arrived from Stromness, in Orkney, 120 miles (193km) away. All local attempts to save the men had failed and this resulted in a lifeboat being stationed at Aith from 1933. Tiptans Skerry in Hamna Voe has claimed a number of Dutch, French, German and Norwegian ships, while increasing numbers of scuba divers are attracted to the wreck of the 3,847-ton steamship *Highcliffe* which sank off Forewick Holm in February 1940. This time all 35 crew members were taken off safely by the Aith lifeboat. When smoke from the grounded ship's funnel wafted over the Papa Stour shoreline one aged woman fled to a neighbouring cottage, saying the Germans had invaded and were trying to gas everyone. In December 1977, the *Elinor Viking* also hit the Ve Skerries, tearing a hole in her side. Two years later the Northern Lighthouse Board put a lighthouse on these treacherous rocks. The tips of the Ve Skerries can be seen, just above the sea surface to the north-west. They might look small, but the shallow *baas*, or submerged reefs, stretch out much further. Offshore to the west of Papa Stour are the exposed skerries of Fogla and Lyra, where relentless wave action has punched huge passages through which the sea surges.

FLORA AND FAUNA

The island is divided by a hill dyke that separates the fertile eastern land from the moorland of the *scattald*, or common grazing, to the west. In the past turf and peat from the *scattald* were removed and used by the islanders for fertiliser and fuel and this has resulted in a scalped heathland of sparse vegetation, including **ling**, **thyme**, **mountain everlasting**, **spring squill**, **plantain**, **heath spotted orchid** and **woolly hair moss**. The open *scattald* provides a perfect environment for ground-nesting birds such as **ringed plovers**, **great skuas**, **Arctic skuas** and **Arctic terns** and Papa Stour is now recognised internationally as an important area for the large number of terns that nest here in the summer breeding season. Some 18 species of seabirds, including **fulmars**, **guillemots**, **razorbills**, **kittiwake** and **puffins**, nest along the coast among clumps of **sea pinks** and **campion**.

Although the distance between high and low tide is only 7ft (2m) turbulent seas keep the shore above high-water mark swept and splashed by waves, which allows marine and shore life to live high up on the shore and extends the intertidal zone by up to 26ft (8m). Seals are regular visitors. **Common seals** haul ashore to pup in June and July. In October, the furry white coats of **grey seal** pups dot the beaches. More difficult to see are **harbour porpoises**, the occasional pods of **killer whales** which swim past the island, and the **otters** which hunt off the low rocky shores of the islands and voes.

GETTING THERE

By Air

Directflight (✆01595-840246) flies to the island from Tingwall Airport (✆01595-810460). The flight takes 10 minutes and departs Tingwall at 9am and 4pm Tuesday (3pm in winter). The return flight to Tingwall leaves at 9.20am and 4.20pm (3.10pm in winter). The return adult fare is £35 (senior citizens £17.60).

By Sea

Most visitors arrive on Papa Stour by boat, less than 45 minutes from West Burrafirth, on the west Mainland to the pier in Housa Voe, on the east side of Papa Stour. There are toilets and parking facilities at West Burrafirth pier. Otters are often seen around the pier and even board boats in search of fish. The Papa Stour passenger-only ferry leaves from West Burrafirth on Monday, Wednesday, Friday and Saturday at 9am, and Friday, Saturday and Sunday (bookings only for these three days) at 6pm. For bookings contact Ulsta Booking Office (✆01957-722259). Confirm 24 hours before departure. All sailings weather permitting. Further information on Papa Stour Services (✆01595-743977). You can also contact

Shetland Islands Council (Town Hall, Lerwick ZE1 0HB; ℂ01595-693535; fax 01595-695590; email sic@sic.shetland.gov.uk).

ACCOMMODATION

North House Guest House: Andy and Sabina Holt-Brook, North House, Papa Stour ZE2 9PW (ℂ01595-873238). One-star, working croft, seashore location, home cooking with local seafood and croft produce. £20 per person B&B. Full board accommodation is also offered. Transport can be organised.

Hostel

Hurdiback: Gwyneth and Alan Thomas, Papa Stour ZE2 9PW (ℂ01595-873229; email gwynalan@gwynalan.fsnet.co.uk), chalet style single storey, sea views. Kitchen area, shower/toilet, sitting room, sleeps eight. Self-catering or meals on request. Advance booking necessary. Open March to October, £12 a night. Member of *Scottish Independent Hostels*. You can also pitch a tent at *Robina's* (ℂ01595-873236) next door to the hostel.

HELP AND INFORMATION

There are **public telephones** at Hurdiback; a part-time **post office** at the Ark; and medical assistance from the **doctor** at Walls, on the Mainland (ℂ01595-809352).

North Mainland

NORTHMAVINE

Northmavine is almost an island in its own right. Only the narrow isthmus at **Mavis Grind** joins it to the rest of the mainland of Shetland. You can stand here on the shore of the North Sea and, with a little effort, throw a stone into the Atlantic Ocean on the other side. Vikings once hauled their longboats across this narrow waist of land to take a short-cut through sheltered waters. This is the gateway to a wild area which can still surprise. In May 1951, the body of a man was found in a shallow grave along the Gunnister road clothed in woollen clothing – breeches, cap, stockings, jacket, coat and belt. In his pockets were a small horn, a knitted purse containing silk ribbon and three late 17th-century coins, one Swedish and two Dutch. He had a birch stick, a small wooden tub, a wooden-handled knife and two wooden tablets. A reconstruction of the 'Gunnister Man' can be seen in the Royal Museum, in Edinburgh.

The vast landscape is dominated by Shetland's highest summit, **Ronas Hill** (1,475ft/ 500m). At the summit there is a fine example of a heel-shaped chambered cairn. On a clear day the view from the top is unsurpassed, taking in all of Shetland from Fair Isle to Muckle Flugga. Below, Ronas Voe cuts 7 miles (11km) into Northmavine. At **Hollanders Grave**, on the south shore of the Voe, is a memorial to Dutch sailors killed in 1674. The slope looking down on Yell Sound is dotted with the chambered cairns and standing stones. The slopes of the Beorgs of Housetter are known as the **Giant's Garden**, an area of jumbled rocks legend says fell from the net of boulders a giant had collected to build a causeway to Yell, where he planned to rustle stock. Locals catapulted him to his death from the escarpment. His grave is marked by red granite stones – 6ft 6 inches (2m) at the foot and an 8ft (2.4m) stone at the head – indicating an occupant around 19ft (5.8m) tall.

Atlantic Coast

To the east lies Sullom Voe, Shetland's largest sea inlet, and to the west is St Magnus Bay and the Atlantic Ocean. The coast at Eshaness, the Ness of Hillswick, Fethaland and the banks around Ronas Hill are home to vast colonies of breeding seabirds. The isle of **Uyea** is a noted nursery for grey seals. Some of Britain's oldest rocks, nearly three billion years old, are at Uyea, which is also said to have the best grazing in Shetland. The volcanic rocks – black basalts and purple andesites – forming the cliffs at Eshaness contain agates and amethysts.

The Atlantic coastline from the Ness of Hillswick north to Uyea displays an unrivalled array of cliffs, stacks, geos, blowholes, natural arches, caves and gloups. From **Eshaness Lighthouse** an easy walk leads you to the **Holes of Scraada** (Old Scratch, or the Devil), which were formed when the roof fell in at the end of a deep, narrow cave stretching in from the sea for more than 130 yards (119m). Further on is the **Grind o' da Navir** ('Gate of the Borer'), a huge, vertical-sided gateway in the cliffs where the sea has torn a huge chunk of rock out of the cliff face and hurled it inland. Nearby is the **Loch of Houlland**, where there is a ruined Iron Age broch. Out to sea on your far left are **the Drongs** off Hillswick, weirdly shaped rocks rising like gigantic teeth from the sea. Closer in is **Dore Holm**, an islet with a natural rock arch big enough for a boat to sail through. There is a car park near Eshaness Lighthouse and an information board. The late Dr Tom Anderson (1910–91), well-known traditional fiddler and composer, was born and is buried at Eshaness. He wrote more than 500 tunes and the one played at this funeral, *Slockit Light* ('Extinguished Light'), evoked the crofthouse lights going out as the Eshaness population dwindled. The main A970 road ends at Isbister, but a track leads to the **Point of Fethaland**, which is a popular but fairly strenuous hike. From the point you can look out to the jagged Ramna Stacks, an RSPB reserve which is thronged by seabirds in summer.

In the 18th and 19th centuries Fethaland was one of Shetland's busiest deep-sea fishing stations, with 60 boats based here. The ruins of 20 lodges still stand not far from a circular mound believed to cover the remains of a 4,000-year-old homestead. The Vikings left their mark on a nearby soapstone cliff where you can make out the shape of bowls and utensils carved from the cliff face. Make sure you are well equipped if you walk in this rugged area. There are other enjoyable **scenic walks** around Fethaland, and the rest of Northmavine – the Ness of Hillswick, between Hillswick and Braewick, along Ronas Voe past Heylor, at Nibon and Mangaster and by Gluss Isle and Bardister, near Ollaberry. All offer wildlife attractions, geological features and archaeological remains. At Hillswick, where the man-made beach was used for drying fish, **the Booth**, a former Hanseatic trading post, has stayed in business for more than 300 years. It is now a vegetarian restaurant.

Aspects of life in Northmavine over the years are well illustrated at **Tangwick Haa Museum** (Eshaness ZE2 9RS; ✆01806-503389). The haa was built in the late 17th century for the Cheyne family, lairds of the Tangwick Estate and elsewhere in Shetland. The manor which houses the small museum was the home of Captain Cheyne, who was killed by South Pacific islanders in 1866. The museum is open from 1 May to 30 September, Monday to Friday from 1pm to 5pm, and Saturday and Sunday from 11am to 7pm. Admission is free.

Crofter John Williamson (1740-1804) of Hamnavoe was better known as 'Johnnie Notions' for his inventive mind. Though uneducated, he hit upon the idea of inoculation against smallpox, saving thousands of local people from this 18th century scourge. A camping böd at Hamnavoe carries his nickname. He is buried at the medieval Cross Kirk, once a principal place of pilgrimage. Snails collected here were dried and used as a remedy for jaundice.

To the east of Northmavine are the districts of **Nesting, Lunnasting** and **Delting**, where in the space of a few miles you can leave the dramatic fjord-like landscape of Dales Voe and look down on the massive oil and gas terminal stretched along the shore of **Sullom Voe**. Every week, millions of barrels of oil from the North Sea oil fields are pumped into giant tankers here bound for refineries worldwide. No visitors are allowed. A few minutes' drive from the terminal and you can stand all alone in a secluded valley, on a tranquil beach or on the banks of a sparkling trout stream.

Ten miles (16km) north of Lerwick is the 'Nesting Loop' side road, which branches off the main A970 road to make a pleasant detour over the moors to Voe. Past the Loch of Benston and its wild swans an even smaller road leads to Vassa Voe and the promontories of Gletness and Eswick. Gletness is home to a stud of Shetland ponies. Scan the tiny isles of Gletness with binoculars and you may spot *dratsi*, the otter. The lighthouse at the Moul of Eswick has a panoramic view of Whalsay and the Out Skerries to Bressay and Noss. The road to North Nesting passes a prehistoric standing stone near Skellister. From Brettabister an offshoot leads to the headland of Neap, the starting point for fine coastal walks out to either the Staney Hog or Stava Ness, where **ravens** and **puffins** nest. For one of the finest views of the islands walk up to the World War I watchtower on top of **Kirk Ward Hill** near the hamlet of Billister.

A couple of miles north of Billister, the crofting township of **Laxo** lies on either side of the Laxo Burn, famous for its sea trout. From Laxo the Ro-Ro ferry sails for Whalsay. In strong south-easterly winds the ferry berths at the village of *Vidlin*, terminal for the Out Skerries ferry. In Vidlin, instrument maker Kenny Johnson of *Skyinbow Fiddles* (The Workshop, Vidlin ZE2 9QB; ✆01806-577234; email info@skyinbow.com; www.skyinbow.com) is especially known for his bright electric instruments, which have been featured in *Lord of the Dance*.

In the days before roads when most cargo and passengers travelled by sea the headland of Lunna was a busy trading and commercial centre. Vessels bound for Lerwick from the North Isles and Westside would call in at the natural harbour of West Lunna Voe. This is overlooked by **Lunna House**, the 17th-century mansion of the Hunter family. Nearby is a watchtower built by them to spy on their tenants fishing offshore and also to watch out for Customs officers. Like most island landowners, the Hunters were smugglers. **Lunna Kirk** was built in 1753 and is one of the oldest churches in Shetland still in use. In one wall is a 'leper hole' allowing the afflicted to take part in services without entering the church. With Scalloway, Lunna is famous as a secret wartime base for Norwegian resistance operatives whose heroic story is told in *The Shetland Bus*, by David Howarth, the British naval officer who ran the operation from Lunna House. Thriving but elusive **otters** have made part of Lunna Ness a Site of Special Scientific Interest (SSSI). Easier to see are **common** and **grey seal** colonies on the skerries between the ness and Lunna Holm and at the Skerry of Lunning. Not far away are the Loch of Stofast and the mysterious **Stanes of Stofast**, a 2,000-ton glacial boulder split in two by frost. This is a heavily glaciated landscape with eerily shaped rocks associated in Shetland folklore with *trows* (trolls).

The Delting district has seen increased prosperity since the discovery of oil off Shetland, with new houses everywhere and modern roads converging on Sullom Voe. **Voe** is a striking Norwegian-looking village with its colourful houses nestling at the head of Olna Firth. Voe was an important 19th-century base for cod fishing. On the north side of Olna Firth is ruined **Olnafirth Kirk** (1714), which is the burial place of the Adies, lairds of Voe, and the Giffords, lairds of Busta. From Voe, the road to the large, modern village of Brae follows Olna Firth past shellfish farms and an old whaling station. **Brae**, on the shores of Busta Voe has a good social amenities, but like all modern agglomerations seems a soulless sort of place.

GHOSTS AND GARGOYLES
Not so Busta House across the water from Brae, which is now a fine hotel. The earliest part of the house was built in 1588 by the Giffords. In 1748, wealthy Thomas Gifford and his wife were horrified when they found that their eldest son and heir John wanted to marry his orphaned cousin Barbara, who lived in as a companion to Lady Gifford. Lady Gifford told a friend she would rather see John dead at her feet than married to Barbara. Once calm May evening John, his three brothers, their tutor and a boatman, set off across the voe to visit relatives. When they did not return search parties were sent out. The boat was found but there was no trace of the six men. Eventually the bodies of John Gifford and the tutor were recovered and the son was laid dead at his mother's feet. Barbara died grieving at 35 and it is said that her ghost appears from time to time in Busta House. The house was bought in the 1950s by Sir Basil Neven-Spence, MP and Lord Lieutenant of Shetland. He was able to rescue and bring to Shetland some gargoyles being tossed out during renovation work at the House of Commons, in London. The gargoyles can be seen in the gardens.

Beyond Busta is the crofting island of **Muckle Roe**, linked by bridge to the mainland. Peat is still cut by hand using a specially shaped spade called a *tushkar*. The **Hams of Roe**, a deserted settlement among red granite cliffs at the north end of the island, is a favourite with walkers. **Sullom Voe** is the longest and most sheltered sea loch in Shetland, and thanks to strict environmental controls, is still a rewarding place for bird-watching, despite the huge tankers, pipelines and gas flares of the massive oil terminal. Sullom Voe – it means 'a place in the sun' – oil terminal and port was built in 1978 and is the largest of its kind in Europe. Crude oil flows through two underwater pipelines from North Sea oilfields about 100 miles (160km) north-east of Shetland to onshore pipeline terminals here, where supertankers are loaded. The flare stack burning off the excess gas can be seen from afar. The construction of the terminal and associated port and storage facilities, power station, and processing plant to separate gas from crude oil was the largest civil engineering project to be undertaken in western Europe since World War II, and is regarded as one of the key achievements of the Scottish offshore petroleum industry.

Victoria Crosses. World War II became a reality in Shetland when the first bomb to be dropped on British soil landed in Sullom. The only casualty was a rabbit, which allegedly inspired the famous wartime song *Run, Rabbit, Run*. During World War II, Sullom Voe was an RAF Coastal Command station for Sunderland and Catalina flying boats. Two Victoria Crosses were awarded to airmen serving there. Flt-Lt David Hornell of the Canadian Air

Force was awarded his VC posthumously on 24 June 1944. He ditched his aircraft in the sea after he had sunk the German U-boat which shot him down. Hornell and his crew did not survive. The other VC was awarded on 17 July 1944 to Flt-Lt John Cruikshank of 210 Squadron RAF who, despite being wounded, carried out a sustained attack on a U-boat. A **memorial** dedicated to RAF Sullom Voe and all those who served and gave their lives can be seen in the car park on the approach road to the Sullom Voe terminal.

At Firth, where the road branches off to the Toft ferry terminal for Yell, Unst and Fetlar, 'oil boom' housing estates look out to ruins across Firth Voe. The crofting townships here lost 22 local fishermen in the 'Delting Disaster' of 1900 and a memorial to commemorate those who died stands at the Mossbank junction, two miles (3km) south of the Toft ferry terminal. The disaster was one of the worst fishing tragedies ever to strike Shetland, sweeping away almost the entire male population of Toft, Firth and Mossbank. The memorial is built with stone from the ruins of the houses where the men lived and shingle from the beaches where they launched their boats and is surmounted by a model of the open Shetland-type rowing boat used by fishermen until early in the 20th century. The headland of Fora Ness is connected to Swinster by an unusual triple ayre, sandspits enclosing the lagoon of **Houb**, a designated SSSI where pollen found in submerged peat reveals that large areas were once covered in thick scrub. Across the racing tides of nearby Yell Sound lie the North Isles – Yell, Fetlar, and Unst – while to the east lie Whalsay and the Out Skerries.

GETTING AROUND

North Mainland bus services are operated by *John Leask & Sons* (Esplanade, Lerwick; ✆01595-693162), Toft–Mossbank–Lerwick, Monday to Sunday; other routes by *Whites Coaches* (West Burrafirth, Bridge of Walls; ✆01595-809443) Monday to Saturday; and *Johnson Transport* (Brae; ✆01806-522443).
Taxis: Archie Jack, Sullom Voe (✆01806-242501).

ACCOMMODATION
Hotels

Busta House Hotel: Busta, Brae ZE2 9QN (✆01806-522506; fax 01806-522588; email reservations@bustahouse.com; www.bustahouse.com). Three-star 16th-century former laird's home, overlooking the sea, 27 miles (43km) north of Lerwick on the A970, 22 rooms en suite. From £50. Cosy bar serving a choice of 160 malt whiskies, bar lunches and suppers, open seven days a week Monday to Saturday midday to 2.30pm and 6.00pm to 9.30pm. List of more than 100 old and new world wines.

Brae Hotel: Brae ZE2 9QJ (✆01806-522456; fax 01808-522026; email reception@brae-hotel.co.uk; www.braehotel.co.uk). Three en suite bedrooms, from £25. Restaurant and *The Northern Lights* bar have a daily menu.

St Magnus Bay Hotel: Hillswick ZE2 9RW (✆01806-503372; fax 01806-503373). The village of Hillswick is dominated by this hotel, a wooden building prefabricated in Norway for use at the Great Exhibition in Glasgow in 1896. It was bought by the North of Scotland Orkney and Shetland Steam Navigation Company and re-erected in Hillswick in 1902.

Guest Houses

Almara: Mrs M Williamson, Upper Urafirth, Hillswick ZE2 9RH (✆/fax 01806-503261; email almara@zetnet.co.uk; www.almara.shetland.co.uk). Four-star B&B from £25, near Eshaness cliffs and Ronas Hill. Open all year, no smoking throughout. Accomplished cooking such as dressed Eshaness crab with Rebecca sauce, and Scallop Arianne: scallop and monkfish tail sautéed in sherry, topped with Parmesan cheese. Unlicensed. Vegetarians welcome.

Valleyfield Guest House: Marina Nicolson, Brae ZE2 9QJ (✆01806-522563; email marinanicolson@hotmail.com). Three-star, homely family-run guest house, £30 per person.

Bed & Breakfast

Lunna House: Mrs Erwood, Lunna, Vidlin ZE2 9QF (✆01806-577311; fax 01806-242850; email stay@lunnahouse.co.uk; www.lunnahouse.co.uk), historic laird's mansion. Former HQ of the *Shetland Bus*. Family home, from £30.

Westayre: Elsie Wood, Muckle Roe, Brae ZE2 9QW (✆01806-522368; email westayre@ ukonline.co.uk; www.westayre.shetland.co.uk). Four-star. Comfortable modern family home on working croft. Quiet area, close to sandy beaches and magnificent cliff scenery. En suite facilities, £26 per person.

Self-Catering

Croft Cottage: Sweening ZE2 9QE (✆01806-577224; email croftcottagesweening@yahoo. co.uk). Three-star, spacious cottage, close to sea. Two bedrooms, sleeps four, from £195 to £310.

Mrs J Mouat: Swinster, Ollaberry ZE2 9RX (✆01806-544275). Two-star, traditional stone-built cottage on working croft, view over Ronas Voe and Ronas Hill, sleeps two, £120 to £160 a week.

Stuytak: Mrs W Balfour, Busta, Brae ZE2 9QN (✆01806-522589; www.nibon.shetland. co.uk). Three-star, overlooking Nibon Isle, sleeps 4, £200 to £260 per week.

Upper Garden: Mrs LM Grains, Ulvik, Skelberry, Vidlin ZE2 9QD (✆01806-577215; fax 01806-577343). Four-star, traditional house with views of Vidlin Voe, sleeps six, £185 to £310 per week.

The *Voxter Centre:* (✆01806-588205). Near Brae the centre provides a good base for a group. It can accommodate 27 people in four six-bedded rooms plus a leader's room/office and a room for disabled visitors. Facilities include a fully equipped kitchen, dining and recreation rooms, as well as a well-equipped field studies area, showers, changing and drying rooms. Open 9am to 12.30pm weekdays. All visits must be pre-booked.

Eshaness Lighthouse is set amidst cliff top scenery. It has three bedrooms, sleeps six, and costs from £200 to £450 a week. To book contact VisitShetland, Market Cross, Lerwick ZE1 0LU (✆0870-199 9440; fax 01595-695807; email info@visitsheltand.com).

Eating

The Baker's Rest: Walls Bakery, Walls ZE2 9PF (✆01595-809308; fax 01595-809701; email wallsbakery@btconnect.com). Family-run tea room, hot and cold snacks, soup, oatcakes, filled bannocks, sandwiches, pies, pastries fresh from the bakery. Open Monday to Saturday 10.30am to 4.30pm, Sunday midday to 4.30pm.

Böd

Johnnie Notion's (www.camping-bods.com), at Eshaness on the north-west coast, is a small cottage associated with the pioneer 18th century smallpox inoculator John Williamson. Nearby are some of Shetland's most spectacular seabird cliffs, freshwater lochs with excellent wild trout fishing, superb hillwalking, and fascinating Tangwick Haa. Open 1 April to 30 September (or by arrangement), one bedroom, sleeps seven, no electricity. Shop within two miles (3km). £5 per person per night. £35 exclusive use (not in July or August).

The *Sail Loft* (www.camping-bods.com), in Voe, once a store for sail fishing boats' gear and later a knitwear workshop, is the largest of Shetland's böds. It stands between the tideline and a handy bakery in a village setting, at the head of mini-fjord Olna Firth. Open 1 April to 30 September (or by arrangement), three public rooms, one bedroom, sleeps 18. Showers, electricity, solid fuel stove. Shop within two miles (3km). Disabled facilities. £5 per person a night. £90 exclusive use (not in July and August).

Camping

Braewick Café & Campsite: Breiwick, Eshaness ZE2 9RS (✆01806-503345; www.eshaness. shetland.co.uk). Views over St Magnus Bay, open all year. Ten touring pitches, 30 tents. Caravans £12.50, tents £6.50.

HELP AND INFORMATION

Police Station: Brae (✆01806-522381).

Doctor: Hillswick (✆01806-503277); and Brae (✆01806-522543).

North Mainland Leisure Centre: Brae (✆01806-522321; email nmlc@srt.org.uk; www.srt. org.uk). Swimming pool, squash court, fitness suite and sports hall. Contact for opening times and charges.

Petrol is available in Hillswick, Ollaberry, North Roe, South Nesting, Vidlin, Voe, Brae, Firth. **Public toilets** at Hillswick, Vidlin, Laxo, Voe, Brae, Toft. **post offices** at Hillswick, Ollaberry, South Nesting, Vidlin, Voe, Brae, Mossbank. **Public telephones** are at most places.

Whalsay & Out Skerries

WHALSAY

Keep a lookout during the ferry crossing to Whalsay and you will see why the Vikings called it *Hvals-oy*, the 'island of whales'. The 390ft (119m) **Ward of Clett** reminded them of a surfacing cetacean. Later it was dubbed the 'Bonnie Isle' by 19th-century Scots fishermen, but it was the Norse name that stuck. Whalsay is about 5 miles (8km) by 2 miles (3km) and lies some 3 miles (5km) east of the Shetland Mainland. The population is around 1,000 and the main settlement is at **Symbister**, whose harbour is the main port for some of the most modern fishing vessels in Europe. Shetland's large purse-seiners are owned and operated from Whalsay, which as a result can also claim to be home to most of Shetland's millionaires. Vessels owned and crewed by local families throng the sheltered dock, from the smallest creel boats to enormous trawlers. The fleet catches herring and mackerel round Britain and Ireland; smaller vessels take whitefish and shellfish. There is a modern fish-processing factory, *Whalsay Fish Processors*, which exports most of its products to Australia and America and has won the Queen's Award for export achievement. Next to the **Whalsay Boating Club**, which welcomes visitors, are the ruins of a former herring curing station. The inner harbour is crowded with colourful dinghies and the distinctive double-ended Shetland model skiffs which compete in local sailing and rowing races. Competitive sailing features strongly in the summer months.

At the harbour is **Pier House**, a Hanseatic böd used by German merchants who traded in Shetland salt fish until the early 18th century. This picturesque old building, was one of two Hansa böds, or booths, in use in Whalsay until the German traders were forced out by import duties imposed following the 1707 union of England and Scotland. Tradition says a smugglers' tunnel ran under 'Bremen Strasse', the road outside the böd, to the cellars of the Auld haa, the former home of the Bruce lairds. The soil in the garden at the haa came from Spain as ballast in the laird's ships after they had landed their fish. The böd is open daily, all year round, and features displays of historical and general information. Along with examples of trade goods, interpretive panels tell the story of the Hanseatic German traders back to 1557. You can get the key from the shop opposite and there is a small entrance fee. Overlooking the harbour entrance is **Symbister House** built in 1823 by Robert Bruce. The Bruces once owned most of Whalsay and ruled the islanders with a heavy hand for more than 300 years, but they were almost bankrupt after building Symbister House, or the New Haa. Despite using tenants as forced labour, construction cost a fortune and the estate's finances never recovered. The former laird's granite edifice is regarded as one of the best examples of Georgian architecture in the north of Scotland. Part of it has been the local junior high school since 1940.

Archaeological Sites

The island has been inhabited since around 3,000BC and evidence of one of its earliest settlements has been unearthed on the east side of the island. This is Neolithic **Hoxie House**, which at one time was thought to be a temple, but is now recognised as being the site of a large farmhouse. In the south-west, near Sandwick Loch, are two Bronze Age burnt mounds. The locally named **Broch of Huxter**, on an islet in the Loch of Huxter, is a ruined Iron Age fort, reached by a rubble causeway. Shetland's record 9lb 4oz (4.2kg) brown trout was caught in this loch. Visiting anglers are welcome and the lochs on the island are controlled by the Whalsay Angling Association. The road runs up the north side of Whalsay to Skaw, and half-way up the south side to Isbister, with a connecting loop across the island. North from Isbister are oval Neolithic houses and, at Pettigarth's Fields, the **Beenie Hoose** and the remains of a heel-shaped cairn with a burial cist. Viking implements have been found at Isbister and can be seen in the Shetland Museum, in Lerwick.

Apart from the Bible, Whalsay is probably the only place you'll ever find **Sodom**. Scots poet Christopher Grieve ('Hugh McDiarmid'), his wife Valda and son Michael, lived in the croft house of Sodom (from the Norn *sud-heim*, or the southern house) above North Voe between 1933 and 1942 and it was here that he wrote much of his finest poetry.

At Skaw, there is a small but well-maintained par 70 golf course, open all year round. **Whalsay Golf Club** (captain, ℂ01806-566483; clubhouse, ℂ01806-566705). **Whalsay Leisure Centre** (ℂ01806-566678; email wlc@srt.org.uk; www.srt.org.uk) at Symbister has a 49ft (15m) pool and offers a range of sporting facilities. Modern pleasure boats can be found at the marina in Baltasound, along with the *Far Haaf* a locally built replica of a *sixareen*, or six-oared boat.

FLORA AND FAUNA

Whalsay is an important landfall for birds migrating from Scandinavia and further afield in spring and autumn. Most of Shetland's seabirds are here, including **puffins**, **ducks** and **waders**. **Red-throated divers** can be spotted on the inland lochs, and the beach at **the Houb** lagoon on Kirk Ness is a good place to watch wading birds. The south and east areas offer interesting walks with **seals** and breeding seabirds along the coastline. At the geos of Yoxie on the east coast one of Shetland's rarest plants, the **sea aster**, grows. **Otters** are common but shy, except around Symbister where they've become used to harbour traffic and can sometimes be seen at close quarters.

GETTING THERE

By Air

The airstrip is near Skaw, at the northern end of the island. There are no regular scheduled air services, although the Out Skerries flight lands there on request. *Directflight* (ℂ01595-840246) also operates charter flights from Tingwall.

By Sea

The ferry terminal for Whalsay is at Laxo, a 20-mile (32km) drive north of Lerwick. The Ro-Ro vehicle and passenger ferry crossing to Symbister takes 30 minutes and the service is frequent (every 40 minutes from about 7am to 10pm), Monday to Sunday, although bookings are advisable in the peak season. Booking office is open 8.30am to 1pm and 2pm to 5pm (ℂ01806-566259). Under certain weather conditions the ferry service operates from Vidlin. For more information (ℂ01595-743973), or contact *Shetland Islands Council* (Town Hall, Lerwick ZE1 0HB; ℂ01595-693535; fax 01595-695590; email sic@sic.shetland.gov.uk).

ACCOMMODATION

Accommodation on Whalsay is limited so you should book well ahead. You can get something to eat at *Oot Ower Lounge* (Livister ZE2 9AQ; ℂ01806-566658; email ootowerlounge@hotmail.com) and visitors can buy snacks in local shops, at Symbister, Harlsdale, Sodom, and Booth Park, or at the leisure centre in Symbister.

Self-Catering

Oot Ower Lounge: Mrs M Anderson, Livister ZE2 9AQ (ℂ01806-566658; fax 01806-566674; email ootowerlounge@hotmail.com), three-star chalet, sleeps five, £150 to £250 a week.

Mrs S. Simpson: 1 Bothies, Symbister, Whalsay ZE2 9AQ (ℂ01806-566429), two-star, modern spacious cottage, sleeps two, £150 to £200 a week.

Böd

Grieve House (www.camping-bods.com) at Sodom, above North Voe, is where Scottish poet Hugh McDiarmid (real name Christopher Grieve) lived for nine years. Open 1 April–30 September (or by arrangement), one bedroom, sleeps 10, solid fuel stove, no electricity. Shop within two miles. £5 per person a night, £50 exclusive use (not in July or August).

HELP AND INFORMATION

Police Station: Gardentown (☎01806-566432).
Doctor: North Park (☎01806-566219); Dr Marshall (☎01806-566501); relief doctor (☎01806-566203).
Ferry booking office: Symbister (☎01806-566259).

There is a **post office** at Harlsdale; **public telephones** at Symbister ferry terminal, and at Brough crossroads. **Public toilets** at Symbister, Skaw, and South Play Park. **Petrol** is available at Symbister and Booth Park.

OUT SKERRIES

Three principal islands make up Out Skerries – **Bruray, Housay** and **Grunay**, although there are plenty of stacks and other skerries scattered around their 540 acres (219ha). The islands are some 5 miles (8km) from Whalsay and 10 miles (16km) east of the Shetland Mainland. The larger islands of Housay and Bruray, often called East Isle and West Isle respectively, are connected by a concrete bridge built in 1957. Fewer than 90 people live on Bruray and Housay, but they make up a friendly community thriving on fishing and salmon farming. Grunay, across Northeast Mouth from Bruray, is uninhabited.

The harbour entrance through the South Mouth is narrow and guarded by imposing Stoura and Old Man's stacks. The little local fishing fleet berths around the jetty where the ferry docks. Historically, the protected natural harbour was crucial to the development of the *haaf*, or deep-sea fishing industry, providing a haven for the fishermen who, in small open boats, powered by oars and a single square sail, fished far out of sight of land. Fishing is still an important activity for islanders, along with the community-owned salmon farm. At North Mills on Housay and Lang Ayre on Bruray you can see the ruins of *haaf* lodges and near the pier is an iron kettle once used to melt fish livers and later to prepare the preservative bark used to coat fishing lines and nets. Man-made **Ling Beach** was constructed for drying fish and gets it name from the once prolific species of cod which was a prime export. The beach is now disused and overgrown.

Islanders still catch and dry fish but today you are more likely to see *piltocks* (coalfish, or saithe) hanging out to dry on washing lines. Smuggling was also once a source of income. The far easterly position of Skerries made it a good isolated landing point for smugglers from Scandinavia and Holland and the caves and inlets were ideal for storing contraband. The coastline is endlessly fascinating and names of local features have interesting historical links. **Tammie Tyrie's Hidey Hol**, for instance, recalls one local who escaped the Royal Navy's press-gang whenever it arrived by ducking into this coastal hole on Housay. For sweeping views of the islands and, in the distance Fetlar, Yell, Whalsay and the Mainland, climb to the top of the Bruray Hill, North or South Hill.

Green Oasis

Croft cultivation is not as intensive now as it once was, but Skerries still has well-preserved *rigs*, narrow strips of land still producing *tatties* (potatoes), *neaps* (turnips) and carrots. Gone, though, is the practice of *runrig*, a system of rotation once essential to ensure everyone received a fair share of good land. Sheep are still plentiful, providing delicate lamb and the wool which many Skerries women knit into shawls and warm *gansies* (pullovers). In spring the island becomes a surprisingly green oasis. Visitors arriving by air are impressed by the shock of **sea pinks** growing on grassy banks and cliff-tops. You are free to walk anywhere on Out Skerries and as you wander around you'll notice intriguing signs of past settlement. The most interesting is a 43ft (13m) Bronze Age stone circle at **Battle Pund**. In Scotland, these were sites where blood feuds were settled in single combat.

There's also plenty to interest scuba divers and marine archaeologists as the rugged coast and its surrounding islets, reefs and rocks have wrecked many vessels, among them great sailing ships such as the 17th-century Dutch East Indiaman *Kennermerland* and *De Liefde*, wrecked in the 18th century, their treasure chests revealed hundreds of years later by finds of silver and gold coins washed up on the shore. At south-westerly **Point of Mioness** a silver ducatoon and a 1711 gold ducat were found in 1960, starting a feverish treasure hunt. Since then the two wrecks and that of Danish warship *Wrangels Palais* have been picked over and are now legally protected. Diving on them without permission is strictly forbidden. Wood from the cargo of the German sailing ship *Norwind*, wrecked in 1906, still clads the walls and floors of many local homes.

In spring and autumn, the islands are noted for visiting rare migrant birds, one of the more unusual being **Pallas's grasshopper warbler**. There is a large breeding population of **guillemots** and a variety of other seabirds, as well as **otters** and **seals** around the shore. The Benelips and Filla, small rocks off the south-west point, are often thronged with seals. East of Grunay, on tiny **Bound Skerry**, is the tall tower of the lighthouse built in 1857 on Shetland's easternmost point. The signature of 19th-century Scottish writer Robert Louis Stevenson appears in the visitor's book. The keepers' old houses still stand on Grunay but the light is now automatic and the dwellings are empty. A Canadian bomber crashed here during World War II and a **memorial plaque** was placed on the island in 1990.

GETTING THERE
By Air
The airstrip is on Bruray. The *Directflight* flight from Tingwall to Out Skerries takes 20 minutes. There is a flight on Monday and Wednesday at 1.30pm (Monday 1.50pm and Wednesday 12.50pm in winter), and Thursday 9am and 4pm (9am and 2.55pm in winter). The return flights are on Monday and Wednesday at 2pm (9.30am and 4.30pm in winter), and Thursday at 9.30am and 4.30pm. The fare is £39 return for adults (senior citizens £19.60) The flight goes via Whalsay on request. Actual arrival and departure times at Out Skerries vary according to number of passengers travelling and whether a stop is required at Whalsay. Enquiries through Tingwall Airport (℃01595-810460) or Out Skerries (℃01806-515253).

By Sea
There is a ferry service from Vidlin, on Vidlin Voe, North Mainland, on Monday (9.30am), Friday (10am), Saturday (10am), and Sunday (10.30am). On Tuesday and Thursday you can take a ferry from Lerwick at 2.45pm. Passengers and vehicles must be booked by 5pm the previous evening. If no bookings are received the ferry does not sail. The small Ro-Ro vehicle and passenger ferry takes 1½ hours from Vidlin and 2½ hours from Lerwick. Vehicles are carried weather permitting. All bookings to GW Henderson (℃01806-515226). For more information contact ℃01595-743975 or *Shetland Islands Council* (Town Hall, Lerwick ZE1 0HB; ℃01595-693535; fax 01595-695590; email sic@sic.shetland.gov.uk). Visiting yachts are welcome, with plenty of space to anchor in calm water. Berth at the marina. Water, fuel, public toilets, showers and telephones are all available and easily accessible. The annual **Round Skerries Yacht Race** is an enjoyable social occasion, featuring music, dancing, and merrymaking at the hall.

ACCOMMODATION
Rocklea: Mrs JK Johnson, East Isle, Out Skerries ZE2 9AR (℃01806-515228; fax 01806-515282; email rockleaok@btinternet.com). Three-star, on the island of Bruray. Two double rooms, one single room, two public bathrooms. Family run. £22 per person.

HELP AND INFORMATION
There is a mile of surfaced road for the island's 20 cars, a community hall, two **shops** – one on Bruray and the other on Housay – and Britain's smallest secondary school. Lack of water can be a problem and in dry summers tankers bring in water from the Mainland. There are **public toilets** at Bruray pier; a **public telephone** at Bruray; a **post office** at Housay; and a resident **nurse** (℃01806-515225).

North Isles: Yell, Unst & Fetlar

YELL

At 17 miles (27km) by 5 miles (8km) Yell is Shetland's second largest island, supporting a population of more than 1,000 people. The island is roughly rectangular and nearly cut in two where the long voes of Whale Firth and Mid Yell almost meet. Most of the island is heather moorland, with considerable depths of peat and patches of green around crofting areas. Blanket peat covers much of the island, providing an important wildlife habitat. Peat is formed by the compression of dead plant matter and in some places on Unst it is more than 10ft (3m) deep, representing 3,000 years' deposit. It is the least fertile of the inhabited islands but it has some of the **best sandy beaches** in Shetland, especially at Hamnavoe, Gossabrough, West Sandwick and the Sands of Breckon. **Grey** and **common seals** often bask on rocks at low tide, particularly on the west coast.

Stop at the shop near the jetty if you need provisions, snacks or petrol. This is your **last chance to fill up** if you are driving. You can also hire taxis and minibuses here. The shop is open daily from 9am (3.30pm on Sundays) to 7.30pm. The main A968 road travels up the west coast, and if you are simply on your way to Unst, use this road. If you want to explore Yell, drive north on the west road and return by the east to see the best of the scenery. To the left of the main road as it curves across the island's pinched waist to Mid Yell is the Herra peninsula, which is superb for walking. At its north-west corner is **the Eigg**, 4,250 acres (1,720ha) of moorland, the last known nesting site (1910) of Shetland's **sea eagles**. Two carnivorous plants – **butterwort** and **sundew** – grow on the moorland, which is alive with breeding birds in summer. **Great skuas**, **Arctic skuas**, **terns** and **eider ducks** nest on the moorland and **whimbrel**, **red-throated divers**, **dunlin** and **golden plover** can also be seen. You might also spot Britain's smallest bird of prey, the **merlin falcon**.

On the beach at Basta Voe is the workshop of *Bayanne House* (Sellafirth ZE2 9DG; ℡01957-744219; email tony.gott@zetnet.co.uk; www.bayanne.co.uk), a pleasant halt if you are interested in textile design, genealogy and archaeology. There is also an internet café. Open all year, Monday to Sunday 9am to 9pm.

The RSPB's 3,954-acre (1,600ha) **Lumbister Nature Reserve** on the west coast has a large and varied population of waders and other species typical of Shetland, including **red-throated divers, merlin, waders, twite, lapwing** and **ringed plover**. There is a flourishing population of **otters** in the reserve. In the deep gorge known as the **Daal of Lumbister**, wild flowers grow in abundance. Standing high above the road at the head of Whale Firth is ruined **Windhouse**. Locals swear that this is haunted. Skeletons were found walled up and under the floorboards when the house, built in 1707, was renovated in 1880.

The **Leisure Centre** (Mid Yell; ℡01957-702222; email ylc@srt.org.uk; www.srt.org.uk) provides various sporting activities and has a free-form 41ft (12.5m) pool. The centre houses *Yell Crafts*, a voluntary organisation established to promote and develop crafts produced socially. Such traditional items as spinning wheels, cradles, chairs and knitwear are available (℡01957-702218; fax 01957-702072). **Mid Yell Boating Club** (℡01957-702317) welcomes visitors. At the entrance to Mid Yell Sound is the uninhabited isle of **Hascosay**, which is said to have magic soil that keeps away mice. At Sellafirth, on the way to Gutcher, is *Suphilan Crafts and Produce* at St Olaf's (℡01957-744327). As the main road approaches **Gutcher** and the jetty for the Unst and Fetlar ferry, a secondary road, the B9082, skirts Bluemull Sound and winds around to **Gloup**, once an important *haaf* station in Shetland. At Gloup is a memorial to the six boats and 58 men lost in the great storm of July 1881, leaving 85 children and 34 widows. Above the list of names is a poignant statue of a woman and child, the woman shading her eyes as she peers out to sea.

Gloup Holm has a large seabird colony and at **Burgi Geos** are the remains of an Iron Age fort. There are toilets at the Gutcher ferry terminal and the *Wind Dog Café* near the pier (℡01957-744321; www.winddogcafe.co.uk) is a good place to wait for the ferry. Open Monday to Friday 9am to 5pm, Saturday and Sunday 10am to 5pm, evening meals 6.30pm. Disabled access. Coffee and homebakes, Internet access. Opposite is **Gutcher post office**, which was bombed by the German *Luftwaffe* during World War II in an attack on the island's communications system.

Otters. Yell is one of the best places in Europe to spot otters and you'll see them all round the island. Much of Hugh Miles' award-winning BBC documentary film *The Track of the Wild Otter* was shot on location at Burra Ness, at the mouth of Busta Voe, where there is also a ruined cairn, ancient boat *noosts*, and the ruins of a well-preserved broch on the north-east promontory.

The B9081 road through the eastern half of the island starts at Mid Yell. In the local graveyard is a black marble slab, set in stone from nearby Hascosay island, commemorating the four men who died when the 1,487-ton German training barque *Bohus* was wrecked at the Ness of Queyon, near Otterswick, on 25 April 1924. Above the shore at Otterswick is the **White Wife**, the ship's reconstructed figurehead. Detour into picturesque **Vatsetter** and walk round the lochs to **Birrier**, one of Shetland's prettiest bays, connected to the mainland by an ayre, a spit of land, topped by a natural arch. Crossing this is dangerous. At Aywick is *Norman Tulloch Knitwear* (℡01957-702410).

On the south-east tip of the island, at Burravoe, is one of Yell's oldest buildings. This is the **Old Haa** (*Old Haa Trust* Burravoe ZE2 9AY; ℡01957-722339), built in 1672 and restored in 1987 as a museum and visitor centre. Open late April to end-September on Tuesday, Thursday and Saturday from 10am to 4pm, Sunday from 2pm to 5pm. Admission is free. There is also a small art gallery with interesting exhibitions and a tea-room with scrumptious homebakes. You can learn traditional hand-knitting at the Old Haa. The **knitting course** is organised by Shetland College and local instructors offer instruction in Fair Isle and Shetland designs. Accommodation is in B&B and guesthouses on the island and local tours are arranged. Cost for B&B is £744 and guesthouse £766 per person sharing for the week's course. For more information contact *John Leask & Son* (The Esplanade, Lerwick ZE1 0LL; ℡01595-693162; fax 01595-693171; email info@leaskstravel.co.uk; www.leaskstravel.co.uk).

A World War II Catalina aircraft crashed on the hill above Burravoe on 19 January 1942. Only three of her 10-man crew survived. A commemorative tapestry hangs in the Old Haa, and outside the building is an aircraft propeller. Not far from the haa are the cliffs at **Ladies Hole**, which is a good place to see **common seals** and breeding seabirds. **Fulmars**, **ringed plovers**, **black guillemots** and **oystercatchers** are common on the shores and **puffins**, **shags**, **guillemots** and **kittiwakes** on the sea cliffs.

GETTING THERE

By Sea

Two inter-island Ro-Ro ferries, *MV Daggri* and *MV Dagalien* operate from Toft (Mainland) to Ulsta (South Yell) daily from 6.30am to 11pm, at about 30-minute intervals, Monday to Sunday. The crossing takes 20 minutes and you might spot **harbour porpoises**, **pilot** and **killer whales** as you cross. The booking office is open Monday to Saturday from 8.30am to 5pm (℡01957-722259). For more information contact ℡01595-743972 or *Shetland Islands Council* (Town Hall, Lerwick ZE1 0HB; ℡01595-693535; fax 01595-695590; email sic@sic.shetland.gov.uk). It is 17 miles (27km) from the Ulsta ferry terminal to Gutcher, in North Yell, where the ferry leaves for Unst and Fetlar.

By Road

RG Jamieson & Son (Cullivoe; ℡01957-744214; fax 01957-744270; email rhjamieson@hotmail.com) provide a connecting service on the island, leaving Cullivoe at 8.20am, arriving at Ulsta at 9.20am. Leaving Ulsta at 9.30am, arriving Cullivoe 10.15am (Monday to Saturday). Also leaving Ulsta on Monday to Friday at 4.30pm (5pm Saturday), arriving

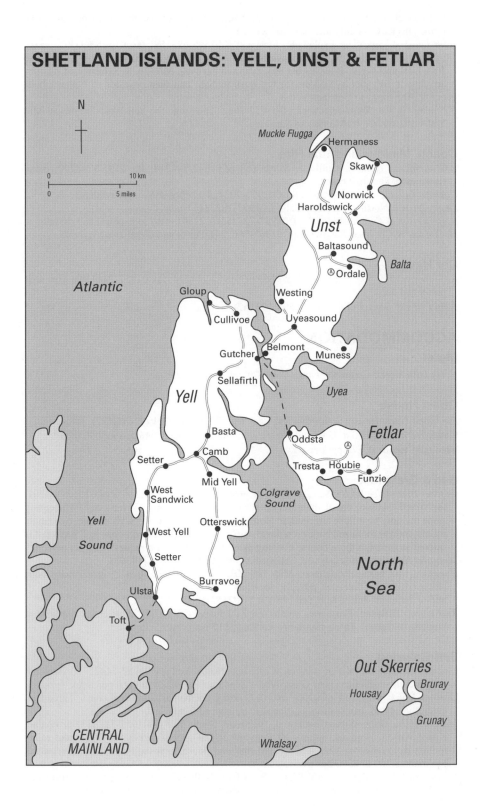

SHETLAND ISLANDS: YELL, UNST & FETLAR

N

0   10 km
0   5 miles

Muckle Flugga
Hermaness
Skaw
Norwick
Haroldswick
Unst
Baltasound
Ⓐ Ordale
Balta

Atlantic

Gloup
Westing
Cullivoe
Uyeasound
Gutcher
Belmont
Muness
Sellafirth

Yell

Uyea

Basta
Oddsta
Fetlar
Camb
Tresta Houbie
Ⓐ
Setter
Funzie
Mid Yell
West
Sandwick
*Colgrave
Sound*
Otterswick

Yell

West Yell

Sound

*North
Sea*

Setter
Burravoe
Ulsta

Toft

Out Skerries
Bruray
Housay
Grunay

*CENTRAL
MAINLAND*

Whalsay

Cullivoe after 4.58pm (5.28pm Saturday). There is also a service on Sunday during school term. Check availability and times of service.

John Leask & Son (The Esplanade, Lerwick; ✆01595-693162; fax 01595-693171; email info@leaskstravel.co.uk; www.leaskstravel.co.uk) operate a service from Lerwick to Yell, Unst and Fetlar. It leaves the bus station in Lerwick, Monday to Saturday, at 7.50am, arriving at Toft pier at 8.55am for the ferry to Yell; and then onwards to Fetlar. Check connecting times to Unst and Fetlar.

H Sinclair & Co (West–Sandwick; ✆01957-766224) operate the Yell-West–Sandwick–Mid Yell-Ulsta service on Monday to Saturday.

Coach, Minibus and Taxi Hire

R.G. Jamieson & Sons: Cullivoe, North Yell (✆01957-744214; fax 01957-744270; email rhjamieson@hotmail.com).

Norman Tulloch: Aywick, East Yell (✆01957-702427). Petrol and diesel available.

Jimmy Nisbet: North-a-Voe, Mid Yell (✆01957-702231).

R. Robertson & Son: Ulsta Ferry (✆01957-722253/722280). Also sells petrol and diesel.

H. Sinclair & Co: West Sandwick (✆01957-766224). Petrol and diesel also available.

Car Hire

R.G. Jamieson & Son: Cullivoe ZE2 9DD (✆01957-744214; fax 01957-744270). Also sells petrol and diesel fuel.

John Leask & Sons: Lerwick (✆01595-693162).

ACCOMMODATION

Motel

North Isles Motel: Cunnister, North Yell (✆/fax 01957-744294).

Guest House

Pinewood Guest House: South Aywick, East Yell ZE2 9AX (✆01957-702427). Two-star, views overlooking Fetlar, Unst and Skerries, traditional home cooking, about 30 minutes from ferry terminal, £22 per person.

Bed & Breakfast

Gutcher Post Office B&B: Margaret Tulloch, post office, Gutcher ZE2 9DF (✆01957-744201; fax 01957-744366; email margaret.tulloch@btopenworld.com). Three-star, 19th-century stone building near ferry terminal, in North Yell. Accommodation for six people, two single rooms, shower room and bathroom downstairs, twin and double bedrooms. Full breakfast is offered as well as a three-course evening meal. Packed lunch on request. £23 per person.

Margaret Hamilton: Westerhouse, Sellafirth, North Yell (✆01957-744203).

Norwind: Mrs Isobel Robertson, Mid Yell ZE2 9BJ (✆01957-702312; email norwind@ btinternet.com). Three-star, peaceful location, from £28.

Caroline Johnson: Setter, Mid Yell (✆01957-702153).

Rita Leask: Hillhead, Burravoe, South Yell ZE2 9BA (✆01957-722274; email rita.leask@ btopenworld.com). Three-star, home cooking, £19 per person.

Self-Catering

Charlie Henderson: Kirks, Gloup, Cullivoe, North Yell (✆01957-744257). Two-star, comfortable croft house near Gloup Voe, sleeps four–six, £120 to £140 per week.

Coel-na-Mara: Mid Yell (✆01957-702102; email coelnamara@hotmail.com). Three-star, centrally located, two bedrooms, sleeps four, from £140 to £280.

Manor House: John Wilson, Skibhoul, Burravoe, South Yell (✆01957-722233) or contact Karen Wilson, Hopkins, Sutton, Nr Petworth RH20 1PS (✆01798-869738; email rod@ redlion-antiques.com). One-star, fine old character house, views to Fetlar, Out Skerries and Mainland, £200 to £300 per week.

Voeview Cottage: Hillend, Mid Yell ZE2 9BJ (✆01957-702307). Two-star, recently refurbished croft house, views of Hascosay and Fetlar. Two bedrooms, sleeps four, from £150 to £300,

The Wilderness: Raga Herra, Mid Yell (✆01595-840598; email margaret.scollay@btinternet. com). Three-star, old family home. Three bedrooms, sleeps six, from £160 to £320.

Mrs Williamson: Gremister, Herra (✆01595-880117; email herra@btinternet.com; www.herra.shetland.co.uk). Four-star, spacious house. Three bedrooms, sleeps six, from £280 to £365.

Böd

Windhouse Lodge (www.camping-bods.co.uk), at the head of Whale Firth, is the solidly built gatehouse to a haunted ruin and is the best-equipped of Shetland's böds. It stands on the edge of the RSPB's Lumbister Nature Reserve. Open 1 April–30 September (or by arrangement), four public rooms, three bedrooms, sleeps 12. Hot water heater, electricity, showers. Shop within two miles (3km), solid fuel stove. Disabled facilities. £5 per person a night, £60 exclusive use (not in July or August).

HELP AND INFORMATION

Police Station: Reafirth, Mid Yell (✆01957-702012).

Doctor and Health Centre: Reafirth, Mid Yell (✆01957-702127).

Ferry booking office: Ulsta (✆01957-722259/268).

Tourist guide: Elizabeth Morewood, Gardiesting, Mid Yell (✆01957-702052; email elizabethahm@aol.com).

Wildlife guide: Terry Holmes, Basta, North Yell (✆01957-702237; email terry.otters@virgin. net).

Yell Leisure Centre: (✆01957-702222).

Post offices at Tulloch of Shetland, Linkshouse, Mid Yell (✆01957-702026; fax 01957-702068); Lawrence & Margaret Tulloch, Gutcher, North Yell (✆01957-744201; fax 01957-744366); RS Henderson, Cullivoe, North Yell (✆01957-744242); and Aywick Shop, Aywick, East Yell (✆01957-702077). Other post offices in Burravoe, Camb, and Ulsta.

Public telephones in Busta, Burravoe, Cullivoe, Gutcher, Mid Yell, Sellafirth, Ulsta and West Sandwick. There are **public toilets** at Ulsta and Gutcher ferry terminals, Mid Yell and Cullivoe piers.

UNST

You can post a letter from Britain's most northerly post office, spend a night in its most northerly hotel, tour its most northerly brewery, and admire its most northerly lighthouse and rocks – but there's more to Unst than that. In an area just 12 miles (19km) long and 5 miles (8km) wide are stupendous cliffs, jagged sea stacks, sheltered inlets, golden beaches, heathery hills, freshwater lochs, peat bogs, fertile farmland, and even a stony desert. The island is a paradise for naturalists, drawn every summer by the rich birdlife and the exquisite alpine flowers. Tiny Shetland ponies run free and the 600ft (183m) cliffs of Hermaness teem with colonies of sea birds. Extensive deposits of serpentine make the island a magnet for geologists and the story of Unst can be traced through prehistoric sites and further unfolded at the Unst Heritage Centre, in Haroldswick. It must have impressed writer Robert Louis Stevenson when he visited in 1869. If you look at his map in *Treasure Island* you'll notice an uncanny resemblance to the shape of Unst. The island is also an excellent base for scuba diving, with many wrecks, from the *Curacao*, a protected wreck which sank in 1729; the *E49*, a World War I submarine and war grave which can be dived only with permission; and the 3,161-ton SS *Tonis Chandris*, which ran aground on Vere Reef off Muness in January 1940 while zig-zagging to avoid an enemy submarine.

Unst is Shetland's third largest and most northerly island and, as it was the closest port on the route of raiding Vikings from the Norwegian seaboard, it is rich in Norse relics. It has a population of around 800. Look for grazing **Shetland ponies** on leaving the ferry terminal. Unst is particularly noted for these hardy ponies and the first stud book states that they 'foaled in the fields, live in the fields, and die in the fields'. The ponies used to be general beasts of burden, as useful for *flitting* (moving) loads of peat as for ploughing and riding.

At **Hoga Ness** to the west of the ferry terminal is a ruined broch. The dilapidated old house at **Belmont** was built in 1775 and is a classic example of 18th-century architecture. A charitable body – the Belmont Trust – has been formed to restore the house to its former glory and is looking for assistance, both financial and volunteer labour. If you'd like to help you can become a sponsor or a Friend of Belmont. For more information contact the Trust at Gardie House, Bressay, Shetland.

There is a fine walk around the south-western corner of Unst to the picturesque village of **Uyeasound**, a busy fish farming centre where there is also a youth hostel. Next to the jetty here is **Greenwell's Booth** (1646), a storehouse once used by German Hanseatic merchants, and the shop of Donald Ritch, 'Purveyor of Fine Meats, Flat Caps, and Turpentine'. The landing is sheltered by uninhabited **Uyea Isle**. The Hall there was once the home of Sir Basil Neven-Spence, the Shetland MP from the 1935 to 1950. St Sunniva chapel (12th century) south-east of the hall suggests that the isle was once well populated.

One of Unst's two prehistoric **standing stones** can be seen along the road to **Muness Castle**, the fortified residence built in 1598 by Laurence Bruce, half-brother of Robert Stewart, Earl of Orkney and Lord of Shetland, who put Bruce in charge of his lands in Shetland in 1571. Like the Stewarts, Bruce is remembered as a laird who 'excelled in avarice'. The baronial castle was put to the torch in 1627 by privateers and although rebuilt it was abandoned early in the 18th century. There is a quaintly worded inscription carved above the entrance doorway which says:

> *List ye knaw this building quha began*
> *Laurence the Bruce he was that worthy man*
> *Quha earnestly his airis and offspring prayis*
> *To help and not to hurt this wark aluayis.*
> *The Zeir of God. 1598*

There is an information panel at the entrance. They key to the castle is available from the white cottage opposite. Close to the castle is *NorNova* (Margaret Peterson, Muness, Uyeasound; ✆01957-755373; fax 01957-755353; email admin@nornova.co.uk; www.nornova.co.uk), which has a range of knitwear, lace, crafts, and souvenirs. Spinning and knitting demonstration and workshop at weekends. Snacks and teas served. Open April to October, Monday to Friday 10am to 4pm seven days a week. A walk from Muness north brings you to the sweeping sandy beach of Sandwick. At Framgord, on the far side of the beach is a ruined chapel with ancient Celtic crosses in its graveyard. Further on is the deserted township of Colvadale.

On the way to Lund is **Bordastubble**, Shetland's largest standing stone, a huge chunk of gneiss more than 12ft (3.8m) high and 9ft (2.7m) thick, standing in the middle of nowhere on a bleak stretch of moor. The derelict 18th-century house at Lund is a dangerous ruin. Locals say the Devil visited one winter's night, leaving his hoofprint on a flagstone. There are the remains of Viking houses in the field below it. A track leads down to a sandy beach overlooked by roofless **St Olaf's Chapel**, a 12th-century kirk which has a leper's window. A Pictish Christian fish symbol carved on a lintel at the church and gravestones of two 16th-century Hanseatic Bremen merchants inscribed in Low German are interesting features. On the opposite side of Lunda Wick bay is an Iron Age settlement and broch at **Underhoull**. A ninth century Viking longhouse has been excavated here and artefacts unearthed can be seen in the Shetland Museum and Archives, in Lerwick. Two Viking excavations are currently underway at sites in Hamar and Belmont (up the hill on the opposite side of the main road to Belmont House). Excavations are under way and visitors are welcome whenever the archaeologists are on site. At Brookpoint, on the road to Haroldswick, there is a replica of the Gokstad Viking Ship. The Skidbladner is also part of the Viking Unst project and during July two Vikings will be based there talking to visitors. To find out more about the Viking Unst Project you can contact the Shetland Amenity Trust (Garthspool, Lerwick ZE1 0NY; ✆01595-694688; email shetamenity.trust@zetnet.co.uk) or visit the Unst Heritage Centre. There is information about the Skidbladner at the Unst Boat Haven, home to a group or more recent, traditional, Shetland boats. The **Loch of Watlee** on the way to the straggling unofficial capital of Baltasound is good for trout fishing and is the setting for another of Unst's 30 Viking longhouses. Near the turn off from the main road to the loch is an ancient **wishing well**.

Baltasound

Baltasound has shops, a post office, hotel, marina and *Unst Leisure Centre* (℡01957-711577; email ulc@srt.org.uk; www.srt.org.uk), which has various sporting activities and a free-form 41ft (12.5m) heated swimming pool. There is also a full-size football pitch, which is home ground to Unst Football Club. Modern pleasure boats can be found at the marina along with the *Far Haaf*, a locally-built replica of a *sixareen* or six-oared boat. The harbour sheltered by Balta islet once challenged Lerwick as Shetland's main herring port during the boom years from 1880 to 1925. In the herring season the local population of 500 rose to 10,000 with the arrival of gutters and coopers working to support up to 600 boats. Today, only the breastworks of the piers remain and otters live along the harbour's north shoreline.

During World War II seaplanes and anti-submarine patrol boats were based in this all-weather anchorage to help protect Arctic convoys. There was also a detachment of Commandos; one of them was famed naturalist Peter Scott. A branch road leads to the long and narrow **Loch of Cliff**, which is popular with fly-fishermen and sailboarders. *Unst Angling Club* (David McMillan, Rockfield, Haroldswick; ℡01957-711224) has information about local trout fishing, boats for hire, and competitions during the season 25 February to 31 October.

The 74-acre (30ha) National Nature Reserve at the **Keen of Hamar** is the largest example of serpentine debris in Britain. Experts believe this is what much of Britain looked like after the last Ice Age. Here, in 1837, local boy botany wizard Thomas Edmondston discovered **Norwegian sandwort**, found in Britain only on Unst and North Ronaldsay, and **Edmondston's chickweed**, which grows nowhere else in the world. Edmondston published *A Flora of Shetland* in 1845 and died the same year aged 20 on a scientific expedition to South America. His brother-in-law, Henry Saxby, wrote *The Birds of Shetland*, published in 1894.

Haroldswick was Britain's most northerly post office until it closed its doors at the end of 1999. The title is now held by the post office at Baltasound. Britain's most northerly brewery, **Valhalla Brewery** (Baltasound; ℡01957-711648; email mail@valhallabrewery. co.uk; www.valhallabrewery.co.uk) takes its name from the ancient belief that when Vikings died they went to Valhalla, a warrior's paradise where they were revived by Norse god Odin's horn of ale. Today, the brewery quenches local thirsts with three ales and a stout, *Auld Rock*, *White Wife* and *Simmer Dim*, and *Sjolmet Stout. Auld Rock* is the islanders' affectionate name for Shetland, *White Wife* refers to a ghost that has been seen near the site of the brewery (usually after tastings), and *Simmer Dim* is named after that magical period in June when you can watch the sun sink below the horizon and rise again within a few minutes, and *Sjolmet* refers to extinct breeds of cattle and sheep with a dark body and white head. Valhalla also does a summer brew called *Old Scatness* to tie in with the archaeological dig at the south end of the mainland, which is open and worked by students in summer. Visits to the brewery by prior arrangement.

The **Unst Heritage Centre** at Haroldswick (℡01957-711528) is both a public museum and an active community centre for traditional music, crafts and local studies. The centre has exhibitions of local history, crofting traditions, fishing, knitting and folklore. Examples of the exquisitely patterned fine lace knitting so admired by the Victorians are also on display. Open May to September. Admission fee. **Unst Boat Haven** at Haroldswick (℡01957-711213) displays an excellent collection of traditional Shetland and Scandinavian fishing and sailing boats, artefacts, photos and documentary material covering Unst's fishing and seafaring heritage. Both the Centre and the Boat Haven are open 1 May to 30 September, Monday to Sunday 2pm to 5pm. Admission is free.

Next door to the boat haven is *Haroldswick Shop*, licensed general merchants, snack-bar, information, souvenirs, petrol and diesel. Open every day, except Sunday, and open throughout lunch during June/July/August and possibly September (✆01957-711371 to check).

Haroldswick is a good place to watch for **seals** and **otters**, particularly at low tide. At Clibberswick, on the eastern side of the village, is Britain's only working **talc mine**, as well as a **Viking soapstone quarry**. North-east of Haroldswick, a single-track road leads to the lovely beach and dunes of **Norwick** and to **Skaw**, where you can photograph Britain's northernmost inhabited house. Norwick has the most northerly church in the British Isles, the Methodist Chapel designed by local architect Frank Robertson. On the nearby headland of Lamb Ness are the ruins of a wartime radar station, forerunner of the modern RAF towers and domes on top of Unst's highest hill, 935ft (285m) **Saxa Vord**, known locally as 'Muckle Poobie'. The RAF station has been prominent in the life of Unst for more than half a century, although it is now being drastically downsized.

BRITAIN'S FULL STOP

In the north-west, Burra Firth voe is flanked on either side by the cliffs of Saxa Voe and Hermaness. At the head of the 3-mile (5km) sea loch is a long sandy beach. Legend says two giants, Herma and Saxa, both fell in love with the same mermaid. They started hurling boulders at each other, which landed in the sea to become Saxa's Baa, or reefs. One particularly large rock became the Out Stack, officially the end of Britain.

Hermaness National Nature Reserve encompasses 2,422 acres (980ha) of moorland and dramatic coastal scenery, with cliffs of up to 558ft (170m), and is internationally known for its 100,000 breeding seabirds, notably **great skuas**, **gannets**, **fulmars** and the largest gathering of **puffins** in Shetland. Moorland species include **skuas**, **waders** and **red-throated divers**. In the reserve a well marked path will take you as far north as you can walk in Britain, to the cliffs overlooking the **Muckle Flugga** rock on which David Stevenson built his 'impossible' lighthouse in 1854 to guide British naval convoys on their way to the Crimea during the war with Russia. The walk from the car park is a 2½-hour there and back slog but it is well worth it for the view of Muckle Flugga, Out Stack, and the boundless ocean. Boots are recommended for this boggy hill walk, which is made easier in parts by wooden boardwalks. Carry warm and waterproof clothing at all times, but remember that it is dangerous to wear waterproof trousers on steep, seaward-facing slopes. If you slip you will slide more easily.

Once the most northerly inhabited spot in the British Isles, Muckle Flugga ('Big Steep Rock') is a 29-acre (12ha) sheer wedge rising nearly 200ft (61m) out of the sea. In the days when it was manned keepers would sometimes find fish in the lighthouse gallery after a severe gale and in spite of its height above water (250ft/76m) winter seas would occasionally break clear over the top. The lighthouse is now automated. A pimple of rock can geographically claim to be the real full stop at the end of Britain. This is **Out Stack**, a stark chunk of rock several hundred yards further towards the Arctic Circle than Muckle Flugga. On this lonely rock in 1849 Lady Jane Franklin knelt to pray for the safe return of her husband, Sir John Franklin, who had sailed north in 1845 as leader of an expedition to search for the North-West Passage through the Arctic ice. Ten years after her visit to the Out Stack Lady Jane learned that her husband had perished in 1847.

If you don't feel like tackling a stiff walk round the reserve run by the Scottish Natural Heritage the nearby **Hermaness Visitors Centre** (✆01957-711278; fax 01595-692565; email hermaness_nnr@snh.gov.uk), open 14 April to 10 September, Monday to Sunday from 9am to 5pm, will give you a potted history display. Admission is free. The centre is housed in what was once the shore station for Muckle Flugga lighthouse.

Seabirds & Seals (✆01595-693434; www.seabirds-and-seals.com) has trips to Unst every day except Wednesday, from May to August. Tours depart from the Victoria Pier Slipway, near the tourist office in Lerwick, at 9.30am and 2pm (returning 1pm and 5pm). Adult fare is £30, under 16's £20, under 5's free. Complimentary tea, coffee and biscuits. **Top of Britain tour** to Muckle Flugga leaves Mid Yell Pier on Wednesday at 10am (returns 5pm). Fare £75 including meals.

Shetland Wildlife (Longhill, Maywick ZE2 9JF; ✆01950-422483; fax 01950- 422430; email info@shetlandwildlife.co.uk; www.shetlandwildlife.co.uk) organises package trips to the northern tip of Britain. An all-day cruise includes close-up views of the huge gannetries and other seabird colonies on Hermaness and Vesta Skerry, the caves and cliffs in the fjord of Burrafirth, a trip around Muckle Flugga and the Out Stack, and a visit to the Hermaness National Nature Reserve visitors centre. Sailings every Wednesday from April to September. A certificate confirming you have rounded Britain's northernmost point at 60° 51.6'N is included. The cruise is not suitable for the frail, the elderly, or children under 10. Booking is essential.

Muckle Flugga Charters (Bonavista, Brae ZE2 9QL; ✆01806-522447; fax 01806-522833; email info@muckleflugga.co.uk; www.muckleflugga.co.uk) has day trips to Muckle Flugga and surrounding areas from June to September. Depart from Baltasosund Pier in Unst, £35 a person. Diving and angling trips by arrangement.

If you play the fiddle and would like to add Shetland's unique style to your repertoire *John Leask & Son* organises **fiddle tours** to Unst. The course, co-ordinated by Shetland College, is run by experienced local instructors. Accommodation is at the Baltasound Hotel. Contact *John Leask & Son* (The Esplanade, Lerwick ZE1 0LL; ✆01595-693162; fax 01595-693171; email info@leaskstravel.co.uk; www.leaskstravel.co.uk).

GETTING THERE

By Sea

The only way to get to Unst is by ferry from North Yell. Two ferries operate every day between Gutcher (North Yell) and Belmont (Unst) on Bluemull Sound. There are sailings just about every half-hour from 6.25am to 10.15pm, Monday to Sunday. For all ferries vehicles should be booked and you must be at the terminal five minutes before departure. Bookings for late night trips must be made by 4pm the same day. The booking office is open Monday to Saturday from 8.30am to 5pm (✆01957-722259). For more information on *Bluemull Sound Services* (✆01595-743971), or contact *Shetland Islands Council* (Town Hall, Lerwick ZE1 0HB; ✆01595-693535; fax 01595-695590; email sic@sic.shetland.gov.uk).

For visiting yachtsmen there is a fine natural harbour and all-weather anchorage at Baltasound, and a new pier and marina. **Unst Boating Club** (P Thomson, Hamar, Baltasound; ✆01957-711695; fax 01957-711445), has launching and berthing facilities for boats up to 10m long and 1.5m draught. Showers in clubroom. Visiting groups of sub-aqua divers can use clubroom facilities. Clubhouse open on Sunday evenings June to September, snacks available.

By Road

Although Unst is as far north as southern Greenland, it's still easily accessible. From Lerwick it's a 45-minute drive north on the main A970 road to Toft ferry terminal. Follow the signs for the North Isles. The crossing to Yell takes 20 minutes. When you arrive at Ulsta in Yell, follow the main road to the Gutcher ferry terminal (about half an hour's drive) for the 10-minute crossing to Unst. Ferries are very busy in summer, so if you are travelling by car you should book a place by phoning the ferry office. *P&T Coaches* (Pat Thomson and Charlie Priest, Baltasound Industrial Estate, Unst; ✆01957-711666; fax 01957-711847) run a bus service, and hire out self-drive and minibus vehicles. Open seven days a week, Monday to Saturday from 8am to 6pm and Sunday 3pm to 6pm. There is a daily bus service (except Sunday) from Lerwick to Unst, all year round. It leaves the Viking Bus Station in Lerwick and collects passengers at the NorthLink ferry terminal, connecting with ferry arrivals from Aberdeen. Check all ferry and bus timetables before travelling.

ACCOMMODATION
Hotels
Baltasound Hotel: Baltasound ZE2 9DS (℃01957-711334; fax 01957-711358; email balta. hotel@zetnet.co.uk). Two-star, Britain's most northerly hotel. Accommodation is available in the hotel or in pine log chalets. Assisted wheelchair access. Meals and refreshments are served in the bars and children are welcome. Open all year except 25–26 December and 1–2 January. £39 per person a night, double or twin B&B.

Guest Houses
Buness House: Baltasound ZE2 9DS (℃01957-711315; fax 01957-711815; email buness-house@zetnet.co.uk; www.users.zetnet.co.uk/buness-house). A four-star 16th-century laird's house on the north shore. Many notable characters have stayed here, including the infamous graverobbers Burke and Hare, who posed as clockmenders. You can watch otters on the shoreline below the house. Lunch and teas by arrangement. Open May to mid-October. £55 per person.

Ordale House: Baltasosund ZE2 9DT (℃01957-711867; www.ordalehouse.shetland. co.uk). Two-star, 19th-century farmhouse, from £25.

Bed & Breakfast
Clingera Guest House: Irene and Tony Mouat, Baltasound ZE2 9DT (℃/fax 01957-711579; email clingera@btopenworld.com). Two-star B&B in a family home situated on a croft. En-suite facilities, full Scottish breakfasts and packed lunches are available on request. Open all year. From £18.

Mrs S J Firmin: Prestegaard, Uyeasound (℃01957-755234; email prestegaard@postmaster. co.uk). Three-star, spacious Victorian house, three-star, five-minute drive from ferry, near bus route, home cooking. £20 per person.

Mrs Nancy Hughson: 4 Ordale, Baltasound (℃01957-711431). B&B, open all year.

Mrs Jamieson: Leagarth, Baltasound (℃01957-711471). No smoking.

Agnes McLeod: Winwick House, Baltasound (℃01957-711433). Taxi service, open all year except Christmas and New Year.

Mrs Joan Ritch: Gerratoun, Haroldswick (℃01957-711323). Evening meal, special diets catered for. From £20.

Self-Catering
Boatman's House: Burrafirth (contact Mrs Nicolson, Bonavista, Wethersta, Brae; ℃01806-522447). Refurbished cottage, next to Hermaness bird reserve, sleeps nine, £150 to £250 per week.

Hannigarth House: Uyeasound (Mrs M Ouroussoff, The Old Rectory, Hasfield, Glouces-ter GL19 4LG ℃079-4474 9265; email mary.ouroussoff@hasfield.demon.co.uk). Traditional croft house, remote, above sandy beach, sleeps 6. £180-£350 a week.

Keenlee: Baltasound (Yvonne Edmond, 9 Fir Road, Doune, Perthshire FK16 6HU; ℃01786-842321; www.unstselfcatering.co.uk). Spacious, sea views. Four bedrooms, sleeps six, from £250 to £400.

North Booth: Westing (Mrs A McPherson, Cockmuir House, Longmorn, by Elgin IV30 8SL; ℃01343-860227; fax 01343-551604; email themcphersons@tiscali.co.uk). Two-star, self-catering cottage, adjacent to beach, sleeps four, £150 to £275 per week.

North Dale: Haroldswick (I & T Mouat, Baltasound ZE2 9DT; ℃01957-711579; email clingera@btopenworld.com). Two-star, modernised croft house, sleeps four, quiet rural set-ting, linen provided, £90 to £250 a week.

Saxa Vord: Haroldswick (℃01957-711711; email info@saxavord.com; www.saxavord. com). 23 units, three bedrooms in each, sleep five-seven, from £250 to £450.

Voesgarth Crescent: 3 Voesgarth Crescent, Baltasound (℃01957-711579; email clingera@btopenworld.com). Three-star, modern detached bungalow, sleeps six, fully-equipped kitchen, linen provided. From £90 to £300 a week.

Youth Hostels
Gardiesfauld Youth Hostel: Uyeasound (✆01957-755259; email enquiries@gardiesfauld. shetland.co.uk www.gardiesfauld.shetland.co.uk). Three-star, historic house, 40 beds, disabled and family facilities, £11 a day for adults. Camping and bicycle hire available. Open April to September. Britain's most northerly youth hostel.

Saxa Vord: Bunkhouse at Haroldswick (✆01957-711711; email info@saxavord.com; www.saxavord.com). Sleeps 14, open all year. Adults £15, children £10.

EATING AND DRINKING
Saxa Vord: Haroldswick ZE2 9TJ (✆01957-711711; email info@saxavord.com; www.saxavord.com). Traditional food using local produce. Open all year, seven days a week.

HELP AND INFORMATION
Police station: Baltasound (✆01957-711424).
Doctor: Baltasound (✆01957-711318).
Ferry booking office: Ulsta, Yell (✆01957-722259/268).
Scottish Natural Heritage: Shorestation, Haroldswick (✆01957-711278).
Shetland Ranger Service: North Isles Ranger, Micky Maher, Unst Heritage Centre, Haroldswick (✆01950-711238). Walks in Hermaness and Keen of Hamar National Nature Reserves, and on Fetlar and Yell.
Unst Community Council: Rockfield, Haroldswick (✆01957-711224).
Unst Leisure Centre: Baltasound (✆01957-711577).
Unst Music and Dance: Rocklea, Uyeasosund (✆01957-755214).

There are **public toilets** at Belmont ferry terminal, Uyeasound, and at the SNH Visitor Centre at Burrafirth. The **post office** is at Baltasound; and there are **public telephones** at Uyeasound, Baltasound and Haroldswick.

FETLAR

The Norse of old gave Fetlar its name. It means 'Fat Land' and with its rich grazing and fertile croftland it still merits the description and is known as the 'Garden of Shetland'. Fetlar lies to the south of Unst and is about 5 miles (8km) long by 2½ miles (4km) wide. It has a population of 86. According to local folklore the first Norse ship to reach Shetland landed in the eighth century at Gruting, in north-east Fetlar. As the longship drifted in towards the shore a young man jumped on to a large rock known as the Holm of Shoos and became the first Norseman to set foot in the new land. Gruting thus claims to be the oldest Norse colony in the islands. Tradition also says that King Harald Fair-Hair of Norway landed at Funzie on his way to chastise the Vikings raiding his kingdom. Cited as proof are two small lochs near Funzie called **Harald's Water**.

Not far along the road from the ferry terminal you cannot miss **Brough Lodge**, built around 1820 by Sir Arthur Nicolson while he was busy enclosing land and evicting his crofting tenants to make way for more profitable sheep. Close to the house, sitting prominently on the site of an Iron Age broch, is a rare Shetland example of a Victorian folly in the shape of a crennelated tower, used at one time as an astronomical observatory. Another folly built in the 1840s by Sir Arthur was the Round House at Gruting. This was said to be haunted by noisy ghosts and he spent only one night there. The local minister suggested that the spirits of the people evicted by Sir Arthur were knocking. The folly was later demolished. Some of the ruined croft houses, particularly in the north of the island, are reminders of the Clearances. Ironically, most of the houses and buildings erected by the laird and his factor, often with stone robbed from deserted crofts, are now also in ruins.

Fetlar Interpretive Centre (Beach of Houbie, Fetlar ZE2 9DJ; ✆01957-733206/7; email info@fetlar.com; www.fetlar.com), at Houbie, is small, but it is packed with interesting stuff and run by a knowledgeable custodian who obviously loves her work. A visit is a good way to start off your tour of the island. The centre is open from May to the end of September, from 12.30pm to 5.30pm, except Monday. Disabled access to all facilities/exhibitions. Admission is free. You can browse through albums of old photographs, listen to recordings of local history, folklore and music or see films of the island dating back to the 1930s. There are also multi-media computer displays on wildlife, local history and general information. Information at the centre is also available in French, German and Italian. Fetlar has been home to several notables, among them the surgeon **Sir William Watson Cheyne**, who grew up on Fetlar and studied medicine at Edinburgh University, where he was a disciple of the famous Joseph Lister. Cheyne assisted Lister in his pioneering work in antiseptic surgery and helped him to ensure that antiseptic methods became a fundamental part of modern surgical practice.

In 1900, Cheyne built impressive **Leagarth House** at Houbie. Around the house he created some of the most extensive and beautiful gardens in Shetland, and although these no longer exist, you can see photographs at the Interpretive Centre of how they looked in their heyday. Among the exhibits is a display of photographs covering Cheyne's life and contribution to antiseptic surgery, as well as some of his medical equipment and memorabilia, including the signed photograph he received from Queen Victoria after he operated on her servant, John Brown. The 7ft 6 (2m) **Ripple Stone** in the grounds of Leagarth House is named after the De Ripels, the stretch of coast on which it stands. The house is not open to the public. There are memorials to the Cheynes and Sir Arthur Nicolson in the graveyard of **Fetlar Church**, built in 1790 on the foundations of an earlier medieval chapel.

Fetlar General Merchants Café (Gord, Houbie; ✆01957-733227) is popular for its light lunches and homebakes. Try the lemon chicken pie or one of the pasta dishes – all cooked with local ingredients. There are no pubs or bars on the island but you can buy alcoholic drinks at the shop, which is also the post office. Open Monday, Tuesday, Wednesday and Saturday at 11am to 1pm; Friday 11am to 2pm. **Smocks** are made to order at *Fetland Crafts* (contact Marie Hallam, 2 Stakkafletts; ✆01957-733232); and **Shetland lace** is knitted to order by Janice Sawford (5 Stakkafletts; ✆01957-733217).

Archaeological Sites

The large Neolithic stone boundary wall known as the **Finnigert Dyke** runs for a mile across the landscape and is regarded as Fetlar's oldest man-made structure. It runs north-south and divides the island into two, and although much of it is now ruined, large sections can still be seen. Two Neolithic heel-shaped chambered cairns on **Vord Hill** (522ft/159m) could be up to 5,000 years old. Close by is an ancient ring of stones known as the **Hjaltadans**. Legend says the two centre stones were a fiddler and his wife playing music for a group of *trows*, or trolls, dancing in a circle when the sun came up and turned them all to stone. The Dyke and the Hjaltadans lie in the part of the **RSPB Statutory Bird Sanctuary** which is closed from May to August, but free guided walks can be arranged on Tuesdays or Thursdays at 11.30am from the Interpretive Centre.

Near Aith, just above the beach at Sjopli Geo, there's a large oval mound known as **Da Giant's Grave**, which is believed to be the site of a Viking boat burial. Several iron boat fastenings have been found here. Successive generations seem to have concluded that as the grave site was huge it was the grave of a giant. The **Byre Chapel** at Aithness is home to Britain's most northerly religious community, the Society of Our Lady of the Isles. On the east side of the island is the ruined **haa of Funzie**, which was the *haaf* station in the late 1700s where fish was salted and dried before being exported to continental Europe. Beyond Funzie, the road ends. On the cliffbound islets of **Strandibrough** and **The Clett** are the remains of hermitages, probably Norse. Around the shores of the Wick of Gruting are the remains of crofts emptied by the Clearances of Sir Arthur Nicolson. There has always been pressure on the land in Fetlar and much of the land is still farmed as estate land or is under conservation order. In the mid-1980s, this led to the formulation of the Fetlar Integrated Development Plan in an attempt to diversify the economy and channel islanders into areas such as salmon farming, tourism and, more recently, information technology.

Some 300 species of flowering plants grow on the island. One of the rarest, in Shetland terms, is the **water sedge** at **Papil Water**, a loch which also provides good angling for **brown** and **sea trout**. Good sandy beaches can be found below at **Tresta**, and the **Sand of Sand**, below Brough Lodge. **Common** and **grey seals** can be seen along the coast, and **otters** hunt the shoreline between Brough Lodge and Urie Ness.

Shipwrecks

There are said to be more sea-chiselled natural arches on Fetlar per mile of coastline than anywhere else in Shetland. There are also plenty of treacherous reefs and records show that they have been claiming ships since 1601 to as recently as 1979. The best-known wreck is the one referred to locally as the 'Silver Ship'. On the night of 18 December 1737 the *Wendela*, a 26-gun frigate of the Danish Asiatic Company, was wrecked and lost with all hands at Heilinabretta, on the eastern side of Fetlar. The ship was outward bound for India and carried with her cargo 79 silver bars, and 31 sacks of silver coins. The ship had battled North Sea gales for nearly three months before finally foundering. Early salvage operations using a primitive 'diving engine' recovered 60 silver bars and 22 sacks of coins, and another attempt in 1971 brought 16 iron guns to the surface, as well as 44 gold and 673 silver coins. A single Danish gold ducat brought £680 when the haul was auctioned at Sotheby's in 1973. The wreck of *Wendela* is one of 14 protected wrecks under the control of the Shetland Islands Council and permission to dive on any of them must be obtained from the council.

Bird-watching

Even in an archipelago renowned for its birdlife Fetlar is famed for the species it attracts. The snowy owls which nested on the 1,700-acre (688ha) **RSPB Reserve** between 1967 and 1975 have, unfortunately, vanished but one of Britain's rarest breeding birds, the **red-necked phalarope**, can be seen at close quarters. During June and July these amazingly approachable, brightly coloured birds feed along the shore of the **Loch of Funzie** (pronounced 'Finnie') and breed at the **Mires of Funzie**, which can be viewed from the RSPB hide. Since red-necked phalaropes have drastically declined throughout the rest of Britain, the population on Fetlar represents more than 90% of the UK population. Along the road to the airstrip is a good place to see the **whimbrels** which breed on Fetlar.

Other species of interest include **red-throated diver**, **golden plover**, **ringed plover**, **dunlin**, **eider duck**, **Arctic skua**, **great skua**, **Arctic tern** and **oystercatchers**. In the late evening and early morning **storm petrels**, **Manx shearwaters** and **great skuas** can be seen on the cliffs of **Lamb Hoga**, a moorland area which until the 1950s provided islanders with their main fuel, peat. **Fulmars**, **black guillemots**, **kittiwakes**, **shags** and **puffins** are plentiful around the coast. Although the Statutory Bird Sanctuary which is part of the RSPB reserve is closed from May to August to reduce the disturbance to breeding birds, there are no species which cannot be seen elsewhere on the island. The rare birds which nest on Fetlar are protected by law, which means it is illegal to disturb or photograph their nesting sites. Contact the warden at Bealance (✆01957-733246) for more information. Signs displayed at Oddsta and at the junction above the warden's house show the reserve area on the map of the island. His house is signposted and is 2½ miles (4km) from the Oddsta ferry terminal. The warden keeps daily records throughout the season of both the breeding birds and non-breeding migrants, and is always grateful for details of your observations, particularly the dates and number of migrants you have seen.

GETTING THERE
By Air
Charter flights from Tingwall, on the Mainland, land at Fetlar airstrip, near Houbie.

By Sea
Two ferries operate at Gutcher, North Yell, so check with the crew before boarding that they are going to Fetlar. The two Ro-Ro vehicle and passenger ferries are the *MV Bigga* and the *MV Geira*, crossing to Hamarsness on Fetlar frequently from Gutcher and daily from Belmont, in Unst. The trip to Fetlar takes 25 minutes. Booked vehicles must be at the terminal five minutes before the ferry leaves. Bookings for late night trips must be received by 4pm the same day (✆01957-722259/268). The booking office is open Monday to Saturday from 8.30am to 5pm. For more information on *Bluemill Sound Services* (✆01595-743971), or the *Shetland Islands Council* (Town Hall, Lerwick ZE1 0HB; ✆01595-693535; fax 01595-695590; email sic@sic.shetland.gov.uk).

ACCOMMODATION
Bed & Breakfast
Gord B&B: Nic Boxall, Gord, Houbie ZE2 9DJ (✆01957-733227; email nicboxall@btinternet.com). Four-star, next to post office, four-star, from £25 a person.

Janet Kelly: The Glebe ZE2 9DJ (✆/fax 01957-733242). One-star, listed building overlooking Papil Water.

Society of Our Lady of the Isles (SOLI): Aithness, Fetlar ZE2 9DJ (✆/fax 01957-733303) or Sister Mary Cuthbert (01957-733280). Two-star, semi-detached cottages and studio flats overlooking the sea. Access for visitors with mobility difficulties. SOLI is the most northerly religious community in Britain and was started in 1984 by Sister Agnes, an Anglican Franciscan, at Aith Ness. Now Mother Mary Agnes, she was ordained a priest in 1998.

Self-Catering
3 Tresta: Colin Mansell (✆/fax 01957-733231; email colin.mansell@virgin.net). Newly refurbished traditional crofthouse, overlooking beach and loch. Two bedrooms, sleeps four, from £180 to £350.

Camping
The Garths Campsite: Nic Boxall, Gord, Fetlar (✆01957-733227). A well-maintained caravan and campsite overlooking Tresta Beach. Open May to September. Six touring pitches and 12 tents. £4 to£7.40 a night.

HELP AND INFORMATION
There is no public transport on Fetlar and you cannot buy petrol or diesel fuel, although a four-seater **Postbus service** (✆01957-733227) operates from the ferry to the post office in Houbie, and to North Dale, South Dale, Tresta, Leagarth, Aithness, Funzie and Everland, Monday to Friday. It leaves for the ferry at 7.40am and 11am; and leaves the Oddsta ferry landing at 7.55am and 11am. Check details at the post office.
Police Station: at Reafirth (✆01957-702012).
Doctor: is at Reafirth, near Mid Yell (✆01957-702127).
Nurse: is Fiona Thomason, Nurses House, Houbie (✆01957-733228).
RSPB Warden: Bealance (✆01957-733246).
Interpretive Centre: Houbie (✆01957-733206).

There are **public toilets** at Oddsta ferry terminal, at the shop in Houbie, the Interpretive Centre, and at the campsite. There are **public telephones** at the Oddsta ferry terminal and in Houbie.

Fair Isle

South of Shetland and halfway to Orkney is Fair Isle – 3 miles (5km) long and only half as wide – which is one of the most isolated inhabited islands in Britain. Fair Isle is a name associated with radio shipping forecasts, but is justly world famous for the intricate noughts and crosses knitting of the island women and for its incredible birdlife, which in spring and autumn can include some extremely rare migrants. Fair Isle's bristling coastline is the result of ancient glacial grinding and the pounding of the sea over millennia on the tilted rocks forming the island. At Buness, softer mudstone in the rocks has been carved by the sea from between hard sandstone layers to create some amazing natural arches. Deeply carved geos, or inlets, on the west coast offer some of the island's most impressive scenery, with cliffs rising to nearly 656ft (200m) in the north-west. Robert Louis Stevenson described the coast as 'the wildest and most unpitying' that he had ever seen. In his diary in 1870 he described how *'continuous cliffs, from 100 to 400ft high, tower by huge voes and echoing caverns, line the bare downs with scarcely a curve of sand or a practicable cleft in the belt of iron precipices. At intervals, it runs out into strange peninsulas, square bluff headlands and plumb faces of stone...'*

ARCHAEOLOGICAL SITES

Neolithic people settled on Fair Isle about 5,000 years ago in their northward expansion through Scotland and its islands and it has been studied more intensively by archaeologists than virtually any other area of its size in Scotland. There are traces of oval-shaped stone houses, perhaps 3,000 years old, and lines of turf and stone walls, or dykes, winding across the landscape. The **Feely Dyke**, a massive turf rampart which divides the common grazings from the crofts, is also thought to be prehistoric. This still rises to a height of 6.6ft (2m) in the west and once cut the island in half. To the north is the more recent **Hill Dyke**, an unmistakable landmark. The best-preserved archaeology is found in the north, and also on the edge of the crofting land in the south, which suggests that early settlers lived in the northern half of the island until environmental changes on the higher ground forced them to move. Eventually only the southern half remained inhabited. Archaeological remains scattered around the landscape include some 20 burnt mounds, piles of blackened stones which appear to have been heated by fire and then dropped into water-filled stone troughs. Near Pund is the largest burnt mound in Shetland, 128ft (39m) by 89ft (27m) and standing 10ft (3m) high. In all, Fair Isle has 14 scheduled monuments, ranging from the earliest traces of human settlement to the remains of a wartime radar installation.

Kirkigeo comprises the remains of a settlement dated at Middle to Late Iron Age, with a possible early monastic settlement. You can also see ancient boat-shaped *noosts* where fishing boats were hauled up for shelter. The *noosts* are still in use. At **Malcolm's Head** are the remains of a watch tower from the Napoleonic era, supposedly made of egg white and clay. In the cliff facing Fogli Stack, is the **Thief's Hole**, once used to conceal contraband and by men hiding from the Royal Navy's Press Gang. The **Rocket Signal Station** was built in 1885 to warn passing ships of Fair Isle's proximity during foggy conditions. You can see the old accommodation block and two rocket-firing stances. The burn of Gilsetter has a series of small horizontal **water mills** and their supply systems. These were working until sometime during World War I. The burn cascades down to the sea at Funniquey, where there is a small beach. **Sukkamir** has a burnt mound and a large number of the post-medieval and more recent small, circular drystone enclosures known as *planticrubs*, built to protect growing kale.

Landberg is an Iron Age promontory fort, near the Bird Observatory. The remains of a round house have also been found on the promontory, with a central hearth and other internal stone features. Pottery finds date this at around 2,000 years. One shard of pottery unearthed has a Greek key design round its rim, a pattern still used in the island's famed knitwear. Stone artefacts found include a lamp, querns and a number of mortars. Clay moulds in later levels indicate bronze working, possibly from the sixth or seventh century. The burn of Furse to Homisdale site holds two settlement areas which probably date back to the Bronze Age. Within this area are at least two house sites, three burnt mounds, several stretches of walling and field clearance cairns, and numerous *planticrubs*. On 712ft (217m) **Ward Hill** are the remains of a World War II radar station. In World War I, Ward Hill was used as a look-out point for spotting German U-boats. The island's two fine lighthouses are also listed buildings. These were built by the Stevenson family and commissioned in 1892. The North Light's sundial was used to check lighting times. Close by is the amazing **Kirn of Skroo**, a 262ft (80m) subterranean passage ending in an inland blowhole. The **South Light** was the last manned lighthouse in Scotland. It was automated in March 1998. Both lighthouses were targets for *Luftwaffe* attacks during World War II. Near the north-eastern tip of the island between Easter Loder Water and Jivvy Geo is a prehistoric boundary dyke which isolated this corner of the island. In the same area is **Mopul**, a prehistoric burial cairn close to the edge of the high cliffs.

The Vikings arrived in the late eighth century, and their legacy lies more in place-names than in any specific Norse sites. It was the Vikings who named the island *Fridarey* ('Island of Peace') and the Norse sagas tell how Kari the Viking spent the winter here on his way to the Hebrides. Viking warlords and the Earls of Orkney used the island as a look-out post and beacon site for sending fire signals to and from Shetland. The island maintains its historic role as a signal station, although today the fires of old have given way to hi-tech relay stations carrying vital TV, radio, telephone and military communication links between Shetland, Orkney and the Scottish mainland.

Armada Wreck. Fair Isle has been a landmark for shipping for thousands of years but in storms and fog its coastline can be extremely dangerous and has claimed many unwary ships over the centuries. Among 100 known wrecks is that of the Spanish Armada ship *El Gran Grifon*, the flagship of the defeated fleet commanded by the Duke of Medina, which foundered in the inlet of Stroms Heelor in September 1588 and left 270 soldiers and sailors stranded on the island. The island at that time could barely support its population of 17 households, far less the influx of Spaniards who spent six weeks living with them. Before the shipwrecked men were rescued in November, 50 had died of starvation. In 1970, divers retrieved one of its 38 guns, still loaded. In 1984, a Spanish delegation in the full regalia of the *conquistadores* dedicated an iron cross memorial in the island's kirkyard to the men who died.

ECONOMY

The island has changed hands many times over the centuries, with crofters of old paying rent in kind, usually to absentee landlords who were rarely seen. It is now owned by the *National Trust for Scotland* (NTS). Until the mid-20th century fishing was the islanders' major source of income. Fish were dried on flat stony beaches and in *skeos*, open-topped drystone structures, while kettles were used to reduce fish livers for oil. Nearly 400 people lived on Fair Isle in the mid-19th century. Now there are 70 or so who live mainly in 18 traditional crofts of 7–49 acres (3–20ha) on the more fertile and low-lying southern third of the island above South Harbour. As landlord the NTS has stemmed further depopulation by initiating a variety of improvements, including a multi-phased renewable energy project, using wind power, with co-finance from the *European Regional Development* and *Shetland Enterprise*. Electricity is provided by two wind turbines of 60 kW and 100 kW, backed up by two 30 kW diesel generators for use when the wind drops.

NTS has also encouraged crafts such as boat-building, spinning, weaving, dyeing, felting, wood-turning, fiddle-making, and the manufacture of straw-backed chairs, spinning wheels and stained glass windows. The island even has its own resident composer, Alastair Stout, whose specially commissioned work evoking Fair Isle (*Classic Fair Isle*) had its world première on the island in 2002. NTS organises volunteer work camps and if you want to take

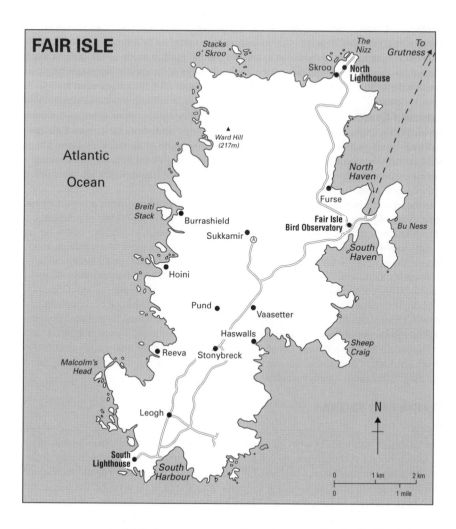

FAIR ISLE

Stacks o' Skroo

The Nizz

To Grutness

Skroo

North Lighthouse

Ward Hill (217m)

Atlantic

Ocean

North Haven

Furse

Breiti Stack

Burrashield

Fair Isle Bird Observatory

Bu Ness

Sukkamir

South Haven

Hoini

Pund

Vaasetter

Haswalls

Sheep Craig

Reeva

Stonybreck

Malcolm's Head

Leogh

N

South Lighthouse

South Harbour

0   1 km   2 km

0   1 mile

part in one you can get details from www.nts.org.uk, send a stamped and self-addressed envelope to Thistle Camps, National Trust for Scotland (28 Charlotte Square, Edinburgh EH2 4ET; ℂ0131-243 9360; email thistlecamps@nts.org.uk; www.thistlecamps.org.uk). For the most part volunteers work with crofters, helping with ditching, fencing, hay or silage making, drystone dykes, weeding, and so on. You might even be asked to paint the markings on the airstrip.

The **George Waterston Memorial Centre and Museum**, in the former Fair Isle School, commemorates the former director of the Royal Society for the Protection of Birds and founder of the Bird Observatory. Known locally as the 'Auld Schule' it displays a wide range of fishing and crofting implements; items associated with the lighthouse and life-saving; knitwear, both old and contemporary; photographs; a reconstruction of a croft kitchen; and glimpses into the archaeological and natural history of the isle. Next to the school is the community hall which offers badminton, pool, bowls, table tennis and a canteen. It is also used for Scottish, Scandinavian and Shetland dancing. All visitors, passing yachtsmen, and work camp volunteers are welcome. It also houses a weekly workshop of the **Fair Isle Crafts Co-operative**.

The Fair Isle Times weekly newspaper was first produced by local school children. Over the years, the readership has grown and there is now worldwide mail distribution. It is now available on the internet at www.fairisle.org.uk/FIT/. There are two churches on the island, a **Methodist Chapel** (1886) and a **Church of Scotland** kirk (1892). Islanders attend each on alternate Sundays indiscriminately. The distinctive holm off the east coast known as **Sheep Craig** provides 10 acres (4ha) of pasture and is reached by a small isthmus. Ropes and chains were once used to haul man and beast to the grazing on top of the craig. A fixed chain drops down the vertical face on the north-east edge of the rock which might help you to reach the 443ft (135m) summit. Islanders used to climb up in their stockinged feet.

Arts and Crafts

For such a small island Fair Isle boasts a surprising range, aside from the famous **Fair Isle knitwear** developed over the centuries and known worldwide for its stranded colour knitting and horizontal bands of geometric patterns. At the beginning of the 20th century commercial haberdasher James Coates gave two kaleidoscopes to the island, which are said to have inspired new geometric designs.

In the past, islanders traded with visiting ships, bartering their home-made jerseys, hats and gloves for things they couldn't make or grow themselves. Traditional colours of red, blue, brown, yellow and white combined by age-old patterns were much sought after and in the early days were the result of experimentation with dyes produced from flowers, lichens, roots and almost anything to hand. A small co-operative, **Fair Isle Crafts** (email fairislecrafts_ knitwear@yahoo.co.uk), uses hand-frame machine knitters and hand-finishers to produce traditional and contemporary sweaters carrying Fair Isle's own trademark star motif. Spinning has been revived on a small scale and garments are produced in the natural fleece colours of *moorit* (brown), *shaela* (grey), black, and natural white. Wooden looms more than 200 years old can still be seen at Barkland, where coloured woollen tweeds and rugs are produced.

The *Textile Workshop* (Upper Leogh ZE2 9JU; ℂ01595-760249; email kathy.coull@btinternet.com) offers demonstrations and tuition in textile techniques, including knitting, hand spinning, felt making, tapestry weaving, patchwork and quilting

FLORA AND FAUNA

Flora

The landscape you'll see is now only a hazy memory in a great many country areas of mainland Britain. Although the variety and range of plants is limited by the island's relative isolation, its small size – just over 2,471 acres (1,000ha) – and it's harsh maritime climate, the island is full of botanical surprises. The 250 or so flowering plant species include several rare and notable ones. Major habitats are heather moorland, marsh and wetland, cliffs and the coastal fringe, and the cultivated areas. The **prostrate juniper** of the moorland is an unusual form rare in Shetland, and the island growths are some of the finest in Britain. Some particularly good specimens can be seen along the road at Byerwall. The rare **lesser marshwort** grows in Gilsetter Burn and at Sukkamir. Magnificent **northern marsh orchids** are found on marshy grassland. In June–July you might be lucky to spot the rare small **adder's-tongue** near the Observatory. The equally rare **oysterplant** and **spearleaved orache** both occur on the shingle above Muckle Uri Geo. At the north end of Burrashield is a narrow valley white with **bog asphodel** in late summer, called **Groggie's Cup**. The name dates back to 1773, when the ship *Caroline* was wrecked in South Naaversgill. By the time she had run aground the crew had given up hope and had broached the ship's spirits. One inebriated crew member fell to his death before islanders rescued the rest.

A wide variety of familiar plants thrive along the verges of roads, in hay fields, cultivated areas and grazing lands. There is no best time to see Fair Isle's flora, but June and July are best for variety and colour. The island is a floral picture well into August, and some special plants are found as late as October. Interestingly, the mudstone at the apex of rock arches around the coast contains the world's best known examples of the Devonian Age plant called *Svalbardia*, a fern-like ancestor of seeding plants, also known as the corduroy plant. The arches at Buness are particularly important for the fossil remains of plants that once grew on the floor of the primeval Orcadian Basin.

Botany buffs can brush up with *The Flowering Plants and Ferns of the Shetland Islands*, by Walter Scott and Richard Palmer (Shetland Times, Lerwick, 1987); and *Shetland's Wild Flowers*, a photographic guide by D Malcolm (Shetland Times, Lerwick, 1992).

Fauna

Eight cetacean species – whales, dolphins, porpoises – and two species of seal are regularly seen around the island. The **best time** to see them is between May and October when conditions are more favourable and because several species move into the coastal waters in summer when food is more abundant. Seals may be seen all year round. On the ferry crossing from Grutness there is every chance of seeing up to 20 **white-beaked dolphins** riding the bow-wave, sometimes accompanied by large schools of **Atlantic white-sided dolphins**. White-sided dolphins are not otherwise often seen. **Harbour porpoises** are also likely to be spotted from the ferry boat, particularly around the *roost* (tidal race) south of Sumburgh Head. **Risso's dolphins** are occasionally seen around the island, and small pods of **killer whales** are recorded fairly regularly hugging the coast-line in search of a seal meal. Occasionally, long-finned **pilot whales** are seen, although this is normally an open ocean roamer. All these cetaceans are toothed whales. The most common of the toothless baleen whales is the **minke whale** and regular sightings occur in July and August.

South Harbour is a good place to see **Atlantic grey seals** and **common seals** and greys can easily be spotted bobbing about in North Haven. Only the greys breed on Fair Isle. Favoured areas include North Gunnawark, Muckel Geo o' Hoini and Guidicum.

BIRD-WATCHING

Seabirds are the main reason why most of Fair Isle's cliffs and moorland are a Site of Special Scientific Interest (SSSI) and Special Protection Area (SPA) and in partnership with the islanders and the Bird Observatory, NTS is also working to achieve a marine protection area around Fair Isle to conserve both marine and terrestrial habitats on which the seabirds depend. Fair Isle is renowned as a twitcher's paradise and is known as the Hilton of the bird world. *Fair Isle Lodge and Bird Observatory* (see *Accommodation*) makes an ideal base, whatever your interests. The observatory was conceived by George Waterston, an ornithologist who, as a German prisoner-of-war in World War II, spent his time planning it. He bought the island in 1948 to make his dream a reality. The NTS succeeded him as owner in 1955.

The Observatory has excellent research facilities and is one of the most important in Britain for the study of migrants, as it lies at the junction of major bird flightpaths from Scandinavia, Iceland and the Faroes. Fair Isle has recorded more than 345 species, including such rarities as the **lanceolated warbler**, **Pallas's grasshopper warbler**, and the **Pechora pipit**. Early migrants start to appear in late March, becoming more numerous through April. May is generally the **best period** for numbers and variety of migrants, although early June is often best for extreme rarities or vagrants. In late July, migrant waders begin to return from the Arctic. By the end of August, the autumn migration is in full swing. September and October are the **best times** for large falls of passerine migrants, and rarities turn up regularly. Migrants continue moving through in small numbers until early November. Fair Isle is one of the best places in Europe to view seabirds at close range, especially **puffins** which, if you are quiet, will waddle to virtually within touching distance. Puffins can be found on almost every cliff top, with Roskilie and Buness the **best places** to see them close up. The cliffs in the north-west at Dronger have tightly packed scrums of **gannets**, **guillemots**, **kittiwakes**, **fulmars**, **razorbills**, **shags** and many other species.

Through their Scottish Natural Heritage-funded Ranger Service, the Observatory organises a variety of structured activity weeks from mid-April to the end of October and with local community help offers a rewarding holiday. Activities vary with the season of the year. On arrival at the Observatory you will be given a pack containing helpful information and a map of the island. A 40-minute walk around the Observatory bird traps with a staff member takes place every morning, except in extremely bad weather. It is ideal for hands-on experience of ringing, or banding, techniques. You will be invited to listen to and contribute to the Bird Log, which is read out by the Warden at 9pm every day. Staff members can arrange visits to local craftspeople and provide lifts. You'll soon hear about the **Red Flag System**. Famous among the birding community, the red flag flying from the window of the Observatory van alerts visitors to the discovery of rare birds.

Activities

The following are guided walks and other activities supervised by the Ranger Service:

Spring. Puffin walks take place until the puffins leave late in July. The ranger will take you up to a thriving colony of puffins close to the Observatory and you might see the ranger catch and ring a puffin as part of an ongoing adult survival study. Fair Isle hosts 18 breeding species of seabird and there is a walk to introduce you to the ecology of some of them, as well as a guided walk to introduce novice twitchers to the skills of bird identification and help experienced birders with the more tricky species.

Summer. The uplands need to be scoured for skua chicks so they can be weighed and ringed. This takes place several times in the summer and you are encouraged to take part. Skua and tern guided walks take place under strict supervision to prevent disturbance to breeding birds – and protect walkers against those 'dive-bombing' intruders to defend their young. Storm petrel ringing means that on calm dark nights from mid-July until early September birders get a chance to release some of these remarkable little birds.

Autumn. The migration walk gives you an opportunity to ask the Ranger to help with the identification of the thousands of migrants that pass through each day.

Tours

Observatory staff can also arrange other events, depending on weather, availability and demand. For a small fee (£30), knowledgeable islanders also provide three-hour guided walks covering other subjects. Subjects available include wild flowers walk with Nick Riddiford or Glen Tyler; archaeology walk with Pat Thompson; crofting and weather walk, with Dave Wheeler; and an illustrated evening talk held at a crofthouse, or a guided walk to learn about maritime history with Ann Sinclair. **Self-guiding leaflets** are also available on archaeology, sea mammals, flowers, seabirds, ringing, geology and crofting. The island ferry and mailboat *Good Shepherd IV* can be chartered for about £150 and carries up to 12 people. The 90-minute trip is a novel way to see the cliffs, coastline and seabird colonies during spring and summer.

Much-needed support for the *Fair Isle Bird Observatory Trust* (FIBOT) comes from *Friends of Fair Isle*. Current subscription of £10 a year entitles you to a copy of the Fair Isle Bird Observatory Report, two newsletters, 10% discount on accommodation during July and August, and preferential booking for peak times in the following year – a good return on investment. Contact the Administrator (Hollie Shaw) for more information (Fair Isle Bird Observatory, Fair Isle ZE2 9JU; ✆/fax 01595-760258; email fairisle.birdobs@zetnet.co.uk; www.fairislebirdobs.co.uk).

GETTING THERE

By Air

The first aircraft to land on Fair Isle touched down in 1937 on the flat cliff-top at Meo Ness, in the south-east corner of the island. An airstrip was built and first used during World War II. This was enlarged in the early 1970s and regular weekly flights from Shetland started in June 1976. Private aircraft can also use the Fair Isle airstrip. The high cliffs can throw up turbulence and fog or low cloud is an ever-present risk, especially during summer.

In summer, *Directflight* (✆01595-840246) flies its eight-seat 'Islander' aircraft to Fair Isle from Tingwall on the Mainland on Monday at 9am and 4pm (9am and 2.45pm in winter), Wednesday at 10am and 3pm (10am and 2.45pm in winter), Friday 9am and 3pm (9am and

1.45pm in winter), and Saturday at 10.55am. There is an additional flight from Sumburgh on Saturday at 2pm. The flight from Tingwall takes 25 minutes and from Sumburgh 15 minutes. A day return will usually give you about 6½ hours on the island. Check in 20 minutes before scheduled departure time – the airline does not wait for late check-ins. The fare is £56 return for adults (senior citizens £28). Charters are available. If you plan to travel by air it is advisable to take out travel insurance well in advance, as flights could be cancelled because of weather, technical problems or air-ambulance needs.

By Sea

The island is served by a modern ferry, *Good Shepherd IV*, owned by the Shetland Islands Council but based on the island and crewed by islanders. This, together with modern harbour facilities, means that even in winter the island is no longer cut-off from the Shetland mainland for long periods.

In **summer**, every Tuesday, Saturday and alternate Thursdays at 11.30am the ferry leaves from Grutness Pier, near Sumburgh, and alternate Thursdays at 3.30am. The ferry leaves Fair Isle on the same days at 7.30am, and 6am on alternate Thursdays. Therefore you must stay a minimum of two nights on the island if you choose the ferry. The ferry carries 12 passengers and takes about 2½ hours. Book through Jimmy Stout (✆01595-760222) and confirm 24 hours before departure. All sailings are weather permitting. Further information is available at ✆01595-743978.

Since the building of the breakwater and new pier visiting yachtsmen can find a sheltered berth in the North Haven in summer. Cruise ships visit Fair Isle between May and September. Among the more regular are the *Professor Molchanov, Professor Multonovski, Shearwater, Explorer, Caledonian Star, Hanseatic, Hebridean Princess*, and *Clipper Adventurer*. Check with your travel agent for more details.

ACCOMMODATION

Most visitors stay at the *Fair Isle Lodge and Bird Observatory*. The Lodge is set in a sheltered spot near the island pier, commanding magnificent views of sea and cliffs. Staff and visitors eat together at large tables, ensuring a family atmosphere. Meals are on a full-board and set menu basis, with the option of a packed lunch instead of the light midday meal. Special diets can usually be provided if requested when booking. The Lodge has a fully licensed bar and is a no smoking area.

The accommodation is single and twin-bedded rooms and dormitories (four–six beds including bunks). Most rooms have washbasins, baths and showers are available. Double glazing and central heating throughout the building help to ensure comfort and there is a drying room for wet clothes and footwear. Slippers or indoor shoes are required for wear inside the lodge.

The lodge is open from late April to the end of October. Booking is heavy during spring and autumn bird migration periods, so apply early. Rates: dormitory £30, sharing twin £39, and single £44 per person per night, inclusive of full board and VAT. *Friends of Fair Isle* are eligible for a 10% reduction during July and August, but remember to quote your membership number when booking. Groups of eight or more adults staying for a minimum of seven nights outside the peak period (15 September to 31 October) and willing to share get a 10% discount. Children under 3 are free, and children 3–11 years inclusive receive a 50% discount if sharing parents' room. Contact Hollie Shaw (The Administrator, Fair Isle Lodge and Bird Observatory, Fair Isle ZE2 9JU; ✆/fax 01595-760258; email fairisle.birdobs@zetnet.co.uk).

Bed & Breakfast

Kathleen Coull: Upper Leogh, Fair Isle ZE2 9JU (✆01595-760248; email kathleen.coull@lineone.net). On working croft, evening meal and packed lunches available.

Mrs Margo Murray: Koolin, Fair Isle (✆01595-760225; email margo.koolin@virgin.net). Also runs the self-catering *Springfield Croft House,* £225 a week.

Youth Hostel

Puffin Hostel: (✆01595-760248) at South Harbour is open April to September, £140 to £160 a week. Previously a stonewalled fish store, this was converted into a self-catering hostel for *International Voluntary Service* and NTS workcamps, which stay for two or three weeks in the summer.

SHOPPING

The revival of the rowing tradition has brought an upsurge in the building and general use of the **Shetland yoa**l, with communities racing every weekend throughout the summer. There is also an increasing appreciation of this distinctive clinkerbuilt boat, pointed at both ends, as a leisure craft. Fair Isle's master boat-builder makes yoals in the old Norse style, and finds customers for them as far away as Holland. Contact Ian Best (Kenaby, Fair Isle ZE2 9JU; ✆01595-760229; email ianbestboatbuilder@fairisle.org.uk).

Straw-backed chairs are hand-crafted from hardwoods and locally harvested oat straw. The base of the chair is traditionally panelled and fitted with twin drawers. Chairs made today by Stewart Thomson of *Fair Isle Straw Crafts* (Quoy ZE2 9JU; ✆01595-760241), are based on the chair his grandfather made for his bride in 1908, which is still in daily use.

Hand-made violins can be viewed by appointment with Ewen Thomson at 1 Aesterhoull (✆01595-760276).

Italian photographer Sergio Mariotti has captured Fair Isle and Foula in photographs and poems in his book *Lights of Islands*, which costs £6.50 at Stackhoull Stores on the island. A video of Fair Isle made by Mariotti is also available.

Fridarey, the family of Fair Isle musicians, has released its first CD *Across the Waters* which can be bought on the island from *Fridarey* (Busta, Fair Isle, ZE2 9JU; ✆/fax 01595-760244; email anne.sinclair@virgin.net).

HELP AND INFORMATION

District Nurse at North Shirva (✆01595-760242). For further medical care patients travel by inter-island air-service to Lerwick. The air-ambulance service is used in emergencies. If you use regular or unusual medication you should bring adequate supplies with you.

Fair Isle Marine Environment and Tourism Initiative (FIMETI): Fair Isle ZE2 9JU (✆01595-760250; fax 01595-760252; email nick.riddiford@fairisle.org.uk).

Ferry booking office: (✆01595-760222).

National Trust for Scotland: Regional Office (✆01463-232034; www.fairisle.org.uk).

For **car rental** or **taxi hire** contact Jimmy Stout (✆01595-760222; fax 01595-760268).

There are **public toilets** at the airstrip and at Stackhoull Stores, which is the only shop and **post office** on the island; **public telephone** at Shirva. Parents with young children should check in advance whether everything they need is stocked at the shop. Photographers should take plenty of film as supplies are limited.

GLOSSARY

Broch – An Iron Age defensive stone tower, named from the Old Norse *borg*, or castle.

Burnt mound – A prehistoric site where food was cooked in a trough in water heated by dropping hot stones into it and then discarding them as they cracked.

Chambered cairn – A Neolithic burial tomb.

Clearance cairn – Stones piled up from land cleared for cultivation.

Cist – A grave or box made from stone slabs.

Crannogs (lake dwellings) – Small islets, usually man-made, on which stone or wooden homesteads were built, linked to the shore by causeways. Some probably date from the late Bronze Age.

Dun – Gaelic for a hill fort, a small drystone fortification usually dating from the Iron Age or later.

Henge – Usually a circular or elliptical area enclosed by a ditch and an external bank and often enclosing a stone circle. Usually regarded as a meeting place for ceremony and ritual.

Iron Age – Final period of prehistory in Scotland, beginning around 500BC and lasting into the early centuries of the first millennium AD, when iron superseded bronze as the preferred metal for tools and weapons.

Mesolithic (Middle Stone Age) – The period between the Palaeolithic and Neolithic ages, from around 7000BC to 4000BC. The Mesolithic groups were hunter-gatherers like their predecessors, but placed a greater reliance on fishing and fowling.

Midden – An accumulation of domestic rubbish, usually built up over a long period.

Neolithic (New Stone Age) – Period between the mesolithic and the Bronze Age in Scotland, dating from around 4000BC to 2000BC and characterised by the introduction of settled farming communities.

Ogam or **Ogham** – A script in which letters are represented by groups of parallel lines meeting or crossing a straight base line. Thought to have originated in Wales or Ireland around AD300. Used by Picts until the ninth century.

Palaeolithic (Old Stone Age) – In Britain, beginning with the earliest occupation by man around 450,000 years ago, and ending with the mesolithic around 7000BC.

Runes – A stick-like angular script developed for carving on wood and stone around AD300. First recorded use was in Scandinavia.

Schist – A coarse-grained rock with a marked layering, defined by flat, broad or elongated minerals. Most schists are composed largely of minerals such as muscovite, chlorite, talc, sericite, biotite and graphite.

Souterrain – An earth-house with a long, underground passage, often having drystone walling and a flagged roof, and sometimes a chamber. Usually attached to a settlement and used for storage. They date from around 800BC to about AD200.

Stone Circle – Circles or ellipses of standing stones, mostly dating from the Bronze Age and believed to be connected with ritual ceremonies and possibly astronomical observations.

Wheelhouse – Round drystone house usually dating from the late Iron Age, in which partition walling, possibly roof supports, radiate in from the wall like the spokes of a wheel.

INDEX

Other titles in this series:

SKYE & THE WESTERN ISLES

The best-selling and most comprehensive guide available to the Western Isles, which include Skye, Lewis, Harris, Uist, Iona, Jura, Islay and Arran.

The Western Isles present visitors with a rich variety of terrain and wildlife from the stark beauty of the Cuillin mountains of Skye to the raging seas off the Butt of Lewis or the palm trees of Arran.

Complete with information on the best walks and climbs, castles and blackhouses, history and culture, music festivals and ceilidhs and the finest food, drink and accommodation.

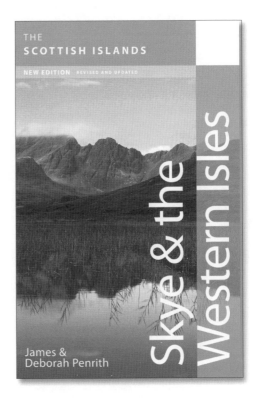

Author: James & Deborah Penrith
Published: July 2007
ISBN: 978-1-85458-370-3